Broken Archangel

Broken Archangel

The Tempestuous Lives of Roger Casement

ROLAND PHILIPPS

THE BODLEY HEAD

LONDON

3 5 7 9 10 8 6 4 2

The Bodley Head, an imprint of Vintage, is part of the Penguin
Random House group of companies whose addresses can be found at
global.penguinrandomhouse.com

First published by The Bodley Head in 2024

Copyright © Roland Philipps 2024

Roland Philipps has asserted his right to be identified as the author of this Work
in accordance with the Copyright, Designs and Patents Act 1988

Maps by Bill Donohoe

penguin.co.uk/vintage

Printed and bound in Great Britain by Clays Ltd, Elcograf S.p.A.

The authorised representative in the EEA is Penguin Random House Ireland,
Morrison Chambers, 32 Nassau Street, Dublin D02 YH68

A CIP catalogue record for this book is available from the British Library

HB ISBN 9781847927071
TPB ISBN 9781847927088

Penguin Random House is committed to a sustainable future
for our business, our readers and our planet. This book is made
from Forest Stewardship Council® certified paper.

For my mother

Contents

Maps

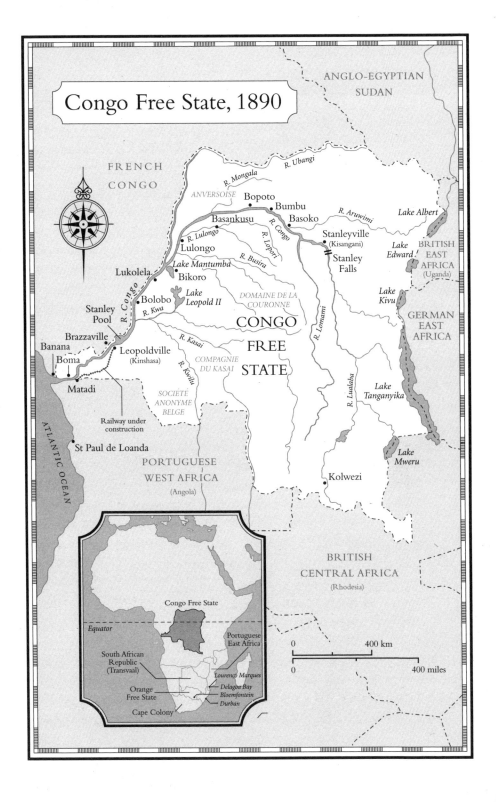

Congo Free State, 1890

ANGLO-EGYPTIAN SUDAN

FRENCH CONGO

R. Ubangi

R. Mongala

ANVERSOISE

Bopoto

Bumbu

Basankusu

R. Lulongo

Lulongo

R. Lopori

R. Congo

Basoko

R. Aruwimi

Lake Albert

Stanleyville
(Kisangani)

Stanley
Falls

Lake
Edward

BRITISH
EAST
AFRICA
(Uganda)

Lukolela

Lake Mantumba

R. Busira

Bikoro

*DOMAINE DE LA
COURONNE*

Lake
Kivu

GERMAN
EAST
AFRICA

Stanley
Pool

Bolobo

R. Kwa

*Lake
Leopold II*

CONGO

R. Lomami

Brazzaville

R. Congo

R. Kasai

FREE

Banana

Leopoldville
(Kinshasa)

*COMPAGNIE
DU KASAI*

STATE

Boma

R. Kwilu

Matadi

*SOCIÉTÉ
ANONYME
BELGE*

R. Lualaba

Lake
Tanganyika

Railway under
construction

St Paul de Loanda

PORTUGUESE
WEST AFRICA
(Angola)

Kolwezi

*Lake
Mweru*

ATLANTIC OCEAN

BRITISH
CENTRAL AFRICA
(Rhodesia)

Congo Free State

Equator

Portuguese
East Africa

South African
Republic
(Transvaal)

Lourenço Marques

Delagoa Bay

Bloemfontein

Orange
Free State

Durban

Cape Colony

0   400 km

0   400 miles

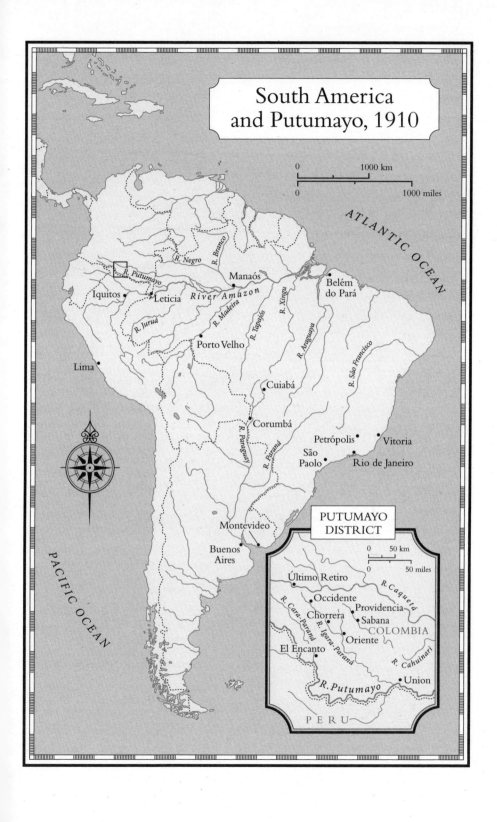

South America
and Putumayo, 1910

0   1000 km

0   1000 miles

ATLANTIC OCEAN

PACIFIC OCEAN

R. Putumayo

R. Negro

R. Branco

Manaós

Belém
do Pará

Iquitos

Leticia   River Amazon

R. Juruá

R. Madeira

R. Tapajós

R. Xingu

R. Araguaya

R. São Francisco

Porto Velho

Lima

Cuiabá

Corumbá

R. Paraguay

R. Paraná

Petrópolis   Vitoria

São
Paolo   Rio de Janeiro

Montevideo

Buenos
Aires

PUTUMAYO
DISTRICT

0   50 km

0   50 miles

Último Retiro

R. Caquetá

Occidente

Providencia

R. Cara-Paraná

Chorrera

Sabana

COLOMBIA

R. Igara-Paraná

Oriente

El Encanto

R. Cahuinari

R. Putumayo   Union

PERU

Author's Note

Some of the contemporary accounts of peoples, events and places in this book use language which is unacceptable to us today. Because such language raises issues that are central to the book's themes, and in the interests of employing the authentic voices of the characters involved, I have included it in limited direct and indirect quotation.

In the second half of the book, I have silently corrected the Norwegian Adler Christensen's idiosyncratic spelling (and grammar when confusing) when quoting from his writings in what was his second language.

Prologue

3 August 1916

Roger Casement walked through the yard of London's Pentonville Prison to the scaffold on a sunny morning. The dark, melancholic good looks that had drawn comparison to the intrepid conquistador Francisco Pizarro had become gaunt through disease, betrayal and exhaustion. Yet his expression was calm: the desperate international political and legal dramas of the last few years had fallen away, his inner divisions had resolved themselves and the secrecy and shame of his double life had ceased to matter. The priest alongside him was struck by the almost regal dignity with which the tall man carried himself. Casement gave the responses to the litany for the dying firmly: he had attended Mass in the prison at 7.30, and received his first Holy Communion at the same time as the Last Rites. As he climbed the wooden steps, he looked up at the sky and remarked in his pleasant baritone that it was 'a beautiful morning'.

The previous day, the Cabinet had decided that the execution would go ahead despite the powerful supplications from around the world calling for his reprieve. A brutal propaganda campaign made his traitor's death a certainty; only five years previously, he had been awarded a knighthood for his humanitarian service on two continents to those without a voice. But even though he had failed in his last great endeavour, Casement could still become a martyr for a cause that he knew would prevail. The romantic reformer was worn out by the idealistic struggles that were now crushed beneath the wheels of world events. He accepted that on his last platform he would 'die the death I sought, and may God forgive the mistakes and receive the intent – Ireland's freedom'.

His inner reaction was one of gentle incomprehension: he was puzzled as to why 'anyone wants to hang . . . one who never hurt a human being – and whose heart was always compassionate and pitiful for the grief of others'. The prison authorities confiscated this last piece of writing, fearful that a charged reminder of his altruism might inflame the public mood, made febrile as it was by the daily death toll from the Battle of the Somme. Just before the hangman pulled the lever, Roger Casement uttered his last words – 'I die for my country.'

Behind the simplicity of that earthly farewell lay a complex man, forced to live a double life by the contemporary legal and moral constraints, whose silencing of his own voice allowed the voiceless to be heard. He had carried himself from an unanchored childhood to barely charted West Africa and the first of his three destinies, yet the same impulses that generated global renown as the first great humanitarian reformer of the century also sowed the seeds of strategic chaos and eventually brought him to Pentonville on this bright August day. He was, in T. E. Lawrence's words, a 'broken archangel', a force for good made fallible by the repressive tenets of the era and his own emotions. He poured those emotions into causes and actions that deflected from his own, mysterious interior being. Roger Casement's life was a surprisingly modern one, driven by moral courage, romantic patriotism and passionate striving, but foreshortened by secrecy, unworldliness and treachery as he was caught up in the great movements of his time. It still arouses disquiet, ambiguity and controversy over a century after his death; perhaps only now can it begin to be understood as a whole.

PART ONE

Reformer

1. Conquistador

In late 1883 the SS *Bonny* moved through the hundreds of miles of ochre silt thrown out by the freshwater force of the Congo River to dock in Boma, on the river's northern shore about fifty miles upstream from the Atlantic. The 5,000-ton cargo steamer's purser was a tall, strikingly handsome nineteen-year-old Anglo-Irish orphan with a thin face, deep-set grey eyes that could be simultaneously soft and blazing, black curly hair and the beautiful, musical speaking voice of a 'cultured English gentleman'. His smitten cousin – and confidante for all but his most closely guarded secrets – considered that the moment he 'entered a room, he seemed to make the other people in it seem commonplace'.

The young man, neither fully Irish nor fully English, neither Catholic nor Protestant, not at ease yet not a stranger in the British Isles, needed to escape the emotionally disjointed, peripatetic childhood that had ended with him a Ward of Chancery under the care of a guardian in Ulster whom he barely knew. After leaving school at the age of fifteen, he went to live with his maternal aunt Grace Bannister's family in Liverpool, where his uncle, an agent for one of the trading companies that made the city the foremost port for the British Empire, introduced him to the Elder Dempster shipping line, owners of the *Bonny*. After this leg-up, the inadequately educated, connectionless Roger Casement 'got every step in life . . . entirely off my own bat'.

Despite the cheer of the Bannister home, Casement had to get away. He felt taken advantage of as a lowly clerk in Elder Dempster. But more significantly, and unacknowledged by his conscious self, his homosexuality – which emerged to his close friends and family, and to the world, in a cataclysmic revelation only in his last weeks – meant that he could not live a conventional life in Britain. His restless energy demanded open spaces or he 'would die', so he made the four-week journey from Liverpool via Plymouth, Hamburg, Madeira and Grand Canary to Sierra Leone and eventually Boma. The captain of the ship had been told his new crew member was 'a noisy, talkative character', so was surprised to find him 'quiet and intense, speaking little'. Casement often confounded expectations: he kept his inner, bifurcated identity hidden even from those that knew him best.

He craved the romance of adventure, but had no inkling of how the first sight of the 'vast and gaunt' waters surrounding Boma would lead to the moral education that would transform the lives of the inhabitants on two continents – and set him on the path to greatness, worldwide acclaim and the scaffold.

In 1877, only six years before Casement's arrival in the port, when it was beyond the frontier of colonial Africa, unclaimed by any European power, four exhausted and bedraggled Africans turned up with a letter addressed 'To any gentleman who speaks English at Embomma'. Its author wrote that he had 'arrived at this place from Zanzibar with 115 souls, men, women and children' who were 'now in a state of imminent starvation' and suffering from scurvy, dysentery and fever; they could 'buy nothing from the natives for they laugh at our kinds of cloths, beads and wire'. Supplies must arrive within two days or there would be 'a fearful time of it among the dying'. The letter was signed 'H. M. Stanley, Commanding Anglo-American Expedition for Exploration of Africa' and it astonished the eighteen or so hard-bitten Portuguese, Dutch, French and English traders who lived in boxlike tin-roofed houses on the bank of the estuary.

The enfeebled Stanley was carried in on a hammock to complete his 7,000-mile, 999-day coast-to-coast journey. He had not been heard from for over a year, and had lost the majority of his men to desertion, drowning, death in battle, dysentery, attacks by cannibal, snake and hippopotamus, thirst, starvation and worms that burrowed through the soles of their feet. Many others were to die in the next few days from sheer exhaustion. Yet the death toll was nothing to that meted out: Stanley boasted that 'we have attacked and destroyed 28 large towns and three or four score villages'.

For Stanley, the arrival in Boma – his purpose being to prove the river link between the vastness of the Congo interior and the sea – was a personal, political and global triumph. The illegitimate son of feckless Welsh parents, he had been raised in a Denbighshire workhouse run by a sadistic schoolmaster before finding his way to America as a deckhand. He was befriended in New Orleans by a wealthy English cotton trader, from whom he took his surname and education, and uniquely served in the Confederate Army, the Union Army and the Union Navy in the American Civil War before deserting to look for adventure as a *New York Herald* foreign correspondent.

Stanley's greatest scoop was finding Dr David Livingstone. Livingstone had discovered the Victoria Falls, Lake Nyasa, the Zambezi River and a previously unacknowledged slave trade; he had seen 400 Africans massacred by an Arab slaver at a market on the banks of the Lualaba River. Livingstone was clear that the unknown heart of the continent had to be cleansed by 'Commerce, Christianity and Civilization', the mantra of the British Empire, then nearing its height as the controller of the world's economies (including those it had not actually colonised, such as China and Argentina) and its policeman, even if the Pax Britannica mostly operated at gunpoint. But by 1871 Livingstone had not been heard from in six years, and Stanley seized his moment to launch his expedition. His book, straightforwardly titled *How I Found Livingstone*, was a massive bestseller, despite accusations that his exaggeration tipped into fraudulence. The exploration authority in Britain, the Royal Geographical Society, sponsor of a competing expedition, put it about that he was 'neither a proper explorer nor a proper gentleman'; the French newspapers, by contrast, declared his discovery to be a feat comparable to Hannibal's and Napoleon's crossings of the Alps. Despite his vexed relationship with the country of his birth, Stanley was a pallbearer at Livingstone's funeral in Westminster Abbey two years later, at which he underwent the dramatic epiphany which convinced him that he had to continue his hero's work. Boma was the endpoint of his crossing of the continent from the Indian Ocean to the Atlantic, to prove that the Lualaba River was the upper reaches of the gigantic River Congo, unconnected to the Nile. He had started to fill in a huge blank on the map of Africa, establishing that the Congo was navigable for a thousand miles and linked 7,000 miles of interconnected waterways, draining a basin of 1.3 million square miles – an area larger than modern India and rich in commercial prospects.

Such discoveries precipitated the astonishingly swift and rapacious 'Scramble for Africa' in the second half of the nineteenth century. Explorers rushed to find the source of the Nile, believing it to be the cradle of civilisation as well as the mightiest waterway for carrying goods to and from Europe. There were dreams of goldfields and diamond mines, and the certainty of ivory in the 10 million square miles of new territory; over 100 million inhabitants offered a ready-made labour force. Europe was in a financial depression in the 1840s and needed new markets for its products, as well as a purpose and prestige that could raise morale and prospects: France had been defeated in the Franco-Prussian War of 1870–1; Italy had just become united and the newly unified Germany was creating its Second Reich. The German Chancellor Otto von Bismarck, embarking on his nineteen energetic years in office, foresaw the possibility of making trouble between France and Britain thousands of miles from home, as well as stemming the flood of emigrants to the United States from his country by giving them new opportunities. He coined the word *Kolonialtummel*, 'colonial whirl', as an apt description for the times.

The imposing, luxuriously bearded, outwardly charming and obstinate King Leopold II of the Belgians was avid for news of Stanley as the journalist-explorer struggled to reach the sea. King of the Belgians was a position created for Leopold's father only forty years earlier and one that always seemed vulnerable in a young country internally divided by its antagonistic Flemish and Walloon citizens, and externally trapped between the warring powers of France and Germany. Leopold had grown up dreaming of an empire from the unexplored world that would give him status among his crowned cousins and prove to his *'petit pays, petits gens'* that they 'could be an imperial people capable of dominating and civilising others'. Leopold I, who had mocked his son's fantasies, had been married to Princess Charlotte, heir presumptive to George IV of England, but she had

died in childbirth. His sister Carlota had married Archduke Maximilian of Austro-Hungary and the couple had been installed as
Napoleon III's puppet Emperor and Empress of Mexico, although
their reign had ended when Maximilian had been executed by rebels
in 1867.

Leopold's jealousy had been intensified by visits to the British colonies of Ceylon, India and Burma, and to the Dutch East Indies with
their crops of coffee, sugar, indigo and tobacco. Yet his ministers
were advising him that free-trading Belgium was strictly business-
orientated and that expensive colonies were not necessarily good for
profits. In one of the more murderous ironies of history, the King
understood that any territory belonging to tiny Belgium had to be
presented as a largely humanitarian venture. He invested profitably
in the Suez Canal Company and looked into buying Fiji, railways in
Brazil, and portions of Argentina several times larger than Belgium;
he tried to acquire the Philippines from Spain in 1875. Now, in envy
of his European cousins and realising that steam transport had transformed the possibilities of exploitation – further enlarged by the
knowledge that quinine was a useful preventative to deadly malaria –
he turned his attention to Africa. In the middle of each night an early
edition of *The Times* was packed into a special cylindrical container in
London, taken by railway from Blackfriars to Dover, carried on to
the Ostend boat and thrown from the Brussels express as it passed the
sprawling palace at Laeken, just outside Brussels. There it would land
at the feet of a footman who hurried it to the royal breakfast table to
satisfy the King's obsession with Stanley.

The Atlantic slave trade had been prohibited in Britain and America in the first decade of the century. Britain had then in 1833 passed
the Slavery Abolition Act, which attempted to formally end the use
of slave labour in the West Indies while providing colossal sums in
reparations to British slave owners; in the US, the 13th Amendment
to the Constitution, which officially abolished slavery, was adopted
in 1865. Although many more were enslaved in Spanish and Portuguese colonies in South America, some millions in Brazil alone, the
French, Germans and British were focused on the African trade as a
part of their purported civilising mission. But in East Africa so-called

Arab slave traders, often Africans from modern Kenya and Tanzania, sold their captives in the markets of Zanzibar for exploitation there, as well as in Persia, Madagascar and the plantations of the Arab peninsula. Leopold was determined to play this to his advantage: in the summer of 1876 he visited his first cousin Queen Victoria at Balmoral and lunched with Angela Burdett-Coutts, an influential philanthropist keen to help missionaries, children without access to education, homeless prostitutes, and thirsty horses in need of water troughs; he sent an aide to Berlin to discover German intentions in Africa. Next, he convened a conference of explorers and geographers which he steered towards establishing the International African Association in Brussels and marking out points on the blank map where 'hospitable, scientific and pacification bases' could be set up. With these preliminaries out of the way, he was invigorated by an account, tucked away on a middle page of *The Times*, of Stanley's arrival in Boma and began to track the explorer's feted return to Europe, even sending emissaries to intercept him when his ship docked in Marseilles, an honour Stanley did not forget.

Leopold's go-between with Stanley was General Henry Sanford, a Connecticut millionaire awarded his military rank in return for his presentation of a battery of field guns to the 1st Minnesota Regiment in the American Civil War. Appointed by Abraham Lincoln as Minister to Belgium, Sanford had become increasingly dependent on Leopold's patronage as he squandered his fortune in disastrous mining and agricultural ventures, and by taking out patents on inventions such as a box to lubricate railway axles with water rather than oil. Stanford became the King's ambassador just as the Scramble intensified and he was despatched to lure the celebrity explorer to Brussels. Stanley negotiated a salary of 50,000 francs* a year and a fully funded expeditionary force to survey the Congo Basin under the aegis of the misleadingly named International Association of the Congo (proprietor the King of the Belgians).

Stanley's first Congo stint for Leopold was also his longest. It was crucial that he took control before the French explorer Pierre de

---

* Nearly £200,000 today.

Brazza could establish the settlement that was to take his name on the river's north bank. In August 1879, he steamed up the navigable 110 miles of the lower stretch of the river to Vivi, and for 'a rental' agreed with the five local chiefs to establish a settlement on the 'barren, mean and worthless', albeit strategically placed, land. He offered £15 per annum in the brass rods that served as currency, with a 'monthly royalty of £2 of cloth' and, as a one-off payment, 'fifty pieces of cloth, three boxes of gin, five military coats, five knives, five cloth waist belts and five ample loincloths of superior quality'.

Stanley's men spent a year breaking rocks as they built the station at Vivi and then began to carve a road linking the Upper and Lower Congo, bypassing 250 miles of rapids, one stretch of which, 200 yards wide, was named the Gates of Hell, its cliffs on either side towering over the white waves as they crashed through the Crystal Mountains. The half-starved, disease-ridden men often covered only a few hundred yards a day, carrying their canoes alongside the torrents that had made all but the coastal areas resistant to exploration in the past. Stanley had five months' start on Brazza, but his workforce was burdened with the parts of two dismantled steamers, the *Royal* and *En Avant*, each one of which weighed over three tons, more than the combined bodyweight of the porters. They bridged ravines, filled in gullies and cut through bush and forest to traverse the rapids with their fifty tons of equipment, including the steamboats and a barge, to reach the newly named Stanley Pool, the key natural harbour giving access to the Upper Congo. The Pool was fourteen miles by eighteen, filled with swirling cross-currents and islands of floating weed as the river roared out of the forest with a force that could uproot trees – the river drops over a thousand feet to sea level in a mere 220 miles, in places surging through its many cataracts into forty-foot waves. On arrival at Stanley Pool, the lowest navigable point of the Upper Congo, the Welsh-American commenced work on a station he called Leopoldville, now Kinshasa, despite being laid so low by malaria that he dictated as his last words an apology to Leopold for failing to carry out his mission.

But by the time the *Bonny* docked with her new purser, the dynamic Stanley had established Leopoldville on his eponymous Pool; the tree-topped hill above it was renamed Leopold Hill, and soon Lake Leopold II and the Leopold River appeared on maps. Stanley had spent around 3 million francs* of his boss's private fortune, but in April 1882 he was ready to set off upstream to establish the great trading empire that he envisaged. The furthest settlement, Stanley Falls, where the river narrowed from two miles wide to under half a mile, its cross-currents throwing up violent jets of foam, was at the midpoint of the entire continent.

Leopold commenced a fresh diplomatic push, adjusting his presentation of the Congo for each audience. He got his new association blessed by London as a 'Society of the Red Cross . . . formed with the noble aim of rendering lasting and disinterested services to the cause of progress', engendering a donation of 50,000 francs from Lady Burdett-Coutts, while in Berlin he spoke of a modern crusade against the Arab slavers moving across the continent from Zanzibar. Sanford adroitly blurred the lines in the United States: on a trip to tend to his failing investments, he gave a speech in New York which promoted Leopold's stated vision 'to found a chain of posts or hospices, both hospitable and scientific . . . ultimately, by their humanizing influences, to secure the abolition of traffic in slaves'. One commentator declared it 'enough to make an American believe in kings forever'.

Leopoldville Station and two others were finished by March 1882, and that autumn the sick Stanley, disillusioned with Leopold's autocratic rule over the Congo chiefs, travelled to Brussels, where he was amazed to be told that the King was prepared to increase his expedition's expenditure fivefold and its manpower from 250 to 3,000 men in return for upping the amount of ivory to be carried out of the basin. Stanley disciplined the workers who had given him 'more trouble than all the African tribes put together'; he used his Zanzibari militia to quash any dissenting Arab slavers; he bribed and cajoled the local chiefs, sometimes encouraging them with demonstrations of his state-of-the-art Krupp cannonry to make their mark on the treaties they could not read, in exchange for more cloth, more

---

* Approximately £11 million today.

gin and more brass rods. King Leopold, Stanley commented, had the 'enormous voracity to swallow a million of square miles with a gullet that will not take in a herring'. There were 200 ethnic groups in the Congo speaking over 400 languages and dialects, but they possessed no gunpowder and no tribe was powerful enough to offer more than token resistance. Soon the new flag of a gold star on a blue background flew above the villages and lands of more than 450 Congo chiefs, and Stanley rushed to write his new work of propaganda, *The Congo and the Founding of Its Free State: A Story of Work and Exploration*. It was soon to be a bestseller that was translated into seventeen languages and boosted Leopold's prestige as well as augmenting his own mythology.

Leopold continued to play the Great Powers off against one another – telling the British government, for example, that if he did not get all the land he wanted he would withdraw from Africa entirely, leaving their rival France with first refusal on the territory or allowing the Portuguese to resurrect their claim on the mouth of the river; at the same time he commissioned an article for circulation to influential Englishmen revealing just how untrustworthy the Portuguese had been over treaties in the past. In order to settle the claims and the division of the spoils, the Berlin West Africa Conference was convened in the slushy winter of 1884–5. It was chaired by Iron Chancellor Bismarck and took place under the huge chandelier in the white, pillared music room, with its red damask curtains, of his Wilhelmstrasse house. Fourteen plenipotentiaries were present, ambassadors from the European nations, Russia and the Ottoman Empire, but not a single African representative, and diplomatically lightweight Belgium did not warrant a delegate. Leopold had to absorb the news sent to him daily while walking in his enormous, tropically heated glasshouses at Laeken, one of which had a massive gold star on its roof. But his manoeuvrings paid off as none of France, Germany or Britain wanted to cede power to any of the others: Britain was keen not to allow the French any control over its oil-rich Niger territory, and Bismarck was determined, despite the recent entente with his neighbours, that France should not expand its colonial reach. The possibility of the International Association of the

Congo remained on the table as a compromise that gave no Great Power too much influence and satisfied the delegates' humanitarian, free-trade-based idealism with its implied benefits for all – including the Congolese.

It was agreed in February 1885 that a huge swathe of Central Africa should become a free-trade zone without slavery. The working map had been drawn from Stanley's sketches of the Congo River and a few hundred of its shoreline villages; Leopold and he added a few sweeping lines in red pencil for approval by the conference. At the mention of Leopold's name during the signing ceremony, all the delegates rose to their feet and cheered. He became King-Sovereign of the Congo Free State on 1 June, ruler of a territory that encompassed a thirteenth of the entire African land mass, was larger than Western Europe and seventy-six times the size of Belgium. Bismarck declared that the state was 'destined to be one of the most important executors of the [humanitarian] work we intend to do' and hoped for the speedy 'realisation of the noble aspirations of its illustrious creator'. The London newspapers treated the conference as a triumph of British negotiation on humanity's behalf: the *Standard* hailed the huge market for 'cotton goods, blankets, crockery, muskets, gun powder, hardware of all kinds, and cheap finery of every description' and the *Leeds Mercury* saluted 'that noble-minded Sovereign who had the wisdom and courage to begin the enterprise of the Congo which would be the bright centre to the new Federation of Freedom and Peace'. A new national anthem, 'Towards the Future', was commissioned. Five years earlier, one of Leopold's subordinates had written to Stanley, 'There is no question of granting the slightest political power to negroes. That would be absurd.'

Between Stanley's near-death arrival in a hammock and Casement's stepping off the *Bonny*, Boma had grown in line with its new significance as the capital and the last point of contact for the riches leaving the continent. Warehouses on cast-iron pilings as protection from rot and termites had sprung up on the dockside and were soon to be linked by a narrow-gauge railway to the government buildings and offices on the cooler plateau above the town. Three times a day the seventy-five white colonial officials were transported down the hill and on through the banana plantations to take their meals in dining rooms at sea level. Leopold himself never undertook the journey, but his birthday was celebrated in the Congo with a review of troops, a shooting contest and a concert by a local Catholic children's choir. The choir had rehearsed in the oven-like cast-iron church, the grandiosely named 'Cathedral', whose wall panels, window frames, roof and spire had all been shipped over from a Belgian foundry.

Rather than eating with the other officials, the Governor General remained in his comfortable residence with its French windows, porches and guards in blue uniforms and red fezzes. Unlike his counterparts in other colonies, he had little to do as the place was run from offices in Leopold's palace. The King picked the top two rungs of administrators himself and the four or five men in Brussels with oversight of the colony reported directly to him. He set up orders of chivalry, including a medal for African chiefs with his profile engraved on one side and the Congo's new coat of arms above the legend 'LOYALTY AND DEVOTION' on the other. He had no need to consult before his decree that 'vacant land' and all the 'raw materials' found in his colossal country were the property of the state. What constituted 'vacant land' in a sparsely populated country without any form of writing or documentation of property ownership, and where agricultural soil often had to be left fallow for years to produce crops, was not considered.

Stanley's rental payments with their sweeteners of cloth and gin were soon forgotten and free trade never arrived. The Congolese were forbidden to sell or deliver ivory to anyone other than one of Leopold's state agents, and even that was set against the King's losses: he told his Prime Minister that the state 'is certainly not a business. If it gathers ivory on certain of its lands, that is only to lessen its deficit.' He had spent his entire fortune of 19 million francs, and started to economise: the man who loved his food to the extent that he had been known to order his next meal in Paris restaurants before he had finished his current one let it be known that he would consume one less course at lunch. He rewrote his will, leaving the Congo to

Belgium after his death in exchange for an immediate loan of 25 million francs plus heavy investment in a railway. He had been granted a mortgageable chattel in Berlin.

Yet Leopold understood the profits that would flow now that the costs of development were sunk. There was a near-insatiable market for ivory billiard balls, piano keys, knife handles, combs and hairbrushes, napkin rings, jewellery, ornaments and false teeth. More significant still was the burgeoning new rubber industry: Leopold estimated that 'if every warrior on the immediate banks of the Congo and its navigable affluents were to pick about a third of a pound in rubber each day . . . £5,000,000* worth of vegetable produce could be obtained without exhaustion of the wild forest productions'. Electrical cabling was using increasing amounts of rubber and a Scottish vet and cycling enthusiast, John Boyd Dunlop, had patented the inflatable rubber tyre in 1888; seven years later the Michelin brothers had put pneumatic tyres on a car in the Paris–Bordeaux race for the first time. Leopold's analysis of his astonishing future wealth was an underestimate. His years of entrepreneurial diplomatic wiles were about to result in an economic boom – albeit at a devastating human cost.

At the start of Joseph Conrad's *Heart of Darkness*, Charles Marlow likens the European rulers of the Congo to the Roman invaders of Britain: 'They were no colonists, their administration was merely a squeeze . . . They were conquerors . . . They grabbed what they could get for the sake of what was to be got.' Roger Casement did not intend to become a member of this victorious administration when his employer's ship docked in 1883 – it was about the escape 'from desk and pen'. His brothers, two and three years older, had already set off for South Africa and Australia, and Roger had even greater reasons than them for feeling a misfit in the British Isles. As a child brought up in gloomy, constricted places, never settling for long, he expressed a yearning for exotic escape by painting scenes of tropical beasts in a made-up jungle and writing adolescent escapist poetry of historical romance; when he was eight, he might have been

---

* Worth nearly 100 times as much at today's values.

stirred by Stanley's celebrated accounts of his discovery of Dr Livingstone. Shortly before the Berlin Conference, aged twenty, after three round trips on the *Bonny* and a decade after Stanley had begun his near-fatal journey of exploration, Roger Casement decided that his future lay in Africa.

He applied to join the International African Association, explaining to his relations in Antrim that it managed 'several large expeditions up the river Congo in south west Africa of which Stanley the great explorer is the head', and, after an initial wobble over the small salary of £72 per annum, signed up as the Berlin Conference was getting under way. After he had made his name as a great humanitarian, it suited him to be vague about his first years in Africa. He probably worked surveying the railway. He also served in the stores at Vivi, loading ivory to be taken downstream to Boma, in the terminology of the time calling the Congolese 'savages' and 'the natives'; late in his life, he merely claimed that the period was spent 'in varied employments'. These were the years that were to give him greater knowledge of the place 'than any man living', as a fellow reformer was to say. By the time of a significant literary encounter a few years further on, his views on the conduct of colonialism in general, and on Leopold's regime in the Congo in particular, were close to being fully formed.

The Free State was administered by about 3,000 Europeans in its early days, approximately half of whom were Belgian, and the new arrival was never short of work. He joined the euphemistically named Sanford Exploring Expedition, alongside virtually all the non-Belgians in the state, in 1886. As a reward for his diplomacy in bringing about Washington's recognition of the Congo Free State, General Sanford was permitted to gather gum copal, palm oil and copper as well as rubber and ivory in the Upper Congo, and was promised more help than was actually delivered with porters, depots and transportation. The twenty-one-year-old Casement was invited to run the expedition's Matadi supply base at an annual salary of £150;* later, he co-ordinated 300 Africans who carried the parts of

---

* Around £16,000 at today's prices.

a steamer, *Florida*, past the rapids and cataracts above the town. It was dull and humid work, but with its compensations: Mounteney Jephson, one of Stanley's men, described dining in April 1887 in Casement's 'large tent . . . Sitting down to a *real* dinner at a *real* table with a table cloth and dinner napkins and plenty to eat with Burgundy to drink and cocoa and cigarettes after dinner . . . in the middle of the wilds'. Three days later they met in the early morning and Jephson 'tucked into his oatmeal biscuits'. Casement, the seemingly conventional colonial figure, was singled out by another colleague at the base as 'a good, hard-working man' and, more significantly, as 'a gentleman, with some principle about him'.

He displayed those growing principles in his first recorded moral turning point. In 1886 and 1887 he often met 'an agent of the State', Lieutenant Franqui, the Commissaire of the Cataract Region, and twice saw him flogging workers. Casement accompanied one of them, who had been 'literally cut to pieces', on the fifty-mile walk to Boma, lending his hammock for the man to be carried in, only to be 'laughed at for my pains' by 'the judicial authority'. He was told he 'had no right of intervention' on behalf of those harmed by Leopold's men because the flogged men were 'poor Portuguese natives from S.E. Africa', despite their being government servants. Franqui went unpunished.

Casement's brief role in Stanley's Emin Pasha Relief Expedition in 1887 gave him insights into the absurdity of colonisation. Emin Pasha, the Governor of Equatoria in south Sudan, was in fact a short German called Eduard Schnitzer, a gifted linguist and eccentric who was gathering a collection of bugs, beetles and stuffed birds for the British Museum. The Mahdists in his territory were a Muslim fundamentalist group who staged a rebellion and killed the British Governor General of the colony, before demanding that Queen Victoria come to Africa, convert to Islam and submit to their rule. The British feared disaster and, being overstretched, they welcomed Stanley's offer of help. The expedition gathered its stores: bottles of champagne arrived from Fortnum's, a new dress uniform was tailored for Emin Pasha, and Hiram Maxim sent the prototype of his latest machine gun, which, Stanley claimed, would be 'of valuable service in helping civilisation to overcome barbarism'. Sponsorship was raised, including £60,000 from the Royal Geographical Society and a sum from Stanley's former employer, James Gordon Bennett Jr of the *New York Herald*, who insisted that the men march with the banner of the New York Yacht Club at their head.

Casement accompanied the expedition for only a week, so he did not venture as far as the cannibal-populated Ituri rainforest, where the vegetation was so thick that they often made only 400 yards' progress in a day; despite that, they were so far ahead of the supply chain that sometimes they had to roast ants for sustenance. Of the 389 men who set off, many of them supplied by the slaver and ivory trader Tippu Tip, over half died from tetanus and dysentery, fell to the poisoned arrows of the terrified forest dwellers or simply got lost. When the rump finally emerged in mid-1889 with their champagne and the uniform that had been made for an imagined six-foot official, and with nearly all the boxes of ammunition stranded elsewhere, it turned out that Emin Pasha preferred to dither between defeatism and resuming his post in order to botanise and store ivory; moreover, the threat from the Mahdists had disappeared since he had written his letters of distress. Tippu Tip retired to Zanzibar and his memoirs, leaving his sons to fight the Belgian incomers set on monopolising the ivory trade. Stanley, with hundreds more African deaths to his name, naturally made journalistic capital out of the expedition, and noted in his journal that Casement was 'a good specimen of the capable Englishman'.

Casement was brought starkly up against inhumanity again when he was promoted to run a new trading station at Equator, on the Upper Congo. On the way to his post, he endured a sixteen-day riverboat journey with the Belgian Captain Van Kerckhoven, a hot-headed Congo veteran who boasted of signing nine treaties with local chiefs in one day. In the next century, the novelist Graham Greene was vividly to describe 'the heat that engulfed them where the river narrowed to a mere hundred metres', the mosquitoes they had to cope with in the evening and the tsetse flies in the daytime; 'Even at night the air was so humid that it broke upon the cheek like tiny beads of rain.' In those conditions, watching Van Kerckhoven's wax-tipped moustache as he boasted how he paid his Black soldiers '5 brass rods per human head they brought him during the course of military operations . . . to stimulate their prowess in the face of the enemy' must have been almost unbearable to the sensitive Casement.

Despite the promise of more responsibility, there was little to do at Equator as trade had not developed. And what developments there were became distasteful as Casement came to realise that the ivory passing through the station was collected with little thought for the elephant hunters – he expressed no opinion about their prey. The ivory and rubber were for Sanford's private commercial ends, as far from the expressed humanitarianism of the so-called Free State as could be, and Casement took the moral course of resigning from his employment rather than going elephant shooting himself.

Casement was photographed with three of his closest Congo friends, and the portrait emphasises both his difference and his diffidence. All are wearing ties and high collars; Herbert Ward and Major William Parminter are in more formal dark suits, Casement and Edward Glave in tweed. However, Casement's clothes look ill-fitting and tropically crumpled by comparison to the others, and he is the only one who does not have the upright stance of an empire builder in front of the camera: he tilts his head to look out sideways, quizzically. He does not appear at ease with these Englishmen and is set apart from them, despite their friendship and many shared values.

Of the group, William Parminter had led the most adventurous life: he had fought in the Anglo-Zulu War of 1879, coming close to being awarded the Victoria Cross; after another period of fighting, he had joined Stanley in 1884. As Governor of Vivi province, he became the highest-ranking Englishman in the colony, with responsibility for finances and transport in the Lower Congo; as such, he was Casement's boss. Edward Glave had explored in Africa, Alaska and British Columbia, before returning in 1893 with a newspaper commission to locate the tree under which David Livingstone's heart had been buried. He was beginning a report on conditions under Leopold's rule when he died of disease at Matadi in 1895: had he survived, 'poor old Ted Glave', as Casement called him when travelling in his investigative footsteps shortly afterwards, might have become a companion in reform as well as in the photograph. The news of his death inspired a forgettable memorial poem from Casement:

> He sleeps himself, whose hand has often made
> The simple grave wherein lost comrades lie
> His last long tranquil slumber, duty-crowned . . .

Herbert Ward was taller even than Casement, and his weather-beaten face is set off by his starched white collar. He too had left school and country at the age of fifteen, working in Australia, New Zealand and Borneo before being picked by Stanley. He joined the Sanford Expedition and met Casement in their early days on the railway. The men became close, with Casement standing godfather to Ward's youngest son. Ward was in charge of the rear column of the Emin Pasha Relief Expedition, with 250 porters and five officers; when the column abandoned its post over a year later, only 150 of the porters and three officers remained. Ward, an accomplished big-game hunter, remained enamoured of Africa and on leaving after five years became a notable sculptor of African figures. Like Casement, he deplored the barbarous slavery of the Congo administration, and at the same time as Casement's conscience propelled him into public action at the start of the twentieth century he wrote campaigning leaflets. He left a beguiling description of Casement as 'a tall, handsome man of fine bearing; thin, mere muscle and bone, a sun-tanned face, blue eyes and black curly hair . . . with a captivating voice and singular charm'. He considered him a person 'of great refinement, high-minded and courteous, impulsive and poetical . . . Quixotic', albeit 'with a certain truth' and no interest in 'personal advancement'. But a few years after this encomium was published Ward was to repudiate his friend and travelling companion, vowing 'to turn him down forever' and changing his son's name by deed poll from Roger Casement Ward to Rodney Sanford Ward.

Casement's disillusion with the administration and regime was mounting by the late 1880s, exacerbated by the impotence he felt after the Franqui episode. The trading station at Equator had been

dull, Sanford's expedition was venal and his own small part in the
Emin Pasha business pointless. He wrote to Sanford to announce that
his work would be finished on the railway by November 1888 and
that he was resigning his employment on the grounds that the Africans under his command were unmotivated by the pitiful wages on
offer, and the money would be better spent on their education,
'quickening their good instincts (and they have many) and repressing
their bad'. It was a bold move by a junior to express his concern for
the welfare of those whose humanity was disregarded by Leopold's
regime. In any case, the Sanford Expedition soon joined the list of
its originator's flops. The general's mounting debts forced the sale of
his art collection and a move to a smaller chateau in Belgium, while
his man in charge in Africa gave up his miserable task and succumbed
to drink; the boilers of the steamboats that had been hauled by porters around the rapids were left rusting in the jungle.

Until the last day of his life, Casement's relationship with organised religion was vexed to the extent that he believed he had been
baptised both Protestant and Catholic, yet he was not comfortable in
either Church. His lifelong search for causes that might fill a lifelong
emotional hollowness expressed itself in a growing spirituality in the
late 1880s. His distaste for the colonial world of Stanley and Sanford
and his desire to help the Congolese rather than be a part of the
system that controlled them and their country led him to his next
role. The first Protestant missions, predominantly British and American, had started arriving in the country in 1878 thanks to Henry
Grattan Guinness of the brewing family and his wife. A few years
later, Guinness's Livingstone Inland Mission Society was merged
into the Baptist Missionary Society, which set up stations, initially
built of stakes, clay and palm fronds and thatched with grass roofs,
throughout the region. The Society commissioned a steamer, *The
Peace*, seventy foot by eleven, from Messrs Thornycroft of Chiswick,
which was shipped out in 1883 and carried piece by piece to Stanley
Pool for assembly; a British missionary boasted of her 'wire network
screens, strong enough to stop spears and slugs, and close enough to
stop even the small poisoned arrows carried by some of the tribes'.
Under the terms of the Berlin Conference, Leopold could keep other

nationalities at bay only through his increasing monopoly of the business of his colony, and he had no way of scrutinising the missionaries' work. Working in a mission was the only way Casement could remain in the country he had come to love and some of the contacts he was about to make, particularly those educated in the East London Missionary Training Institute, were to become his confidants and informers in his great work over a decade later.

William Holman Bentley, who had been in the Congo himself since 1879 and had hacked his way through the jungle as ruggedly as any explorer, vetted Casement's candidacy with care. He heard that he was 'very highly esteemed by everyone out here, a perfect gentleman, and very good and patient with the natives', as well as being 'the fittest man we could find anywhere to help'. Toughness and robust health were essential as hostile Congolese, the weather, insects and disease exacted their toll, and building the stations was as exhausting as laying the railways. Casement's moral and physical courage had been clearly demonstrated: he had been a strong swimmer since his teenage years on Ireland's north coast, and his feat of being the first white man known to swim across the hundred yards of the Nkisi River, avoiding its hidden whirlpools and its killer crocodiles, became the stuff of local legend, while his emerging reputation as a man who did not regard Africans as inferior made him a potentially valuable mission worker.

He was posted to Wathen Station, on a plateau 1,750 feet above sea level and eighty-five miles upstream of Matadi, near the town of Ngombe. The extensive settlement, funded by a wealthy Bristol wool merchant in 1884, consisted of a two-storey brick house and numerous other buildings raised on iron pillars. One of these consisted of a dormitory, chapel and schoolroom for 120 boys, another the same for sixty girls; a hospital, dispensary, printing office and farm buildings stood near by. By the time Casement arrived in 1888, mango, banana, plantain, cashew, alligator pear, orange, lime, coconut and breadfruit trees were flourishing and bringing in some income, and an English flower garden was developing thanks to the generosity of Sutton Seeds of Reading. The workers grew cassava, groundnuts, beans, onions, yams, millet, pumpkins, spinach, aubergines, 'tough native cabbages' and many local vegetables; they also kept chickens, goats and sheep, although their pig-rearing resulted in 'measly' animals. A square mile was under cultivation, and guineafowl and pigeon were shot to supplement the diet.

The station was managed by four men and three women, and the new arrival was welcomed. He was hired for £10 per month (with board deducted) until the end of the rainy season to take over 'the transport, building, planting, accounts, correspondence and general work'. Bentley was soon reporting back to London that the mission 'could not have done better either in terms or type of man'. As did many of those that met Casement in the Congo, Bentley declared that he was 'a gentleman' and was relieved to observe that his 'treatment of the natives is all that can be desired . . . there has been nothing in his manner of life out here which would cast reflection on us'. The only flaw he could find in his new worker was 'how fair, generous and good-hearted he was' in his unwillingness to haggle up the price of the station's surplus produce in the local town, and in his willingness to pay twenty brass rods for an item where others would haggle down to twelve. When he left the station, Casement gave the mission £3 10s from his meagre savings.

At the end of the rainy season of 1889, the perennially restless Casement found himself without employment. He had been away from the uneasy confines of Britain for six years on and off, and had made a name for himself as a hard-working, reliable and sympathetic figure. As Herbert Ward said, he was 'a good man to have near in Africa where situations were always in one way or another critical'; his fellow adventurer Fred Puleston commented on his 'emotional, tender and sympathetic nature' when dealing with people and animals, 'condemning cruelty and injustice in any form', and stressed that he was 'honourable and loyal', the sort to see a cause through. He was widely revered as he tried to improve the lives of the Congolese – they gave him the names *Swama Casement*, 'Woman's God', and *Monafuma Casement*, 'Son of a King'.

He felt useful as he found his feet and a cause in Africa, he had 'made friends with the natives . . . poor souls' – although any corroborative Congolese voices are lost to us – and unlike most Europeans he picked up the essence of their many dialects. He spurned his fellow white officials: while they travelled first class on the two-day train journey to Stanley Pool, he went second class, which would 'in an ordinary European community be held cruel for the transport of hardy animals', partly out of parsimony but more 'as an example to all my countrymen out here who think it *infra dig* to go 2nd with blacks'. As he steamed back across the Atlantic on leave, he reflected that he had made 'no enemies, only friends'; those friends were to prove loyal when he later took on the all-corrupting greed of the colonial regime.

At this time, Leopold was rapaciously ramping up control. The King-Sovereign forbade the sale of ivory to anyone but his own agents, who in turn were encouraged to drive a savage bargain: for ivory purchased for eight francs a kilo, an agent would get 6 per cent of the much higher European market price; there was then a sliding scale which gave 10 per cent of the same market price for ivory purchased at four francs per kilo. It was a powerful incentive to negotiate at gunpoint, especially given that the elephant hunters were paid in beads, cloth and brass rods. The free-trade declarations of the comparatively recent Berlin Conference which gave the Congolese an income from their own country had been categorically pushed aside.

Brutality was on the rise. Thousands of porters were needed to carry the agents' food, ammunition and building materials into the interior, and the ivory and rubber the other way, where the river was unnavigable. *Chicottes*, whips made of twisted hippopotamus hide, were used to keep the conscripted men, and often boys, in line; a punishment beating could consist of anything between 25 and 150 lashes. As a Congo official wrote without shame in his memoirs: 'There were about a hundred of them, trembling and fearful before the overseer, who strolled by whirling a whip. For each stocky and broad-backed fellow, how many were skeletons, dried up like mummies, their skin worn out . . . seamed with deep scars, covered with suppurating wounds . . . No matter, they were all up to the job.' Of the 300 porters conscripted by a district commissioner to set up a new trading post 600 miles upcountry, not one returned.

In 1888, only three years after the Berlin Conference and while Stanley was still struggling through the Ituri rainforest, Leopold formalised his control. The Force Publique, a grim hybrid of a violent military police unit, a mobile guerrilla force and Leopold's private army, came into being alongside the labour-contract system under which all Congolese were forcibly employed by the state for up to seven years. By the end of the century the Force was the most powerful army in Africa with 19,000 officers, many of them scoundrels, ex-convicts, fugitives, adventurers and sadists who signed up for their own ends, and tens of thousands of conscripts. The Force consumed more than half the state's budget and was scattered throughout a network of small military posts, each with one or two white officers, exemplified by Van Kerckhoven, commanding dozens of Black soldiers. The conscripts were forced to fight vicious battles against rebellious warrior tribes, who were sometimes their own people. These clashes, won by superior European firepower, were barely mentioned in official reports.

Whether or not Casement's conscience had been fully shocked into wakefulness, whether or not he believed that the atrocities he had witnessed or heard about were isolated instances of brutality, he felt, quite simply, that he had 'all the love of Africa still upon me' and was anyway unemployed. He decided to recommit to the Congo. The indomitable Major Parminter offered a route back by issuing an invitation to join him in the work for the Société Anonyme Belge – in effect, Leopold – which had taken over the assets of the Sanford Exploring Expedition, to organise transport on the lower river. Casement took a few months' leave in 1889 and went to Brussels to negotiate his one-year contract (it was a sign of his standing that he was not required to commit to the usual three years) before setting out for New York at the start of the following year to accompany Herbert Ward on a speaking tour of the United States. The bookings were made by the J. B. Pond Lyceum Bureau, the premier agency for anyone with a reforming bent, including the author Mark Twain, the African-American educator and presidential adviser Booker T. Washington and later the suffragette Emmeline Pankhurst.

Casement rarely shone in public performance, so his uncredited role was probably as Ward's off-stage support.

On his return, he stayed briefly in London, attending with his sister Nina, eight years his senior, a public lecture given by Stanley before returning to Africa. He strode out into the grassy scrub above Matadi, walking up to twenty miles a day, 'squatting somewhere or other' to hold a palaver, an improvised conference between Europeans and village chiefs, before moving on to scout out the best spots on which to build the stations that enabled the spoils of the interior to be sent on their path to Europe. In the course of this work, his experience and feeling for the country gave rise to an encounter that would reverberate in literature.

When Captain Johannes Freiesleben of the riverboat *Florida* was killed after a trivial quarrel with the inhabitants of Tshumbiri, a village a hundred miles upstream of Leopoldville, the Société du Haut-Congo sent 370 soldiers to massacre all the inhabitants and burn the settlement to the ground. A Polish master seaman, a stocky, black-bearded man with intense, narrowed eyes, was appointed as a replacement. Konrad Korzeniowski was thirty-two and had spent a decade in the British merchant navy after a troubled childhood partially spent in France. While job hunting in London, he had heard tales of the Emin Pasha expedition and his youthful attraction to Africa was reawakened. He docked in Boma in June 1890, carrying with him the manuscript of a novel, and by the time *Almayer's Folly* was published five years later, Korzeniowski had taken the name Joseph Conrad. His six months in the Congo transformed his outlook on life: as he was to tell his publisher years later, 'he had not a thought in his head' and was 'a perfect animal' before his arrival.

The day after he landed at Boma, Conrad went upriver to Matadi, where he was to stay for three weeks before the trek to Leopoldville and command of the flimsy, rectangular fifteen-tonner *Roi des Belges*; it turned out that the *Florida* had been laid up for repairs. Matadi had grown, but 'the town of stones' was no more salubrious: it consisted of rusty corrugated iron shacks on high crags overlooking the rapids, and the European settlement was thronged with prostitutes, drunken sailors and adventurers hoping to make their fortunes in the booming ivory trade. As Conrad arrived, the ivory exchange in Antwerp had surpassed that of Liverpool, with over 75,000 kilos passing through each year – five years later again it had quadrupled in size, selling the tusks of thousands of elephants. The new arrival hated the place and considered the ivory trade an 'idiotic employment'; he was therefore relieved to meet a tall, handsome, weathered man employed as a surveyor for the Matadi–Leopoldville railway, who shared his sense of alienation. Conrad told his diary that it would be 'a great pleasure under any circumstances' to make the acquaintance of Roger Casement, but in in his first hours in King Leopold's colony it was a 'positive piece of luck'. His immediate impressions of the Congo veteran were that he 'thinks, speaks well' and was 'most intelligent and very sympathetic'.

The two men spent a couple of weeks in a shared room, talking until the early hours and going on 'short "palavers" with neighbouring village chiefs' made possible by Casement's fluency in the 'coast languages'. Their objective was to procure porters for the caravans around the cataracts and rapids between Matadi and Stanley Pool. Conrad reckoned his dashing new acquaintance had 'a touch of the Conquistador in him' as he strode into the 'unspeakable wilderness' swinging his stick and always accompanied by his two bulldogs, one white named Paddy, the other a brindle, Biddy.

Conrad, the great chronicler of human motivation in the political and social currents of the times, was to remain fascinated by the younger man's enigmatic, often contradictory, personality, his charm and emotional energy, and the intensity of his conversation – in contrast to his own watchful, ironic wariness of display. When both men became internationally celebrated in the early years of the new century, he wrote that Casement, who by then 'had as many years of Africa as I had months . . . could tell you things! Things I have tried to forget, things I never did know.' It is not hard to imagine Casement's influence on Conrad's masterpiece of colonial degradation, *Heart of Darkness*, drawn from his travel journals and published nine years later. The tales he heard in Matadi in those weeks of the likes of Captain Van Kerckhoven, with his gruesome collection of heads, might well have helped inspire the fictional Mr Kurtz, the prolific ivory trader who starts out intending to bring civilisation to the upriver Congolese but becomes corrupted in his powerful isolation, goes mad and induces them to worship him as a deity; his last words are 'The horror! The horror!' When Conrad disowned Casement in later decades, he cited his 'emotional force', the driver of his sympathetic understanding, as the factor that had both brought him to greatness and 'undone him'.

Casement himself did not report on what he saw on his marches or heard in his palavers, simply referring in one letter to his cousin Gertrude that the native village of Luvituku was 'not a jolly place' for 'a wee girl' like her, before describing his dog Paddy snoring at his side and telling her how much he missed his other bulldog a hundred miles downstream. But Conrad's account of his encounter with the 'pious Protestant Irishman' and their late-night conversations about 'things' the newly arrived sailor had 'tried to forget, things [he] never did know' makes plain that the charming, softly spoken, sympathetic twenty-five-year-old with the 'limpid personality' had changed. He was no longer the restless youth longing to escape the complications of his upbringing and the boredom of a clerkship in Liverpool who had first set eyes on Boma; he was emerging as a man of compassion, morality and sensitivity to the sufferings of others. The *agent exceptionnel* had taken the first steps that would shape his future; his next move was into the service of the government he would come to despise.

2. Breakfast with Leopold

Roger Casement was to spend the rest of his working life in the employment of the British Crown. Initially a keen, creative servant of empire, his questing romanticism, secrecy and rootless upbringing were starting to fertilise his humanitarianism, which found its first expression in the clash of European powers constantly playing out in its African colonies.

Shortly after his return to Africa in 1890, Casement the surveyor and mission worker was demonstrating his standing in the small British community, as well as his naivety about Leopold's control: he suggested to Stanley that 'there is scope for an English trading company on the Lower Congo on a fairly big scale' and that 'any well conducted English house with a business chief at its head could still do wonders on the Upper Congo'. The latter proposition rested on the unlikely premise that 'the [Belgian-controlled] State gave it fair play'. Nothing could come of this, but the stint in Africa of this most unbusinesslike of men and the respect in which he was held in the colonial establishment were recognised by the Foreign Office, which returned him to the continent in 1892 to serve in the Niger Oil Rivers (later Coast) Protectorate* in the trading port of Old Calabar, tucked into the Gulf of Guinea. The territory with its immense liquid assets had first been carved out by British gunboats burning the villages and sinking the canoes of the African middlemen who had ferried the oil to the coast; then, in a diplomatic tussle with the French which was settled at the Berlin Conference, the Niger Delta was recognised as a protectorate, 'with no further assumption of territorial rights than is necessary to maintain the paramount authority and discharge the duties of an occupying power'.

* As Nigeria was known from 1885 to 1893, after which it became the Niger River Protectorate until 1914.

Casement's own duties, for which he was paid £400 a year,* were mainly in customs but also required him to serve as 'travelling Commissioner and in other capacities for the Govt.', including exploring routes for palm-oil trading. Immediately after his New Year's Eve arrival, he set off on an expedition with Sir Claude MacDonald, the Commissioner and Consul General, 'to make a short reconnaissance of our frontier here with the German Colony of Cameroons ... the frontier has not yet been delineated, and my journey will be the first visit made by either side'; they were accompanied by 'a botanical man' as they mapped the new colonial borders. By the October of his first year, Casement was signing himself 'Acting Director-General of Customs', responsible for regulating the export of palm oil, palm kernels, rubber, ivory and ebony and the import of European goods, primarily cotton and railway-building materials.

As in his early days in the Congo, he spent much time on foot among the creeks and swamps that fed into the mighty river. He maintained that this country should be opened up slowly and peaceably, explaining to MacDonald that any militaristic show would lead to loss of life and a 'widespread feeling of hostility and resentment'. He was calm when his party were surrounded by warriors who seized some of their bearers while 'clashing swords and machetes in our faces'; his composure paid off when they were granted a brief palaver and allowed to continue on their way.

He expressed himself in verses all of a piece with his role as a colonial officer which tended to be about heroes from his schooldays or about his periods of leave in Ireland. In 1893 a group of mercenaries in the pay of the mining magnate and politician Cecil Rhodes mowed down the army of a Matabele leader which inspired an epic lament, 'To Lobengula, In His Flight After the Slaughter of His Impis', in which Casement addressed the 'Old King of Zulu sires':

> Tho' England brave blood shed in that far field,
> Her heart is sick with lust:
> The gold she wins is red nor can it shield
> Her name from tainted league with men of broken trust.

* Approximately £37,500 at today's values.

For all its questionable scansion, the poem points to Casement's understanding that the colonising Englishman aims to gain 'gold' for his country unaided by force and untainted by greed. Sir Claude Mac-Donald acknowledged in his despatches to Whitehall that, although the use of the Maxim gun could sometimes produce results, Casement's soft-spoken, diplomatic approach frequently paid off; 'it would have been difficult to find anyone in any way more suited to the work'.

Despite generally seeming content to serve country and conscience simultaneously, at other times the thirty-year-old official could sound like an unreformed colonialist. After a description of an exploration on foot through flooded country in the face of sullen hostility, he reported that 'The natives . . . have made evil their good; they cling to their cruelties and superstitions . . . and symbols of fetish power . . . Our roads into their midst, and the good we seek to do them are equally hateful, for both foreshadow the end of their own power to do after the fashion of their fathers.' He explored far inland, dispassionately reporting customs that others might have judged detrimental to trading relations: he wrote, for example, of the Anang tribe and others in their area who used to kill and eat many of their slaves when a king died.

In 1894, he became involved with a humanitarian organisation that might have been considered at odds with his government position, yet it too combined patriotism and compassion. The Aborigines Protection Society had been founded by Quakers in 1837 to protect the rights of indigenous peoples; its Secretary was the elderly, asthmatic, zealous Henry Fox Bourne, who had kept the Congo in the public awareness as best he could since publication of his book *The Other Side of the Emin Pasha Expedition*. This was a savage attack on Stanley for failing to observe the rights of Central Africans as enshrined in the 1890 Brussels Convention, whose declared objective was to 'to improve the moral and material conditions of existence of the native races'. Casement wrote to Fox Bourne about the German severity that had followed an insurgency in Cameroon: soldiers who had been purchased as slaves mutinied and seized government buildings after several of their wives had been flogged for disobedience; he requested that Fox Bourne 'raise a protesting voice in England against

the atrocious conduct of the Germans', who had retaliated by executing the mutineers and their wives. In an official document, Casement
balanced his place in the imperial hierarchy against his innate compassion to write that 'we all on earth have a commission and a right
to defend the weak against the strong, and to protect against brutality in any shape or form'. He added that 'the opinion of every
Englishman in this part of the world is . . . dead against the German
government'.

When the Niger appointment ended in 1895, Casement entered
another period of purposelessness. He made his way back to the
mouth of the Congo to a mission station run by his friend T. H.
Hoste, but on finding Hoste departing for England decided to go
home too as he had 'absolutely nothing to do'. He needed to work
hard, preferably outdoors, and had also been weakened by his prolonged stay in Africa; he underwent bouts of malaria for the rest of
his life as well as suffering from other health issues. Two years earlier
he had been operated upon for an anal fistula at St Thomas's Hospital,
London, and was to suffer from intermittent rectal troubles, their
possible causes a posthumous matter of gleeful and barely disguised
innuendo among his determined pursuers.*

He used this time to start exploring his roots, twelve years after his
escape on the *Bonny* from the confusion they had engendered. His
mother's maiden name had been Jephson, and on his way out to perform his Niger role he had met a Louisa Jephson-Norreys in Las
Palmas, to whom he now wrote: 'I should wish to establish my
mother's connections with the Jephsons so often mentioned in Irish
history if possible. She died when I was quite a child.' Given the
shadowiness of his maternal history, he did not even know his
grandfather's first name or where he had lived, but wanted to establish
some sort of rooted status for himself beyond 'the occasional remarks
of a long-dead mother'. His hoped-for cousinage to Mounteney

---

* Anal fistulas have been the subject of medical fascination and experimentation
for thousands of years, and remain difficult and painful to treat. There are some
specific sources of fistula, such as Crohn's disease, but neither anal intercourse nor
sexually transmitted diseases are among these.

Jephson, his dining companion in the Congo bush, could not be established and Louisa Jephson-Norreys's genealogical table did not include his mother; she added, maybe euphemistically, that the Dublin Jephsons had been 'dissipated, reckless and brave'.

This research had to be put aside when Casement was summoned back to official service. His reports from Niger were published as a White Paper, confirming his position in the Foreign Office without the usual requirement of the Civil Service examinations. He was needed in Uganda, to the north-east of the Congo, where Cecil Rhodes's British South Africa Company, despite its recent government charter to exploit mineral wealth in Africa, was in difficulties. The region was so geographically ill-defined that it was coveted by the British, French, Germans and Italians as well as by Leopold, and men of 'courage and quality' were needed to secure its commercial potential for the Crown. But the change of government to Lord Salisbury's Conservative–Liberal Unionist coalition in June 1895 prompted a rethink at the Foreign Office, and instead Casement was asked to proceed at once to Lourenço Marques in Portuguese East Africa,* there to act as Consul. The new official displayed the full etiquette of the Victorian establishment when he wrote that he was 'deeply sensible of the honour the Queen' had done him and that he hoped he might prove himself 'not unworthy of this gracious expression of Her Majesty's pleasure'.

His first actions on the other side of Africa were to insist that London provide less mouldy premises for the consulate and that the contents his predecessor had sold should be replaced; he also wanted more land, as befitted its status. He went on to request new flags so that they could be flown to celebrate the Queen's birthday within view of the ships in Delagoa Bay. Even so, he recognised that many problems were best dealt with by informal palavers with the local authorities rather than by insisting on his diplomatic standing. He looked after the interests of British subjects who were there to get ahead of the Portuguese in trade, and honed his skills in taking down depositions and handling legal issues. He worked furiously, 'writing

---

* Now Maputo, capital of Mozambique.

from 7 a.m. until 5.30 or 6 p.m. at trying reports, adding up figures and interviewing people on business in the intervals'. He had no secretary to help him, and often advanced money from his own pocket to help the distressed arrivals from the 230 British steamers and sailing ships that arrived in port each year. The town was 'full of wretched Englishmen seeking work', two of whom had recently died 'of the results of hunger and exposure'; this meant yet more paperwork for the harried Consul, who was frequently ill himself and fell behind in his duties. He complained that he found it a 'severe strain' upon his 'time and temper . . . to be forced to interview anyone . . . often upon trifling business or in quest of unimportant details'. But his accelerated appointment to this charmless backwater was not purely for routine work: as the Queen to whom he had sworn loyalty grew ever older, fractures were appearing in the intricate power balance of African colonisation.

Lourenço Marques's natural harbour was strategically vital: Cecil Rhodes, against the wishes of his government, was planning to seize it as a sea passage for the Cape Colony's northward expansion. Meanwhile the Boer Republics of Transvaal and the Orange Free State to the Cape Colony's north – which acted as a block to the British desire to form a federation of territories in South Africa similar to Canada or Australia – needed a port that was not under British control. In December 1895, Rhodes took matters into his own hands and ordered Dr Jameson, the administrator of Rhodesia, which fell under the British South Africa Company's charter, to raid the Transvaal with 500 troopers. A 'series of thunderbolts' shot out from the Colonial Office in Whitehall at this provocation, but too late to prevent Jameson's failed attack. On the first day of 1896 he raised the white flag just outside Johannesburg, and the German Empire's erratic Kaiser Wilhelm II sent President Kruger of the Transvaal, the face of the Boer cause, a congratulatory telegram.

These early rumblings of what became the Second Boer War* had already been anticipated by the alert Consul after Kruger had sent an emissary by the name of Leyds for a stay in Lourenço Marques,

---

* The First Boer War had been fought in 1880–1.

purportedly for his health, a month before. Casement realised that
Leyds was working out a plan to exploit a railway line from Pretoria
in the Transvaal to the sea at Delagoa Bay – the only possible route
that would not traverse British territory – which brought on his witti-
cism that if Leyds had indeed come for a rest cure, 'such a visit would
be without parallel in the annals of the admittedly unhealthiest port
in South East Africa'.

Casement became involved in espionage: by now the Foreign
Office was making anxious enquiries about whether German troops
and supplies were being landed in Lourenço Marques, to which he
replied that nothing landing from Europe looked military, but he
was not allowed to inspect anything in transit to the Transvaal clearly
labelled 'Government Goods'. Tensions were already running so high
that the consulate had been stoned, so it was risky to carry out illegal
acts against a rival European power. But he found some way around
this protocol, possibly by bribing a railway official, and was able to
report that sixty-five cases of rifles, a hundred cases of Maxim guns
and 4 million cartridges were on their way to the Boers. This dangerous intelligence could do nothing to forestall the looming war, but at
least he was able to write that the Foreign Secretary has expressed his
' "entire approval" of the "very satisfactory settlement" I had obtained
to a certain question, so that is pleasant'.

On matters of less pressing military importance, Casement felt
that local people mattered rather more than colonisers: the American
journalist Poultney Bigelow, a friend of the Kaiser since they had
played Cowboys and Indians at their Potsdam school, echoed Conrad's commentary from Matadi days as he described how the Consul
'would wander away for weeks and months with merely a black
attendant or two, trekking along the Swazi frontier, studying the
language and the customs of the natives, establishing relations with
the chiefs, and sounding them as to their feelings in matters interesting in Downing Street . . . [he] knew more of the natives between
Basutoland and the shores of Mozambique than any other white
man'. Casement's posting may have lacked prestige, but his inquisi-
tive natural sympathy was laying the ground for his greatest work.

The new Consul was right about the health prospects of Delagoa Bay. It was a fetid, swampy place reeking of sewage; it had the distinction of having a fever named after it, an attack of which had meant that he had had to take a month of sick leave in Cape Town soon after his arrival. He did not fully recover, returning to Britain in March 1897, and again for four months at the start of the following year. A Dublin doctor produced a certificate citing 'effects of recent malarial fever, Neurasthenia, Haemorrhage and weak circulation', a potently debilitating combination. 'Neurasthenia' was a much diagnosed but indefinite illness of the era which encompassed depression, lassitude and forms of 'emotional disturbance'; lassitude itself was an inevitable side effect of malaria and the climate, but the other symptoms might indicate Casement's desire to avoid a further stint in Lourenço Marques as well as being a harbinger of his mental state in the Great War.

He spent much of his home leaves between Herbert Ward and Ward's friend Richard Morten, later to become his own closest friend, in the Thames Valley. He stayed with the Bannisters in Liverpool and with his cousin at the Casement family home, Magherintemple in Antrim, reading history and poetry and marking time until his return to work. At the end of July, the Foreign Office decided that he should go to St Paul de Loanda, the principal port of Portuguese West Africa, now Angola, one of the nine countries neighbouring the Congo. On the face of it, this was a lesser posting in terms of British interests and international intrigue – Casement called St Paul 'the City of Sleep, a month behind the world' – but his skills had been recognised in Whitehall, where they wanted to know about French machinations in a trading post south of Khartoum. He stopped in his old haunts in Matadi, just over the border from the Portuguese colony, where he learnt that 'considerable numbers of French officers and men, and large quantities of ammunition . . . have recently been despatched' to Sudan, but by the time this report had reached London the French had withdrawn rather than face any sort of armed conflict with Kitchener's soldiers, ending their hopes of connecting their West African colonies to the Nile and the Mediterranean. More significantly, the government were becoming disturbed by the commercial arrangements in the Congo Free State.

The questions over Leopold's governance were to put Casement on the international stage. The King-Sovereign had come up with a solution to his debt problem: huge tracts of the Congo were to become a Domaine Privé on which the Crown alone could reap and exploit the 'fruits of the land'; the Domaine encompassed an area from the mouth of the river to Leopoldville, over half of which was equatorial rainforest covered with lucrative rubber vines. Only a small portion of the inaccessible Upper Congo was open to competitive trade. Within the Domaine Privé was the Domaine de la Couronne, hidden from outside scrutiny and whose profits went straight into Leopold's exchequer. Other concessionary companies to split their profits with the Belgian Crown were the Société Anversoise du Congo and the Anglo-Belgian India Rubber Company, known as ABIR, although after British capital had been withdrawn in 1898 this became a misnomer. These last two controlled an area slightly larger than England and Wales. A £20 share in ABIR on its foundation in 1892 was worth £725 at the end of the century, had it been available on any stock exchange – the Congo government and leading rubber brokers had no intention of selling.

The devastating basis for these grants was that the concessions were also the agents of taxation: in an economy in which there was no currency aside from brass rods and cloth, the only way of exacting taxes was to force local people to work in lieu, ensuring that pressure was on to produce as much rubber as possible. Leopold's 1897 instructions to his district commissioners were far from that of a free trader: 'These peoples must submit to new laws of which the most imperious, as well as the most salutary, is assuredly the law of labour.' Between 1890 and 1904, Congo rubber earnings increased by a multiple of ninety-six, while each kilo of the sap collected could be sold in Antwerp at a profit of 700 per cent. The value of a Compagnie du Chemin de Fer du Congo's share rose from 320 francs to 2,850 in just one decade.

The overseers forced the workers to maximise production. Rubber vines up to a hundred feet high were tapped, nearly always resulting in the death of the plant and so necessitating even deeper penetration of the dense, thorny, insect-infested jungle to find untapped resources. The most chilling reaction to this inevitable destruction came from a district commissioner and future Great War hero named Jules Jacques, who – in ignorance of the production process – asked his officers to 'Inform the natives that if they cut another single vine, I will exterminate them to the last man'. In *Heart of Darkness*, Kurtz writes a seventeen-page document on the suppression of savage customs, to be disseminated in Europe, but his supposed desire to 'civilise' is contradicted by the scrawled postscript: 'Exterminate all the brutes!' *Heart of Darkness* was published in 1899, when the concessions had full control of the commercial life of the Congo.

The King had fulfilled his key Berlin pledges – he had expelled the Arab slave traders, opened up the trading stations on the river and set up riverboat and telegraph systems. These, alongside his lavish spending on his mistress and the construction at Tervuren of a new palace to outdo Versailles, had brought him close to bankruptcy. He had already ensured that all rubber was sold to his agents through a system which negated the notion of a free state; now there was a threat that the price of latex would decrease as accessible, repeatedly tappable trees flourished in managed plantations in Latin America and Asia, often in British colonies. This tension added to Leopold's merciless economic stranglehold, exemplified by the case of Charles Stokes. In 1895, the English Stokes had been arrested for alleged gun-running by the Belgian Captain Lothaire, a hero of the campaign against the slave traders; Stokes was subjected to an illegal trial, sentenced to death by hanging and denied an appeal. Under British pressure, Lothaire himself was sent for trial in Belgium, but the prosecutor threw out the brief as he could not try 'this brave Belgian officer'. It emerged that Stokes's real crime had been to trade ivory in violation of Leopold's illegal, monopolistic regulations. Lothaire returned to the Congo as Director of the Société Anversoise, at which point Casement discovered that the concession transferred its profits* not

---

* These totalled 4 million francs, approximately £158,000 in 1899; around £20 million today.

to a bank but through the state Finance Department in Boma. His conclusion encapsulated the hazy corruption of Leopold's enterprise: 'Lothaire is nothing less than a State Official, of special and undefined powers.'

Some 450 Protestant and Catholic missionaries, of whom about a hundred were British, were often the only independent witnesses to the horrors. A missionary alerted his organisation about new Force Publique brutalities: since 1892, the state required a severed human hand, smoked for preservation if it had to travel far, for every cartridge expended, an imposition designed to prevent native soldiers squandering ammunition. 'Each district is forced to bring a certain quantity [of rubber] to the headquarters of the Commissaire every Sunday. It is collected by force; the soldiers drive the people into the bush. If they will not go, they are shot down, and their left hands taken as trophies to the Commissaire . . . These hands, the hands of men, women and children, are placed in rows before the Commissaire who counts them to see the soldiers have not wasted cartridges.'

Another missionary reported in 1899 that 'all the people of the villages run away to the forest when they hear the State officers are coming. To-night, in the midst of the rainy season, within a radius of seventy-five miles . . . I am sure it would be a low estimate to say that 40,000 people, men, women, children, with the sick, are sleeping in the forests without shelter.' William Parminter, the Lourenço Marques incumbent after Casement, gave an interview to Reuter's in which he recounted that freed slaves were now being forced into seven-year servitude as 'sentries' for the Force Publique. One evening, he had seen a group of these take off after some fleeing Congolese; they returned triumphant with a necklace of human ears, on which they were congratulated by the Commissaire.

Casement heard posthumously from another of his former companions: Edward Glave had died upriver, and in his last days had entrusted his papers to an American missionary who published them in the *Century Magazine* four years later. Glave had been revolted by how the Free State had become a slaving country in all but name; he described for the first time the hippo-hide *chicotte,* 'trimmed like a corkscrew, with edges like knife-blades, and as hard as wood'. Not only men but women and children were subjected to its lashes, and 'small boys of ten or twelve, with excitable, hot-tempered masters, are often most harshly treated'. The rapid moral decline of the country was matched by the growing global market for its major export: 'rubber and murder, slavery in its worst form'.

The narrow-gauge railway between Matadi and Stanley Pool on which Casement had worked a decade earlier finally opened in 1898 amid much celebration. A bronze monument was erected of three porters, one with a box on his head, the other two prostrate with exhaustion, above the caption 'The Railway Freed Them from Porterage'; there was no memorial to the thousands who had died during its construction – local legend claimed one for every sleeper. By the turn of the new century, more than 5 million kilos of rubber were arriving at the sea from the steamboat docks of Stanley Pool without the attritional delay of three weeks of foot transportation past the cataracts. While Leopold could make it hard for most Europeans to get proper insight, missionaries continued to bear witness and Fox Bourne's Aborigines Protection Society had long since dropped the King of the Belgians as its President. Leopold even paid a personal visit to the editor of *The Times* to try to persuade him to stop printing Fox Bourne's allegations.

Leopold attempted to bolster his credentials by sophistry: he set up the Commission for the Protection of the Natives, staffed by Church leaders and missionaries; he ensured that Stanley wrote of 'what great gratitude the civilised world' owed the King 'for his matchless sacrifices on behalf of the inhabitants . . . who can doubt that God chose [Leopold] as His instrument to redeem this vast slave park?' Privately, Stanley predicted that were he to return to the Congo he would see 'the effects of an unerring and ignorant policy' on its inhabitants. The King-Sovereign, who never visited Africa, continued to build his palace to outdo Versailles at Tervuren with his spoils; for the 1897 Brussels *exposition*, a £300,000* African pavilion complete with an art nouveau wooden jungle was erected in the

* Over £30 million today.

grounds. At the turn of the century in London, Prime Minister Salisbury opened a Congo Atrocities file.

It was against this background that Casement returned to West Africa in the autumn of 1898. His dutiful and overlong reports reveal little of his character, but other writings offer the first hints at his sexuality: he bought fresh sole for four young Englishmen he encountered at the submarine cable station who had been surviving on 'Famine Onion', a bitter wild vegetable; a few days later he annotated a poem 'On Youth' as having been composed 'after watching some fine young Portuguese naval sailors' hauling a net, and signed it 'His heart was ever tutor to his hand. R.C.'

The Second Boer War (1899–1902) was the bloodiest and most costly conflict since the Napoleonic Wars, and at its outbreak Casement's sympathies were patriotically aligned as he advocated 'having it out once and for all with the Boers & S. Africa generally'. He wrote to his cousin at Magherintemple that there had 'been so much sniping by Brother Boer', and expressed the wish that the war were over, 'altho' it can only end on *our* terms never on the Boers' terms'. He loathed the Boers for their treatment of Black South Africans – and, with an irony that can be appreciated with hindsight, despised them for attempting to raise a 'Brigade' of Irish prisoners of war to fight on their side: it was 'another proof of the methods of those in power in Pretoria to leave no weapon untried to induce men loyal to their Queen to be false to their own allegiance, and to be false to themselves'. Yet a fragment of a poem written a few months later offers a glimpse inside a mind attempting to hold harmony above nationality in some sort of borderless, dynamic nation:

> Come, brother, come: this was not of our seeking.
> We each have stood from each other too far apart,
> And listening each to hostile prompter's speaking
> Neither hath heard the beating of his heart.

The sixteen-line draft is headed 'Briton to Boer at Stillenbosch [*sic*] early May 1900'.

Casement's dislike of the conflict was aggravated by the climate

and his general state of health: Matadi in early March was '*very* hot –
too hot for words or for sleep. I am not well, altho' not ill. The heat
is too great and the sleepless nights – night after night panting like a
dog – are too much.' His own dog, an English collie named Rags,
was dying of a tropical sickness. He let his mask slip further to Dick
Morten towards the end of 1899. He had decided that he would 'like
to conclude Africa', he was 'sick of the place'; he felt 'old and grey'
and wanted 'peace and music – and nice people around me – and old
friends'; he had had enough of 'truculent savages – and dirty bad
servants – and worse food'. The Congo was 'a Horrid Hole'.

Despite these complaints, he conjured up a daring scheme when
he returned to Lourenço Marques in the first week of January 1900 to
report again on the arrival of arms. Bribes to dock workers yielded
no fresh intelligence, so he again considered the importance of the
Pretoria railway as a link to Boer territories, and proposed mounting
a commando raid on a vital bridge to disrupt the movement of con-
traband. He asked that he be permitted to remain absent from his post
to 'take a more active part than by merely assisting in discussions' in
the urgent business 'of such transcendent importance', even travelling to Cape Town to solicit the approval of the military chiefs Lords
Roberts and Kitchener, and of High Commissioner Milner, whom
he regarded as 'a fine specimen of an Englishman' who would not
shrink from 'a very big fight'.

He was never strategically adept, and the Foreign Office did not
share its employee's confidence in his venture, drily minuting that 'if
the bridge had been blown up, it would have been repaired in a fortnight', and anyway 'smuggling by road would not have been stopped'.
Officials nevertheless gave the expedition its operational go-ahead at
the end of March. Two weeks later a patriotic gift from the Scottish-
born Canadian businessman Lord Strathcona docked at Cape Town:
a force made up of twenty-eight officers, 512 men with 500 bullets
each, nearly 400 horses (200 had died on the voyage from Canada)
and three Maxim guns with 150,000 rounds. Strathcona's Horse then
split into two parts, one heading towards Durban and the other,
accompanied by Casement, to Kosi Bay. But neither half of the
expedition reached its destination as Milner realised its expensive

pointlessness and recalled them both. It was an adventure that had less devastating consequences than the next occasion he was caught up in war.

Casement's disillusion with Africa and officialdom was brought to a head by illness. He arrived in London on leave in late July and almost immediately suffered a bout of jaundice. His doctor ordered that he should not return to the continent for at least two months, later extended by another month. Instead the patient travelled to Paris to see Herbert Ward in his studio before heading to Magherintemple and his Ulster routines of walking, swimming, reading Irish history and writing poetry. He was nearly thirty-six and needed to find a role and an identity that would make his internal divisions irrelevant: he was an Irishman in an imperial Foreign Office; an Englishman who had just been awarded the South African Medal by the Queen; a professed Christian who was unclear whether he was Protestant or Catholic; a Congo expert who could do little to combat the abuses there and who was now disenchanted by the European influences on the country he had once believed an 'Early Paradise'. He was an anti-colonial colonial officer. But his most significant period in Africa was yet to come, as the first of his three great causes which brought him both fame and disgrace crystallised.

His public humanitarian work began alongside a man with whom he had a lot in common. The exuberant, barrel-chested Edmund Dene Morel was ten years his junior, and already had a shock of white hair and a moustache which accentuated the blaze of his dark eyes. Morel's feckless French father had died when he was young and he too had left his sketchy English education at the age of fifteen; after a short period supporting his English mother, a prim, shy woman of Quaker stock, in Paris, he followed in Casement's footsteps to become a clerk for Elder Dempster, with its monopoly on the Congo route. At first, Morel celebrated Leopold's rule, writing articles in the shipping press claiming that 'a great future is in store for the Congo' thanks to 'the foresight of King Leopold II'. He travelled frequently to the colony, but it was as the Company representative in Antwerp that he put together two observations to become Leopold's most relentless critic. The first was the sheer quantity of armaments bound for ostensible trading companies being loaded on to Congo-bound ships in conditions of some secrecy; the second was that only about 20 per cent of the rubber and ivory arriving in Belgium was disclosed to customs. Morel's damning deduction was that as the Congolese did not use money and the ships were not returning to Africa with much in their holds except the weapons, the Congolese were not benefiting from their labours. Rather, they were being placed in active danger. As he put it in the most basic of economic terms, 'Nothing was going in to pay for what was coming out.' He thought it unlikely that the Congolese were working 'for the love of Leopold', but when he voiced his suspicions, Elder Dempster attempted to buy his silence with offers of lucrative consultancies. He resigned to run his campaign; he 'had launched the boat, and there could be no turning back'.

Casement read Morel's journalism and realised that this was the moment to extricate himself from inactivity and put his experience to good use. He wrote to Sir Martin Gosselin, a senior diplomat who had negotiated at the Berlin Conference, quoting evidence from two unnamed Baptist missionaries about Force Publique savagery, to point out that everything in the Congo 'is subordinated to the lust of gain'. He advocated undoing the neutrality provisions and international oversight enshrined in the Berlin resolutions after the Boer War, and establishing an alliance with Germany to 'deal with Belgian brutality' and end 'the veritable reign of terror which exists'. He suggested that the Lourenço Marques consulate be split into two, with a vice-consul in Portuguese West Africa under a consul in the Congo State itself. He was given the latter post at a salary of £1,000.

Leopold's Native Commission was a sham. Its six members all lived on such far-flung stations, none of them in a rubber-producing area, that they had never even met. Nevertheless, its creation had had the desired effect in European capitals as the King's motives were deemed as lofty as fifteen years before at the Berlin Conference. He donated a triumphal arch in Brussels of Napoleonic proportions to commemorate the founding of his country in 1830, alongside a hand-some public park at Ostend and a Congo Museum at Tervuren, as well as his two (greatly enlarged) royal palaces, in which he continued to live. He spent lavishly on his mistress, Caroline Delacroix, a former prostitute aged sixteen to his sixty-five, awarding her the title of Baroness de Vaughan. When Casement passed through Brussels on his way to his new posting in October 1900, he naturally called on the British Minister, the obsequious and vain Sir Constantine Phipps. Phipps could see no wrong in Leopold or Belgians, they were 'a cultivated people'; he loathed the mutterings from the likes of Morel and Fox Bourne. Phipps had tipped Leopold off about the new diplomat's leanings, resulting in the first, and most challenging, British Consul in Boma being summoned to Laeken.

Casement arrived for 'breakfast' at the recently extended palace at 1.00 p.m. to find a peculiar gathering: Leopold himself, his estranged wife Queen Marie-Henriette, in town for the opera, the Duke of Aosta, various court dignitaries, Princess Clementine and the man she was in love with but not allowed to marry, Prince Victor Napoleon of France. The conversation was politely pointless as the imposing Leopold sought to cultivate the influential visitor, his equal in height if not in girth. He 'spoke of his object in Congo Country . . . to put his desire for the well-being and good government of the natives' first, as 'was continually being impressed upon his officers'. He wanted to 'induce [the Congolese] to develop their country by working its India rubber, to their own benefit and to the profit of the Companies interested'. When Casement asked in that case why not pay and tax the Congolese rather than use them as 'forced labour', the King replied that it was, in fact, 'labour in lieu of tax', as well as apparently in lieu of salary. Casement ventured that it must be hard to govern such a vast country, to which Leopold retorted that the Congo was not a colony, and anyway nothing compared to British, French or German territories. He asked Casement to return the following day in the hope of throwing him off the noxious scent that the British diplomat seemed to be following.

But the next morning Casement wasted no time as he asked outright about the amputation of hands and the other rumoured atrocities. The King, now without his disjointed family around him, admitted that there had been some 'cases of misconduct', but it was not always possible to select the right people, not least because the climate 'seemed to frequently cause deterioration in the character of men previously deemed of the highest standard'. His example was a German prince who had murdered his servant. Although the evasive King feared some of the comments were well founded, he was sure that most of the stories that had reached Casement's ears were greatly exaggerated. The revenue from the colony was used for the public good and never, 'as was sometimes untruthfully asserted, for His Majesty's pocket'. Was the King not 'right to try to help my people – my two millions of workmen to find a little sugar, a little tea – a few added comforts to their daily bread?' He was anxious to claim that Germany was the real danger to both their countries, and that Britain should not be worrying about the Free State. All he wanted for his tiny kingdom was 'a few – only a few – of the crumbs that fall from your well-stocked British table. And yet in England you are suspicious of us, you are sometimes mistrustful of me.'

Casement was unswervingly knowledgeable in the face of Leopold's charm. After his display of fearful defensiveness, the King's final request was that Casement should 'write to him privately at any time, and to write frankly, should there be anything of interest' he could 'unofficially advise him of'. It was a feeble ploy from the ruler who might have sensed that he had just given an audience to his nemesis. Casement himself concluded the meeting with the solemn half-truth that he 'trusted [he] should always be found trying to facilitate good relations between my countrymen and Your Majesty'. But for a man of his humanity, the plight of the Congolese would always override diplomatic niceties. Of his nineteen years in Africa, the next three were to be the most tumultuous as he entered the heart of darkness for himself, cementing his own identity and the fate of millions.

3.   A Man among Thorns

During the Boer Wars, Roger Casement had seen his country fighting for territory that did not inherently belong to it, and his support had frequently clashed with his empathetic nature, accentuating the divisions within him. He later acknowledged that, until this period, he 'was on the high road to being a regular imperialist jingo – although at heart underneath all and unsuspected almost by myself I had remained an Irishman. Well, the war gave me qualms at the end . . . And finally when up in those lonely Congo forests where I found Leopold, I found also myself, the incorrigible Irishman . . . I was looking at the tragedy with the eyes of another race.' The same events, insights and traits that were to establish him as one of the greatest English reformers were also to move him towards rebellion and martyrdom as he began his courageous, resonant work in the post-Victorian century.

The 'regular imperialist jingo' organised a memorial fund after the death of the Queen Empress in 1901, telling his Magherintemple cousins that Victoria had 'lived her life – lived it splendidly and beautifully every day of it – and she has left a memory I suppose no other Monarch in the world ever left before'. But two trade reports composed by him three years apart and sent from Angola to the Foreign Office displayed the morality he was starting to bring to his work: in 1899 he had written disparagingly of the rubber-gathering 'native' of Angola that 'where he gathers for one day he sleeps for two and loafs for four'; on a journey in 1902, hundreds of miles of which were on foot, he established that contract workers were being brought in from the Congo Free State, sold to plantations and then forbidden to leave. His exposure not only encouraged England's predominantly Quaker chocolate magnates, including William and Emmeline Cadbury – generous supporters for the rest of his life – to source ethically produced cocoa, it also brought him to the attention of Fox Bourne and Morel.

Yet he was low. The Congo remained 'a beastly hole' and he complained of fever, and of chiggers that left him lame. He despatched a sarcastic memorandum attached to a newspaper clipping about a theft from the Brussels Transvaal Legation of £1,000 worth of furniture and plate, commenting that he would be hard put to 'realize £50 upon all the furniture' he owned. In the wake of these gloomy pronouncements, he roamed the river basin with a dog or two for company, crystallising his thoughts about the misdirection and future of the Congolese. His reports to London, although not yet as intemperate as they would become, were increasingly critical of Leopold's regime: in June 1901 he stated that 'The unquestioned rule of an autocrat whose chief preoccupation is that autocracy should be profitable' was morally and politically unsustainable.

On leave that autumn he explored a potential solution to his ambivalence about his employment, as well as displaying his lifelong financial unworldliness, when he came to an arrangement with T. Fisher Unwin, Conrad's publisher, to bring out a privately printed volume of his poetry, *The Dream of the Celt*, with a personal subsidy of nearly £50. The title heralded the content: the first group of verses, including the Ossianic central poem, was on Irish heroic subjects, such as one on the Ulsterman Hugh O'Neill's 1598 victory over the Earl of Essex's army which opened, 'Since treason triumphed when O'Neill was forced to foreign flight . . .' A second group was African in inspiration, and the final dozen poems were about love. The title poem – with its opening lines:

> Large limbed were they and of a mightier race
> Than Greek or Phrygian of the tale divine . . .

– had been started on his voyage to Angola in a clear signal of his turning towards the romanticism of an imagined Ireland before it became England's first colony. Unwin could not have been more discouraging: 'We have been reading your MS and I think I ought to say at once that I do not look forward to a remunerative sale.' He wrote 'somewhat frankly', attaching four pages of his reader's notes which criticised Casement's grammar, conventional imagery and ' "bluggy" expression', even using the term 'minor poet' to puncture his dreams.

The wounded author composed three 'tortured ripostes', each with heavy rephrasings and crossings-out before the final acknowledgement that the reader might have been right to find so little to praise; he was 'grateful to this man, whoever he is, for his kindness in going thro' my verses with such attention and care'. He always yearned to find a new outlet in literary form, and continued to write occasional and unspecific or repressed poetry to the end of his life. On the eve of his final Congo journey, he sketched the plot of a novel, 'a splendid story', but events overtook anything even Conrad's fiction could provide. Although his prose was only once to achieve stylistic heights, at his last public appearance, he was now poised to take up his official pen to lasting effect.

The return to Africa in April 1902 after another extended leave brought a single-minded, undiplomatic outspokenness as Casement wound his anger against the Free State regime ever more tightly. In his first despatch to London, he went against the Aborigines Protection Society's scheme of setting up an international conference, advocating instead direct action to expose the 'organised system of plunder', adding that he hoped to see the 'rotten system of administration either mended or ended' soon. The reforming Liberal MP Sir Charles Dilke, loathed by the late Queen as a republican, was demanding a gathering of the countries that had signed the Berlin Agreement of 1885 to discuss the 'evils' of West Africa but was met with official stalling from the Unionist Foreign Secretary, Lord Lansdowne, who used the time-worn formula that the matter was 'engaging his serious attention' and that as far as the government were concerned the British labourers throughout the region were 'thoroughly contented, happy and well-treated'. When Casement pointed out that seven Sierra Leone men had died of brutal ill-treatment in a Matadi gaol, Lansdowne agreed that it was 'a terrible story', but was persuaded by the blinkered Phipps that Leopold could be trusted to take appropriate action on behalf of the British subjects. Phipps as usual ignored the wrongdoing of his hosts, declaring that he 'should be sorry to become the apologist of King Leopold or his regime, but there surely must in that country be some progress!' Lansdowne preferred to side with the complacent, well-born diplomat rather than with the little-known, wayward Consul; he remained unpersuaded in the winter of 1902 that any action was desirable or necessary. As Conrad put it to Casement three years on from *Heart of Darkness*, 'It is an extraordinary thing that the conscience of Europe which seventy years ago has put down the slave trade on humanitarian grounds tolerates the Congo State today. It is as if the moral clock has been put back many hours . . . In the old days England had in her keeping the conscience of Europe.'

The tall Consul cut an eccentric figure as he strode around his vast territory: in protest against the high fares he often refused to take the railway he had helped to build, leading to a bemused report to Brussels from a watchful Free State employee which noted that on his travels Casement was 'always accompanied by a big bulldog with large jaws'. His formal letters often ran to twenty pages on trivial matters and raised a few mocking eyebrows in the stuffier corridors of the Foreign Office, yet he went further and talked to the Congolese more frankly than any white man outside the missions. He analysed every aspect of the administration, its postal service, its judicial system, its prisons and hospitals, and the Force Publique. His language became unguarded and explicit as his anger mounted: 'There is no free trade in the Congo today . . . There is ruthless exploitation at the hands of a savage and barbarous soldiery . . . in the interest of and for the profit of the Sovereign of the country.'

The Foreign Office circulated this indictment. Some of the more restrained mandarins took exception to Casement's heightened rhetoric, but he was powering the shift to action as public awareness grew; the 'dense fog of mystery surrounding the Congo' identified by Morel was lifting now that the Boer War had ceased to dominate the news from Africa and more evidence emerged: for example, a state officer, Simon Roi, had bragged to an audience that included an American missionary of his killing squads which had used 6,000 cartridges, and therefore killed or mutilated 6,000 Congolese, as well as clubbing children to death with their rifle butts. In 1902, Morel's book *Affairs of West Africa* launched an excoriating attack; Fox Bourne subtitled the Aborigines Protection Society's *Civilisation in Congoland* 'A

History of International Wrong-Doing' and Dilke wrote a preface denouncing the Free State as 'the home of appalling misgovernment and oppression'. But there was little appetite for international scrutiny and still no concrete evidence: one Foreign Office official lamented that 'The newspapers are practically our only source of information', because Belgian control of Europeans entering the Congo minimised the risk of first-hand reports.

Parliament eventually stepped up. On 20 May 1903, Herbert Samuel, a new MP on his way to becoming Home Secretary and leader of the Liberal Party, moved a resolution asking the Balfour administration to 'intervene in the affairs of the Congo Free State for the purpose of mitigating the evils under which the Congolese suffered at the hands of the government'. Samuel laid out just what free trade involved for Britain: in 1892, declared Congo exports totalled £2 million,* of which Belgium received £1,860,000 and England £11,400; Leopold's 'one great company' paid dividends of 270 per cent in 1899, 470 per cent in 1900 and 245 per cent the following year. Samuel cited a despatch from Casement the previous August which proposed that to 'break the system' the government need only insist on the free-trading terms of the Berlin Agreement; the Consul recalled Stanley's mid-1880s pledges that there would also be 'paternal care of its subjects' rights, whether black or white' and the explorer's blandishments that the pre-Berlin exports of British cotton to the Congo could climb to £25 million if the state was opened up. In fact, Casement reckoned, the value of cotton exports to the country in 1901 had decreased to £100,000, about half that of sixteen years earlier before transportation improved. Herbert Samuel commented that 'King Leopold has said that "the wealth of a Sovereign consisted in the prosperity of his people". They might suspect that there were sometimes other sources too!'

The reformers' language in Parliament became unrestrained as Dilke concluded that 'as to the question of natives, the whole anti-slavery world has been swindled by the Administration of the Congo', although Britain, 'the mother country of the liberty of the native,

---

* Approximately £250 million today.

and the leader in the abolition of slavery', had been 'honest in [her] original intention'. The Conservative-led government equivocated, declaring that they could not assent to the motion, and asserting in the perennial defence of empire the civilising effect of the 'very high degree of a certain kind of administrative development' – railways, steamers, hospitals and 'all the machinery of elaborate judicial and political systems'; they believed that the Belgian administrators 'had taken the ordinary steps of a civilised government to punish the perpetrators' of crimes. The conclusion of the debate was that 'His Majesty's Government [should] confer with the other . . . signatories of the Berlin General Act . . . in order that measures may be adopted to abate the evils prevalent' in the Congo Free State, but solid proof was needed to empower the Berlin signatories. An investigation by the Consul was approved.

Casement returned to Africa for the last time shortly before the government's change of heart. He was again suffering from malaria, had had a debilitating attack of 'near dysentery' and passed blood on board ship; he was also anxious about his bulldog John, who had congested eyes and had wrought messy mayhem after drinking salt water. But, above all, he was relieved to hear about the Parliamentary proceedings: 'At last they are taking action!'

Lansdowne despatched three cables to Boma after the debate: the only one for which Casement had the cypher ordered him 'to go to interior as soon as possible' to gather 'authentic information'. In order not to be visible to Leopold's spies, and without clearance from the Foreign Office, the following day he chartered the American Baptist Missionary Union's steamer *Henry Reed*,* a long low boat with small cabins at the stern behind the single funnel and an awning running the length of the deck. The investigation was to last fifteen weeks, bestow fame on him and fully awaken his rage.

If some of his writings of 1903 were to bring Casement acclaim as one of the greatest investigative reformers of the century, others

---

* The ABMU refused to take payment when they recognised the nature of the *Henry Reed*'s journey.

provoked infamy and lasting controversy. The notes of his defining year have survived in a small, blue-green leather Letts Pocket Diary and Almanack, a very ordinary item to have had such strange and devastating consequences. His entries are simultaneously laden with moral courage, dull recountings of daily events and annotations of both humanitarian atrocities and sexual encounters. In its surviving form, the diary starts on 14 February, when he was being briefed in London. The pages covering 1 January to 13 February were torn out thirteen years later to cement his fate.

The entries lack any expression of feeling and are thin on commentary of any kind until its author started his mid-year explorations. He went to a performance of *Aladdin* with his sister Nina in London, 'terrible', but offered no opinion on *La Bohème* a few nights later. His frequent sexual encounters are laid out baldly: the first was on 20 February with a man named Arthur whom he had met at a Sailors' Home in London. Arthur's penis was 'monene monene' and taken 'ma nua ami', 'very big' and 'taken in the mouth' in the disguise of the Congolese Kikongo language. Arthur was paid 11s 6d. Casement's long experience of Atlantic travel is reflected in his jottings about crew, distances, winds, menus, porters, innkeepers and officials, as well as sexual opportunities. On his arrival in Madeira, he lunched with a titled Briton and then cruised in Funchal's Old Town, receiving 'two offers. One doubtful. The other got cigarettes.' By 5.00 he was on a losing streak in the casino. Two days later, he went up a mountain, met the 'delightful' Lady Wilton and on his descent noticed a 'beautiful creature' by a stream, who inspired him to call on a nineteen-year-old, 'Hogue', also paid in cigarettes. The rest of the day involved a friend for dinner, the loss of three more dollars at the casino and going to a café in the main square before 'turning in early'.

None of Casement's annotations of his sexual encounters in port cities carry any personal freight, as shame overwhelmed the possibility of any analysis of emotion, and there seems no practical reason for listing them as he does. They accentuate his anonymous lack of romantic intimacy, just as throughout his life he had no friends to whom he disclosed his inner thoughts. The dislocations and lack of emotional nurture stemming from his childhood perhaps militated against an ability to look into himself and process whatever he might find there; the paucity of such insight also inhibited his poetic ambitions. As well as the money or cigarettes that changed hands, he often established penis size, either in inches or by a brief description such as 'enormous', so possibly the journal was to serve as a reminder of those fleeting pleasures when he was alone in Africa; possibly, as with his small gambling losses or grocery expenses, they were noted down merely for their transactional value, the result of a recording mind and a thin wallet. The rising official with a shameful secret could make no emphatic distinction even in his journal between being given a hymn book by a Miss Somerset and his wistful eyeing up of handsome young men on his chaste walks with her.

We cannot know if Casement ever had Oscar Wilde in his mind as he 'took offers' in London, Lisbon and Madeira, but his fellow Anglo-Irishman's disgrace and imprisonment for gross indecency in 1895, with its maximum tariff of two years' hard labour, might well have resonated with him as an example of English prejudice against the Irish as much as it was a contemporary indictment of homosexuality. Successful prosecutions had declined in the course of the nineteenth century, even after the death penalty for sodomy had been abolished in 1861, when the lesser crime of gross indecency was more often the charge. Seven years after capital punishment had been removed from the statute books, the word 'homosexual' was first coined in Germany, eventually replacing pejoratives such as 'invert' or 'Uranian' – at least within the medical and legal establishments. The oppression of secrecy and twisting of shame remained.

Wilde's second trial after the failure to reach a verdict in the first occurred at the high water mark for cases in the later decades of the nineteenth century, 855; sixty years later there were 2,322 prosecutions, and even in 1990 there were 1,159 recorded cases of 'indecency between males', more than two decades after homosexual acts between consenting males in private had been legalised.* The Metropolitan Police often hung back from exposing indecency unless it was

---

* By 2000, the figure had fallen to 167.

flagrant: on one occasion in 1854, two men were arrested outside a drag ball at the Druids' Hall in Turnagain Lane, City of London; one was 'completely equipped in female attire of the present day', the other, a man of sixty, was 'in the pastoral garb of a shepherdess of the golden age'. The Irish prostitute Jack Saul played a prominent role in the Dublin Castle Scandal, in which nationalists alleged homosexual orgies took place among the country's Protestant administrators; Saul also had a role in the Cleveland Street Scandal of 1889, which involved male brothels, the activities of Post Office telegraph boys and, by rumour, a royal prince. When Saul was interviewed, he stated that the police 'have had to shut their eyes to more than me'.

Wilde had built his career on mocking the English class system, and his sexual encounters took place without regard to its codes: he was berated in court for his 'disgraceful audacity' in dressing up a boy he had picked up on the beach at Worthing 'in public school colours'. He taunted the establishment from the dock, and the poet W. B. Yeats commented that 'the rage against Wilde was also complicated by the Britisher's jealousy of art and the artist'. Others were punished for sins seen to be stemming from or coexisting with their sexuality: Lord Arthur Somerset's were being upper class, exploiting the workers and fleeing from justice when he was implicated in the Cleveland Street Scandal. A popular rhyme after his escape to Boulogne in France went:

> My Lord Gomorrah sat in his chair
> Sipping his costly wine;
> He was safe in France, that's called the fair;
> In a city some call 'Boo-line'.

Other homosexual scandals relating in part to attitudes towards Ireland included Prime Minister Lord Castlereagh, who before his suicide in 1822 was accused of seeking an 'unnatural union' between Britain and Ireland; the first man to be tried under the Labouchere Amendment of the Criminal Law Act in 1885, which tightened the laws further, was a vociferous Irish MP who had complained of the brutality of British policemen.

Casement's only extant statements on the subject appear in his 1903 diary, written en route to the Congo: he heard the 'pitiably sad' news about Sir Hector MacDonald, a popular general who had risen from the ranks and been ADC to both Queen Victoria and King Edward VII. MacDonald was a married man who had returned from Ceylon to face a court martial on indecency charges involving a party of Sinhalese boys and two Anglican clergymen on a train in Kandy. When he saw in an American newspaper that his story had gone public, he shot himself in a Paris hotel room. His Edinburgh funeral took place in private at dawn, a source of popular resentment as thousands afterwards travelled to his grave to pay their respects to 'Fighting Mac'. Casement considered that the general's suicide was 'the most distressing case . . . surely, of its kind and one that may awake the national mind to saner methods of curing a disease than by criminal legislation'. Arthur Conan Doyle too characterised homosexuality as outside the control of the individual when he wrote of Oscar Wilde 'that the monstrous development which ruined him was pathological, and that a hospital rather than a police court was the place for its consideration'. Casement, rarely given to introspection, then referred to MacDonald's death twice more: two days later he was 'very sorry at Hector MacDonald's terrible end', and ten days on he was in 'a dreadful' hotel in Banana in the Congo, unable to sleep: 'Sandflies. Did not close my eyes. Hector MacDonald's death very sad. 5 francs per room.' If sex was never far from his mind, judging by the little evidence we have, it was necessarily a compartment he had to keep closed, albeit with little self-torment. This cut the romantic man off from any sort of intimate relationship until near the end of his life.

He left a poem he called 'The Nameless One' depicting this romantic solitude. He scribbled 'Lines written in Very Great Dejection at Genoa. November 15 1900 before sailing . . . for Barcelona' on the back of the manuscript, but with no indication of why or about whom he was cast down in the Italian port. The poem itself is his most personal, a cry of loneliness about his quest for fleeting, anonymous sex; it also more broadly might concern 'the love that dare not speak its name', in the phrase coined by Wilde's lover Lord Alfred Douglas implied in the title. It begins with the lament that he has:

No human hand to steal to mine
No loving eye to answering shine . . .

As he pursues the love 'Where God had writ an awful no', he questions whether he can live 'loveless' despite it being 'death to give / My love'. In the last of the seven stanzas, Casement asserts his own religious sensibility to contradict what he has just said about God's writ, to claim 'God made this love; there let it rest', although his unspecified 'broken heart' must not be seen 'To heavenly eyes'. The poem is a startling and uncharacteristic window into the solitary pain underlying his sexuality, as well as an expression of his powerful inner emotional life which was soon to find an outlet in his exertions to help the oppressed.

Casement was in no doubt about the perils of his journey, telling Poultney Bigelow that he was certain 'to endure bitter days . . . and in the end perhaps ruin *if I told the truth*'. Nevertheless, he was determined 'to speak the truth straight from the heart' about the 'revolting things' he expected to unearth. He showed how far he had moved from being a traditional diplomat when he quoted a Yoruba proverb: 'A man doesn't go among thorns unless a snake's after him – or he's after a snake . . . I'm after a snake and please God I'll scotch it.' He had spent nearly half his life in Africa, long enough to know that 'the Congolese authorities are past masters in the art of innuendo and the basest forms of *tu quoque*';* they reckoned 'the easiest way to refute the truth of my observations or diminish their significance is to – vilify the individual'. He was also aware that he was 'a dangerous man' in the context of his inquiry, and even overheard one official remark that ' "*cette canaille*† *d'un Consul*" was on their track' as he embarked on his radically modern exploration.

On his first day on the river, just after the 'old Queen's birthday' in May 1903, he was surprised to find the 'country a desert – no natives left'. He was told by one of Leopold's commissaires that the ratio of five women to each man on his territory was down to 'Sleeping

* A retort accusing the accuser of doing what he criticises in others.
† Scoundrel.

Sickness!' He retorted that another likely cause was 'Transports!!' From then on there are only brief mentions in his diary of the terrible stories he hears, with more on the health and antics of his bulldog John than on the administration of the Free State. It is as if his journal was a refuge from the daily horrors; the notes that formed the basis of his devastating indictment were kept separately.

His final journey to the heart of the Congo lasted ten weeks. From his previous visit to the region as part of the Sanford Exploring Expedition, he was able to compare the Congolese living 'their own savage lives in anarchic and disorderly communities, uncontrolled by Europeans' and those 'created by more than a decade of very energetic European intervention', including the river steamers, the stations and the railway. These 'energetic' benefits had been both the engine of trade and the driver of depopulation: the Congolese workers had little use for the cloth they were paid in, selling it on at a fraction of its value in order to buy salt and other staples. Meanwhile, he pointed out that the majority of the government employees in Leopoldville were drawn from the Upper Congo and served 'the authorities not primarily at their own seeking', mostly on the river steamers.

As he moved upriver, he started to record the words and voices of those he was interviewing, and their desperation emerges unadorned through his – at that stage – balanced and unemotional prose. A man called Moyo described how his village was paid in cloth 'and a little salt' for rubber, but 'the Chiefs eat up the cloth, the workers get nothing'. As ever more vines were tapped, the gatherers had to go deeper into the forest, and many starved. If they were late with their stipulated twenty baskets, each filled as high as Casement's walking stick, every ten days, they were killed. 'Wild beasts – the leopards – killed some of us when we were working away in the forest, and we begged the white man to leave us alone, saying we could get no more rubber, but the white man and their soldiers said "Go! You are only beasts yourselves, you are *nyama*"' – meat.

At Chumbiri in early July, he found the area that had contained 4,000–5,000 inhabitants in 1887 reduced to '500 souls', with whole villages deserted and overgrown. Those left behind had to keep the

telegraph lines free of undergrowth, cut wood for the steamers and
supply *kwanga*, the staple food of the Upper Congo laboriously made
from the boiled root of the cassava plant. Despite the decline in the
local population, the demand for *kwanga* for the Force Publique
remained the same, meaning that the women left behind in the villages had no time to cultivate the fields and gardens, accelerating the
downward spiral of their existence: one told him how three of the
ten inhabitants in their settlement had to grow the cassava to make
forty *kwanga* loaves, between 180 and 270 pounds in weight of food,
every week, and carry it a day's journey to the workers in return for
a payment equivalent to two francs in brass rods. If the cakes were
'too small or not well-cooked', or if the inhabitants complained that
the brass rods were too short, they would be beaten by the state
employees and often kept for days to cut wood. Their previous
income from selling ivory or dried fish to Europeans downriver was
now denied them, and disease was taking its toll; many were crossing
the river to its northern banks and the comparatively benign French
Congo.

The Consul complained about his own diet of 'chicken, chicken,
custard, custard every day. Come Sunday, God knows . . . Soup,
boiled sugar for change and custard – Hot in morning – same one
cold in eveg.' At the same time, he was writing to a Lisbon friend
about his travels among cannibals in 'the heart of this poor, benighted,
savage land': how a Pygmy tribe, now known as the Twa (eradicated
in the Rwandan genocides ninety years later), 'dispense with cooking
pots and eat and drink their human prey fresh cut on the battlefield
while the blood is still warm and running'. Neither these domestic or
nor these dramatic observations made it into the controlled prose of
his report.

The further inland, the darker the stories. Sometimes people were
too scarce or too frightened to provide testimonies. At the end of
July, he found only a few hundred inhabitants in Lukolela, compared
to the 5,000 of his visit sixteen years before, and a local missionary,
the Reverend John Whitehead, handed over copies of his unacknowledged letters to the Belgian Governor General detailing the
settlement's story. Whitehead had concluded that there were now

352 people in the area, over half of them women, 'not many capable of hard and continuous work' yet expected to make unrealistic quantities of *kwanga* for small quantities of brass rods. The population was shrinking daily, and existed in 'fear and trembling' because the 'pressure under which they live at present is crushing them' as they laboured to make baskets and haul the rubber from the inland districts. Any lapses meant shackling in chains, and a downward spiral in farming, food preparation and health. The main foods were dried fish, usually maggoty, elephant meat and dog-headed bats which brought on diarrhoea, while hippo meat led to constipation. Whitehead reckoned that, within the preceding nine years, 'the people quite lost heart and felt their homes were no longer secure . . . and then hunger, improper food, fear and homelessness increased the death rate from sleep-sickness and other causes most appallingly'.*
The fewer the inhabitants, the proportionately higher the mortality rate, as the demands of the administration remained the same. Whitehead could 'see the shadow of death' over many of his flock.

At the start of August, Casement was investigating around Lake Mantumba, about 600 miles from Leopoldville, in the King's Domaine Privé. His entry for the 1st of the month masks his anxiety about his expected findings: 'Rained in night – but later a beautiful day.' John caught three goats. He then has a sentence that does not reference anything at all ('Nothing in particular') before another description of the changeable weather, 'Rain again – but afterwards delightful.' The final entries for the day carry his romantic distraction and his yearning for physical contact on the bold and lonely enterprise he has undertaken, feelings perhaps triggered by sunshine after a rainstorm on an August day: 'Roman soldier. Coliseum. August 1900. Carte de Visite. Fortunato.'

Such reveries had to be put aside. He knew that 'large bodies of native troops' from the Force Publique had been quartered around the 300 square miles of the lake, but was unprepared for the evidence

---

* It was only discovered that year that sleeping sickness is caused by the tsetse fly. Some 80 per cent of deaths from African trypanosomiasis still occur in the Democratic Republic of the Congo.

of abandonment he encountered. His first stop was a burnt-out village; at the next three the few remaining inhabitants fled at the sight
of the *Henry Reed* despite her crew's entreaties. Once it was established that this was a mission boat, and that the strangers were not
Bula Matadi, men of the government, Casement was reminded that in
the hopeful early days of the Free State 'the people flocked from all
sides to greet a white stranger'.

The gentle, experienced man won enough trust to elicit pent-up
stories far worse than even he had expected. He heard Frank Eteva, a
'native teacher at Ituta on Lake Mantumba', speak of the savagery
meted out by Monsieur Svenson, chief of the post at Bikoro in 1894.
For no apparent reason, Svenson had two men and four women in a
canoe on a creek murdered; Eteva 'saw them killed' but 'they did not
cut the hands off, because [Svenson] was there looking on' so did not
require the evidence. The bodies were left in the water, while the
ducks found in the canoe were taken by Svenson and the *kwanga*
given to the execution squad. Eteva told of a chief crying with pain
as he was whipped with a *chicotte* for refusing to hand over a fowl, and
of eight men of the Mwebi tribe who were bound in tight chains for
eight days as hostages after they had fallen short of their fish quota;
their canoes had been taken from them by Monsieur Daneels, the
local Belgian functionary.

A young woman called Elima recounted her childhood experiences: soldiers attacked her village under orders from 'the white
man', as she called Lieutenant Durieux of the Force Publique. Elima
encouraged her sister to run, but the girl was too exhausted. One soldier proposed 'keeping them both', but others thought it too much
trouble to have the younger along, so she was shot in the stomach. At
the next town Elima's captors took an old woman prisoner, were
granted permission by Durieux to slit her throat, 'divided her' and
ate her in front of Elima. The rampage continued, with more ampu-
tated hands taken to Durieux as proof of the men's murder of their
own countrymen. After two weeks in captivity, Elima escaped and
made it to a mission station.

Another girl, Ncongo, was left orphaned in charge of her brother
and sister. They were caught and her charges were left to die of

starvation in the bush; another half-sister was killed and her hands and feet cut off for the rings on them; Ncongo saw a basket of 200 severed hands counted in front of Durieux. A little child was beheaded for laughing at the soldiers, and other children sold into slavery to a different tribe. Mola Ekulite was captured alongside other men from his village and their hands so tightly bound that, after a night in the rain, the thongs had cut through to the bone; the soldiers, in full view of a white man known to him as 'Leopard's Paw', beat their hands to a pulp against a tree with their rifle butts. Mola Ekulite staggered back to his village. A boy of eleven or twelve had had his right hand severed at the wrist while 'perfectly sensible' after a gunshot wound; he played dead, 'fearing that if he moved he would be killed'. Casement was shown an anonymous letter begging for help for another boy whose right hand was severed, and his left beaten on the side of a canoe until 'all the fingers were destroyed'. As he wrote up these testimonies in the heavy rain, his malaria flared up again to the point where he understatedly felt 'not at all well' and took nine quinine tablets. When the *Henry Reed* pulled off to continue her slow progress upriver, more Congolese paddled behind in their canoes, desperate to tell the shivering, trusted man their stories of degradation, destruction and mutilation.

Throughout his journey Casement heard of iniquitous food taxes and brutal punishments. Village chiefs were obliged to provide maize, sorghum, groundnut oil, nuts, workmen and soldiers on the instructions of the district commissaires, but the mandated numbers remaining behind to cultivate crops were either non-existent or referred back to a time when the population was ten times greater. A chief described how he had bought a seven-year-old boy, nephew of the neighbouring chief Botolo, for 1,000 rods, the equivalent of fifty francs, to enable Botolo to meet a fine imposed by the Commissaire-Général to penalise a shortage in that week's supplies. Two days later, the Consul walked to Botolo's village to find that it now had a population of only eight men, two of whom had been imprisoned for failure to meet quotas: the weekly demands were 700 pounds of *kwanga*, ninety-five rations of fish, two canoeloads of wood for steamer fuel and 900 palm-thatch mats, as well as 'two fowls for the European table'. Pawning his nephew could stave off the fines for only a few days; imprisonment and worse would inevitably follow for Botolo.

Casement was to hear these stories time and again as he made his way upstream in the pungent atmosphere given off by the water hyacinths and marshy vegetation in the heat. But it was when he reached the most productive rubber-producing districts far upstream that the worst emerged. The Lulongo River and its two great feeders ran for 350 miles through richly forested country to form a gigantic, fertile basin, inhabited by the Mongo tribe. The rivers united at Basankusu, the headquarters of the ABIR concession, about 120 miles above the Lulongo's entry into the Congo. Casement arrived there on 28 August. ABIR employed fifty-eight Europeans in 1903, overseeing what was effectively a slave-labour force of 47,000; it was currently enjoying its peak production year of a thousand tons of high-quality rubber, up from an average of 700 tons. Casement reckoned that, at the lower range, 'its annual yield may probably be estimated at not less than £150,000',* for which was bartered 'the usual class of Central African goods – cotton cloths of different quality, Sheffield cutlery, matchets [machetes], beads and salt'. He lapsed back into contemporary colonial language to comment that 'the latter is keenly sought by the natives of all the interior of Africa', before adding that he believed ABIR also imported a considerable quantity of guns 'which are chiefly used in arming sentinels', for forest guards who were quartered in the native villages in considerable numbers. While he was there, one of the largest concession companies wrote to Brussels to ask for more ball cartridges for the Albini rifles each 'factory' was allowed; the inventories stated that the 72,000 supplied three years earlier had been used 'in the production of india-rubber'.

The La Lulanga Society, a small concession bordering ABIR's, had nearly exhausted its vines, and 'it is only with great difficulty' that the 'natives' could produce enough 'to satisfy their masters', leading to widespread evidence of 'murder and mutilation'. The taxes levied were pointless. The Congolese supplied the companies not only with all their exports, but also with their 'food and

---

* Approximately £19 million at today's values.

material', while the Congo government 'itself requires no contribution to the public revenue'. After noting the number of armed men in the area, Casement reported the dry observation that the profits which appeared in the annual budget for the Congo as a *'produit de porte-feuille'* might 'more correctly be *"produit de porte-fusil"* ', a return on the use of arms rather than on investment. The concessionaries' convoluted explanations that the workers were paid for their labours, or maybe taxed on their productiveness weekly, or maybe offered their services in return for protection, were 'so obviously untrue . . . that they could not be admitted as having any real relation to the things which came before me'.

If Casement's exasperation was now seeping into his prose, his next stops induced an icy rage. He travelled 120 miles up a tributary of the Lulongo, back in ABIR territory, to witness for himself men and women being struck and locked up as hostages for not bringing in enough rubber, while those who fulfilled their quotas were paid in glass beads, a little salt and wooden-handled knives; he visited a mission where he could hear the cries of those being flogged with the *chicotte* in a *maison d'otages*, a hostage compound, 300 yards away. By the time he returned to the main river, Congolese from the surrounding country were rushing to him: he met two six-year-old boys, one of whom had been wounded by gunfire when his father had refused to pay over 1,000 brass rods to some rogue soldiers, the other had had his right hand severed at the wrist. When he interviewed the teenaged Epondo – whose stump of a wrist had 'scarcely healed' and was wrapped in an insanitary rag – alongside the boy's mutilator, a sentry called Kelengo, his almost legalistically, officially dispassionate questions were translated by a missionary into the local language.* Kelengo, unique in being willing to speak at all, denied that was his name, that he had ever seen Epondo before, that he had shot and mutilated him or that he had exacted brass rods as hostage money for women in the villages – every charge brought by Casement should be aimed at his predecessor, a bad man. The interview had no need

---

* Today there are an estimated 220 languages in use among 250 different ethnic groups in the Democratic Republic of the Congo.

of any further commentary: it succinctly encapsulated the wilful blindness of the authorities to the atrocities carried out by those empowered by Leopold and the Force Publique. Although Casement had only 'touched on the outmost fringe of this horrible reality', he had seen enough and, distraught, exhausted and paranoid about being 'shadowed', he ordered the *Henry Reed* downstream towards Stanley Pool.

On 15 September, he anchored in the dark waters of the Pool, irritable and unwell. He was so altered by his journey that the regular bulletins about the antics of his bulldog had been absent from his diary for nearly three weeks. His sympathies were transposed to those he had encountered. That day's entry ends: 'Wrote F.O. all night.' The result of this sleepless outpouring was Casement's description of himself 'as a self-appointed Criminal Investigation Department', going far beyond his brief to establish the extent of free trade as he gathered plentiful evidence of 'wholesale oppression and shocking misgovernment'. He had 'broken into the thieves' kitchen', his fury ignited by the atrocities his courage and his compassion had enabled him to uncover; he was about to expose a European country's murderous corruption. He sensed that his discoveries were so momentous that he would 'pay for [them] in my own future'.

4.   Those in High Places

Casement was both drained and overwrought in the wake of his investigation. A photograph of him taken on his homeward voyage in São Tomé with one of Stanley's great admirers, the American journalist May French Sheldon, shows that his natural ranginess has become gauntness, accentuated by his height and white Irish linen suit bleaching out in the sunshine; his eyes are large and intense above his sharpened cheekbones. He grasped that he had reached his life's turning point: he had 'burned my boats deliberately' with the Congo authorities and 'would have to go overboard', exceed his brief and pour out everything he had seen.

He could not hold back the horrors of the 'unhappy people whose sufferings I have witnessed, and whose wrongs have burnt into my heart', until he had left Africa; their cries of 'Protect us from our protectors' were ringing in his ears; he was the only person who could make their voices heard in the halls of power – and it was urgent that he do so. He wrote to Lansdowne from the mouth of the Congo that, at the risk of 'incurring your Lordship's displeasure', his greater 'duty was to serve the persecuted beings who had far and wide appealed to me for help'. One Foreign Office official languidly commented on 'the rather exuberant diction for which Consul Casement has a weakness' but agreed that this was the basis of 'a far more effective weapon of attack on the Congo State' than the Office had been able to wield before; another took a more traditional view of his emotionalism, considering that 'we ought to have as British representative someone not harder hearted, but harder headed'. The Foreign Secretary understood the shock of Casement's discoveries, and declared that even 'making every allowance for the strength of his feelings, these papers are a terrible indictment'. What all were agreed on was that Casement had to come home.

The battle lines were drawn up before his ship *Zaire* had begun her voyage to Lisbon. Casement urged Morel, the campaigner against Leopold's regime whom he had yet to meet, to get in touch with Conrad, describing the now-famous author as 'a Pole, a seaman, an ex-Congo traveller . . . one or two of his short stories – such as "The Heart of Darkness" [*sic*] – deal with his own view of Upper Congo life'. It was just after this introduction that Casement encountered Sheldon, who was travelling under the aegis of King Leopold and Casement's first employer, Sir Alfred Jones, Chairman of Elder Dempster, Director of the Compagnie Belge Maritime du Congo and Consul for the Congo in Liverpool. Sheldon was the first of many journalists the monopolists sponsored for propaganda purposes, and officials took great pains to show her 'the territory's delights'; hostages were freed ahead of her and a prison was demolished at Bangala. One local station chief blundered when he confused her with a visitor from the Liverpool School of Tropical Medicine: he lined up the worst cases of disability and disease he could find, but by that time Mrs Sheldon had fallen in love with a steamboat captain and was generally enamoured of the country. She gave speeches and slide shows in Britain, and wrote articles claiming that she had 'witnessed more atrocities on the streets of London than I have ever seen in the Congo'. Leopold added her to his payroll at 1,500 francs* a month as a Parliamentary lobbyist. Meanwhile, once word got out about Casement's upstream travels, letters and telegrams from Belgian diplomats began thudding into the Foreign Office, claiming 'vagueness . . . complete lack of evidence', and pointing out that Britain was guilty of 'numerous and bloody wars against native populations' in Sierra Leone, Nigeria and Somaliland.

Casement disembarked in Liverpool at the start of December; there he boarded the night train and proceeded straight to the Foreign Office from Euston Station. He was angry and confident: he lambasted his colleagues in his diary as 'a gang of Stupidities in many ways'. This view was slightly tempered when he was summoned to Lansdowne House in Mayfair two days later to hear the Foreign Secretary declare of his 'dire tale' that it was 'Proof of the

---

* Approximately £7,500 at today's values.

most painfully convincing kind'; he was instructed to start his official report at once. Jordan the 'type man' came to his temporary home in Herbert Ward's house in Chester Square, Belgravia, to begin work. The typist must have been fatigued, as well as shaken, as the softly spoken, emaciated author tersely and unsparingly began to dictate. Two more days and he was 15,000 words in; by the end of the week, it was done, complete with Casement's estimate that Leopold's regime had caused 3 million deaths. Morel's best guess to the *The Economist* in 1912 was that 'Twenty-five years of unbridled tyranny has reduced the aboriginal population . . . by at least eight millions'; the American author, humorist and campaigner Mark Twain reckoned 8–10 million. In the evenings of these productive days, Casement went out to dinner at his club or at a restaurant, often alone, walking back to Belgravia. Once again anonymous in a big city, he sought out anonymous sex, noting of one partner, 'Dusky – depredator – Huge', and one undeciphered as 'D.W. 14 C.R. £1'. These entries again sit alongside references to his international mission, to remote family matters and to a momentous meeting: 'E.D.M. first time I saw him'.

Arthur Conan Doyle described the encounter between Morel and Casement as 'the most dramatic scene in modern history'. The two men talked for hours, before going out to a late dinner at the Comedy Restaurant which had, according to the diarist, who rarely commented on such matters, an excellent new French chef; they then repaired to Chester Square to converse until two o'clock in the morning; Morel slept on a couch in Ward's study. He was awestruck by his hero, waxing about 'one of those rare incidents in life which leave behind them an imperishable impression. I saw before me a man my own height, very lithe and sinewy, chest thrown out, head held high – suggestive of one who had lived in the vast open spaces. Black hair and beard covering cheeks hollowed by the tropical sun.' He commented on the sunken dark eyes and the 'long, lean, swarthy' face, 'extraordinarily handsome and arresting . . . graven with power and withal of great gentleness'. He felt 'mutual trust and confidence', and the 'feeling of isolation' his crusade had aroused fell away from the moment of their first handshake. He was transfixed by the 'monologue of horror unfolding in a musical, soft, almost even voice, in language of peculiar dignity and pathos'. Casement would interrupt himself to 'murmur beneath his breath, "Poor people; poor, poor people"', as his narrative threatened to overwhelm him. Morel was in the presence of 'a man indeed . . . who would convince those in high places of the foulness of a crime committed upon a helpless race, who would move the bowels of compassion as no one else could do'. Casement, rarely given to exuberance in his diary, merely noted that Morel was 'as honest as day', mirroring Ward's testimonial to him that 'No man walks the earth who is more absolutely good and honest and noble-minded'.

Fired up, and after a final day's read-through, Casement took his typescript and his heavy cold to the Foreign Office on 12 December 1903, where he saw the 'despatches from Brussels by bag – Congo have begun their anti-Casement campaign'. Leopold was fearful and threatening: even before Casement's report had been delivered, he had sent Sir Alfred Jones, whose shipping contract was up for renewal, twice to the Foreign Office to warn that 'the attitude of HMG in regard to the Congo administration might drive him into the arms of the Germans. He . . . might even be forced to hand over everything – he meant himself and Belgium – to Germany.' Jones cleverly flew the kite of the European power balance: Britain was planning a rapprochement with France to end centuries of enmity and twenty years of African disputes, primarily in Morocco and Egypt, not least over the vital, jointly owned Suez Canal link to South Asia. Edward VII had made a successful diplomatic (and gastronomic) state visit to Paris just before the House of Commons Congo debate and the Foreign Office was delicately negotiating behind the scenes for what would become the Entente Cordiale in April 1904. The Entente deftly avoided the two countries being caught up in the looming Russo-Japanese War as formal allies of Russia in France's case and of Japan in Britain's. All of this was alarming to surrounded, isolated Germany, which accelerated its shipbuilding programme in the arms race with Britain, France and Russia.

The Belgian press fought back with disinformation. *La Dépêche*

Coloniale insisted 'that the cases of mutilation discovered by Mr Casement are the result of intertribal warfare anterior to the commencement of operations'; *La Tribune Congolaise*, a paper allied to business interests, claimed that the mutilated people Casement had seen 'were unfortunate individuals, suffering from cancers of the hands, whose hands thus had to be cut off as a simple surgical operation'. In order to paint him as a hypocrite, Leopold republished Casement's own 1901 encomium to the Governor General of the Free State expressing his and his countrymen's 'very sincere appreciation of your . . . efforts to promote goodwill among all and to bring together the various elements in our local life'. But the mandarins ignored the propaganda and were 'all agreed that Mr Casement's report must be laid', perhaps not least to avoid the charge of condoning colonial atrocities while ruling over so much of the globe themselves.

In its final form, the 50,000-word paper was 'terse, full of matter, and written in a quite dispassionate style . . . free from all trace of exaggeration', as Assistant Under-Secretary Francis Villiers was surprised to note, having read some of Casement's more highly wrought missives. Its understatement made it all the more powerful: Morel saw that its 'moderation of language' – in many cases its verbatim record of what witnesses had said – 'threw the facts recorded into the boldest relief. . . There was a subtle quality about it which stirred profoundly [and] one rose from its perusal in a sweat of rage.' The presentation of the protagonists in their own words moved some of Morel's acquaintance to tears as it 'brought home the human effects'.

Casement revised his work in December, adding appendices to back up his findings, and on the 21st crossed to Dublin on the night boat. He met up with a former lover, 'J.B.', in the city before going on to Belfast and Ballycastle on Christmas Eve. A handsome letter from Joseph Conrad awaited him: the novelist had always had 'a high opinion' of Casement's courage, dismissing his own *Heart of Darkness* as 'an awful fudge' by comparison, and weighed in on the side of right in his condemnation of 'one small country' and its actions 'in defiance of international treaties and in brazen disregard of humanitarian declarations'.* Despite this accolade, Casement was 'miserable' over Christmas and New Year. He found Ballycastle 'cold and black', although his spirits were revived by seeing his sister Nina and hearing some cottage entertainments such as a recital of 'Paddy in the Butter'. He was unwell and was exhibiting the dissatisfaction that was to become familiar for the rest of his life at times of under-employment and, above all, when he was not engaged in principled emotional endeavour.

But by the time the *Correspondence and Report from His Majesty's Consul at Boma Respecting the Administration of the Independent State of the Congo* was published as a Government White Paper on 15 February 1904, its author was raging bitterly against his employers for their betrayal of those whose stories he had so painfully set down. His professional demeanour had again evaporated in what had become more of a personal than an official campaign, leading him to the exaggerated claim that his former 'certainty that truth will win in this campaign' was endangered.

The issue was the identification of agents and locations, tribes and individuals. He was clear that witnesses had to be named to avoid Belgian accusations of fabrication and to honour the victims' injuries. He had believed the issue settled before he left for Ireland, and was outraged to find out that identities had been suppressed by the Foreign Office – it showed his unfamiliarity with Whitehall that he had ever considered he might have the final decision. He bombarded his employers with telegrams and letters expostulating that 'the report will cease to be a faithful record . . . you make the report absolute fiction and worthless . . . the timidity of not speaking out . . . will only do harm'. Writing to friends, he called Villiers an 'abject piffler' and the Foreign Office as a whole 'a wretched set of incompetent

---

* Chinua Achebe and others have made the case that *Heart of Darkness* itself is racist for propagating the contemporary tropes of Europeans being superior to Africans, who are treated as objects rather than thinking people, with 'Darkest Africa' the antithesis of Europe and therefore of civilisation. Achebe also points out that some of the carved wooden sculptures from the Congo were to have a profound effect on Braque, Matisse and Picasso, and were influential in the birth of Cubism.

noodles'. He abandoned this playful tone in his vituperation against Phipps, whom he called a 'cur' who was 'beneath contempt'; he would like to set about him 'with a good thick Irish blackthorn'.

Lord Salisbury, Lord Privy Seal and son of the recently dead Prime Minister, was adamant that 'all names should be suppressed both of tyrants and victims', and the matter was settled. The report was published with letters standing for proper nouns, leading to passages that read absurdly, such as Casement's interview with Epondo and Kelengo:* 'The Consul, through WW, speaking in EF, and XX repeating his utterances both in FG and in the local dialect . . . asks II who cut off his hand . . . The sentry denies the charge, stating that his name is TTT and not KK.' Although the Foreign Office was used to Casement's undisciplined despatches, they must have been astonished to receive from him at such a moment an eighteen-page letter of outrage. They had 'issued a cooked and garbled report' that left him 'a good deal disgusted'; 'Ringing changes of the alphabet' did not even serve its stated purpose as 'in many cases the identity of the individual is still quite clear to anyone with local knowledge'. He could no longer 'continue to serve a department which has so little confidence in me and so little regard for my opinion as . . . to make such vital changes in face of my strong protest'. It was clear that a 'resignation is called for'. He went, as he knew he would have to before he embarked on the *Zaire*, 'overboard'.

The publication of the White Paper was a publicity anticlimax. Among the major newspapers, only the *Morning Post* grasped the significance of the moment, according the report a four-column summary and an editorial which concluded that the Free State was 'not a state at all, but a gigantic trading concern, a monopoly run for the benefit of its shareholders'. Influential writers rallied, including Ford Madox Ford, who opined that the state was 'on the whole the most horrible institution that the world – or let us say Christendom – has suffered to exist', full of atrocities sanctioned by that 'redoubtable

---

* Quotations in this book are from Casement's first draft of his report, with identifying details present.

tradesman' Leopold that were 'revolting beyond belief'. But liberal voices carried little weight. Phipps went so far as to claim that the effect of any outcry would be to put public opinion firmly behind Leopold in Brussels, where the report was considered a sop to the Commons rather than a cause for alarm. He 'was loath to believe that Belgians, members of a cultivated people . . . could, even under a tropical sky, have perpetrated acts of refined cruelty and of systematic oppression'. When Casement saw these despatches, his usually eloquent use of insult failed him: 'How Phipps can believe all these people tell him puzzles me, or rather it doesn't.'

Leopold went on the offensive, but stopped short of publicly criticising the British government and potentially igniting an international incident. He commissioned a former Congo administrator from the 1880s to write *Notes on the Report of Mr Casement*, a strange document that was simultaneously aggressive and defensive: it postulated that, since the Consul's trip had been 'hasty and rapid', his observations were inevitably 'superficial'; and that as he had presented himself as a 'redresser of wrongs', the Congolese felt able to air any grievance, real or imagined. In the end, the Belgians had no problem in identifying 'II' as Epondo, and announced that the boy now admitted that his hand had been bitten off by a wild boar rather than hacked off by soldiers. So if this critical testimony was false, how could the rest be trusted?

The Belgian press reasserted itself to claim that Casement was a tool of British commercial interests, specifically Liverpool shipping companies looking to break into the monopoly. A long letter was sent from the Bachelors' Club in Piccadilly to *The Times* by James Harrison, who had been on a 'shooting trip' to the Congo; he had 'wandered about, visiting 50 different tribes and hundreds of villages, armed as a rule with a camera, umbrella and at times a collecting gun'. Harrison implied that Casement was biased, a 'trader' looking for business; he himself had 'had no unpleasant experiences' but was 'received with kindness far different to any I ever met with when hunting among British African natives'. The newspaper was vigorous in its leader column's rebuttal of Harrison on the same day, asserting that his narrative was 'local and partial in character' with 'an unavoidable incompleteness'. 'The Thunderer' argued its case to its readers: 'The alleged misgovernment of the Congo is exactly one of those subjects which appeal not, as the Congo government insinuates . . . to the jealous cupidity of Englishmen, but to their strong inherited instinct of fair play and compassion for the weak.' Enquiries established that Harrison was a big-game hunter who traded propaganda for the requisite licences.

Phipps seemed to be on Casement's side for once as he urged his employers to produce more evidence to counter the views expressed in the Belgian press that the English were looking for 'justification for the benefit of Liverpool merchants who have organised the campaign against the Free State', but Lansdowne refused on the grounds that the reports aside from Casement's in his now bulging files were 'hearsay' and 'lacked the authority of personal observation, without which H.M. Government were unwilling to come to any definite conclusion unfavourable to the administration of the Congo State'. Casement scrawled 'a deliberate lie!' in the margin of his copy of Phipps's letter. Religious cross-currents in the run-up to the Entente Cordiale must also have baffled Casement: many Irish Parliamentarians took a nationalistically religious path, exemplified by the MP for South Armagh who 'deprecated the Protestant attacks on Catholic Belgium', while some Catholics, notably Belgian bishops, even claimed that Casement's report was some sort of Protestant plot to offer 'an alternative power structure' in the Congo.

Casement could not return to the Congo, and the reaction to his report convinced him that he had no future as a diplomat. But Eric Barrington, Lansdowne's private secretary, was firm that 'Nobody [in the Foreign Office] wants you to resign'; he had 'never heard of such a thing'. Casement was now 'intended' as Consul in Lisbon; the comfortable, undemanding, disease-free and well-paid European berth was a plum reward for African work. But Casement's honourably grudging reply was that, although he would accept the post if offered, it still 'might relieve the Foreign Office of some embarrassment were I to resign from the Service'. There was no intention of letting him go, however, and he had no alternative employment:

their abrading relationship still had much more embarrassment to undergo.

Casement could not bear the slow workings of government in the face of the need for urgent assistance in the Free State. In his simple and morally direct view, 'Leopold = Hades = Hell' and immediate action was required so that 'all will work out straight & white & clear'. A few weeks after their first meeting, he went to stay with Morel on the Welsh border to propose an organisation that could circumvent officialdom. Morel was at first reluctant to cut across the Aborigines Protection Society's campaigning strengths, but his wife was in 'fervid support' of Casement as the men once again talked through the night.

Just before the report was published, Morel travelled to Ireland, and the two men had dinner at the Slieve Donard Hotel in Newcastle, County Down; it was the start of the practical collaboration that helped pressure the world into change. The choice of venue was symbolic: Morel said of the encounter, in which they 'conspired further . . . and drew up a rough plan of campaign', that it was significant that it took place on 'Irish soil . . . fertilised by so many human tears'. He echoed his new ally's heightened diction as they concluded that 'the Congo evil was a special and extraordinary evil calling for special means of attack' and that if Britain, which had combated slavery successfully in the past, was 'really roused', then so would the world be; the only question was whether they 'could raise a throbbing in that great heart of hers'.

The first step was the practical one of funding. Casement wrote a cheque for £100, a significant portion of his annual salary while he remained on half-pay during his leave, and Morel used the money to buy supplies, including a typewriter and notepaper on which to write to potential patrons – peers, businessmen, MPs, bishops, the great-grandson of William Wilberforce, members of the Gladstone family and prominent Quaker families and shipowners. The Congo Reform Association held its first meeting in Liverpool's packed Philharmonic Hall in March 1904 with Casement absent: partly because he was still a supposedly impartial government employee, possibly because he had just seen the Belgian *Notes*, and certainly because of his dislike of personal publicity. As his and Morel's friendship deepened, they began to refer to each other as 'Tiger' and 'Bulldog', pitted against Leopold, the 'King of Beasts'. They were men of unimpeachable conviction – a noble, if at times febrile, attribute which was to land both of them in Pentonville Prison a dozen years later.

Joseph Conrad declined to join the new organisation, disingenuously writing that he was 'only a wretched novelist inventing wretched stories and not even up to that miserable game'. In his time in the Congo there had been a less corrupted rubber trade and no Force Publique, and during his 'sojourn in the interior, keeping [his] eyes and ears well open too, I've never heard of the alleged custom of cutting off hands amongst the natives'. He may have believed that novelists should let their fictions speak for themselves; or he may have been wary of campaigns against a powerful international enemy following his parents' futile struggle against tsarist Russia in Poland; or he may have wanted to be apolitical in the country whose citizenship he had now acquired. He may have been beginning to entertain the doubts he was later to express about Casement's increasingly uncentred, emotional passage through life.

Notwithstanding, Casement threw his energies into the Congo Reform Association. When Fox Bourne refused to merge his Aborigines Protection Society with them, Morel begged him not to 'shoot at Casement . . . one of the finest fellows in the world, and consumed with a passion for these wretched people . . . a noble trait'. Casement remained in the background of the CRA until May 1904, by which time he had been disheartened by the official follow-up to his gruelling report. He regretted that 'no further action is likely to be taken by the Foreign Office in the matter, and the reason intimated to me was that neither Parliament, nor the press of this country has displayed the slightest interest . . . the whole thing has fallen flat.' By September, he was so wounded by the lack of support and by Leopold's lobbying that he was complaining that 'It is Villiers, Phipps and Co. who have got control of the Congo question, and they are now vindictive . . . They are sincerely sorry I was born.'

The Foreign Office and the Liberal opposition in Parliament,

including contributions from Casement's future boss Sir Edward
Grey, had, in fact, been pushing Leopold to set up an independent
commission to investigate the abuses. But without more international
support the government had their hands tied even as Leopold's propaganda campaign ran aground. The King had spent the spring financing
a supposedly philanthropic organisation in Brussels which published
information about the Free State, another cover for paying foreign
and domestic writers to churn out articles portraying it in a rosy
light. Phipps sounded rattled at the end of June when he complained
that 'the saloons and sleeping cars throughout Europe at this travelling season are full of pamphlets, amended periodically and entitled
La Vérité sur le Congo . . .'

The counter-campaign got off to a good start in America in April:
over the headline 'Congo Charges False', the *Washington Post* claimed
that the *Notes on the Report of Mr Casement* provided 'a most convincing testimony to the humanitarian work which King Leopold has
accomplished in Africa'. But Senator Morgan of Alabama, a former
slave owner, was outraged by the stories he had heard from a business
partner whose missionary son had died in the Congo. Morgan told
the Senate that Casement's report was 'entirely just and correct', and
arranged for the *Congressional Record* to include fifteen pages about the
atrocities. US newspapers added pressure on Leopold, urging him to
set up an independent Commission of Inquiry if he had nothing to
hide.

The unlikely final straw came from Italy. The Free State employed
Italian officers as mercenaries and Leopold believed he would have an
easy time of it there. But on 6 July *La Tribuna* carried an article about
a lieutenant who had killed himself shortly before he was brought to
trial at home in Italy on Congo brutality charges, which led to questions in Parliament and demands for an investigation. Leopold had no
option but to announce his Commission, which consisted of two
judges – a Belgian and an Italian – and the head of the Department of
Justice in the Swiss canton of Lucerne. Fox Bourne pointed out that
Casement should at least attend the Commission's hearings in Brussels, but Lansdowne chose not to press the point, instead instructing
Phipps to inform the Free State authorities that without a British

representative the Commission could not feel 'surprised or aggrieved if the result should be to destroy in advance all the moral authority which might otherwise attach' to it. Despite these promising diplomatic manoeuvrings, Casement's earlier sense that he had been slighted by the Foreign Office was the start of a resentment that gathered speed with damaging consequences in the years to come.

Casement's promised Lisbon consulship was a fiasco exacerbated by his health, and it increased his dissatisfaction as a servant of the Crown. He arrived in the Portuguese capital in July 1904, but by mid-September was once again on sick leave. He told his cousin Gertrude that he was 'seriously unwell', fearful that he would not recover in Portugal and might have to go to hospital, adding that he did '*not like Lisbon at all* and [was] not sorry to be leaving it'. Although he was never well after his first years in Africa, other factors in Lisbon might have aggravated his dissatisfaction. The first was that the work in the consulate was tedious: there was a legation to undertake the sort of business over which he had had personal sway in his African postings, and he was left to the dull side of the job, including clearing British ships in and out of port, dealing with drunken citizens who had been arrested and registering seamen's deaths, all of which must have felt trivial after his adventures of the preceding years. The other reason for his disgruntlement was his ongoing perception of Whitehall's lack of support against the attacks from Belgium: Antonio Benedetti, an Italian chancer who had worked for the Free State, approached the Congo Reform Association to write an exposé of the conditions there. Casement warned Morel that Benedetti 'looks like a rascal' and that they should steer clear, but it was too late. Benedetti took his contract with the CRA to a Belgian newspaper as proof that he was being bribed to tell lies on the Association's behalf, and Casement was appalled to find that the Foreign Office had known about the Italian's relationship with Belgium but had not thought to warn Morel.

However, despite – or possibly because of – the lack of official recognition, which left the Congolese in their dispossessed nightmare, Casement's next extended leave began to give him inner sustenance for the last tumultuous decade of his life. He was disillusioned with the government that seemed not to appreciate him, and with diplomacy and England in general. He was hard up, unwell, forty years old and a man of strong emotions who had never been fulfilled by a romantic relationship. He had returned to his roots immediately after delivering his report a year earlier; now he chose to have an operation, possibly for another anal fistula, and undergo his convalescence in the country of his birth. He always needed a mission to fill the void within his hidden, divided self, and from this low point he began to gather information, strength and passion from Ireland.

5. Foundations

Casement's foundations were insecure, shadowy and shrouded in secrets. The only settled part of his fractured upbringing was when, as an orphan, he seized upon the legendary heroes of Ireland's past in his uncle's library at Magherintemple, just south of Rathlin Sound in the country's north-east corner, thus taking the first unrecognised steps towards creating an identity for himself. His father, also Roger, came from a family of landowners and public officials, one of many sons of a Protestant Ulster shipping merchant who had lost his capital when several cargoes of Australian grain failed to reach dock. After serving in the army, he existed on a captain's precarious half-pay. Casement's mother, Annie Jephson, claimed to be descended from a notable Ascendancy family, but the relationship was mysterious to her children: she was possibly a love child of her father, who she believed had been killed in a hunting accident when she was young.

Roger David Casement was born in 1864 in Doyle's Cottage, Sandycove, a small terraced house in a respectable part of Dublin. He was the youngest survivor of his mother's eleven pregnancies: his siblings were Agnes (Nina), Charlie and Tom; eight years separated him from Nina, two and three from his brothers. Their father had gone into the world as a son of empire with a commission in the 3rd Light Dragoons in India for eight years, fighting in the Sikh Wars, before selling his commission at a loss. A less narrow-minded figure than many Ulster Protestant soldiers of his time, he was the author of a long essay on Hindu mysticism. The republican captain's only other extant piece of writing dated from 1870, and proposed that the Siege of Paris at the culmination of the Franco-Prussian War be alleviated by 10,000 horses carrying supplies to the besieged members of the Paris Commune before themselves being eaten.

Captain Casement's most memorable, barely corroborated exploit helped to instil a notion of heroic romanticism in his children. He had left India to aid Hungary in its struggle for freedom from Austrian rule. The reforming but defeated Lajos Kossuth and his 5,000 rebels were trapped in Widdin in 1849; Kossuth was petitioning the Turkish government for sanctuary but suspected that Austrian counter-pressure would cause them to back away; he realised that only the British could save him and his men. Just then, Captain Casement arrived, unsolicited, at his headquarters. The captain swiftly remounted and rode back across Europe to deliver Kossuth's letter to Lord Palmerston's London dinner table; the Foreign Secretary intervened and the rebels survived. One detail that the captain never omitted in his retelling was that Kossuth did not even know his name, and years later in a chance encounter between the two men at Niagara Falls he handed over his card with a pencilled scrawl: 'I gave Palmerston the message from Widdin.' After his death, Kossuth's confirmation of the heroic episode in his memoirs militates against the story being a much practised fiction.

Nothing else in the elder Roger's life contained even a hint of the glamour of his dash across Europe. He married Anne, sixteen years his junior, in 1855, and three years later resigned his second commission, in the North Antrim Militia, on health grounds, possibly a cover for financial irregularities. The tall, striking couple and their growing band of children then led a peripatetic existence, moving between the Isle of Man, Boulogne, possibly Italy, Jersey (where young Roger became hooked on swimming, according to his sister) and Dalston, Surbiton and Dorking on the outskirts of London. Letters from rented rooms made their way to his uncle John* in Ulster, one of them asserting that 'your most kind and welcome Xmas box of £5 . . . will stop the mouths of the two tradesmen who threatened me', and lamenting that he cannot get 'any sort of employment', even as a 'copyist'; he never received an answer to his application to be a subeditor on a local Hastings newspaper. When his uncle did not respond, Roger self-pityingly wrote from a different Surbiton address

---

* Roger (born 1819) was the grandson of Roger Casement (of Harryville) by his first marriage; John (1825–1902) was Roger Casement of Harryville's son by his second marriage.

to say 'how very black' things were looking as winter brought on his usual bout of ill-health 'from which death would be a merciful release'. There were constant complaints about landlords charging for extras before the inevitable notice to quit. The captain acknowledged that he kept his family in 'a shocking position' financially, and a relation did not mince words in describing him as 'an insinuating idler who lived on his debts'. The eleven-year-old Roger and the thirteen-year-old Tom appeared in court accused of stealing books from a Lambeth newsvendor in 1876, admitting to the court that they had planned to resell them. Their father, 'a respectable-looking man', testified that he gave the 'inveterate readers of juvenile literature' pocket money, and he could only assume that they had intended to pay the vendor 'another day'. The beak ordered the boys 'to be given up to their father on his entering into recognisances for their future conduct'.

All the children lived geographically unsettled and financially insecure lives. Charlie and Tom were both funded by John Casement to leave for Australia – a country their father had once hoped to make a fresh start in himself – when Casement was sixteen; he did not see Charlie, who worked for the Melbourne Omnibus and Tramway Company, again. So deeply was any hint of homosexuality hidden that when Charlie was asking for a gift to help him furnish his Melbourne home in later years, he divulged that he had 'often wondered, is it because you have such a lot of poor relations that you are helping that you never got married yourself?' Tom married and separated twice and worked in Australia and South Africa variously as a sailor, miner and hotelier before his post-war return to Ireland. Both brothers suffered from periodic mental-health issues, and both borrowed money from their generous, but never flush, youngest brother, who also paid an allowance to their sister Nina.

Casement was baptised a Protestant in the Isle of Man a year after his birth, the lateness of the ceremony a sign of the chaotic family circumstances. But he and his brothers were also baptised Catholic, secretly, at their mother's instigation in Rhyl, North Wales, when they were holidaying there. Anne was not of that faith, but her daughter Nina said the baptism took place 'as she always had strong leanings towards the Catholic Church'. Casement, aged four at the time, had to be reminded of the event as an adult, and although his family, education, confirmation and churchgoing, which included putting his fine voice to use as a chorister, were Protestant, this change of faith to a man who was always alert to spirituality represents one of the buried contradictions that he turned into a strength: a later goal was to unite Protestant and Catholic, as well as Dissenters, in an independent Ireland.

The movement between lodging houses came to an end with the death of Anne Casement in October 1873. Roger was nine. He always believed that she had died in childbirth, but her death certificate tells a different story: the primary cause of death was cirrhosis of the liver, implying that she was an alcoholic. According to his much younger cousin Gertrude's memoir, 'Roger constantly spoke of his mother's gentleness, beauty, bright disposition and religious feeling.' Gertrude always took the most rose-tinted view of her Casement relatives, claiming that her aunt's 'nature was too expansive, too beauty loving, too vivacious to find consolation in a religion that cramped, that denied, that suppressed'; but neither the only surviving photograph of her nor the circumstances of her death corroborate such an uplifting description. She died apart from her family shortly before her fortieth birthday in a boarding house in Worthing, and her alcoholic absences, both emotional and actual, would be a critical factor in her son's make-up: his inability to regulate and override his emotional responses as a result of the lack of guidance in early years was one of his campaigning strengths, but also a significant catalyst in the tragedy of his last years. None of his poetry, even 'The Nameless One', carries much psychological perspicacity, and many of his actions from the turn of the century on were fuelled by pure emotion without profound thought. He had no conditioning in how to process his feelings, nor in how to look at them with the paradoxical detachment that a true poet requires.

It is possible that Casement's father's inability to find work, his need to keep moving on and the begging letters to the uncles who had no desire to have him back in their Irish fold, were symptoms of his own alcoholism; if so, it would have further increased the psychological burden on his children. In December 1873, the captain reminded John Casement of his 'great pleasure' in hearing from him a year earlier with the 'most welcome "Xmas Box" even before the day arrived'; since then he had 'experienced a variety of trouble, but none equalling, or approaching to that which I and my poor children have had to bear' in the loss of Anne. He complained of the 'great extra expenses' occasioned by this, only partially alleviated by hand-outs from other relations, lamenting that if he could have afforded 'a more experienced and expensive Medical adviser . . . the result would likely have been different'. Another £5 would tide him over, and he reassured his uncle that he was 'trying very hard to get something to occupy me, even slightly remunerative'.

Captain Casement did not cope well as a widower. He was iras-cible, a strict disciplinarian who was 'stern and harsh with his children', particularly the two elder boys, though he 'nevertheless inspired them', declared his youngest in a loyal afterthought. The children spent more time with their mother's sister, the kindly 'wee auntie' Grace Bannister, in Stanley, Liverpool, in the only stable family home in Casement's life. He became close to Gertrude, the loyal protector of his reputation as a man of 'gentleness and tender-heartedness', one who abhorred cruelty to man or beast in any form. Gertrude's father, Edward Bannister, was the West African agent of a Liverpool trading company, which struck his nephew as 'a poor sort of life'; but when Casement wanted to halt the drift of his dislocated childhood, Bannister had the right connections to enable him to take a role in the same line of work.

Captain Casement 'drifted from lodgings to lodgings' following his wife's death, but returned to Ulster to await his own death. His relations had taken on his young son; Roger was enrolled as a student at the Diocesan School, Ballymena, and lodged with his great-uncle John's daughter Catherine Pottinger. The broken captain moved into the Adair Arms Hotel in Ballymena, and six months later a 'haemor-rhage arising from a long continuing pulmonary disease', possibly tuberculosis, carried him off. He had been conducting seances in the hotel, and writing a long, unpublished and not always comprehen-sible piece, 'The ultraordinary spiritual phenomena of modern times in America and Europe and their connexion with science, religion and human needs generally, traced and explained by a former officer of the British army in India'. They were sad final months for the man who had reputedly galloped across Europe to try to secure Hungary's freedom.

Roger Casement was an orphan at twelve years old after a disjointed and bewildering childhood that left him emotionally hollow and with a carapace of withdrawn self-sufficiency. He became a Ward of Chancery of John Casement and Catherine Pottinger and continued to board at the Diocesan School. John Casement was fifty years older than the boy, while Katie Pottinger lived in Ballymena, some twenty-five miles from Magherintemple; the latter house was being rebuilt at the time, so the bereaved Roger continued to live with her outside term time. Roger informed Katie that he had been decently schooled, although he was only just starting Latin at thirteen, late for the time, was deemed good at history and geography and was poor at arithmetic. He learnt to love Keats, Shelley and Tennyson. There was no point in his remaining in education for long, and the family were soon lining him up for emigration to Canada, 'the Constabulary, or a Bank Clerkship or in a mercantile house'.

Although his headmaster was one of the leading Gaelic scholars and the first translator of the Book of Common Prayer into Irish, Casement learnt the history of Ireland only as recounted by the Protestant incomers. When in later life the school asked him for money, its most celebrated alumnus replied that he was refusing as 'the word [Ireland] was never mentioned in a single class', and that was far from 'a good and healthy state of mind in which to bring up the youth of any country'. The house at Magherintemple had been a modest Georgian farmhouse with its tree-lined frontage and sea views until John Casement attached a Scottish baronial granite and sandstone two-storey residence, complete with crow-step gables, finials and chimney stacks alongside the previous plain façade. He built a gatehouse lodge and changed the name from Churchfield to the Irish Magherintemple, 'the church in the field'. The admonition 'In all thy ways acknowledge Him and He shall direct thy paths' was carved above the front door, and the family motto was *Dum Spiro Spero*, 'While I Breathe, I Hope'. Roger was to note in his diary in his disgruntled winter of 1903–4, not long after his uncle's death, that it was a 'miserable place to stay in' and a 'very miserable place during the day', but his uncle's 'dark old library' was where he began to imbibe Ireland's distant history, and on his long walks in the surrounding countryside he explored his Ulster roots. He later sent a handsome jacaranda chest of drawers from Boma as a gift to the family home.

John Casement proved a warm figure in his great-nephew's life: Roger sought his opinion before his changes of jobs in Africa, and was able to write to him from Old Calabar when his brother Tom was 'in difficulties in Australia' and he was 'not in a position to help him to the extent . . . desirable'. He proposed that John bail out Tom to the tune of £40, repayable at £5 a month, a structured approach very different to their father's begging letters. Roger asked to borrow fifty guineas* from his uncle for a pre-Calabar fistula, an 'expensive surgical operation', and three years later thanked him for the handsome gift of £100. He always asked affectionately after John's wife Charlotte, to whom he often brought 'curios' from his travels, and also enquired about the farm, hoping it was 'returning . . . good for evil' in its crops. At the start of 1893 he wished them 'good wishes for a very happy Bright New Year', signing off 'I remain my dear Uncle, Your affectionate nephew'.

His periods of leave in Ireland in the 1890s inspired some of his earliest and least memorable verses, such as 'Dunluce Castle', a poem about the seat of the McDonnell clan which now consisted of 'ruined turrets so hoary and grey', able to inspire 'Grief's wasted hand' to 'strike a chord' in the poet's heart, 'Whence the murmur of sorrow shall never depart'. It was on a visit to Magherintemple in the spring of 1895 that he 'loafed and swam and walked and scribbled' and contemplated living as a poet before that dream was stolen by Unwin and his reader. In 1899 he was asking his cousins for books to be sent to St Paul de Loanda from the Magherintemple library, works such as the 1630s *Annals of the Four Masters* (in

---

* Nearly £5,000 today.

translation) or an Irish-language history of Ireland from the biblical flood up to 1616.

Casement left Ulster at the age of fifteen to settle with the welcoming Bannisters in Liverpool, and Gertrude remembered that his attic room was 'papered with cartoons . . . showing the various Irish nationalists who had suffered imprisonment at English hands'. He always identified with the underdog: as a teenager taking the side of wounded, overburdened or otherwise suffering animals; as an adult the weaker nations, sometimes regardless of moral or political stance. Three years after his school education finished, he was ready to make his first Congo voyage on the *Bonny*.

In the summer following his Congo report, Casement became active in Irish politics and the promotion of Ireland's historical life for the first time. It was a psychological turning point as well as a geographical detachment from the London establishment, which was moving too slowly in taking vigorous international action over his findings. He helped organise the Feis na nGleann, the Festival of the Glens at Cushendall on the Antrim coast, a recreation of a festival which harked back to the sixth-century gatherings of the chiefs of Ulster in Tara. It had been revived by the Gaelic League, formed in 1893 to promote the Irish language and culture, under the auspices of Francis Joseph Bigger, a Belfast solicitor, antiquarian and editor of an archaeological magazine who was to become a friend to and influence on Casement. Also part of the Feis was a radical Ulster Quaker with a grasp of economic theory, Bulmer Hobson. The apolitical Gaelic League's first President, and later the first President of Ireland, was Douglas Hyde, himself a Protestant. The occasion encouraged Casement: 'all the old hopes and longings of my boyhood sprang to life again'; they had 'dozed on underneath all & unsuspected almost by myself' to emerge when he had no other cause.

He championed the fourteen families of Rathlin Island, the Irish-speaking enclave in Ballycastle harbour visible from Magherintemple. He chartered a tug to bring them to the Feis and was delighted when his charges took first prizes in the pipes and dancing competitions. Other nationalist cultural themes were Irish storytelling, spinning and knitting tweed and flannel, wood carving, singing and hurling; there were prizes for the best-written copy of the Lord's Prayer in Gaelic, the best oral knowledge of the history of the Glens, the best hank of Irish yarn and the best telling of a story in Irish. Moira O'Neill, author of the sentimental ballad 'The Boy from Ballytearim' (and future mother of the novelist Molly Keane) was among the donors. Another of the organisers and a keen promoter of the Irish language, Ada ('Ide') McNeill, was a teenage friend of Casement's with whom he used to walk the Glens. She was four years older, and had always had feelings for him: she described their first conversation as like 'meeting a friend of a long time ago, not a stranger'. Later, to Casement's embarrassment, she declared those feelings.

The disillusioned diplomat was brought to life by the activity surrounding the Feis, and was described by the Irish Nationalist MP and writer Stephen Gwynn as 'strolling down after dinner, in evening clothes but with a loose coat of grey Irish frieze thrown over them and a straw hat crowning his dark, handsome face with its pointed black beard'. Gwynn thought Casement 'one of the finest-looking creatures' he had ever seen, 'his countenance had charm and distinction and a high chivalry'. The festival suited his aesthetic, imaginative devotion to an Irish cause which was not yet quite his by upbringing or politics.

Fired up by the Feis, Casement helped fund the Irish Languages College in Cork with money saved by resigning from his London club after the *Morning Post* criticised the waste of Parliamentary time in debating the teaching of Irish, which had 'as much relevance to Imperial concerns as the teaching of "kitchen Kaffir" has with the administration of the War Office'. He read issues of the *United Irishman*, a radical newspaper set up by Arthur Griffith to promote the Irish language, sport and industries: the paper championed Michael Davitt's Land League, campaigning for Irish tenants to own their properties; so long as land remained in British hands, the Irish would be 'effectively enslaved' whatever the concessions given by politicians, exactly as Casement was arguing about the Congolese. He wrote in under his Gaelic name of Ruairí Dáithí Mac Easmainn. W. B. Yeats, a fellow contributor, detected 'among the young men who hold the coming years in their hands, a newly awakened inspiration and resolve'.

When Griffith founded the Sinn Féin* movement in 1905, its eponymous newspaper ran a series of articles as a parallel manifesto about how Ireland should emulate the example of the Hungarians forty years earlier, when they had boycotted the Imperial Parliament in Vienna in order to peacefully achieve their first steps towards independence. As a result, Casement was politically and personally drawn to that publication too: he retold his father's role under the pseudonym 'Kossuth's Irish Courier', overstating his father's patriotism, acknowledging the dichotomy of his own situation and presaging his own future: 'Although an officer in the British Army, [he] was throughout his life an ardent and sincere lover of Ireland . . . [who] never wavered in his loyalty to her National claims . . . [and had] an overmastering love of freedom born of a close perception of the evils of Irish misrule.'

He published 'The Irish Language' in the *United Irishman* in 1904. It opened:

> It is gone from the hill and the glen –
> The strong speech of our sires;
> It is sunk in the mire and the fen
> Of our nameless desires.

He revisited the poem in his last days, commenting in its margin that he had composed it in Glenshesk, one of the ruggedly peaceful Nine Glens of Antrim, as he chafed for action on his report, and that it was in that spring he 'found Ireland again & the Gaelic League'. As well as *Sinn Féin*, he supported other new nationalist publications, including Bulmer Hobson's the *Peasant*. He strode the countryside while learning quite basic Irish himself; the language was unfashionable (even when Yeats had set up the Irish Literary Theatre in 1899, its output was all in English) and Casement never came close to mastering it, but 'if Ireland is to remain Irish in thought, in hopes, in generous emotions', it was essential. His optimism survived any setback, such

---

* 'We ourselves'.

as the manager of the Ballycastle branch of the Northern Banking Co. refusing 'to undertake any correspondence in Irish'.

He poured his hopes into these new causes to offset the bitter anticipation that his report would change nothing. As Leopold's Commission of Inquiry began its deliberations, he again turned on the Foreign Office, denouncing Villiers as 'the physical embodiment of vacillation' and accusing Lansdowne of supporting 'this bogus commission' as an unspecified means of reconciliation with 'the Evil One' and his 'extraordinary success'. Leopold's propaganda campaign continued: Casement's first employer, Sir Alfred Jones, paid £3,000 for Jones's friend Lord Mountmorres and May French Sheldon to visit the Free State; Mountmorres wrote a fawning book which included such sentences as: 'It is astounding to witness the whole-hearted zeal with which the officials . . . devote themselves to their work.' Jones forwarded the peer's account of his trip to the Foreign Office expressing regret that the Congo should have been condemned 'on the statement of one man – Mr Casement'. Casement's 'blood [was] boiling' following the book and letter, he was 'injured in health' and 'most depressed in spirit and nerves', in sharp contrast to his demeanour at the Feis, but he still maintained that even if the Congo Reform Association were to 'go under . . . it *must* end in a betterment of things'.

He was once again resolved to leave the Foreign Office when he went into hospital for another fistula operation in January 1905. He had exhausted his sick leave and was now without pay until either he was called back or he returned of his own volition. He considered his employers had used him, the 'honest and fearless official they deliberately thrust forward'; they were 'not worth serving . . . what sickens me is that I must go back to them, hat in hand, despising them as I do, simply to be able to live'. A full year had passed since he had delivered his report and there had been no action around the 'Congo cads' and 'Congo cannibals'. At the same time, he was being person-ally attacked by Leopold's paid adherents, in the latest case the editor of the *Catholic Herald*, for being British Consul and supposedly an 'impartial person' while simultaneously 'a subscriber to the funds of this very Congo Reform Society'.

He spent part of his convalescence in England with his friend from the 1880s, Dick Morten, whose warm, red-brick medieval home, The Savoy, in Denham, Buckinghamshire, was to be a constant refuge for him. While there, he met the journalist H. W. Nevinson, recently returned from 'trying to expose the abominations of the slave traffic in the Portuguese provinces of Angola and the Cocoa Islands of San Thome and Principe'. Casement was an inspiration to Nevinson, and his recognition that the distinguished war correspondent and campaigning journalist's account was 'unexaggerated, but understating the horror of the truth' was critical to Nevinson's standing. Although it was never a friendship with the depth of that with Morten, Nevinson amply repaid the debt of loyalty at Casement's time of greatest need.

Perilously short of funds as well as deficient in health, Casement joked about going into the workhouse, considering himself and Morel 'a wretched pair of paupers' in their enterprise. Money was never far from his daily concerns, evident in the obsessive accounting for even trivial sums in his diaries, yet he was self-denyingly generous to siblings and causes. He even wondered whether he might join his brother Tom in South Africa. He could leave government service 'with a happy heart' and get away from his 'overmastering contempt' for his employers, but lack of self-confidence as the perpetual outsider held him back. 'All men are snobs', he averred, who 'worship assurance and position', and he reckoned he would be unable to earn even £50 per year out of the Foreign Office; that would prompt his so-called 'friends' to look askance at him as a 'begging pauper'. He lodged with Bigger in Belfast, and in his correspondence with Gertrude Bannister ramped up both his poetic and his political rhetoric as if to persuade himself of the rightness of his course: he spoke of 'the spirit of enlightened conviction welling the Irish heart' as well as criticising the Conservative Prime Minister Arthur Balfour as 'a dirty soap bubble . . . and please God we Irishmen will blow him into suds'.

The British establishment were oblivious of his pseudonymous attacks. As far as the Foreign Office was concerned, one of their shining, if irksome, lights was absent for health reasons. Casement was therefore astonished when in the 1905 Birthday Honours the King appointed him a Companion of the Most Distinguished Order of St Michael and St George, an award for those who had performed outstanding service in foreign affairs. He received the news while walking the shore at Cushendall with Bulmer Hobson and a naval cousin, and became deeply troubled. Hobson pushed him to overcome his reluctance to accept and to keep his Foreign Office boats unburnt, and Casement followed his advice. He nevertheless expressed his feelings in a letter to a colleague in Whitehall that reiterated his 'oft uttered contempt . . . for distinctions and honours and principalities and powers', and his embarrassment that as 'a confirmed Home Ruler' seeking devolved powers for Ireland he 'would now be regarded askance in every respectable quarter of Ireland'. He spent the rest of the year contorting himself to avoid having to go to Buckingham Palace to be invested: he managed to postpone twice, and eventually the insignia were despatched by post. When they had to be returned eleven years later, the wax seals on the package remained unbroken.

Despite Leopold's best efforts, the ripples of adverse opinion were spreading. In September 1904, Morel travelled to America to charge the government with a special responsibility, as the first country to have recognised the Free State, for bringing to an end the King's rule in Africa. He was received by President Theodore Roosevelt at the White House, and established the US branch of the Congo Reform Association: its first board included Church leaders, Mark Twain and Booker T. Washington. Washington, a former slave who had been an adviser to several presidents on African-American matters, urged Roosevelt to act, lobbied the Senate Foreign Relations Committee and spoke at rallies alongside Twain, now aged seventy and widely regarded as the father of the literary establishment. The next year, Twain published his excoriating fifty-two-page pamphlet *King Leopold's Soliloquy*, which drew heavily on Casement's report to hammer home its savage satire: the pious Leopold's only aims were to 'root out slavery and stop the slave raids, and lift up those twenty-five millions of gentle and harmless blacks out of darkness into light'; he had got 'not a compliment' for the millions he had spent on 'religion and art', whereas his opponents, through Casement, 'spy and spy and run into print with every foolish trifle'. Twain donated his considerable royalties to the CRA.

Leopold's reactions to these unwelcome developments followed the usual pattern: an anonymous pamphlet of the same length appeared, entitled *An Answer to Mark Twain*, alongside an offer to Washington for an expenses-paid trip to the Congo; when that was met with silence, an excursion to Belgium was proffered. The King offered Congo trading concession rights to American powerbrokers including John D. Rockefeller and the Guggenheims, and once again tried to suborn the Catholic lobby into his camp by claiming the attacks were religiously inspired by Protestant Britain. But it was obvious that American political and moral opinion was turning against him.

The self-effacing and thin-skinned Casement was embarrassed at being named in Twain's polemic, and his shift of interest was plain when he wrote to Morel that 'the Congo question is very near my heart, but the Irish question is nearer' as a result of his immersion in Ulster. But he was galvanised back into action by Morel's success. Morel told him that in his opinion the new Foreign Secretary, Sir Edward Grey, was too much in thrall to Germanophobic MPs to take vigorous action. Casement avoided the Foreign Office on his return to London in April 1905, instead launching into feverish planning for a CRA meeting in Holborn Town Hall designed to cement the Association firmly in the wider public consciousness as it unveiled 'the true inwardness of the CONGO EVIL'. They corralled well-off supporters, including the West African merchant John Holt and the chocolate magnate William Cadbury; the Association was now backed by MPs and peers across parties, by churchmen and atheists, by colonialists and writers.

Casement's most important contact in this period, the one who would introduce the cash, the connections and the intellectual heft to underpin his future, was Alice Stopford Green. The seventh child of the Archdeacon of Meath, Alice was the scholarly widow of J. R. Green, whose *Short History of the English People*, one of the first histories to concentrate not on kings and battles but on unknown individuals, earned her handsome royalties even thirty years after its publication. She had travelled to South Africa and become outraged by the British treatment of the Boers, launched an investigation into prison conditions on St Helena and set up the African Society with the publisher George Macmillan. She was in her upright late fifties, and had just finished a book which posited that the Anglo-Norman conquerors of Ireland destroyed a civilisation rather than delivered one. It was published as *The Making of Ireland and Its Undoing 1200–1600*, provoking considerable literary debate and appealing strongly to her new acolyte, at that stage more of a romantic than a rebel. Green was 'a mordant, well-educated, civilised woman of startling will-power and dazzling wit . . . vinegar-sharp' who drew to her Kensington Square drawing room the likes of Florence Nightingale, the explorer Mary Kingsley, the novelist Mrs Humphry Ward and her learned husband, and the young politician (and staunch imperialist) Winston Churchill for evenings of vigorous discussion. When she received a letter from Casement stating 'we have so much in common in our love for Ireland that I need not go to Africa to seek an introduction to you', she invited him to her salon.

'Tiger' Casement deployed his pent-up energy in arranging the press for the Holborn meeting, soliciting donations (Alice Green gave £5, Herbert Samuel half that), overseeing the programme and sending out the tickets, but his aversion to personal publicity and his understanding that he had 'seriously compromised my career in the public service by my attitude on the subject' again kept him from speaking himself. He wanted to hold the meeting at the Mansion House, but was dissuaded by 'Bulldog' Morel on the grounds that the Lord Mayor could not be seen to host an attack on a king; Holborn Council agreed a fee of one guinea for the use of their town hall. Morel spoke for half an hour and the meeting ended with a resolution that the Free State be placed under 'international control' with 'guarantees required from Belgium'.

The following day's *Morning Post* noted the large audience and acknowledged the resolution as a significant development. The same issue carried a story about an Italian Dr Baccari who had been sent to the Congo in the wake of Casement's report and made the mistake of broadcasting his findings while still in the country; one evening, he found his wine tasted odd and on analysis realised it had been laced with a corrosive sublimate. Phipps faithfully sent the Free State's response that a Congolese boy had found a beetle in the bottle so had decanted the doctor's wine into another which happened to have contained poison. Unfortunately, the doctor's last letter home had commented on the rumours he had heard that Europeans who looked too deeply into the Free State were poisoned, and if his family and country never heard from him again, they should assume that had been his fate. Whether or not Dr Baccari's story was a series of accidents or untruths, it was a signal of how even rumours were feeding the reformers.

By the time of the Holborn meeting, Leopold's commissioners had been back from the Congo for four months. The King delayed publication of their findings, but by November 1905 could obfuscate no longer. 'FROM PHILANTHROPY TO SLAVERY BY SUCCESSIVE STEPS' ran the sub-headline in a special supplement to the *Official Organ of the Congo Reform Association*. The *Manchester Guardian* was clear that the 'the King had been denounced by his own hirelings' and that 'the result is a complete vindication of those who have carried on a ceaseless agitation for investigation and reform'. Casement's own reaction was notably less whole-hearted as he described the report as a '*very* queer production . . . a series of half-truths each followed by its qualifying whole untruth!' But in the *Morning Post*'s challenge the only question now was whether British statesmen possessed the 'moral courage' to right Leopold's 'atrocious international wrong-doing'. William Randolph Hearst's newspaper empire led the journalistic charge in the United States to lay out the Commission's findings of 'Infamous Cruelties' and expose the shenanigans of bribed government influencers in devastating and sensational terms.

In Britain the change of government that December to the Liberal administration of Sir Henry Campbell-Bannerman gave Casement hope that events might start to accelerate. Lansdowne, whom he had regarded as 'honest but weak', was replaced as Foreign Secretary by Sir Edward Grey, the sportsman, fisherman and ornithologist who was to be an admiring and admired and vilified figure for the rest of Casement's life. Casement initially shared Morel's fear that Grey would become 'more or less a friend of Leopold' but was heartened when Phipps was instructed to make a protest to the Free State government about their failures: when the Minister came back with 'a barely civil reply' from Leopold's Secretary of State, Phipps was finally withdrawn, to be replaced by the more talented Sir Arthur Hardinge, an eloquent diplomat who was resolute about the need for international pressure for regime change.

The seventy-year-old Leopold was worn down by the bad publicity. He realised that he had no option but to bring forward to his lifetime the disposal of his huge, fabulously wealthy colony, rather than make it the grand bequest he had envisaged. He began negotiations in 1906, but the secrecy surrounding its finances made the business a convoluted one; in his opinion the state was still 'not beholden to anyone except to its founder . . . No one has the right to ask for its accounts.'

Morel came up with the peculiar idea that Casement should return to the Congo to carry out an 'independent investigation' for the CRA just as things were starting to unravel for Leopold. He responded that that was '*far* better than idling and eating my heart out'. He could travel via Angola to arrive undetected – but, even if he was discovered, 'one couldn't do better than be hanged in order to end that den of devils'. The drawback to such a scheme was that it would not pay him; he had claimed a full salary for 1904 for his two months' work in Lisbon but had been paid a mere £40 for 1905 and the first half of 1906, a fact which he begged Morel to keep quiet. His bankers were starting to press him, pointing out that the £25 allowance he paid quarterly to Nina could not be covered by the £3 in his account without some form of security. He again toyed with the notion of making a career as a writer, particularly now that he had a degree of fame, but Nevinson tactfully dissuaded him by pointing out that 'One's best and most valuable work is shamefully treated . . . it is always very discouraging.' Later, Casement wrote that he would have left the Foreign Office then were it not for his obligations to the sister who had helped bring him up.

He still had at least one supporter in Whitehall, Sir William Tyrrell, now the Foreign Secretary's précis-writer. Tyrrell persuaded Casement that Barrington, now Assistant Under-Secretary for Africa, did not wish him ill, which did not stop a fractious correspondence between the two about his inclination to reject the Lisbon post. Eventually, in July 1906, the Foreign Office made the offer of the dull consulship in Bilbao, at a salary of £650 a year plus an allowance of £350. Casement was on the point of accepting, when the same post in the Brazilian city of Santos fell vacant, with its £600 salary, £200 rent allowance and £500 office allowance. Although he was only ever really interested in money for what it could do for others, telling Bulmer Hobson in September 1907 that if he had no employment beyond his nationalist interests he 'would be seriously handicapped in life and grievously injured too', the extra £300 settled it.*

Although Santos was 'a hideous hole, and very expensive', the post would enable Casement to finance 'one or two small Irishisms of my own'. Chiefly he was leaning towards backing Sinn Féin. Until 1916 the party was more of an irritant than a political force that was taken seriously; it advocated a totally autonomous republic at a point when the new government in London, with the support of the Irish Parliamentary Party, were considering limited devolution rather than giving the country full responsibility for its affairs. Casement's long stay in Ireland, the contacts he had made, the struggles he had had with the English establishment, many of them of his own making, and above all his new sense of rootedness after his disconnected childhood and far-flung, often secret adult life had brought him to a point of certainty – that 'we create a governing mind again after 106 years [since the Acts of Union between Britain and Ireland] of abstraction of all mind from this outraged land'. Ireland had become the anchor to his imagination.

Yet the diplomat still had a measure of control over Conrad's man

* Until 1919, there was a minimum private income requirement of £400 per annum (around £50,000 in today's values) to follow a full diplomatic career. Consuls would frequently take a position purely for its remunerative value.

of emotion, and still hoped for a peaceful political resolution over Ireland. As he sailed for Santos in September 1906 he realised that his eighteen months of leave had 'moulded all [his] subsequent actions'. He sent a last postcard to Gertrude Bannister, a picture of the Euston Hotel in London, with the Union flag blacked out, and wrote to Alice Green from the ship on the first leg of his voyage to Brazil, asking that his address be written as 'Consulate of Great Britain and *Ireland*'.

In 1908, after Casement's career had moved on and two years after Leopold entered into discussions with his country, Belgium acquired the Free State in exchange for assuming its 110 million francs of debt (much of it in the form of bonds held by Leopold, the mistress he was to marry on his deathbed in 1909 and his family) and paying the King 45.5 million francs for his building projects in Belgium, which included more work on the grandiose Tervuren palace, and another 50 million francs* 'as a mark of gratitude for his great sacrifices made for the Congo'. These sums were raised from the colony itself rather than from the Belgian taxpayer in a final, ironic snub to the Free State's founding principles.

Casement's 1903 journey and his experiences preceding it had paved the way for the first great international reform of the century. His name would always be associated with it, regardless of the disappointments, the anger and the debates that had followed delivery of his report five years before. But those years of indecision about his future and his turning to Ireland to fill the emotional gap came at a cost to his sense of self. Even his steady fellow campaigner Morel was writing in May 1906 that he was 'very sorry for him, and his troubles have made him unreliable'. Although Morel did not specify in what 'his troubles' consisted, there is a sense that Casement's growing intemperance against the establishment, however strongly induced by the desire to make life better for others, did not always help the often delicate nature of their work.

* It is hard to establish exact equivalents, but 50 million francs approximates to £170 million today.

In his turning towards Ireland, Casement was letting his dislocated upbringing infect his emotions, and he increasingly expressed a more simplistic view of the relationship between coloniser and colonised. He seemed to take little pride or pleasure in his moment of success, writing to Alice Green that, 'The Congo will revive and flourish, the black millions again overflow the land – but who shall restore the damaged Irish tongue?' He continued his work for the CRA, most notably in fundraising, for years to come, and after Leopold's death in 1909 he recognised that, as 'the break-up of the pirate's stronghold [is] nearly accomplished', it was time to start the work of reconstruction. By 1911, he was impractically, yet gloriously, urging Morel to make the organisation 'a movement of human liberation the world over . . . the cause of human freedom is as wide as the world'. When the Congo Reform Association was eventually wound up ten years after its originator's journey upriver had awakened the world's conscience, Casement's global ambitions had narrowed. For Henry Nevinson, 'In the camp of the fallen he always was . . . and for that camp no Irishman need look abroad.'

6. The Devil's Paradise

Casement's most distinguished predecessor in Latin America's biggest port city, then with a population of 45,000, had been the African explorer, adventurer and polyglot orientalist Richard Burton. Isabel Burton, as forthright as her husband, described Santos, on a substantial island off the southern coast of Brazil's São Paolo state, in words that rang true forty years on: 'the climate is beastly, the people fluffy. The stinks, the food, the vermin, the [inhabitants] are all of a piece . . . one way, you sink knee deep in mangrove swamps; another, you are covered with sandflies.' For much of the previous century it had been known as 'the port of death' owing to the high incidence of yellow fever.

Casement was writing to Gertrude within an hour of his arrival in September 1906 that he loathed the town and expected to be 'a failure in this environment'. His heart remained in rediscovered Ireland; he continued to send small sums of money to the Rathlin Island School and the Ulster Gaelic League even though his salary and allowances dwindled in a city that was three times as expensive as London. The consulate itself was a bare room in a coffee warehouse, open to the street; the last Consul had put up netting to prevent stones and other missiles being hurled in. He paid £90 a year for the place, enough for a comfortable home in England or Ireland, and commuted by train from his lodgings some thirty miles inland in the mountainous city of São Paolo. Such papers as existed were in a disastrous muddle.

The consular district covered the states of São Paolo and Paraña, but the Consul's major role was to look out for British interests in Santos, which shipped £15 million worth of coffee (in itself 47 per cent of Brazil's total exports) each year, as well as bran, bananas, hides and rubber. Casement was chiefly occupied with British sailors who 'get drunk & come ashore & desert in shoals & the place is a pandemonium'; he reckoned the town would be better served by a 'bar keeper's chucker out' than a consul. He was diligent in filing the annual trade report to London and took care to promote Irish interests: he made a pointed reference to the consumption of Guinness in his territory, imbibed on local medical advice, and suggested that English and Irish exports be separated out in the paperwork, rather than being lumped together as *Ingleze*. After two months he concluded that Brazil was 'the least interesting country in the world' and this the most 'futile and absurd post'. Sir Edward Grey was informed directly that Santos 'is quite the nastiest place I have ever been in'. It was a '*Hole*', requiring only a consul who could discuss coffee.

Dissatisfaction moved him even further from his English upbringing: when Alice Stopford Green suggested that he might be pushing his luck in writing long letters to Whitehall defending a Congo colleague fired for incompetence, he replied that he regarded it as 'a mistake for an Irishman to mix himself up with the English' because 'if he remains Irish', he would inevitably 'go to the wall'; the alternative was to 'become an Englishman himself'. He reckoned he had nearly gone down that wrong road at the time of the Boer War and the Strathcona's Horse venture in South Africa, but his reconnection with Ireland and the frustrations over the Congo report – still unactioned, as he saw it – determined that he was, prophetically, 'an Irishman, wherever that may lead me personally'. But even as he balked at his re-employment and nailed his identity to the country of his birth, he had another complex and courageous humanitarian mission to undertake on the new continent.

The Foreign Office had suggested him for Santos with good reason, including concerns about slavery, legally abolished in Brazil only eighteen years earlier, but had offered him an option to quit early, telling him that they were looking for an alternative post for one of their best consuls. He did not have to spend much of his first leave in the summer of 1907 deliberating. After a few days in his rented rooms in Philbeach Gardens, Earl's Court, he headed for Ballycastle and then on to Donegal and the Irish College at Cloghaneely, hoping to progress his Irish studies, and suggesting an article to Bulmer Hobson arguing that Ireland should have its own Olympic team for the forthcoming games in London. In August, shortly after publication of Alice Green's *The Making of Ireland and Its Undoing*, which Casement claimed would restore 'Irish national self-respect', he was offered the congenial and well-paid post of Haiti, only to have it snatched away when the needs of a disabled Boer War veteran trumped his. His main disappointment was that he would not be able to give the extra salary to family and Irish causes: during his time at Santos, there had been numerous disbursements to schools and colleges in Ireland, to 'the Irish Consumption Crusade', to Sinn Féin, to a prize at the Feis of the Glens, as well as handouts to Nina and to his brother Charlie for a 'Suit of Clothes' – all of which left him with little for himself. A Foreign Office letter about Haiti has the jotting in his hand: 'Rec'd 24/Augt/07. Just before Millar came!' An exclamation mark often signalled a sexual encounter; but even if Millar Gordon meant some-thing deeper to Casement than the run of fleeting partners, he was in no position to refuse to go back to another Brazilian position.

He arrived in Santa Maria de Belém do Pará, the Atlantic port at the mouth of the Amazon, at the end of February 1908, to take com-mand of another consular district larger than Western Europe. He travelled to the northern coast of Brazil on the same ship as the Peruvian rubber magnate Julio César Arana, soon to become his for-midable enemy. Pará was a city of 120,000 inhabitants which was prospering amid the booming rubber trade to the point where Case-ment's predecessor was able to announce that he would be its first Consul not to require an earth closet. Nevertheless, the premises were again in a dire state, without even a bottle of ink or a pen, and Casement was threatening resignation after a few days for reasons of expense and irritation at the prostitutes who hung around his hotel at all hours. He was given permission to select a more salubrious base, but his depression still mounted to the point where he was writing to Ger-trude in his passionate, hyperbolic style that his life was a 'penance' and his thirteen years in the service had been 'utterly wasted and mis-placed' – an exaggerated claim from the author of what was now known simply as 'the Casement Report', which was within weeks of forcing Belgium's acquisition of Leopold's killing grounds. He was in the 'domestic scullery of the F.O. officials – to be portioned out amongst the menials and bottlewashers'. But a letter of resignation suggesting that the Brazilian consulates were pointless remained unsent.

Despite feeling unwell throughout his brief time in rain-sodden Pará, Casement was diligent in the performance of his duties, and gained valuable insights. He came to appreciate the place, to the point where he wrote to London that 'The people are too good-natured and cheerful to make trouble . . . The town is pretty and beautifully laid out and the people are the most charmingly immoral in Brazil', intimating that he had found sexual partners there. In April, he made his first trip upriver to inspect the railways and to look into the production of banana flour as a possible food source for tropical countries, observing the falling off of the production of turtle oil and cocoa through poor agricultural practice. A month later he flagged up what would become his next great campaign when, in his commentary on the rubber industry in the Putumayo region at the meeting point of Peru, Colombia and Brazil, he mentioned 'the horror in the interior – this time between Peruvians and Colombians'. He questioned 'whether the universal subjection' of the Amazon Indians 'to the spell of rubber production is altogether good for the people or for the future of their country'.

He sent anteaters and ocelots to Dublin Zoo from Brazil; his own collection of blue morpho butterflies was remarkable. He was ahead of his time when he spoke out about the deforestation of the Amazon as the destruction of a renewable resource, and also made the parallel with the English logging of Ireland as an act of colonial vandalism. This train of thought led him to give an eccentric lecture in Pará which took issue with the polymathic Alexander von Humboldt's proposition that the word 'Brazil' came from the trees felled along the Atlantic coast of the country; instead, he offered the Irish revivalists' case that it derived from the search for the utopian paradise island of Hy-Brasil somewhere off Ireland's west coast, the inspiration for St Brendan's voyage in the sixth century.

He continued to complain – about his health, the food, his insomnia, but most of all about the cost of living, which meant he would have to 'give up my servant, hair-cuts, laundry, even a cauliflower occasionally'; his only satisfaction was that if he died he would be buried at government expense. He was seriously ill with acute gastritis in June, and ordered to Barbados to recuperate; he had to be carried on board ship, 'a loathsome sight – blotches and sores and eruptions'. Even the voyage and the medical expenses in the West Indies were a saving on lying in bed in Brazil, he reckoned, for the two months of his recovery. After a brief stop to pick up his possessions in Pará, he once again returned to Britain, pausing in Rio where the Vice-Consul heard out his 'tremendous monologue on Irish Home Rule', before going straight from Liverpool to Ireland. He asked the commercial Mozambique Company if an offer he had previously turned down was still on the table, but that came to nothing.

The Foreign Office at last acknowledged his value when on 1 December they offered him the senior post of Consul General in Rio de Janeiro, with its income of £1,600. He had no hesitation in accepting, which did not stop him writing 'I hate Brazil' on his arrival in February 1909 after leave spent in Dublin, in Paris with Herbert Ward and in his old sexual haunts in Lisbon. Rio was to be his last posting in the service of the Crown, and would garner him honours and renown.

Rio was more congenial: he had assistants in the office and consuls and vice-consuls under him in the major ports to handle quotidian matters, while the climate meant that he, and most of the diplomatic community, lived two hours away in Petrópolis, far from the improvisational, multinational chaos of the capital. His despatches contained the now familiar grumbles about the cost of living and the inadequacy of consular expenses alongside tirades about the Brazilian treatment of British subjects, but the replies from London were more often along the lines that he had 'handled an awkward situation with tact and good judgement'.

Yet after the emotional drama of his Congo journey, the strenuous campaigning of the CRA and, above all, his increasing involvement in Ireland, this period of comparative stasis led to an outpouring of frustration. He was never really able to moderate his linguistic pitch when caught up in his unregulated feelings and his cousin Roger at

Magherintemple received a more candid assessment that Brazil was 'an abominable country and the towns are disgusting . . . The climate is all right but the daily life hideous and the cost of everything ridiculous.' Above all, he found the Brazilians 'over-dressed, vain, empty-minded humbugs with extraordinary vanity and arrogance', particularly compared to the Congolese, a 'far nicer people, sincere and real', even though they 'had no clothes'. He had been 'fourteen years a Consul', was in one of the top postings and was fed up.

He diverted his attention towards Ireland, championed Alice Green's book, became a £50 shareholder in Arthur Griffith's new, daily edition of *Sinn Féin*, expecting to lose his stake, and took risky opportunities to denigrate England and the English. One of his vice-consuls, Ernest Hambloch, was startled to hear him 'pour forth a torrent of violent abuse . . . of everything British from the Crown downward' at a dinner party given by the general manager of the British-owned railway which ferried him to and from Petrópolis. Hambloch portrayed his superior as 'yellow-skinned' after his decades of tropical exposure, but still striking; he was an 'odd man out . . . difficult to classify'. He had been described as 'a typical Celt' but that did not fit; on the other hand, he was 'certainly not a typical Englishman'. He found Casement 'elaborately courteous . . . as though he was afraid of being caught off guard' – the ingrained deflection stemming from his sexuality was exacerbated by the growing gap between his consular duties and his true patriotic interests. Hambloch found Casement's musical voice 'purrs at you'; and although without profundity in argument, his boss had 'great powers of persuasion', to the extent that he sometimes lost his 'sense of proportion' when his emotions outran his reason.

Hambloch was English to his core, and recorded Casement's criticisms of his country faithfully as he became more outspoken and more easily offended by the divisions between his Irish and English heritage. When Ernest Shackleton, who had been born into an Anglo-Irish family but had moved to Sydenham at the age of ten, was acclaimed as an 'English' hero and knighted after his 1909 South Pole expedition, Casement railed that 'if he had cut a cow's tail off . . . of course he would have been an Irishman right enough'; the similarities of his own upbringing were not mentioned. More significantly, he turned against John Redmond, the Jesuit-educated leader of the Irish Party in Parliament, a man never given to extremism who had now become part of the Westminster establishment; out of touch with feeling in Ireland, Redmond was supporting the retention of Ireland's representation at Westminster after Home Rule. As it was, in the years before war broke out, two days of the Parliamentary year were given to debating Indian affairs, and one to other colonial matters, but every debate involved at least one heated mention of Ireland. Casement reckoned that Redmond's liberal imperialism 'abandoned every principle of Irish nationality and sacrificed our birthright not for a mess of pottage but for a promise of a chance to lick the plates in the scullery of John Bull's basement'. Irish MPs 'should be the foremost champions of a poor people against misrule'.

For the first time, Casement was to be heard singing the praises of Germany as a colonising power with a comparatively unsullied record and 'honest clean laws and institutions', although he did have aesthetic reservations about the military class of Prussian Junkers with their 'thin pork chops of cheeks, criss-crossed as if for cooking'. In his enthusiasm, Casement made no mention of his 1893 complaint to the Aborigines Protection Society about the repression of the Cameroon insurgency, nor of the ethnic massacres waged by the German Empire against the Herero, the Nama and the San peoples in German South West Africa (now Namibia) between 1904 and 1908. With a death toll of 65,000–75,000, they represented the first genocide of the twentieth century, as acknowledged by the German government in 2021.

Casement was on home leave in the summer of 1910, and his journals for that year survive to give an insight into his secret sexual life: he was a more prominent figure than he had been in early 1903, with the correspondingly higher stakes perhaps fuelling his defensive intemperance about other areas of his life. His sexual appetite was still prodigious, but the encounters were occurring further apart yet more frequently once one had taken place, almost as if he was trying to suppress an addiction to risk, bingeing when he gave in once. On a night in London he dined with Conan Doyle and Morel before

going on to see the former's *The Speckled Band* in the theatre; at 1 a.m.,
and again forty-five minutes later, he paid a total of 16s 6d for sex
with two men described only as 'H.B.' and 'Jamaica!' A week on he
once again had two encounters in a single evening, with 'Welsh Will'
and 'Japan'. When he was in Ireland in June, he had many casual
encounters but also picked up more romantically with Millar Gordon,
mentioned three years earlier. He entertained Gordon at the Northern Counties Hotel and bought him a tie pin at a cost of two shillings
before going on to sleep with him at his mother's Belfast house. The
next year, he gave him a second-hand Triumph motorbike which set
him back £25.

The greatest difference with the earlier diaries was his sex life outside Europe. In South America his journals show as much sexual
activity as in London or in the staging ports to Africa. On one day in
Rio in January, he had encounters with Gabriel Ramos, a young
'caboclo' (a mixed-race Indian), a '(thin) dark gentleman of Icahary'
and once more with Gabriel at the end of the day; after two weeks
without any sex recorded, he met Mario and a 'perfectly huge'
eighteen-year-old on the same day; in Buenos Aires in March he
spent a lot of time with Ramón, to whom he was attached enough to
write. There was an excitement and exuberance in his records of
these encounters, such as in Rio: 'Lovely. Young – 18 & glorious.
Biggest since Lisbon July 1904.' Possibly the European atmosphere
and influences in the South American ports made such rendezvous
more usual than in Africa; it is possible that fleeting, frequent sex was
a distraction from the gloom of his working life.

In May he saw many old friends in Dublin, and sent a postcard of
Phoenix Park Zoo to Ramón in Argentina. In Belfast, he discussed
politics with Bigger and Bulmer Hobson before moving on to Antrim
in June. On the 17th of that month, in Ballycastle, he opened a letter
'from Anti-Slavery People about Putumayo River & the Amazon
Rubber Coy. Answered by wire and wrote also.' It was an appointment to a vital new commission, which hastened his return to
London. He was revivified by the new sense of purpose and had a
'splendid talk' at the office of the Anti-Slavery Society attended by
Sir Charles Dilke, Josiah Wedgwood and other Liberal MPs before

his evening at *The Speckled Band*. After a few days' fundraising for a testimonial for Morel, he was on his way back to South America and his second great humanitarian campaign.

Julio César Arana del Águila was a heavy-set, grey-bearded Peruvian with receding dark hair and a confident, distinguished demeanour. The trader was the same age as the new Consul General, whom he had met on the ship to Pará in 1908, and he had grasped the potential of the future demand for rubber as a bare-footed Panama-hat salesman in the 1880s, when the trade was in its infancy. In an echo of Leopold twenty years earlier, he had played off the unresolvable territorial tensions of Peru and Colombia to be granted a concession over an area larger than France in the Putumayo region bordering Peru, Ecuador and Colombia, with its many rivers draining from the Andes into the Putumayo and then on to the Amazon. His monopoly in steamers enabled him to boast by the end of the decade that he effectively held sovereignty over the vast territory. He intended to wring the maximum profit from the 'black gold' through the use of slaves, still legal in Amazonia. With his brother, the well-named Lizardo, Arana calculated that the best overseers for their workers would be those used to cracking the whip on the British sugar plantations of Barbados.

Headquarters were in the Peruvian port city of Iquitos, 2,000 miles from Pará and onward shipment to Europe. The jungle town contained cafés serving ice cream and no fewer than three cinemas screening the latest Westerns or films about New York high society, as well as a Company-controlled market in young girls. Casement considered Iquitos 'a pigsty' and so corrupt that, although it raised £300,000 in customs dues each year for the Peruvian government, less than £2,000 was spent on improvements for the city's inhabitants. The Peruvian Amazon Company had listed on the London Stock Exchange in 1903 with four British directors but the majority Peruvian, and over £1 million* from investors attracted by the projected returns. It was on the journey back from the flotation that Casement encountered Arana as his shipmate.

---

* Approximately £125 million at today's values.

Rumours had been circulating for some years about brutal practices in the Putumayo. Priests and liberal Lima newspapers had
filtered back tales of floggings and executions, accounts which were
dismissed by the Peruvian authorities. But in the autumn of 1909,
articles by 'Scrutator' appeared in *Truth*, a weekly periodical set up in
Britain to expose financial fraud. 'Scrutator' was Walter Hardenburg,
an American railway engineer who had travelled in the region a year
earlier: not even his alarming encounters with spectacled alligators
and huge tapirs that continued charging despite being hit by four
revolver rounds had prepared him for coming under fire from a Peruvian government vessel as his canoe neared Iquitos. He was hauled
aboard to be 'kicked, beaten, insulted and abused in a most cowardly
manner' by an army captain before being imprisoned in a Peruvian
Amazon Company hut.

He saw the 'poor Indians who loaded and unloaded the vessels . . .
so weak, so debilitated, so scarred that many of them could hardly
walk'. They were branded with 'the infamous *marca de Arana*'. When
they collapsed under the weight of their loads, they were kicked back
on to their feet. At noon, each group of four men collected a handful
of cassava flour and a tin of sardines to sustain them through their
sixteen-hour working day. 'Involuntary concubines' aged between
nine and thirteen were 'the helpless victims' of the Company men
who either 'murdered them or flogged them and sent them back to
their tribes' when they tired of them. Corpses were chucked into the
river.

As in the Congo, the slaves had to penetrate ever deeper into the
lacerating depths of the jungle as the more accessible vines gave up
their sap, which was hauled out on the backs of the men, women and
children. If the overseers' scales tipped the mark, the workers would
'leap about and laugh with pleasure'; if they failed, they would
'throw themselves face down upon the ground to await their punishment' of a savage flogging or being placed in stocks, sometimes face
up, sometimes face down; either way, their legs would be spread an
agonising yard apart, often for days on end, with regular beatings
under the burning sun. The children of those undergoing punishment were tethered to make them watch; their brains might be bashed

out on trees with their pinioned parents looking on. When wounds turned putrid and maggoty, the victims could be doused in kerosene and set alight, or mutilated by machete or simply released into the jungle to die. Any pretext served: unpunctuality, incomprehension of Spanish or just to 'practise target-shooting . . . to fill other Indians with a fear of the "whites" '.

Hardenburg, afraid for his life, persuaded Miguel Loayza, the 'copper-complexioned, shifty-eyed half-breed' manager of the Company's chief post on the Caraparaná River, in pidgin English that he was the representative of a huge American syndicate that would send search parties and punish those responsible for his disappearance. After a few more apprehensive weeks, sustained by watery tea, stale bread, stinking butter and a 'repugnant preparation of codfish', he was delivered to Iquitos on the Company steamer, ironically named *Liberal*. He eventually came to London and *Truth*, the only outlet that would overcome the fear of libel to publish his article 'The Devil's Paradise: A British-Owned Congo', linking the appalling revelations from the Belgian rubber industry to Britain.

The Company counter-attacked with accusations of blackmail over Hardenburg's claims for loss of property; it alleged (truthfully) that he had forged a cheque in Iquitos, but did its cause no good when its manager in London, H. L. Gielgud, tried to bribe a reporter to put its side of the story. As an international outcry over the actions of a company on the London Stock Exchange loomed, Foreign Secretary Sir Edward Grey requested corroboration for Hardenburg's account, and a Captain Whiffen, who had been travelling in the Putumayo to put together a photographic book, was tracked down to Harrogate. Armed with the upright Whiffen's unimpeachable evidence, the Foreign Office approached Gielgud for an explanation. Gielgud, who had himself just returned from the jungle, reported that the Indians seemed to him to be 'simply children of a happy disposition', well treated by the 'Company's kindly agents'.

The renamed Anti-Slavery and Aborigines Protection Society and other bodies had heard enough. The media pressure mounted to the point where shareholders began to worry about the stock price, and although the Company had insisted that any investigation was a matter for the disinclined Peruvian government and not the Foreign Office, it now capitulated. In June 1910 Arana proposed a Commission of Inquiry that included R. H. Bertie, lately of the Royal Welch Fusiliers and a close friend of a director, a tropical agriculturist, a rubber expert and Gielgud. The balance of this group, reminiscent of the now dead Leopold's weighted Commission, was unacceptable to Grey and the Anti-Slavery Society, and a letter was sent to Casement to divert him from his leave at Cloghaneely summer school to London to read the file on the case and join the new Commission. It was a signal of the resolve underpinning the dangerous investigation.

The Commission sailed from Southampton on the *Edinburgh Castle* on 23 July 1910, arrived at Madeira on the 27th and set off again four days later on the SS *Hilary*, which carried a cargo of granite and railway-building materials, and three boxes of silver pound coins bound for Bolivia, to Casement's former home of Belém do Pará. After a week's delay, the *Hilary* continued upstream, although Colonel Bertie had to disembark at Manaós with acute dysentery – a blow to Casement who had come to admire the soldier. Following a further two-week layover in Iquitos, which he disliked for its European pretensions, the rest of the party travelled on a fast boat provided by the Peruvian Amazon Company, but Casement felt that to accept such hospitality would compromise him; certainly the other investigators dined with Lizardo Arana on more than one occasion, toasting 'health and prosperity to Peru', while he went slowly up the often miles-wide river on a 'beastly . . . old and smelling' ship, with only one toilet for its twenty-seven passengers. He developed a painful eye infection and a fever, and even his romanticism could not prevail in the heavy heat amid the swarms of mosquitoes and sandflies. 'The formation of the country . . . leaves nothing to the imagination. The eye falls on unending lines of trees walling in a vast flow of discoloured waters, and behind the trees are no regions of the unknown . . .' The Foreign Office was irritated to receive the bills stemming from his principled stance.

Lizardo Arana brazenly expressed the hope that the result of the Commission's inquiry, rumoured to be costing the Company

£10,000, would be an injection of fresh capital, a signal to Casement that it would take all his determination to see what the Aranas wanted to keep hidden, as the Commission had no powers to summon witnesses under oath and was not being supplied with 'proper interpreters and guides with some local knowledge of men, places and affairs'. He could at least get direct testimony from the Barbadian overseers, one of whom, Frederick Bishop, confessed with relief and in graphic detail that he had been ordered to flog Indians and hide the whips and stocks when Gielgud was due to audit. Over the next week in the torrential tropical rain, Bishop and others told Casement of floggings, of Indian women being trussed up over fires, of decapitations, of a firework being inserted into a girl suffering from venereal disease and other horrors. They reported some of the Peruvian overseers gaining bonuses of as much as £1,000 by dint of terror tactics to increase production, as well as fiddling the books. As in 1903, Casement's personal diary entries are initially dispassionate, mingling Bishop's stories with the mundane winning of bridge rubbers and his observations on handsome young workers.

The Commission was met in mid-September at La Chorrera by the Company's chief overseer, Juan Tizón, the 'one decent man up there'. Casement observed on the Indians the 'mark of the Aranas' inflicted by the floggings, and one of the five Barbadians at the station told how the most vicious overseer, Armando Normand, who would stand in Casement's report as the exemplar of the abusers, had forced him to beat a man between the legs before shooting him when he was unable to carry his load. On hearing this, Tizón 'practically chucked up the sponge' before promising sweeping reforms. Once the dam of silence had been breached, the recitals of the atrocities poured out, including Indians lined up to see how many a single bullet would pass through, thrown into fires, buried alive, limbs and heads cut off.

As the Commission travelled upriver and Casement's horrified indignation mounted, so did his annoyance with his fellow investigators: they were not getting first-hand material like him, preferring to remain reading in their rooms or engaging only with the commercial and corporate issues rather than the human ones. He was uncomfortable as the guest of those he was investigating, loathing their food and the abominable weather. Even the squalor of Pará appeared 'a delicious dream up here in these awful crime-stained forests'. To compensate, he worked ever harder: he measured the Indians and the stocks to prove that the size of the holes was an additional torture, he struggled under the standard fifty-kilo load of rubber and took numerous photographs with his box camera. Over 90 per cent of the Indians bore livid weals from the tapir-hide whips with their five-foot-long, three-inch-wide lashes – the Amazon *ronzal* lacerated even more than the Congo's *chicotte*. He heard about slaves being held underwater, being flogged with the flat side of machete blades so as not to open the skin, and begging for scraps and crumbs. He found it hard to keep up his consular demeanour knowing that the London registration of the Peruvian Amazon Company gave it a 'cloak of respectability, and the guarantee for cash', and that the 'horde of infamous ruffians' would remain in charge whatever the report said. In an irrational expression of this resentment, he wrote that it was 'infernal cheek' that Gielgud, the Company man, called him 'Casement' as if they were equals. He came round from a 'dreadful nightmare' one morning to write on his blotter that he had yelled for help and woken the whole house.

The party returned to La Chorrera near the end of October, with a full catalogue of cruelty. Casement drew up a 'Black List' of the criminal elements within the Company, and wrote out fair copies of the Barbadians' statements for their signature. Just after he had taken down a deposition about José Fonseca, an overseer, killing a young Indian in the stocks at Último Retiro by 'smashing his testicles and private parts', he 'shuddered' as he shook the murderer's hand. He found letters and newspapers waiting, many sensationalising the arrest of Dr Crippen and his mistress. The worldwide attention directed towards the Kentish Town wife murderer was a 'farce' – he had been dining with 'lots and lots of gentlemen . . . who not only kill their wives, but burn other people's wives alive – or cut their arms and legs off and pull the babies from their breasts to throw in the river'. He ended this entry with the lament of every humanitarian crusader: 'Why should civilisation stand aghast at a Crippen and turn wearily away when the poor Indians of the Putumayo, the

The infant Roger
with his parents.

Roger's sister
(and substitute mother) Nina.

Magherintemple, Co. Antrim, the family home which Casement
was not to visit until after his mother's death.

The explorer, journalist and recorder of his own remarkable feats Henry Morton Stanley, whose arrival on the Atlantic shore of Africa at Boma in 1876 helped fuel Leopold's territorial ambitions.

Even though he was not present at the negotiations, King Leopold II of the Belgians was granted the spoils of the Congo Free State at the Berlin West Africa Conference of 1884–5.

Roger Casement and thousands of other Europeans
got their first sight of the Congo at Boma.

Souvenir de l'Etat Indépendant du Congo.

La Vue de Matadi.

Matadi, the town below the cataracts and rapids around which
Casement helped build the railway early in his career.

Casement resigned from his work on the railway in 1888 on the grounds that the money spent on it would be much better invested in its workers' education and welfare.

Colleagues who left their mark on the Congo, and it on them:
Edward Glave, William Parminter, Herbert Ward and Roger Casement.

Casement was praised for his mission work at Wathen Station.

April 25th 1890.

Your affectionately
Rod Casement.

Roger Casement (left) in 1890, the year he met the as yet unpublished Joseph Conrad (above) in Matadi.

In his consular uniform. His first appointment was in Lourenço Marques, Portuguese East Africa.

E. D. Morel, Casement's fellow campaigner whose work as an
Antwerp shipping clerk opened his eyes to the Congo atrocities.

Rubber workers left for dead and mutilated by Leopold's private army,
the Force Publique, for failing to meet their quotas.

The steamboat *Henry Reed* commissioned by Casement for his horrifying expedition up-river in 1903.

An encounter with one of Leopold's paid journalists, May French Sheldon, on his journey back to England to write up his findings. His experiences left him haunted and gaunt.

Bantu of the Congo, turn bloodstained, appalling hands and terrified eyes to those who *alone* can aid?'

There had been many opportunities to observe naked young men on the Amazon, and Casement recorded some of these in his diary. But he refrained from any sexual activity on the trip, no doubt aware that discovery would destroy the trust placed in him. Now that he was in La Chorrera and finalising his interviews before the return to Barbados, accompanied by many of the relieved overseers who had concluded their service, he took the extraordinary step of acquiring a young man and a boy. He was calculating the load/weight ratio of the enslaved porters when he came across a 'dear wee thing called Omarino', of an undisclosed age and weighing only twenty-four kilos. The boy's parents had been killed 'by this rubber curse', and his brother shot by one of the villains on the Commission's list. It was suggested that Casement give a 'present' of shirt and trousers to Omarino's *capitan*, Macedo, in return for which Macedo 'with great unction' made a 'present' of his young charge. Casement simply wrote 'Bought Omarino' in his diary.

That same afternoon, an older boy who had been watching 'with a sort of steadfast shyness' as Casement made his calculations and distributed tins of salmon followed him home and asked to be bought as well. Ricudo was nineteen and married, but his wife was with her parents and would be 'no issue in the case'. Casement admired his 'beautiful coffee limbs' and believed that Herbert Ward would want to sculpt a South American group in bronze with him as a model. If the honesty with which he wrote about his urges elsewhere is to be believed, he had no sexual intentions towards either of the boys – but also very little idea what he was going to do with them. It is not possible to form a definitive judgement on why he took the pair to Europe, but it is likely to be a combination of using them as exhibits of the beauty and innocence of the Putumayans when his report was being discussed, an overflow of his pent-up compassion and his desire to rescue during the trip, and simply the irrational impulse by an overwrought man who did not always pause for thought. His fear of the exposure of his private world was always terrifying enough for him to overcome his impetuosity, so if he had apprehended accusations of impropriety he would never have taken the step that looks so bizarre today.

He sent the boys, who seemed miserable, ahead to Iquitos, and when he reached the town towards the end of November found them in rented quarters in the care of Barbadians who had escaped the Aranas. Mrs Caze, the Consul's wife, 'sniffed' at their presence and suggested they should have a good bath, to which Casement replied that they were a good deal cleaner than most whites. Following this exchange, they do not seem to have been a topic of much conversation in the Consul's residence – the three Britons passed the time in interminable games of dummy bridge, while Casement seethed about how little the Consul must have passed on about the Aranas. When he left to deliver his 'ghastly and horrible tale', Omarino and Ricudo, with some cash and a letter for the Governor, were dropped off in Barbados in the care of the Jesuit Father Frederick Smith pending their future travel to Europe. The priest's reports of Ricudo drinking rum and wanting to return home because 'Indians as a rule do not like to stay in any one place for long' did not encourage Casement to think he had made a good decision.

Casement had his first sexual encounter since the journey upstream with the *Liberal*'s young pilot, with whom he had been bathing and flirting for days. Afterwards, he dreamt of a purer time, before he had witnessed the abominations of the last few years and before his prominence made secrecy more necessary and more repressive: he 'waked with vivid dream of 1887–88 going up Mozamba Hill – Oh! God – to think of it – "the fields of heaven" – 24 years ago in the heyday and glowing flush of my youth – just 23 years old – more than half my life gone since then'. He had seen too much and buried too much ever to feel such innocence in his conscious life again, as he contemplated writing up the detail of what he recognised was 'a bigger crime than that of the Congo', even if one that involved 'only a few thousands of human beings, whereas the other affected millions'.

The Putumayo was a genocide in progress. Casement calculated that the indigenous population had reduced from 40,000–50,000 in

1908 to 12,000, and within a decade would be extinguished. Normand and the other six 'monster' overseers named in his report had directly killed 5,000 slaves by 'shooting, flogging, beheading, burning' in the seven years of the Arana reign. After his Congo experiences, Casement braced himself for more official dilatoriness as he wrote up his findings, and this time expressed his anxiety in extreme nationalist terms: 'The white man's world' was populated by two groups, 'compromisers and Irishmen'. Only Irishmen, in which category he included Hardenburg, Whiffen, the Foreign Secretary and a few other officials, but not the unstirred Englishmen on the Commission, who were incapable of compassion towards other races, could relieve 'these enormously outraged Indians . . . from their cruel burden' by abolishing the Company and expelling the Aranas from every part of English life. To him, compromise was an undesirable English characteristic too often shared by those fellow Ulstermen who wanted to remain under Westminster rule.

He left Iquitos in early December after an interview with the Prefect of the town who begged him not to publish a report that would bring down 'international obloquy' on Peru; Casement thought the Peruvian government's conniving blind eye to the Aranas was an international disgrace. The whole place was so corrupt that his photographs of the Putumayo victims got mysteriously lost while being developed in Iquitos. He landed in Cherbourg on the last day of 1910 and spent New Year's Eve in a 'vile' and noisy hotel in Paris. The next day involved a renewal of acquaintance with friends and lovers, listed in his diary as Denis Hilaire, Dick (Morten), 'Noisy Nick' (a boisterous retired naval captain called Harry Nicholson, married to Morten's niece) and Pierre, with whom he had oral sex for forty francs. He visited Herbert Ward and his family, but failed to mention in his diary the imminent arrival of Ricudo as a potential model; he collected a coat from his tailor, and was relieved of ninety-two francs by a mugger he was attempting to pick up before lunching at the embassy.

His reception at the Foreign Office was entirely positive. Grey had read his despatches and the Assistant Under-Secretary Louis Mallet even hoped that Normand and others would be hanged. Casement considered this unlikely, yet went against the other members of the Commission (who had eventually earned his respect) to suggest capital punishment as a step towards ending 'this long martyrdom and hellish persecution of the Indians'. Julio Arana wrote to Casement twice to ask for an early meeting, but he did not reply, dismissing him in his diary as 'The swine!' Yet the Foreign Office was hamstrung as Britain had no jurisdiction in nor treaty with Peru and was hampered by the Monroe Doctrine, dating back to the fifth US President in 1823, which explicitly stated that any European power attempting to control 'in any manner the destiny' of an American country which had gained independence would be considered to have 'an unfriendly disposition towards the United States'. Nevertheless, when Arana was appointed the official Peruvian representative at the International Rubber Exhibition in London as befitted Britain's largest supplier, Mallet forgot the diplomatic niceties enough to reiterate that he was 'an appalling criminal' who 'ought to be hanged'.

In contrast to his frenzied outrage in the winter of 1903–4, Casement wrote his report slowly, finding himself ' "full up" with horrors at times . . . it is only the thought of those poor, hunted, gentle beings up there in the forests that keeps me going'. Despite his traumatised exhaustion, his damaged eyesight and the hopelessness of the agency typist, his 120-page manuscript was delivered on St Patrick's Day, and even when toned down on Foreign Office advice it did not shirk the descriptions of the stocks, floggings, wounds, starvation, incineration and putrefied bodies. It came down unequivocally against Normand and the worst of his cronies in its tale of 'unrelieved barbarity', with testimony from 'British subjects' as well as the evidence of the Commissioners' own eyes. He described how determined the Amazonians were not to give away the hiding places of their colleagues, even undergoing fatal limb amputation rather than betray. This 'fortitude in the face of impending torture and death . . . speaks for itself of the excellence of some of their qualities'. Hardenburg wondered 'how so much goodness still survived'.

The facts were stark: in the six years to 1910, Putumayo rubber, all of it transported in British ships, had a value of £1 million on the London market but came at a cost of upward of 30,000 lives ended 'by deliberate murder, by bullet, fire, beheading or flogging to death'. Casement had his focus fixed on those who had been brutalised, but he combined that with an unusual worldliness and strategic maturity to advise that the government should not cut loose from the Company, which was 'in the hollow of our hand', but reform it from within to prevent Arana restarting 'with as many of the spirits of evil as he can gather round him', and to stop lone traders rushing to fill the vacuum without any oversight. In the middle of May 1911, Grey told Casement that the Company knew, 'unofficially and privately', that he was prepared to advise them, but he was nevertheless surprised to be invited to the next board meeting. He fruitlessly demanded that a note-taker be present, and found the experience chaotic and dispiriting, detecting no desire for reform; the villain of the piece had even written to thank him and to express astonishment at the report's revelations. Mallet decided he would have to involve the Peruvian government, especially after the new Consul in Iquitos transmitted the dispiriting news that Arana's chief agents had all fled across the border to Brazil with several dozen Indians they were planning to sell for around £50 a head in the slave markets. The report was translated into Spanish and despatched to Lima, without any great hope of change. For that, its author's diplomatic skills would be tested to their utmost.

Casement spent little time in Ireland in the five months after he delivered his broadside. His frequent meetings with Alice Green in London involved discussions that were more historical and aesthetic than political, albeit with Home Rule always in the background since H. H. Asquith's Liberal government were now propped up by the Irish Party. He was euphoric about his exposure of the Amazon criminality, writing to Green that 'life is more beautiful than data, and the world we live in more lovely than all the plains of heaven. There can be no heaven if we don't make it here.' He made plans for Ricudo and Omarino to arrive towards the end of June, lining up a place for the younger boy at the school set up by the nationalist barrister and poet Patrick Pearse, progressive St Enda's in Dublin, aided by a £50 gift from William Cadbury, despite the philanthropist's complaints that he was being nipped by Polly the Amazon parrot he was looking after for Casement. This aside, Casement seemed less emotionally connected to Ireland than he had been for years, after pouring his zeal into the Putumayo.

When he was awarded a knighthood in George V's Coronation Honours in mid-June, his reaction was quite different to his dismay at the CMG. He doodled 'Sir Roger Casement CMG' on a blank page in his diary to see how it looked and knelt before the new monarch on 6 July. He let Grey know that he was 'much moved at the proof of confidence and appreciation', and grateful for the Foreign Secretary's 'personal esteem and support'. His sincere and loyal words were to rebound against him, but for now they signified an acceptance of the public acclamation, a fitting acknowledgement of his great humanitarian efforts and growing international influence. He displayed an enhanced level of confidence which overcame his previous public withholding when he met the pre-eminent African-American intellectual W. E. B. Du Bois in London, after which he spoke out against racial prejudice and lynching in the USA. On the other hand, he told Alice Green that 'until Ireland is safe and her outlook happy no Irishman has any right to be accepting honours or having a good time of it anywhere'; and he hated 'the thing'. W. B. Yeats, less ambiguous in his national identity, refused such an honour as he did not want his countrymen to say 'only for a ribbon he left us'.

Casement's involvement with the Putumayo was to last another two years. It became his final humanitarian and diplomatic monument. He undertook a complicated mandate to help reform and keep afloat a crucial British company, and attended more board meetings to persuade the directors to send representatives to Iquitos to look after their interests before action was taken against them; this earned him a supportive letter from Arana. But the wily Chairman informed the next meeting that the Peruvian Amazon Company was close to bankruptcy, at which point intervention would be impossible. Grey countered this threat with one of his own, that the Commission's report would be published in full. Finally the Peruvian government were forced to take action.

Following this successful outcome, Casement's emotional involvement with his cause dovetailed with his ambition for it. He went so
far as to tell Cadbury that 'The F.O. are doing and have done everything a great department could possibly attempt'; they were being
'splendid' – a far cry from his sentiments at the same stage in the
Congo investigation. Alongside his official work, he set out to raise
£15,000 for a Christian mission in the Putumayo. In July, when 200
warrants for arrest were issued, many of them for murder charges
and including one for Arana's brother-in-law, he courageously asked
to be sent back to Iquitos to see the thing through.

He concluded that Ricudo and Omarino would be better off at
home after their unsatisfactory interlude in London: they had been
introduced to the Anti-Slavery Society, to the board of the Peruvian
Amazon Company and to some close friends, but ultimately the
strange, honest experiment in human propaganda, questionable on
many levels to modern eyes, was not the publicity success he had
hoped for, despite delighting his landlady Miss Cox and all who met
them. Casement commissioned Sir William Rothenstein to paint the
pair, and the distinguished portraitist even came to the docks to see
the party off in mid-August.

From Barbados, Casement was accompanied by the Briton H. S.
Dickey, a former Company doctor at El Encanto, who had witnessed
the cruelty of Loayza and others and confirmed Casement's estimates
of the population decline. Dickey had resigned when his salary was
halved, having already noted that 'the very humblest rubber gatherer' could earn $25 per day through the efforts of slaves. He had
suffered his own torture at the hands of a neighbouring tribe to the
friendly but enslaved Weetotos. Having taken himself into the bush
for a few days to get away from his colleagues and look for exotic
birds, he was set upon by Indians who had every reason to dislike
white men; they suspended him from a tree by his hands, dislocating
both shoulders, before cutting a wide gash in the trunk. Two Wee-
toto girls gathering berries found him twenty-two hours later,
covered from eyes to feet by ants marching in their thousands towards
the sap running over him.

Dickey and Casement spent two weeks in Pará waiting for the

local customs officer to release their luggage. They passed their days
reading, doing jigsaw puzzles and in dull conversation with their
acquaintances in the port; at night, Casement cruised the streets
looking for fast sex. For the first time, he wrote about memories of
past encounters with adjectival pleasure: he recalled Stanley Weeks in
Bridgetown who had a 'beautiful specimen' which he was 'glad' to
show in his 'youth and joy'; it was a notable change from the previous crisp descriptions of financial and physical transactions. Alongside
this febrile sexuality, he exhibited some sartorial eccentricity in the
ninety-six-degree heat: the doctor was dressed in the standard colonial outfit of white pith helmet, shirt and trousers, while the Consul
was doing everything possible to distance himself from imperial
British uniform by wearing 'a thick and very dark brown suit of Irish
homespun . . . [and] a straw hat that looked as if it had been taken
from an ash can many years before', and carrying a 'very knobbly
walking stick . . . that must have been two inches in diameter'. When
they were finally bound for Iquitos, the boat's captain requested that
Casement at least wear his shoes and socks at the dinner table but was
defiantly rebuked. As Casement had taken a slow boat rather than a
fast, British-owned Booth liner after one of the Booths had refused
to associate the family with reform in the Putumayo, it was an
uncomfortable voyage.

On arrival, they discovered that the Company had indeed gone
into liquidation, with Arana as liquidator. The worst of the criminals
remained in Brazil, while many of the indicted had been released; the
judge who had issued the arrest warrants, including that for Arana's
brother-in-law, had been dismissed. For the fourth time, Grey threatened to publish the report to shame the Peruvians, but first he took a
bold decision: since Washington and its Monroe Doctrine were such
a block, Casement would go on to America.

The liberal British Ambassador, James Bryce, an Ulster Irishman
writing a book about South America, wanted to hear everything. He
engineered a gathering with President Taft at the embassy and 'let
[Casement] loose' on him in 'a quiet corner'. It was a 'queer picture . . .
the tall Celt, haggard and livid from the Putumayo swamps, fixing
with glittering eyes the burly rubicund Anglo-Saxon'. Casement's

passionate discourse had the effect of 'a black snake fascinating a wombat', and a few days later the Secretary of State cabled Lima that unless the court actions over 'that iniquitous system' were reinstated, the United States would come to believe that Peru had proved itself 'unable properly to exercise sovereign rights over disputed regions'. In other words, America would side with Colombia over the ongoing boundary arguments.

Nearly two years after Casement first steamed up the Putumayo, Peru made a last attempt to block the report by taking a leaf out of Leopold's book to announce its own Commission. America was supportive; the Foreign Secretary hung back yet again. However, Casement was not in a mood to fight just then: he had a throat infection, then took a much needed motoring holiday in the Rhineland with Dick Morten followed by a fortnight in Falmouth with Nina. On his return he finessed the Peruvians by proposing that they should welcome the document if, as they claimed, they were serious about reform. His report was published in full by the Stationery Office on 13 July 1912 at 1s 5d, and Sir Roger Casement became a household name. Thomas Fisher Unwin, who had damaged his poetic ambitions twenty years earlier, followed up with a trade edition of the government publication, entitled *Putumayo*, in December.

No section of the press held back this time. *The Times*'s leader stated that the findings 'must stir the anger and compassion of all those who are not utterly dead to the sense of humanity and of right'; the article made the connection with 'King Leopold's infamous *régime* in the Congo' and declared that 'Sir Roger Casement has deserved well of his countrymen and of mankind by the ability and the zeal with which he has investigated under very difficult circumstances an appalling iniquity'. Morel embarrassed his friend by writing in the *Daily Star* that he had passed 'through the highest test of mental and physical endurance to attain the most conspicuous point of human achievement'. Publishers approached him to write 'a great and good book' on his 'public life and experiences' to cash in on the wave of public outrage, but Casement refused 'civilly . . .pointing out [that he was] too "unsettled" to write a book yet'. Pope Pius X issued an encyclical asking for more humanity to be shown to South American

Indians, and a sermon was preached in Westminster Abbey. Casement was justified in his boast to Gertrude Bannister that he had 'blown up the Devil's Paradise . . . a great step forward in human things – the abodes of cruelty are not so secure as they were – and their tenants are very scared'.

Casement heard about the report's reception in Ireland, where he was involved in a fresh campaign to alleviate the plight of the impoverished, typhoid-suffering, Irish-speaking people of a corner of Connemara; as his campaigning focus shifted, he called this 'an Irish Putumayo' and returned from a visit there to claim that the 'white Indians' were weighing more heavily upon him than 'all the Indians of the rest of the earth'. He raised £2,000 to enable the infant-school children on the islands of Connemara to have a free meal every day for a year, provided Irish was the language of the classroom.

Prime Minister Asquith and Attorney General Sir Rufus Isaacs, soon to play an even greater role in Casement's life, set up a Select Committee of Inquiry to look into the situation with regard to the Peruvian Amazon Company's directors, which sat thirty-two times between the autumn of 1912 and the spring of 1913. Casement attended twice, once waving a Winchester rifle above his head as a comment on the arms industry's potential to destroy indigenous peoples, and supplied yet more first-hand material for the official record.

A year to the day since his landing in Europe, Casement left England at the end of 1912, travelling to South Africa in search of warmth to alleviate his arthritis. He stayed with his brother Tom in a hotel he and Cadbury had helped fund, but the venture was doomed to failure. He was exhausted, with an 'ever-recurring desire for retirement' in the country, but was 'overborne' by his friends to 'return home' for the time being at least. By the time Casement returned from his last visit to Africa, in mid-May 1913, Julio Arana had given his evidence to Parliament. The Committee ignored his blustering accusations that Casement and Hardenburg had fabricated evidence, and staged a dramatic coup by confronting him with Hardenburg. But they could do little to punish the villain in Britain once the Company was liquidated. They concluded that Arana 'had knowledge of and was responsible for the atrocities perpetrated by his agents', and pointed out that he was 'the last person in the world' who should have dissolved his own company. Conan Doyle had written to his 'affect. friend' while Casement was in South Africa to say he had done 'a great deed. Will these villains never be punished? My head is bitter against the London directors – callous, surely, if not criminal.' Arana was to live another forty years and serve as a senator in Lima, but when the Putumayo territories were handed to Colombia as part of the Salomón–Lozano Treaty in 1927, he was left penniless.

However, the Committee's eventual recommendations were diplomatically and legally lasting: a more professional consular service ensured protection of the Indians from slavery and abuse, and company directors would be held responsible for the consequences of their actions; the Peruvian Amazon directors were culpably negligent for their ignorance of what went on, but as they were not personally responsible for any overt act of slavery, their only punishment was public disgrace. If it had not already been dissolved, the Company itself would have been closed by judicial order. The Anti-Slavery Society continued to receive complaints about the treatment of Indians until late into the twentieth century, but the Amazon rubber industry was already in decline as managed plantations sprang up in Malaysia and South Asia.

The Congo Reform Association was also winding up in 1913. At its final meeting, Morel paid tribute to his absent co-founder, conjuring a 'vision of a small steamer ploughing its way up the Congo just ten years ago this month, and on its decks . . . a man of great heart, great experience, great knowledge of African races; a man of great insight . . . If he had been another kind of man than the man he was . . . I shudder to think what might have happened.' Although Casement had failed to secure any long-term safeguards for the Putumayans, his courage in the exposure of evil saved countless lives and much suffering, and cemented his reputation around the world. A century after his report was published, the governments of Peru and Colombia held a ceremony at La Chorrera and put out a statement acknowledging that what had happened there was a crime of ethnocide. Pope Benedict XVI reconfirmed his predecessor's encyclical.

Casement finally resigned from the Foreign Office in August 1913 after two decades that had been marked by ill-health and dissatisfaction, but above all by unparalleled moral courage as he took his place as the first and one of the greatest humanitarian reformers of the century. Tyrrell and Grey recommended him for a pension commensurate with the 'long, valuable and distinguished services made to the Crown', which was settled at a handsome £421 13s 4d.* Thirty years after he set eyes on Boma from the deck of the *Bonny*, he exuded a justified satisfaction in having 'done my work anyhow . . . & *some* evils will never again be quite the same'.

At the end of the previous year, he had asked a friend for counsel as his 'future depends on the decision' he would come to 'in the next few days'; he did not want 'to leap impetuously or follow my impulse alone'. Although that letter was about leaving his career as a diplomat in the service of the Crown, his concerns ran much deeper; he ended it by admitting that he was 'in much trouble of mind'; a later instruction was added in a different ink to keep the missive 'Private & Confidential'. His great task now was to turn to himself, to settle his historic, internal divisions and find reconciliation between his practical and emotional sides. Any chance of such fulfilment would take total immersion in the cause closest to his confused background and to which he had been referring with greater frequency as he witnessed, and alleviated, suffering elsewhere in the world.

---

* Around £50,000 at today's values.

PART TWO

Patriot

7. The Soul of a Felon

Sir Roger Casement's near-fifty years had brought him honour and fame as the author of two reports which had changed, and saved, the lives of those without voice in the imperial European capitals. Both his river trips were comparatively brief, even if the first was the culmination of decades of experience; by contrast, the last period of his life had a frenetic pace and many scene changes, reflecting the fast-moving tides of the times which swept him up and on which much of his reputation still hangs.

The turning point occurred on a grey afternoon in May 1914 in Alice Stopford Green's house overlooking the Thames in Westminster. Casement was in a meeting with Eoin MacNeill, the Celtic archaeologist, co-founder of the Gaelic League and Chairman of the secret, oath-bound Irish Republican Brotherhood, the Fenians, to discuss gun-running. Also present was Darrell Figgis, a former tea broker who had moved to Achill Island off the coast of County Mayo to immerse himself in Irish culture, and who reckoned that he 'had never met any man of so single and selfless a mind, or of so natural and noble a gesture of soul' as Casement. Figgis had offered to be the go-between 'to all the addresses on the continent' where weaponry might be acquired. Casement was looking out over the coal barges lying on their sides in the mud at low tide and the warehouses on the further bank of the Thames vanishing in the dusk; Figgis was struck by his handsome profile silhouetted against the grey, rising mist: it had worn its habitual expression of 'apparent dejection', an impression intensified by the 'great hole' in his left boot 'for he gave his substance away always'. Yet his face was 'alight with battle' as he said, 'That's talking.' His normal loquacity was silenced in the charged seriousness of the moment. The previous day, he had been giving evidence to the Royal Commission inquiring into the consular world to which he had added lustre; now he was setting up an arms-running operation. His 'brevity betokened an end of talking', as patriotism slipped over into illegal nationalism.

Casement's return from the Putumayo and his move towards leaving the Foreign Office coincided with the cause which he had been culturally exploring since the start of the century becoming the most significant disruptor of British party politics. In 1885, the Liberal Prime Minister William Gladstone, in a minority government with Charles Stewart Parnell's Irish Nationalist MPs holding the balance of power, had taken the decision to overturn the 1800 Acts of Union which had suppressed Ireland's Parliament and made the island part of the United Kingdom. Gladstone's Home Rule Bill offered limited devolution – the country would still be ruled by the King, defended by British forces and policed by the Royal Irish Constabulary; foreign policy, taxation and customs would be managed from Westminster. Despite Gladstone's exhortations that it was best to take the initiative in the face of an inevitability, some broke away from his party to form the Liberal Unionists and in the ensuing general election the Conservatives were returned to power.

The Second Home Rule Bill was introduced by the next Liberal government in 1893 but rejected by the House of Lords, and the Conservatives again took office the following year. The period spanning the turn of the century saw the foundation of the National Irish League, the launch of Griffith's *United Irishman* and *Sinn Féin* and the reunification, after its division between Parnellite nationalists and Home Rulers, of the Irish Parliamentary Party in the Commons under John Redmond, as well as calls for an Ulster Unionist Council to be established for the northern, mainly Protestant, counties with the aim of keeping them ruled from London. The Liberals were returned in 1906 and hints of another Home Rule Bill began to occur in ministers' speeches when the reactionary House of Lords rejected the November 1909 'People's Budget', with its unprecedented taxes on wealth and land to fund social reform; this precipitated a constitutional crisis centring on the power of the elected government to enact legislation. In the resulting general election of January 1910, Asquith's Liberals won 274 seats (down from 397 in 1906), the

Conservatives 272 and the young Labour Party 40: the Irish Parliamentary Party's 71 seats tipped the balance for Asquith to go back into Downing Street with a promise of Home Rule. A few months later, the Parliament Act, under the threat that the King had agreed to appoint sufficient peers to ensure its passage, denied the Unionist Lords their veto; and in a second election held in December similar numbers prevailed in the Commons. A Cabinet committee that included Winston Churchill and Sir Edward Grey was established in January 1911 to plan for Home Rule.

With the Lords routed, the Conservatives gathered themselves to oppose Home Rule as the guardians of landed property and the empire. They elected a new leader in the unlikely guise of Andrew Bonar Law, the former iron-merchant son of an Ulster Presbyterian minister, damned by the handsome, cultivated Asquith's description of him as 'meekly ambitious'. Bonar Law's connections ensured that he would listen to what were now the Ulster Unionist members who were determined to defy Parliament. While Casement was leading his own crusade on behalf of the Putumayo Indians, this resistance to Home Rule among the predominantly Protestant community in Ulster acquired Sir Edward Carson as its leader. The powerful frame and defiant scowl of the successful King's Counsel and former Conservative Solicitor General may have belied a self-doubting hypochondriac, but he was a formidable speaker who never entirely lost his Dublin brogue and whose open-ended cross-examination of Oscar Wilde in his libel trial had destroyed for all time the reputation of his childhood playmate and university friend.* Carson, whom Casement found 'gloomy, dark and foreboding', sincerely believed that Ireland could not prosper apart from the rest of the United Kingdom, and became Ulster's champion when Asquith's government introduced the Home Rule Bill for the third time in April 1912. In September, Carson addressed a packed rally in Belfast City Hall. Standing in front of William of Orange's tattered standard, which

---

* Wilde had hoped to have Carson on his own legal team; when he heard the news that he was acting for the other side he quipped, 'No doubt he will pursue his case with all the added bitterness of an old friend' (Sturgis, *Oscar* p. 550).

recalled the Protestant King's victory over the Catholic James II at the Battle of the Boyne in 1690, he announced that he would be back, 'whether for peace, I prefer it or, if it be to fight, I shall not shrink'. A volley of shots 'bade him farewell'. Thomas Andrews, Secretary of the Ulster Unionist Council, assured 'waverers in England' that if the north of Ireland was 'deserted by Great Britain I would rather be governed by Germany than by . . . John Redmond and Company'.

The elegant, quick-minded, provocative and frequently melodramatic F. E. Smith MP was also a barrister, and worked so closely alongside Carson that his nickname of 'Galloper' stuck to him throughout his political career, which would encompass becoming Lord Chancellor and Secretary of State for India. But first he was to play a lacerating role in Casement's life as Attorney General. A rally was held in Smith's home town of Liverpool to whip up the Unionists, in defiance of Parliament, at which Carson spoke of 'the possibility of grave and official operations in Belfast and in Ulster . . . If that is inciting to riot, here I am.' Smith supported him, declaring that 'Ulster . . . would be right in resisting . . . Nationalist domination under a trick' and should go to any lengths to oppose having legislation foisted upon it. Bulmer Hobson realised that Carson 'had opened a door that could not easily be closed again'.

Asquith foresaw that he would have to make a bargain over Ulster even if his Bill effectively only promised local government powers under the Crown, but he did not want to negotiate before the arguments had been thrashed out; yet before the Bill was even introduced, loyalist Orange lodges all over Ulster began to practise route marching, drilling and semaphore. Carson had held discussions with the tall, ruddy MP for East Down, Captain James Craig, a landowner and Boer War veteran with formidable organisational skills,* which resulted in a gathering in September in front of his house on the shores of Belfast Lough. Fifty thousand Orangemen heard Carson's ringing words: 'We must be prepared . . . the morning Home Rule passes, ourselves to become responsible for the government of the Protestant Province of Ulster.' The following Easter, Bonar Law

---

* Craig was later to become the first Prime Minister of Northern Ireland.

marked the merger of the Conservative and Unionist parties at a gathering outside Belfast, during which he expressed the view that Home Rule was nothing less than an assault on the very notion of imperial Britain and exhorted his audience to 'hold the pass, the pass for the Empire'. The poet of that empire, Rudyard Kipling, published 'Ulster 1912' in the *Morning Post* on the same day:

> The dark eleventh hour
> Draws on and sees us sold
> To every evil power
> We fought against of old.

Twenty-three thousand men of the province signed up immediately to the Ulster Volunteer Force, and eventually the signatures, some of them in blood, of 447,197 men and women were bound into the Ulster Covenant, their pledge to refuse 'by all means necessary' to recognise the authority of a 'Home Rule Parliament' under the 'present conspiracy'. His Majesty's Loyal Opposition had in effect endorsed a paramilitary organisation formed to defy British law.

Civil war became a distinct possibility as sectarian skirmishes flared up, and the government were trapped: if Home Rule proceeded, there would be armed rebellion in the north; if Ulster was excluded, the government would have given way to threats. They lived up to Casement's characterisation as 'compromisers' by choosing to do nothing: neither using the thousand soldiers and the demoralised and ineffective police force in the province against the UVF, nor pushing Home Rule legislation forward. Casement wrote to the pacifist William Cadbury that Carson had proclaimed and gloried in the illegality of the Volunteers, challenging the government 'not to touch a hair of their heads'. He foresaw that the nationalist movement would have to become an 'anti-English' rather than a co-operative party as legislation proceeded, but as always he was most unbuckled in his prose when he wrote to his cousin Gertrude about the betrayal of his own tribe:

> I *love* the Antrim Presbyterians ... they are good, kind, warm-hearted souls; and to see them now, *exploited* by that damned Church of Ireland – that Orange Ascendancy Gang who hate Presbyterians

only less than Papists, and to see them delirious before a *Smith*, a *Carson* (a cross between a badly reared bloodhound and an underfed hyaena, sniffing for Irish blood in the track) and whooping Rule Britannia thro' the streets is a wound to my soul . . .

His heightened metaphors, like those he had used about the evils of Leopold's Congo regime, demonstrated the passion that had transformed his earlier cultural nationalism into a profound anti-imperialism.

Casement's own entry into the new arena was on his Antrim home ground of Ballymoney in October 1913. His speech to a hall packed with 'smiling, good-faced farmers . . . in hundreds & a magnificent table of *reporters*' was 'a *grand* success' according to its deliverer. But the organ of the Anglo-Irish ruling class, the *Irish Times*, in its report of the gathering stung by describing him as a 'romantic Nationalist' and a 'Citizen of the World'. The next day he went to Rathlin Island with Alice Green and was hurt again when the owner of the island from which he had brought the Irish speakers to the Feis nine years earlier gave him a 'cold and derisory reception' for his interference with 'her island' and 'her people'. The two occasions highlighted changes that had taken place while his attention had been on the Amazon: he had become famous and had been knighted for working for the British establishment, while the increasingly strident, partisan and militaristic nature of the debate over Ireland left less room for romanticism. He was forty-nine but sometimes felt older owing to his recurrent malaria, eye infections, arthritis and stomach complaints. He had allies in the highest echelons of the religious and political establishments, including the Pope, members of the US Senate, newspaper editors and leading thinkers, yet the questing figure of the first decade of the century still needed to find self-certainty, to fill the emotional hole left by his upbringing, to move in from the often unrealistic intellectual edges and take greater risks in the increasingly fraught drama of the times.

His active campaigning for Home Rule rekindled his energising morality and gave him focus as he managed to overcome his dislike of personal appearances. The Ballymoney meeting, 'A Protestant Protest', had been organised by Captain Jack White, the Antrim-born son of a field marshal and himself a Boer War hero, who for many years had lived in the utopian Whiteway Colony in Gloucestershire, visited by Mohandas Gandhi in 1909. About 500 attended the heavily policed gathering, which was accompanied by the menacing beat of a drum from a nearby Orange hall. White's trenchant opening speech claimed that Home Rule was 'a question of human rights in which the Catholic hierarchy had intervened to hinder rather than help' and was followed by Alice Stopford Green citing historical examples of Protestants helping out Catholics. Casement's own measured speech continued this theme, to which he was to return frequently: the island had become divided 'where a hundred years ago there was only one Ireland. The Wexford Catholics and the Antrim Presbyterian were then equal rebels.' In a first public statement equating imperialism with the current state of affairs, he made a direct correlation between the success of the 'expanding and consolidating' empire and Ireland 'contracting and falling apart'.

The Times employed the same slur as its Irish counterpart when it wrote of the 'Protestant Home Rulers' romantic nationalists like Sir Roger Casement and Mrs Green', neither of whom could be called 'a typical citizen of Ulster'. Casement was sufficiently energised by his new campaign to retort with unusual, justified sarcasm and hauteur in the newspaper's letters page that 'It was doubtless an enthusiastic attachment to romantic humanitarianism that led my footsteps from Ulster up the Congo and Amazon rivers.' He glossed over many of the ambiguities of his upbringing to point out that the difference between himself on the one hand and Carson, Smith and other Unionists on the other was that he was 'by family, and education, an Ulsterman'. He was able to present his past great works, and that on which he was now embarked, as all of a humanitarian piece.

He suppressed the possibility of romance in his necessarily limited personal life as he rebuffed Ada McNeill's declaration of her feelings for him after his return to Ireland. One of the organisers of the Cushendall Feis, she had now fallen 'passionately in love' with her childhood friend. She had a show of her watercolours in Belfast that autumn, and Casement asked his erstwhile lover Millar Gordon to choose one for up to £5. Gordon managed to buy two for that price, but in his own name so as not to encourage McNeill's hopes. Casement hoped the 'poor old soul' would leave him alone; despite his 'strong feelings of friendship, and goodwill and brotherly Irish affection', he wished she 'would leave other things out of the reckoning'. In an uncharacteristically hard-hearted way, he kept many of his future visits to Belfast and Antrim from her. Yet Ada, along with Alice Stopford Green and other female friends, was to prove a staunch supporter when his hidden life was exposed.

Although rebellion in Ulster seemed more likely than war in Europe as late as May 1914, Germany had for a decade been perceived as a potential menace. The 1904 Entente Cordiale was signed between France and Britain largely to settle imperial rivalries in North Africa and to formalise the end of centuries of warfare; the Kaiser regarded the Entente as creating an unwelcome new constellation in Europe, and signalled his discontent by backing the Sultan of Morocco against the French in 1905. The German Navy had been expanding since 1897, and from 1905 became the benchmark for British naval strength. Casement had been toying with the notion of Germany breaking the structures of empires as far back as his unhappy Pará posting: he had wondered whether Germany might intercede in South American affairs in order to undo the Monroe Doctrine and the United States' 'tutelage . . . over this vast, unoccupied, misused earthly Paradise', and in his anti-imperial, pro-German perorations to Hambloch had argued that Britain would need to go to war to protect its trade monopoly. He had sent a brief, hurried outline for an 'Impossible Novel' to Gertrude Bannister; his fiction had the potential to be *awfully* funny' in its depiction of Germany as the sane saviour of the oppressed and misunderstood: 'The Germans . . . advanced rapidly on Dublin, received everywhere as deliverers and friends' to form a provisional National Government. From this point, events moved swiftly, 'the terrified Unionists everywhere accepted the inevitable', the USA recognised the country, the '*Daily Mail* went into deep mourning' and the British government fell after recognising Ireland as 'a friendly state'.

Now he returned to the theme without the joviality of a family letter and a fantastical synopsis. In July 1912, Britain had moved battleships from the Mediterranean to the North Sea in response to the German build-up and increased its own naval budget to a record £45 million. Two months later Casement wrote an article under the name Batha MacCrainn for the newly founded *Irish Review*, set up by the Dublin poets Joseph Plunkett and Thomas MacDonagh, both of whom were to be executed in 1916. In the article, entitled 'Ireland and the German Menace', he argued that England was granting Home Rule to Ireland to ensure the country's allegiance against Germany; he feared that Germany might mistake Ireland for a loyal territory of the Crown.

The use of pseudonyms had enabled him to maintain his anonymity to Whitehall as well as to emphasise the Irish credentials of the authorship of his articles, but immediately after his resignation from the Foreign Office he used his own name as he went further and more cogently with 'Ireland, Germany and the Next War'. This was a riposte to Conan Doyle's 'Great Britain and the Next War' in the *Fortnightly Review*. Doyle was a supporter of Home Rule who had appealed to Ireland 'to recognise that her interests are one with those of Great Britain in the eventual defeat of [Germany]'; Casement offered the extreme alternative that Britain's defeat might 'result in great gain to Ireland' which might 'emerge into a position of much prosperity', his rationale being that Germany would bring its administrative skills to the country and was better equipped 'intellectually and educationally' than Britain and would take pride in 'advancing Irish well-being' and autonomy. A newly liberated Ireland could become 'an Atlantic Holland' or 'a maritime Belgium', a hub with 'a restored communion with Europe' rather than remaining 'an island beyond an island'. His own liberation from his employers gave him licence to be unambiguously, imaginatively himself, as well as to take the first steps of disloyalty towards the country he had served.

The outspokenness was the product of his rage against the Unionists. He was incensed by the 'infuriated and selfish bigots, who have suffered no wrong' yet who 'go out in thousands to break the law, to arm and drill against Crown and Parliament'. He was whipped up enough to write that he now 'loathed' Englishmen collectively; their country had 'been a curse . . . transcending all the maledictions of history'. In November 1913 he told Alice Green that confronting the proponents of armed rule would be 'far better than to go on lying and pretending – if only we could be left free to fight out our battle here ourselves'. Three months later, he linked the Irish cause to the rest of the 'Elsewhere Empire', surmising that even if 'Ireland *might* be bought or bribed' by the English, the same could not happen to the '35,000,000 of Indian mankind' who were equally crushed. The British Empire was a 'creeping, climbing plant that has fastened on the limbs of others and grown great from a sap not its own, of the sort found in 'the great swamps at the mouth of the Amazon'. He prophesied that its conquerors were 'upon the horizon . . . London, like Rome, will have strange guests' and 'The birds of the forest are on the wing.' Britain might turn to America for support in the coming war with Germany, but if such 'an alliance were ever consummated . . . the most distracting and disastrous conflict that has ever stained the world with blood' would ensue. The only solution 'for all who love peace is the friendly Union of Germany, America and Ireland', with Ireland the critical link.

By the time *Irish Freedom* published 'The Elsewhere Empire', the race for arms was not only taking place between the Royal Navy and the German High Seas Fleet. Eoin MacNeill had put out an article at the end of the previous year in the Gaelic League's newspaper, *An Claidheamh Soluis*,★ which aligned with Casement's Ballymoney position to acknowledge that the Ulster Unionist situation changed everything: 'the British army cannot now be used to prevent the enrolment, drilling and reviewing of Volunteers in Ireland. There is nothing to prevent . . . citizen forces.' A few days later, Bulmer Hobson, a Council member of the Republican Brotherhood, joined MacNeill in discussing a paramilitary movement, and on 20 November the *Daily Chronicle* published a front-page story about the 'citizen force', naming Casement and White as two of its leaders.

A grand inauguration was held in the room at the Rotunda Rink

---

★ 'The Sword of Light' of Gaelic myth.

which had been constructed in the 1870s as an asphalt skating arena and which had also hosted the foundation meeting of Sinn Féin. Four thousand Irish Volunteers signed up on the spot. Although Casement was not present, he was electrified by the movement, his mind racing until 3 a.m. when O'Neill, who became its President and Chief of Staff, first approached him about it. Within days he had drafted the *Manifesto of the Irish Volunteers*, which specified that the duties of the men and women who signed up 'will be defensive and protective, and they will not contemplate either aggression or domination' as they sought to 'secure and maintain the rights and liberties common to all the people of Ireland'. To emphasise patriotism rather than politics was the key theme, the organisation's name should not include 'nationalist'.

In December, MacNeill and Casement took the Volunteers' message to Galway, where a torch-lit procession followed their rally; and then on to Cork, where Casement had other business to transact. The ships of the British Cunard Line no longer used Queenstown (now Cobh) on their way to and from the United States on the grounds that there were too few Irish passengers, as borne out by the numbers: the country still had a falling population, with the census total declining from 4,458,775 in 1901 to 4,381,591 in 1911. Yet in 1851, after the six years of the potato blight and subsequent famine during which a million died and another million emigrated on the so-called coffin ships that had given the independence movement such impetus, it had stood at 6,552,385. The British government were reviled for paying £20 million in compensation to slave owners, but only £7 million in relief to a starving Ireland, while the treasury mandarin in charge of the funding opined that 'the real evil with which we have to contend is not the physical evil of the famine, but the moral evil of the selfish, perverse and turbulent character of the people'. Nationalists saw the cessation of passenger ships as an isolating tactic, and Casement spent some months negotiating with the Hamburg-Amerika Line to land in the port as a provocative symbol of the Irish link between Europe and America. He organised a march of the Volunteers to coincide with the arrival of the *Hamburg* on 6 January 1914, only to learn that the line was postponing the arrival of the first vessel, now the *Rhaetia*, for two weeks. He planned to charter a tug flying the Irish and German flags, with Bigger, Alice Green, Volunteers and students from the University of Cork aboard and a band 'to give the ship the proper welcome', but on the same day as he outlined this jamboree he heard that the Germans, sensitive to the international situation, would prefer no fuss. Two days later the message came that 'no notice whatever [should] be taken', and shortly afterwards the *Rhaetia* was cancelled altogether.

Casement was 'in despair. Sean Buide* has won!' The incident, over which the British government had taken no position, added weight to his conviction that 'no English government . . . was capable of treating Ireland with justice' if it preferred one part of its islands to another. In his mind, Cunard's original decision came to represent 'underhand diplomacy . . . unfriendly to a foreign state'; he was unable to credit any commercial imperatives for the shipping line itself as he lost sight of diplomatic nuance. He wrote three bitter articles in the *Irish Review*, under the name 'An Irish American', entitled 'From "Coffin Ship" to "Atlantic Greyhound"', equating the British shipping company's actions with the Great Famine, stressing that emigration had boosted profits. He employed accounting skills learnt from Morel to calculate that, of £63 million worth of exports from Ireland in 1910, Britain had taken £52 million; and of the £11 million worth of goods shipped to other countries, only £700,000 was shipped directly from Irish ports; the rest was handled in Britain before 'steaming back to the shores of the Ireland it had just left'. He blamed the government in general for their anti-Irish attitude and Churchill, First Lord of the Admiralty, in particular for his plans to refocus Queenstown as an imperial naval base.

Just before the Ballymoney meeting of October 1913, Casement had met an ally who had also joined the Home Rule struggle after achieving distinction elsewhere. The Anglo-Irish Erskine Childers was another Boer War veteran who had also been orphaned young. He was educated at Cambridge before continuing his establishment route

---

* John Bull.

by becoming a clerk in the House of Commons, and was on the point of election as Liberal MP for Devonport in 1912 when he left the party in the face of its likely concession to the Ulster Unionists. His ground-breaking thriller *The Riddle of the Sands* had as far back as 1903 warned of the growing strength of the German Navy and imagined the possibility of an invasion of Britain – he was a keen sailor; Winston Churchill credited the novel with bringing about the establishment of naval bases at Rosyth, Invergordon and Scapa Flow. Childers might have recognised echoes of his protagonist, Arthur Davies, when he eventually met Casement: a man who ignores physical discomfort for the sake of doing right, burning with 'a fire of pent-up patriotism struggling incessantly for an outlet . . . a humanity, born of acute sensitiveness to his own limitations, only adding fuel to the flame'. In 1911, Childers wrote *The Framework of Home Rule*; in its review the *Times Literary Supplement* described him as 'a clear thinker who deals honestly with facts and is not afraid of his own conclusions', yet whose bias meant that his book ignored 'the depth or the significance of the opposition of Ulster' and the obvious 'danger of civil war'.

Childers observed that his exhilarated new friend was 'a Nationalist of the best sort and burning with keenness' but feared he was 'unpractical'. On the same day that Casement heard about the *Rhaetia*, he wrote to Alice Green complaining that Britain 'has again locked the door & shut us off from that friendly people coming to our shores', and declared his intention to 'certainly go to USA *now* & burn all boats and compromise and raise this issue . . . We'll wreck the "Anglo-Saxon" Alliance anyhow.' He was again displaying his instinctive, emotional tendency to rush to extremes when disappointed by what he considered immorality against his cause. In past crusades, that seemingly impractical passion had propelled him into vanquishing wickedness; now he was pushing against major political currents.

The year 1913 ended badly for the government: it was discredited when some of its members profited from inside knowledge of the future plans of the Marconi wireless company; there was increasing labour unrest; and, above all, there was Ulster: Carson and the UVF had effectively taken the Home Rule question out of Parliament's hands and Redmond was in despair at the founding of the Irish Volunteers with their potential to destroy the prospect of a political solution. He was under pressure to exclude Ulster from Home Rule to avoid bloodshed; Carson threw down the challenge: 'if you want Ulster, go and take her, or go and win her. You have never wanted her affections; you have wanted her taxes.' King George V came close to political involvement when his Private Secretary called on Carson to 'express the King's hope that he would refrain from delivering a bitter speech' which would make it hard for the Prime Minister to broker a Parliamentary settlement with the Unionists. In early December the importation of arms into Ireland or their transport along the coast was banned, to the fury of nationalists; they pointed out that the UVF had been arming for a year and were now claiming enough weaponry to resist Home Rule by force. Asquith held secret meetings with Bonar Law and Carson, but announced to the Cabinet in January that Carson had 'flatly refused anything except the exclusion of Ulster' from Home Rule.

Casement spent New Year's Eve of 1914 at Bigger's house in Belfast, where the Irish Volunteers, known as Fianna after the ancient warrior bands, processed through the streets. He then rented rooms in Malahide, outside Dublin, and attempted to gain wider support: articles and letters poured from him and he attended Volunteer recruitment rallies. The Royal Irish Constabulary monitored his movements, although his thoughts on the consular service were still welcomed on his last visit to London as a free man in May.

America became key as the Home Rule movement shifted away from Parliamentary control and faced conflict with the UVF. Casement had been corresponding with John Devoy, head of the hardline sister organisation to the IRB in the United States, Clan na Gael,* and editor of its newspaper, the *Gaelic American*. Devoy was twenty years older than Casement, and was known to the Irish as 'Sean Fear', the Old Man. Born in Kildare, he had served in Algeria with the French Foreign Legion at the age of eighteen, before returning to

* Family of the Gaels.

become the Chief Organiser of Fenians in the British Army in Ireland, with a brief to enlist soldiers into the Irish Republican Brotherhood. Devoy calculated that by 1866 he had 80,000 men and was calling for an uprising, but the British moved the regiments concerned abroad and imprisoned him for treason before exiling him to the United States in 1871. He built up Clan na Gael to be the most important Irish republican organisation in America, closely aligning it with the insurrectionist IRB before the end of the century. By early 1914, he was fundraising and working to persuade Irish-Americans – of whom in 1910 there were 4.5 million either Irish-born or with an Irish parent, a number greater than the population of Ireland – to support physical force in the cause of nationalism.

Bulmer Hobson travelled to New York with a memorandum written by Casement, which Devoy described as 'an able document'. It outlined plans for close Irish–German relations in the event of war, with the promise of a manuscript to follow which Casement believed would expose the true, devastating picture of the British administration of Ireland. He characterised this manuscript, the work of a disgruntled government secret agent called Joyce and now lost, as explosive: 'the corruption is there, the shamelessness is there, the debauchery of the "public service" by the higher servants of the State is there: all for political ends against Ireland'. Casement was more than ever convinced by the Hamburg-Amerika debacle that 'it is in the U.S.A. we must hold up the hand of Ireland'; he linked the fight for independence with his earlier campaigns, in order to charge that 'if John Bull' betrayed his country again, as he was 'quite sure he means to do, then with the help of God and *some* Irishmen, he'll learn that all Irishmen are not slaves, and there is fight in us still'.

Months touring Ireland had galvanised Casement. His fame went before him, and he was received with a near-religious fervour as he spoke to packed meetings (although, as he was still publicly diffident, he was unable to manage without notes). He reported that in Limerick, where he appeared alongside Patrick Pearse, soon to become an IRB Supreme Council member, the 'faces were handsome, strong and good', and he assured these stalwart patriots that the Volunteers had no intention of disrupting the Home Rule Bill, still to him the constitutional plank. By the middle of 1914, there were 200,000 Volunteers, although Casement still believed that the Unionist position was a diplomatic challenge to which he could rise if he could only meet Carson: both men were 'honest, and sincere, and fearless', after all. But any hope of such a settlement turned out to be fantasy, as Redmond conceded in the Commons that 'a peaceful solution of common good will for this great problem must be found, or else they must see the thing through . . . For every week makes the task more difficult, and every week is adding to the fact that we in this country are becoming the laughing-stock of Europe.' This speech came on 31 March, ten days after the so-called Curragh Mutiny, in which sixty officers of the British Army at their base outside Dublin threatened to resign rather than go to Ulster to coerce Unionists to accept Home Rule by force, a profound embarrassment to Asquith's government. Casement and MacNeill wrote a joint letter to the *Irish Independent* to claim that the 'mutiny' indicated that 'the Curragh military junta', to which the British administration in Dublin Castle was 'a sort of vermiform appendix', was dictating 'the policy and future of Irish government'. Casement threw off his last vestiges of loyalty to Britain and any remnant of diplomatic caution when he concluded that 'Liberalism . . . will not and cannot free Ireland from British military domination . . . Nothing should take place to cloak the naked truth until the Irish people fully realise the duty imposed upon their honour and their patriotism.'

If the threats of conflict from the UVF were anything other than a 'gigantic game of bluff and blackmail', as Redmond reckoned, both sides would need arming. Major Frederick Crawford of the Ulster Unionist Council had made various attempts to get weapons into Ulster from Germany or England but was thwarted by patrol boats and the Hammersmith police until he rented the SS *Fanny* in Hamburg in March 1914 to import 19,000 guns and 5 million rounds of ammunition. As the *Fanny* neared Ireland, the cargo was transferred to the newly acquired *Clyde Valley*, which evaded the Royal Navy to land in Larne on 24 April, from where the shipment was moved to arms dumps around Ulster in a well-planned road operation. When war was declared in Europe, the government requisitioned these caches but none of the rifles was handed over, and they continued to appear up to the 1970s. Carson had backed Crawford 'through this business, if I should have to go to prison for it'; less than a year later, he was Attorney General, before finishing his career as Conservative Leader of the Opposition.

The Irish Volunteers had been parading with wooden guns and whatever shotguns and rifles they owned. At the least a show was needed to prevent the Ulster Protestants wrecking their goals, and only by possessing arms could the Volunteers seize the agenda after Redmond had splintered the movement by his demand that the Provisional Committee of the Volunteers contain twenty-five representatives of the Irish Parliamentary Party. It was, in effect, a takeover of the public face of the movement, but Hobson was forced to agree even as it looked as if the Ulster cause would be lost. The twenty-five Redmondites were middle-aged and uncommitted compared to the young zealots they replaced, further angering the hardliners. Casement resigned his seat with bitter frustration as he felt 'The country *is* being sold – for place and posts and profit – into the hands of the English.' He was clear that Redmond and his supporters 'do not want Irish freedom – they want merely majority rule, i.e. Catholic rule'. If this came about, 'England will more and more strangle Ireland & emasculate the minds of the people'.

Roger Casement, Eoin MacNeill and Darrell Figgis travelled to London and to the critical meeting on that grey afternoon in Alice Stopford Green's room overlooking the coal barges, the one in which she had held her intellectually sparkling salons. They agreed that illegal arms were needed to persuade the Republican Brotherhood that the 'existence of an armed force . . . would bring the practical control into their hands'. Another, unarguably illegal, line being crossed towards conflict brought on Casement's 'apparent dejection', as noted by Figgis. O'Neill was under suspicion and his mail was being intercepted, but Figgis was unknown to the police, so he undertook to travel to the continent to secure the weapons.

The nationalists were short of funds, 'lean and naked' where Carson was 'clad in soft raiment'. They raised £1,523 19s 6d, a proportion of which came from Alice Stopford Green's royalties from her husband's bestseller, and Figgis arranged for a Hamburg firm to send him two samples of rifles, 'one of an ancient pattern, the other of a pattern downright antique', but they would also need money to charter a ship. The daughter of an Irish peer, Mary Spring Rice, suggested her father's fishing smack, but as the boat was in a creek near a police barracks, its disappearance might be obvious. Erskine Childers, whose Bostonian wife Molly had been a prominent subscriber to the fund, offered Casement his forty-four-foot, Norwegian-built yacht *Asgard*, lying in Criccieth, North Wales. The vessel was modelled on Nansen's Arctic exploration ship and was seaworthy in all conditions. When Casement passed on this news, Figgis was initially sceptical that 'an Englishman should desire to bear these risks in our service', but soon came to see that Childers's standing and contacts with the Liberal Party 'were safeguards not to be thrown lightly aside'. In early May, Casement introduced the pair to the agent of an arms dealer he knew in the City, following which Childers and Figgis set off for Northern Europe. There was initial resistance in Hamburg, where the dealers were nervous of being seen to jeopardise the fragile peace between Britain and Germany; but a pretence of being Mexicans arming for revolution enabled proprieties to be observed and they were soon making arrangements with an Antwerp shipping house to transport a paltry 1,500 rifles and 45,000 rounds of ammunition in crates labelled 'machine parts' to rendezvous with the *Asgard* and the intellectual aristocrat Conor O'Brien's *Kelpie* in the English Channel.

The *Asgard*'s crew consisted of Childers, Molly, Gordon Shephard, who later became the youngest brigadier in the Royal Flying Corps, and two Donegal fishermen who sailed in ignorance of their mission. In mid-July, the yacht rendezvoused with a tug in the fog off the white cliffs of Dover and until the early hours a precarious human chain loaded 900 guns packed in straw and wrapped in canvas; it was too great a load for the *Asgard*, and some ammunition was jettisoned. After being nearly run down by a destroyer off Plymouth, they made for Dublin. They managed to avoid the naval cordon put in place by that 'bumptious ass' Churchill, and coastguards who questioned them seemed satisfied with their shouted answers, but a vicious storm nevertheless forced their return to the Welsh coast.

The Irish Volunteers diverted the attention of the authorities during these delays by marching in their overcoats and flat caps with rifles on their shoulders; they were parading in Howth on Dublin Bay as Molly steered the yacht into harbour at midday on 27 July. The telephone lines had been cut, so the coastguards who saw hundreds of armed men could not summon help, and within an hour the *Asgard* had been unloaded. The new weapons were on their way to their hiding places under floorboards and in roof spaces by taxi and bicycle. By the end of the day, Erskine and Molly Childers were sailing back to England.

Government minds were on weightier matters than Irish gunrunning that day: Germany and Austria-Hungary were warned that Britain would side with Russia and France in the event of war; a week later Casement's supporter Sir Edward Grey was proclaiming, 'The lamps are going out all over Europe; we shall not see them lit again in our life-time.' By then, one of the chief architects of the arms shipment had left Europe. Casement's intensive, country-wide recruitment drive for the Volunteers that last peacetime summer, in which he preached 'nationalism against imperialism' so hard that he did not have time to repair his shoes, left him exhausted, barely sleeping, eating little and 'writing all day with nervous agitation . . . an extremely suffering and burdened man', as observed by Alice Green.

Casement had made his last public speech in Ireland a few days after the shot that killed Archduke Ferdinand in Sarajevo made war inevitable. He concluded two years of hectic activity as, escorted by a piper, he stood on the cairn at Cushendun dedicated to Shane O'Neill, one of the heroes of the resistance to Elizabeth I, and 'harangued in a cracked voice' an audience of Antrim Volunteers about O'Neill's life, diplomatic skills, courage and desire for peace. Nine months after the foundation of the Volunteers, his focus on these traits fully acknowledged that if Ireland was to break away from the greatest empire the world had ever seen, it would need financial and military backing from overseas. The supporter of the Gaelic League, of the Feis, of traditional Irish crafts, and the advocate for cheques being written in Irish was now taking his next irrevocable step – becoming an international, militaristic, fundraising political agent.

The following day, 4 July 1914, he embarked on the ominously named SS *Cassandra* in Glasgow for the twelve-day journey to Montreal. The only people who knew he was travelling were 'Mrs G – vaguely and not precisely – Bulmer Hobson (precisely), F. J. Bigger (precisely) and possibly Erskine Childers', who was then at sea with the rifles. His last letter from Mrs Green had been addressed to 'My good champion of Ireland . . . my dearest friend'. She said that she was 'broken-hearted' at the way events were going, aggravated by his 'illness and overwhelming sorrow'.

On his arrival in North America, Casement used a degree of self-bolstering hindsight to ruminate on his career so far. All his courage and his triumphs had been a preparation for this moment:

> Some day I may try to write the story of the Congo, and how I found Leopold; of the Putumayo, and that abominable London Company, and of the 'inordinate wild Irishman' who went out on both quests in the garb of a British official, with the soul of an Irish felon. If the English had only known the thoughts in my heart and the impulses I obeyed when I did the things I took pride in . . . I wonder would their press have praised my 'heroism' and 'chivalry' or . . . have referred to me . . . as 'one of the finest figures in *our* Imperial history'?

There was no going back after the last two heated years. He was to spend only one more night in the country of his birth.

8. Circle of Treachery

Sir Roger Casement mused on the fate of the Native Americans as the train to New York jolted along the edge of Lake Champlain on 18 July 1914. Generalising about 'the savage' and 'the white man', he suggested that the former 'lives and moves to be, the other toils and dies to have'. The 'savage' was happier, he had '*life* – your white destroyers only possess *things*'. The 'civilised man' made the 'greater world'. Casement rarely mentioned the dispossessed now without equating them with the Irish, but his analysis was more aligned with the contemporary hierarchy of thought about indigenous peoples: he was not witnessing genocidal abuses towards 'savages' as his mind dwelt on the 'civilised man' then mobilising in Europe.

He was unaware that John Devoy wished to cancel their meeting in his rage at the capitulation to Redmond over the Volunteers Committee, the postponement of Home Rule and the enrolment of Irish soldiers into a pointless war: 'all that gang' were 'real liars and rascals & the debauchery of the Irish mind by this atrocious imperial appeal will have fatal results', as Devoy told Alice Green, who had complained that the war 'will do nothing good for our cause, it may ruin it'.

Casement stayed in the Belmont Hotel next to Grand Central Station; he was pleased to find that many of the staff were Irish, some with 'the brogue still lingering round the shores of that broad estuary of smiles' and with an anti-British mindset. As the day cooled, he strolled along Broadway to rediscover some of the sights he remembered from nearly half his lifetime ago in 1890, when he had been a little-known Congo hand accompanying Herbert Ward on his lecture tour.

He had not gone far when he was accosted by a burly, blond young man with 'grey eyes very small and close together', a gap between his front teeth and a 'fleshy, dissipated appearance', in the disdainful words of a British diplomat. Eivind Adler Christensen was a twenty-four-year-old from Moss, Norway, who had left home at the age of twelve to stow away in an English collier before becoming a foreman on Norwegian steamers. He may have been selling his favours and did not necessarily confess that he had lodgings on 38th Street as well as a wife, Sadie, and a young son in Philadelphia as he explained that he was 'out of work, starving almost and homeless'. According to Christensen's account, Casement, always generous to those in distress and presumably attracted to his importuner, asked him to call at his hotel the next morning, when he hired him as a manservant. It was the start of the most intense, fulfilling, treacherous and occasionally farcical relationship of his life.

Casement called at the cluttered downtown offices of Devoy's *Gaelic American*. The newspaper, which had been founded in 1903, differed from many other weeklies in that rather than aiming to turn Irish immigrants into better Americans, it ran thoughtful articles on European politics and from countries where British rule and influence held sway, targeted at the educated, literate leaders of Irish America. Although Devoy had thought well of Casement's work in recent months, the Clan na Gael chief did not hold back: the chances of raising money in the US were poor following Redmond's manoeuvres, which included a speech in Wicklow maintaining that it was a Volunteer's duty to enlist in the British Army. The Irish Party was a failed political force: Devoy was adamant that Redmond had 'lost the faith of all the Irish here – they spit his name out of their mouths'. Casement reined in his emotions to 'listen attentively' before putting forward his case; Devoy had little time for romantics preaching nationalism, so was struck by his visitor's 'calm and friendly manner' as Casement 'undertook to persuade me that I was mistaken' and that the '*only* thought influencing Hobson' to agree to the new make-up of the committee was 'to save the Volunteers from disruption and Ireland from a disgraceful faction fight, in which all original issues would have gone by the board'. Devoy and his colleagues were impressed by the 'sincerity of the man', although Devoy privately considered that his visitor was both 'highly intellectual' and 'very emotional and trustful as a child' – to his mind not an ideal combination for a rebel.

He took Casement to lunch at Mouquin's, a fashionable artists' hang-out, and gave him introductions to two men essential to American support for the Irish cause: Bourke Cockran, an Irish-American politician, friend of and rhetorical inspiration for Winston Churchill; and John Quinn, a successful lawyer, art collector, champion of modernism, adviser to the poets T. S. Eliot and Ezra Pound, backer of *Ulysses*, and virulent anti-Semite. Quinn allowed Casement the use of his huge penthouse apartment at 58 Central Park West, which was bursting with books and 'the strange new pictures of the School of Paris'. Casement was not a great reader, but might have appreciated knowing that Yeats and Conrad were frequent guests.

Despite Quinn's warning that he should not fall prey to Devoy's 'especial bug . . . that England has paid spies all over the place', Casement detected surveillance everywhere, even believing that his mail was opened by British intelligence, which had little interest in him at that stage. After two days in Manhattan, he travelled to Pennsylvania to meet Joe McGarrity, who was to become his closest Irish-American friend. In 1892, aged sixteen, McGarrity had walked from his home in Tyrone to Dublin, before catching a cattle boat to Liverpool and stealing a ticket to America. The brawler and civil rights activist made one more fortune than he lost in the liquor and real-estate businesses in Pennsylvania, and was to emerge as Éamon de Valera's right-hand man in the US, the first to declare him President of the Irish Republic in 1919. McGarrity urged Casement to go to Norfolk, Virginia, to address the national convention of the Ancient Order of Hibernians as the representative of the Irish Volunteers. At the convention, Casement was 'cheered repeatedly' when he said he was a Protestant, and he concluded that the American Irish were 'mad for a Protestant leader'.

All the while there was an undertow of anxiety about his gun-running operation. Alice Green cabled that 'our friends are on the sea', and on the evening of the expected day of delivery, Casement and McGarrity lay on the grass in front of the latter's Philadelphia house; it was hot and they had their watches in their hands as they waited for the telegram that would tell of success or disaster. At nine o'clock an informant on a local newspaper rang the house to announce the worst – that the rifles had been seized by British troops and several Volunteers killed. McGarrity rushed to the Hibernia Club for confirmation, only to find that he had been misinformed. The confusion had arisen because, as the Volunteers marched back into Dublin, there had been a brief scuffle with a contingent of the King's Own Scottish Borderers. The Volunteers broke away across the fields, but, lacking orders, the flustered soldiers fired into a crowd of civilians at Bachelor's Walk, alongside the Liffey at O'Connell Bridge, killing three and wounding others. 'Remember Bachelor's Walk' became a rebel cry and an instant propaganda coup that resulted in $5,000 of donations in the US alone the following day, more when O'Brien's yacht unloaded at Kilcoole, County Wicklow, the next week. Casement wrote in triumph to Alice Green (addressing her as 'Dear Woman of the Ships' and signing himself 'The Fugitive Knight'), recounting that he had been 'in anguish first – then filled with joy – and now with resolute pride in you all. We have done what we set out to do! And done it well.' 'Old J.D.' was also 'in a glow of joy', calling the operation 'the greatest deed done in Ireland for 100 years'. No matter that the rifles were barely adequate compared to those of the UVF: 'May this bring a new day to Ireland . . . new hope, new courage on the old, old manhood.'

Reporters from the evening papers clamoured for interviews with Casement about Bachelor's Walk; he put the 'murder of women and children' 'fair and square on the shoulders of Mr Asquith'. A protest meeting was set up for 2 August in Philadelphia at which he was to be the chief speaker. It began with a spectacular piece of theatre, 'a triple funeral with hearses, coffins and mourners but no corpses' as the *Gaelic American* reported, followed by over a thousand marching men, many wearing the new green uniform of the Irish Volunteers, its tunic buttons embossed with a harp. Casement and Devoy were in an open car, although Casement tried to turn away when they were photographed: he lamented that the picture might damage his chances of 'escaping detection by the English' if he wanted to go on a 'mission unknown to them'. He realised that the events of the week meant that 'whether I liked it or not, I was now in for it up to the neck'.

He publicly aligned himself with the armed insurrectionists to claim that the Irish-Americans 'are sick of talk & Parliamentarianism & will give their strength and hearts only to some leader who will fight'. He preached unity, looking forward to the day 'when all Irishmen will march under one banner', and was told on all sides, 'You are the man we want.' But even as he was carried along by the acclaim at this highest point of his campaign, the imminent declaration of what he termed 'the War of Devils' was squeezing him out.

It had become clear over the summer that the Ulster Unionists would set up a provisional government if the Home Rule Bill was implemented, but on 30 July James Craig, now Unionist leader in the Commons, suggested that Home Rule be set aside for the duration of the crisis to avoid internal strife; he hardly needed to add that the UVF would help the British 'see the matter [of the war] through'. To Unionist surprise, Redmond, without pause for consultation with nationalist leaders, replied, 'If it is offered to us, in comradeship with our brothers in the North we will ourselves defend the shores of Ireland.' He calculated that a united victory in what would be a short war should bind the two sets of Volunteers, leaving the nationalists in good odour and so helping Home Rule to apply to all of Ireland in the peace. The Secretary of State for War Lord Kitchener founded the 16th (Irish) Division in September, and the Ulstermen signed up in large numbers while the Irish Volunteers began to split between those who wished to continue the struggle at home and those who joined up for patriotic or economic reasons.

Casement's dreams evaporated as loyalty to the United Kingdom government became an option for his former supporters. He was 'raging, like a caged animal' at 'Redmond's treachery, and the deplorable state of things in Ireland'. He was enraged anew when the Home Rule Bill was passed and immediately suspended on 18 September, 'in the openly avowed hope of entrapping thousands of young Irishmen into the British army, on the grounds that England had at length granted "national freedom" to Ireland'.

On 4 August, Germany declared war on Great Britain, which

joined with Russia and France in the Triple Entente. Meanwhile Casement met the former President Theodore Roosevelt to explain the situation in Ireland. Roosevelt was a supporter of Home Rule, but turned out only to care what America could get out of that support. Two fundraisers in Baltimore and Buffalo followed, but by the end of the month Devoy was dejectedly noting 'the almost universal approval of John [Redmond]'s pledge' among Irish-Americans. He had hoped Casement's presence would raise $50,000, but the total was more like $7,000, nearly all from the days following Bachelor's Walk. With Home Rule suspended and Ireland committing to war, the Supreme Council of the Irish Republican Brotherhood broke with the Home Rulers to pass the seismic resolution that there must be an Irish insurrection before the end of hostilities. The following year a satirical song went the revolutionary rounds:

> Full steam ahead John Redmond said
>   That everything was well, chum,
>   Home Rule will come when we are dead
>   And buried out in Belgium.

Casement, for whom Belgium had been abhorrent since his Congo experiences, was doubly furious at the way the invasion of that country was used as a pretext for war. One of the few options open to him was to appeal to his enemy's enemy.

Casement had championed Germany back in his Pará and Rio days, and in the journalism of 'The Elsewhere Empire' and 'Ireland, Germany and the Next War'. When the artist John Butler Yeats, father of the poet, visited him in Park Avenue after the German defeat on the Marne in the second week of September, he found Casement, 'afraid of no one . . . and the soul of honour . . . a very fine gentleman . . . a prince of courtesy', lamenting ' "Poor Kaiser. Poor Kaiser," almost with tears in his voice.' Yeats likened him to 'a very nice girl who is just hysterical enough to be charming and interesting among strangers and a trial to his [sic] own friends'. The next week, the day before the Home Rule Bill was suspended, Casement took the step that could not be ignored.

Up to that point, the establishment saw him as an asset that could be used to advantage: a letter had been sent by Lord Aldenham, Chairman of the Patriotic League of Britons Overseas, asking him to join the many titled members of its committee to help mobilise the 'three million British subjects in the USA' to form 'a fighting unit' as part of the 'armed forces of the Crown'. Casement noted in the margin that the 3 million were 'mostly Irish!' and did not bother to reply. His 'Open Letter to Irishmen', published the following month in the *Irish Independent*, got a more threatening reaction: he stated that no Irishman should join the British Army because the country had suffered at the hands of 'British administrators' more than 'any other community of civilised men'. Ultimately, 'Ireland has no blood to give to any land, to any cause but that of Ireland.' Home Rule was 'being offered on terms that only a fool would accept' and it was the duty of his countrymen 'to save their strength and manhood . . . to build up from a depleted population the fabric of a ruined national life'. As Ireland had been left by Britain with only half its population and no commerce, it had no stake in the destruction of the German Navy. Some three weeks after this broadside, Sir Arthur Nicolson, Permanent Under-Secretary at the Foreign Office, reminded him that since he was 'still liable, in certain circumstances, to be called upon to serve under the Crown', he needed to confirm that he was the author of the piece.

Casement did not receive Nicolson's letter until he was well beyond any possibility of loyalty and in no doubt that he was a marked man. When it eventually caught up with him, he reacted exaggeratedly, as so often at moments of discovery and change, to propose that his erstwhile supporter 'Sir E. Grey should be hanged' alongside the King and all others who had committed the country to war. By mid-October, he had grown even more passionate in attacks fuelled by his lonely desperation: he railed against Grey as a 'wicked, stupid, obstinate fool', one of the worst of the 'gang of unscrupulous anti-Germans', a category that included Sir William Tyrrell, Grey's Private Secretary, who had made such efforts to ensure Casement was well treated in the 1900s. Grey was dithering over whether to stop Casement's pension when a Parliamentary question on the subject made the decision easy. The last of the ties to Casement's ground-breaking, life-changing official career was now severed. He was on his way to becoming little better than an outlaw.

If August had started with the high point of the Philadelphia rally, by the end of the month Casement was rudderless. He drafted a letter to the Kaiser, to be sent 'by a special Imperial messenger' from the German embassy, which he hoped would be signed by the Irish-American leaders, expressing 'sympathy and admiration for the heroic people of Germany' who 'did not seek this war' but had it 'forced upon her by those jealous of her military security, envious of her industrial and commercial capacity and aiming at her integrity as a great World power'. It pleaded for the Emperor to recognise the importance of Ireland to Britain's seafaring capabilities and ensure its post-war independence. The letter was approved by Clan na Gael, although Quinn, a dedicated Francophile who loathed Germany, refused to sign. There is no record of whether the Kaiser received or read it.

In the discomfort of his failing mission, Casement started to lash out against his hosts: they were 'ignorant and unthinking', credulous of their 'rotten papers', materialistic and self-obsessed. He told a group of Irish-Americans in New York that he had 'tumbled into a party of English Liberals' and that if they were 'not good enough Irishmen to help arm' their countrymen he would 'go to Germany and get arms there'. In October 1914, he told friends (possibly to throw off any spies reading his mail) that he was expecting to end his days as an editor in America; but he was already committed to another course – by that stage he could regain his equilibrium only when he had a plan, and hope.

He began collecting his essays under the title *The Crime against Ireland and How the War May Right It*. In one of his last letters, he would claim that the collection 'was the foundation and inspiration of the [Irish] Rising'. But in practice he could change little and, once involved in a campaign, inaction was anathema to him. He apologised to Quinn for his 'cranky letter' to the *Irish Independent*, and suggested to Devoy that he go to Berlin to act as the movement's lobbyist in the capital of England's enemy before returning to Ireland to use his skills to keep 'some of the poor boys from this abominable sacrifice of Irish manhood to English mammon'.

In response to this purposeful prose, Devoy introduced Casement to Count Johann Heinrich von Bernstorff, the German Ambassador, and his Military Attaché, Franz von Papen, at Manhattan's German Club. Papen had been trying to ship weapons from North America to Germany, but had been thwarted by the British naval blockade; he was currently plotting industrial sabotage in America alongside a possible invasion of Canada. The future Chancellor was an ideal conspirator-comrade for the Clan members: even before he read Casement's 'How Ireland Might Help Germany and How Germany Might Help Ireland', it might already have crossed his mind that an effective subversion of British attention and military effort would be to offer men and arms to Ireland. He was so struck by Casement's certainty that he mischaracterised him in his despatch as 'the leader of all Irish associations in America'.

Papen's support enabled Devoy to overcome his strategic misgivings in order to sanction the trip and pay $1,000 for expenses; Bernstorff wrote an introduction to the Imperial Chancellor, Theobald von Bethmann Hollweg. A Clan member with a passable resemblance to a clean-shaven Casement, James E. Landy of Orange County, New York, gave up his passport and coached him in the nature and concerns of his business; and cards were printed in that name with Quinn's office address in Nassau Street. An official in the Austrian consulate bought a first-class ticket on the Norwegian steamship *Oskar II*, and Casement persuaded Devoy that a second-class berth should be acquired for the seeming fixture Adler Christensen, ostensibly to visit his parents after twelve years away. Devoy mistrusted Christensen: he might have grasped the nature of their relationship, or felt that Casement seemed to be impervious to any suspicion, but he could see the advantages in having the supposed manservant along as guard and interpreter.

The man who had been a near stranger to underhandedness and who always wore his emotions on the outside now emerged as a subtle deceiver. On 15 October, he checked into a Manhattan hotel as

R. Smythe of London, laying a false trail by telegraphing ahead to reserve a room at the La Salle Hotel, Chicago. Two days later, he sent Devoy an emotional 'farewell word and grip of the heart', praising his 'life of unceasing devotion to the most unselfish cause on earth' and ending with the hope that they would meet in a free Ireland. After he had settled his bill and engaged the hotel clerk in talk about his Chicago plans, Casement shaved off his beard, washed his face in buttermilk to lighten his complexion and used the back stairs to exit into a side street en route to joining the *Oskar II* as a visitor to the real James Landy. Christensen had already taken his few suitcases aboard and Landy disembarked just before the ship sailed, leaving his documents behind. As they cast off from their berth on Manhattan's west side, Casement threw his diaries of the last few months into the Atlantic.

The single-funnelled *Oskar II* was stopping at Christiania (known as Oslo from 1925) before her arrival in Copenhagen. Although Norway and Denmark were neutral, Northern Europe had been undergoing unheralded turmoil since Casement's departure three months before. Belgium had been overrun with the help of the new German fleet of Zeppelins dropping bombs on civilians and the massive howitzers nicknamed Big Bertha; Austria-Hungary had been defeated at the Battle of Cer by Serbian troops in the third week of August, the first Triple Entente victory, leaving Germany to conclude that it was 'shackled to a corpse'; by the end of the month General Paul von Hindenburg had rebalanced the tally by routing the Russian Second Army at the Battle of Tannenberg. Sir John French had wanted to withdraw his British Expeditionary Force after the unexpected French retreat led to defeat at Mons, but was overruled by Kitchener. After further losses in the Ardennes and at Charleroi, the Entente armies regrouped to fight the First Battle of the Marne, which resulted in shocking casualty figures – a quarter of its 2 million combatants – but halted the German advance twenty-five miles short of Paris. Germany's target of victory within six weeks disappeared and Bethmann Hollweg temporarily shelved his *Septemberprogramm* setting out Germany's goals in the war, which included the destruction of Britain's hegemony in world affairs, the foundation of one huge German colony across Africa called *Mittelafrika*, and a *Mitteleuropa* economic association of France, Belgium, the Netherlands and Austria-Hungary (plus possibly Italy, Sweden and Norway) dominated by Germany. The armies were now digging in on the Western Front in North-Eastern France and into Belgium, preparing for the grinding attrition of trench warfare, which was to continue over the next four years: the First Battle of Ypres began on 19 October 1914; the Fifth ended on 2 October 1918.

Bernstorff had warned Berlin of Casement's arrival, unaware that his transmissions were being intercepted by the British: a team of secret servicemen disguised as fishermen had cut the undersea cables between Germany and America on 5 August, meaning that all messages had to be sent by interceptable wireless. With great good luck, MO5(g) – as the War Office named the Counter-Espionage or Special Intelligence arm of the nascent Security Service – received a codebook captured by the Australian Navy from a German ship on 11 August; on 6 September, the Russians found a second codebook on a battleship and on 30 November a third was located by a British trawler. By the end of October, at least one of the German codes had been cracked and Room 40 in the Admiralty had been set aside for cryptanalysis under the command of the benign-featured new Director of Naval Intelligence, Captain (later Admiral Sir) Reginald 'Blinker' Hall, so nicknamed because of a twitch which caused one eye to blink like a navy signals lamp. Hall was a gifted interrogator and subtle agent runner who regarded co-operation between the intelligence services and Scotland Yard's Special Branch as essential; he soon became a key player in Casement's war and its aftermath.

Eleven days after departure, with the *Oskar II* lying off Christiansand, Casement clumsily dissembled as he described his journey in a letter to Nina. He posed as a woman who had had her hair done before boarding at the request of 'that dear good cousin Jimmie', Landy, who had helped him aboard; 'even father and mother would not have recognised their own child'. He was seated at the table of the Austrian Ambassador, but everyone seemed 'afraid to speak their mind' and they were further disappointed when the crew of the SS

Lancaster, rather than passing close to them, went to help a ship that was sinking after a collision just out of New York: all her fellow Americans wanted to see 'those nice Britishers we've been reading about so much'.

Five days out, he noticed that the ship was changing course and the 'dear kind Captain, such a nice Dane with a beard just like cousin Roger's', announced that he was heading for the Faroe Islands to avoid British cruisers around Shetland and Orkney, but the *Oskar II* was halted when HMS *Hibernia* fired a shot across her bows. A month earlier, the sea war had come to Scotland when HMS *Pathfinder* was the first ship to be torpedoed, in the Firth of Forth by the submarine *U-21*, and the Royal Navy was on the alert for Germans aboard neutral ships. The *Oskar II* was boarded by marines and diverted to Stornoway in the Western Isles to await orders from, as Casement put it, 'the London week-enders' in the War Office. 'Landy' had explained away his British accent by pretending he had been schooled in Europe, but 'there was a regular spy fever on board' and his fellow passengers jested that he was 'a British spy to betray the poor fellows who had false passports on board', while his Norwegian servant must be spying on the second-class passengers. Casement inwardly 'split his sides'.

Nevertheless, at the first sight of the *Hibernia*, he had gone to his cabin with his 'maid' who 'stowed all the old hair pins'. After two days of searching and interrogation, a British officer took away six German nationals – two stowaways, two crew members, the second cook and the chief bandmaster, who to Casement's outrage had 'Danish papers of a sort'. Before the *Oskar II* was allowed to steam on, Casement, true to form, extracted a promise from the arresting officer that the men would be well treated until the war was over and got up a collection for the prisoners which raised $65. The letter to Nina was no place to express his relief at the completion of the first part of his mission – although his sense of security on European soil had only a day to run.

At 2 a.m. on 29 October 1914 Casement and Christensen took neighbouring rooms at Christiania's Grand Hotel. Later that morning,

Christensen was sent to wire James Landy news of their arrival while Casement bought a few necessities and strode to the German legation with Bernstorff's request that he be furnished with 'facilities to enter Germany'. As he walked the streets he was convinced he was being shadowed. Despite remaining undiscovered during the search of the *Oskar II* in Stornoway, the reality of his move into treachery was ramping up his fears. His papers would not be ready for twenty-four hours, so after his return to the hotel around lunchtime he lay low, writing letters in his room. He despatched Christensen to complete the purchases for the next leg of the journey.

Christensen was instructed to return by 5.30 but rushed in earlier 'in some excitement' to confirm that Casement was being spied upon 'by the British authorities'. He recounted how he had been crossing the hotel lobby when 'a strange man accosted him in good English' to suggest they 'take a stroll together'. Even though 'his suspicions were aroused', Christensen agreed; in his own account he did not seem alarmed when his new acquaintance summoned 'a large touring car, with a chauffeur in private livery' who was instructed to take them to 79 Drammensveien, a large house standing in substantial gardens. 'The conductor' went to a room off a capacious hall, and a short man with greying black hair emerged to ask Christensen to come upstairs; 'the conductor' now seemed more like a 'man servant', behaving towards the 'short gentleman with great deference'.

In Christensen's breathless report, the door of the upstairs room was locked behind them, and he was interrogated about the voyage from America and about 'a tall, dark gentleman, an Englishman', on board. He said he 'knew no Englishman, but only an American gentleman whom he had known slightly in New York'. His interlocutor quizzed him about his finances, asking him if he had 'done well in America', followed by a repeated request for the 'tall dark gentleman's name and address'. Christensen stonewalled a bit longer, the interview terminated with his refusal to leave his contact details, and he returned to the Grand.

A glance at the telephone directory told Casement that 79 Drammensveien was the address of the British legation. He dashed off a panicked note to Count von Oberndorff, the German Minister, insisting that his travel documents be expedited for that evening. Christensen was instructed to 'take every precaution' against being followed as he took the letter, and on his return he gave an elaborate description of his tradecraft in changing trams three times just before the doors shut to throw off any watchers. Casement was told to be at the side door of the German consulate at 7.00 that evening, and the two men came up with a deft manoeuvre: they set off together in a taxi, Casement jumped out as it turned into a side street and Christensen drew after him the pursuing 'man servant' from earlier in the day.

Oberndorff had not heard from Berlin. Casement urged him to action, as usual putting his mission above his personal safety when he claimed that he 'did not regard the danger' to himself as of any consequence but was aware of what might happen to the cause he represented if they 'succeeded in kidnapping or waylaying' him while he was using false papers. The Count promised to summon him as soon as there was any news. On Casement's return to the Grand, Christensen announced that it was surrounded. He had been accosted in the restaurant by a man who offered him two bottles of beer and declared that 'English gold had never been quoted at such a high rate of exchange as now'. This unsubtle bribe decided the panicking Casement: they would hire a car and drive the eighty miles to Sweden. But as Casement was pacing his room at midnight, Oberndorff's messenger arrived to 'reassure' him that he would be departing late on the following afternoon.

That day of drama, paranoia and impending catastrophe had been engineered by Christensen, whose fabrications and betrayal were to colour the ensuing year. Yet the Norwegian would continue to be believed and forgiven by the romantic who had finally found someone he could trust, even love; suspicion was not a trait of the passionate, emotionally untutored man. In an environment in which he was anyway leading a distasteful life of subterfuge – without his levelling confidantes Gertrude Bannister and Alice Stopford Green – it was easier for him to suspend all suspicion, not to ask questions about why Christensen had agreed to board a luxurious car instead of 'taking a stroll', or why he was asked for his contact details by the British when they knew where he was staying, or why as a servant he had been in the hotel dining room at a time when the place was under surveillance.

Francis Lindley, a junior official at the British legation, was sending a 'Most Private and Secret' telegram under cypher for the personal attention of Sir Edward Grey just when the two travellers were executing their taxi manoeuvres. It told of 'a young Norwegian . . . with a strong American accent' who had called in at the legation and demanded to talk to the Minister; he 'finally consented' to see Lindley instead. The visitor had arrived by ship 'in the company of a highly placed Englishman, a nobleman who had been decorated by King Edward', travelling on a false passport. Christensen did not conceal the fact that his 'relations with this Englishman were of an improper character', as if to give away that illegal confidence would boost the credibility of the rest of his treacherous evidence.

This was that 'the Englishman was there because of letters from the German Embassy in Washington to Berlin' and that he, Christensen, had been entrusted with these letters as 'the Englishman was afraid of being searched'. Christensen might have stolen the papers that morning; or Casement's reference to his 'maid' stowing 'the hair pins' on the *Oskar II* might be decoded as his entrusting them to his companion. Either way, Lindley could see that 'the informant had steamed them open before returning them and made pencil copies'. They were addressed to the German legations in Christiania and Copenhagen and to the 'Reichskanzler' in person; Lindley noted that the English used in the letters was 'natural' and all the complexities of German styles of address and titles were correct, so assumed they were genuine. Christensen confided that 'the Englishman was going to Germany about trouble in Ireland'; Lindley was puzzled about his 'very anxious' informant's motives, as he 'did not state why he gave me this information and did not ask for money'; maybe the lack of venality was what convinced him that the 'story was true', although Christensen's fabrication that evening about the hotel agent's remarking on the value of gold implies a pecuniary motivation for his betrayal. The financially unworldly Casement would not have known that gold was not hitting any particular peaks just then.

Casement noticed a 'night watcher' outside the Grand at dawn. At around 7.00 Herr Hilmers from the German legation delivered a message that Count von Oberndorff would call at noon with the details of their departure, and Christensen was sent down at around 9.00 to 'walk about and keep his eyes open'. He came back near midday 'in state of great excitement [and] threw down some paper money (25 Kronen)', which he had been given in the Legation in exchange for 'absolutely incredible . . . proposals'. Casement was convinced by Christensen's 'anger and resentment' – after all, he had trusted him enough to give him the papers for safekeeping at Stornoway, as he had done with some gold coins from the IRB in New York; he was sure of Christensen's 'fidelity to and affection for' him in return. Christensen had once again injected the maximum drama into his tale to shock his master's credulity: this time he had been 'brushed against' by a stranger in the hotel lobby, and told to ring 11460 from the telephone booth in the hall. A voice told him to take a taxi to 79 Drammensveien and then hung up. He had even noted down the taxi's licence number.

On arrival at the legation, Christensen met 'a very tall man, clean shaven except for a short, greyish moustache, with his hair brushed back straight, and dressed in a tweed suit'. Mansfeldt de Cardonnel Findlay, by some inches the tallest figure in the diplomatic corps, locked the door and announced himself as the British Minister. He knew who Christensen was, and whom he was travelling with. Christensen handed over the cable to 'Cousin Jimmie', which was soon on its way to London for a handwriting comparison. The Minister then apparently pointed out that Casement was 'going to be fooled by the Germans; they don't care anything about Ireland and only want to make trouble for England'. If this was a fabrication by Christensen, it was an accurate one. According to Christensen, Findlay rounded off the meeting by surmising that he was 'a necessary ruffian who would carry out his wishes for a suitable reward'. Christensen retorted that

Casement had been good to him; Findlay countered by pointing out that as nobody knew Casement was in Norway he could be discreetly murdered; if Christensen were the person who 'knocked him on the head', he would be paid enough to have 'an easy time all the rest of your life'. He handed over the twenty-five kroner* 'for taxi fares' and requested another meeting at 3.00 the same day.

It was altogether a cunningly improvised set-up that flattered, enraged and frightened Casement, cut off as he was from his Irish and American support and moving into the most dangerous waters of his life. It also deviated from the Foreign Office telegram sent that second day under cypher to Whitehall in almost every detail. In Findlay's 'Most Secret' account, Christensen had travelled to the legation to present 'more papers written by his English friend'. Findlay qualified the last two words by adding, 'with whom he evidently has unnatural relations', although this was crossed out before the telegram was enciphered. 'The principal idea' Findlay took from a confused glance at the papers was that the 'invasion of England by Germany . . . was an impracticable or at any rate almost desperate enterprise', but that there might be 'a surprise invasion of Ireland by Irish-Americans' which 'was quite practicable'. Eventually, and apparently after 'much pressure', Christensen confirmed that his companion was Sir Roger and that he had been given the papers during the Stornoway interception with instructions that, if Casement was taken ashore, Christensen should get in touch with Francis Joseph Bigger, Solicitor, in Belfast.

Although Casement, puzzling through the calamity later in the day, 'knew that a British Minister . . . would not use kid-gloves in dealing with a man bent on such a journey' as his, he was 'hardly prepared for the outrageous character of the suggestion' made to his 'man' that he be 'knocked on the head'. Christensen, promising that he could be 'as big a blackguard' as Findlay, returned to the legation for his afternoon appointment, leaving the trusting and frightened Casement 'in some anxiety' that he would give in to temptation after his life 'of very great hardship'. The price offered would be 'a high

---

* About twelve shillings.

one', and he hoped that Christensen would accurately pass on the story they had rehearsed: that Casement was on his way to stay at the Hotel Bristol in Copenhagen, and that Christensen was joining his parents in Moss. Casement laid out these false plans in conversation with the hotel staff, but was deeply worried when Christensen did not return until 5.00.

When he did, he had another bundle of banknotes and now claimed that he had agreed to persuade Casement on to a boat 'anywhere on the Skagerrak or North Sea' where he could be 'taken by force' and carried off on a British destroyer. He was to pass on Casement's letters and as much 'proof as possible against [him] and [his] Irish associates'. On the day his 'body was procured', Findlay would pay him £5,000, a sum which should have been incredible to a more rational Casement, but oddly one that came into play, to lasting British shame, in the months to come. Findlay gave Christensen a name and address to which he should deliver his findings, and a simple code by which he was to write a 'harmless letter about anything at all, of which only every fourth word counted in the real message intended'.

After this debriefing, the two men rushed for the station. They boarded the Copenhagen train with Richard Meyer, a German diplomat who was to be their escort to Berlin and, in effect, Casement's government liaison; Casement had met his brother Kuno, a former professor of Celtic languages at Liverpool University and now a German spy, in America. Meyer was confident they could shake off any watcher by moving quickly down the train, as it split at Ängelholm Junction at 5.45 a.m., into the carriages which would carry them to Swedish Trelleborg. From there, they were on the morning steamboat to Sassnitz, just inside Germany, ending their frantic, threatening two days in Norway. Findlay's latest telegram stating that the 'alleged Casement' had set off reached London just before midnight. His personal opinion of his former consular colleague was that there could not 'be many blackguards of that class'.

Casement trusted Adler throughout his double-dealing; this was already the most enduring relationship of his life. The often lonely man now had a companion in a period of considerable peril; he was so focused on his own mission that he could never have suspected

that he was being betrayed in turn; and he was fired up by the sense
of his importance to the British, who were evidently so alarmed by
what he was up to that they were even prepared to sanction his
murder – a fiction that was so outlandish it might paradoxically have
increased his trust in Adler's loyalty that he should have been told it.
For now, he seemed not to mind that, despite his instruction that the
Norwegian should stay awake while he himself got some sleep, his
servant-lover was snoring on the top bunk as the train puffed through
the Swedish night. The British Naval Attaché further down the carriage was under orders from Minister Findlay to warn a King's
Messenger on his way to Denmark not to approach the 'dangerous
rascals'; there was no need as Findlay had already 'arranged that
informer should let [him] know what passes in Germany and should
be paid by results'. They had a spy in place watching the former Foreign Office hero who was on his way to meet the enemy's Imperial
Chancellor in the annihilating war that was not quite three months
old.

PART THREE

Rebel

9. On Manoeuvres

Tom Casement was tactful in his letters home. In July 1914 he echoed his brother in saying that 'the only thing that will bring peace and prosperity in dear old Ireland . . . is some blood spilling'. He possibly knew that Roger had left for America, but would have been dumb-struck to learn that he was on his way to Berlin when he wrote from his farm in South Africa in August – in a letter that only reached Casement months later – that 'one has to be careful at home in what one says. You can't lash out at John Bull now. It would not be wise.' Ten days later, Alice Green tried to ameliorate Casement's disap-pointments with America by offering, 'Do not let hope fail you. We will keep a flame alight to warm your heart when you come back.' 'Home' was a tricky prospect to Casement because he believed that he could not be loyal to Britain as he would be 'in jail within a week, or in a Concentration Camp or in flight to the hills'. Neither the warning from his brother nor the comfort from Alice Green could alter his situation anyway as he pursued his irreversible quest to Berlin. The harder-headed John Quinn considered the German expedition 'a silly thing to do. It has absolutely cut him off from any usefulness in Ireland.'

The oddness of Casement's position took human shape on the train from Sassnitz to Berlin, as 'two ugly Junkers landlords' boarded. Meyer translated their mutterings about the 'extraordinary inso-lence' of 'an Englishman' travelling in Germany and quickly defused the situation by pointing out that his companion was, in fact, Ameri-can. He explained to Casement that to men like these a 'hatred that exceeds anything ever felt in Germany' hitherto was directed towards England. It was an introduction to what would be Casement's home for the next, cut-off eighteen months, which highlighted the peril-ous nature of his plotting.

★

As the train drew in to Berlin's Hauptbahnhof at around 7.30 p.m. on the last day of October, Casement saw bandaged men lying on stretchers or limping about the platform on crutches in the first manifestation of the struggle he was now joining. A taxi took the party to the Palast Hotel, convenient for the Foreign Ministry on Wilhelmstrasse, but that was closed for the duration, so they went to the Continental, where Casement registered as Mr Hammond of New York. He was anxious about the cost of his and Christensen's rooms given the limited funds and uncertain duration of his stay: they were four doors apart but his larger room, with bathroom attached, was eighteen Marks* a night compared to four for Christensen's. After dinner alone and 'a talk with Adler', he was apprehensive, wondering if the Germans would 'see the great cause aright and understand all it may mean to them, no less than to Ireland'.

Meyer demonstrated Casement's importance when he announced that, as both the Chancellor and the Foreign Minister were visiting the front line, they could not see him immediately, but he had made an appointment with the Under-Secretary, Arthur Zimmermann, for the following morning. Meanwhile, the dreariness of the hotel was alleviated by the service he was shown after Christensen spread the word below stairs that his master was an American millionaire with a 'fine steam yacht', a fantasy he was soon to recreate in a more threatening context.

As Casement walked down Unter den Linden towards Wilhelmstrasse with Meyer, he noted the shuttered British and Russian embassies, and was disappointed by the street and the size of its eponymous trees – 'it is not a fine thoroughfare and the shops do not impress one' – but he cheered when they crossed Friedrichstrasse, which was 'full of life'. In general, he found Berlin 'not imposing . . . but fine. It is extraordinarily well kept and clean' and, although the buildings were not 'lofty', they were 'massive and well built'. He was delighted to be introduced to Princess Fürstenberg as they passed by, remembering her family's 'splendid château' in the Rhineland from his 1912 holiday with Dick Morten. Once in the Foreign Ministry, as

---

* Approximately £75 at today's values.

he sat 'on a big sofa in this centre of policy of the German Empire' waiting for his appointment with Zimmermann and Count Georg von Wedel, the head of the English Department, he told himself that he had 'no regrets, no fears' – before correcting that in his diary to 'some regrets, but no fears'; he pushed away the wobble with the bolstering axiom 'victory or defeat, it is all for Ireland'.

He considered that his scheming with the enemy meant it was likely he 'should almost fatally never see' Ireland again should Germany be defeated. Even so, his plans could bring about the 'blow struck for Ireland [that] must change the course of British policy towards that country', place 'the Irish Question' properly into the international debate and enable 'a people lost in the Middle Ages [to be] refound and returned to Europe'. Sitting in the marble hall brought on a potent mixture of nerves, defiance and historical wistfulness. He allayed his turmoil through moral righteousness: he 'should be a traitor did I not act as I am doing'; the real turncoats were the likes of Grey and Asquith who had 'surely betrayed their country to glut the greedy jealousy of the British commercial mind'.

Arthur Zimmermann's 'fair-haired, very good-natured face' and 'warm and close handshake' were reassuring. He acknowledged Findlay's perfidiousness in supposedly waylaying Christensen as 'Dastardly!' and typical of the English. Casement hoped the Germans would work up the outline of a 'declaration' he had composed that morning in his pyjamas which contained a summary of the 'cruel calumnies' the British were 'spreading through Ireland' to defame Germany and encourage 'Irish youth' to join up; with contorted logic, 'the German government could quite legitimately defend itself from these atrocious charges of evil intent towards Ireland' by making a 'formal declaration of its attitude towards my country'. The cheerful Herr Zimmermann, keen to distract Britain by fomenting revolt among Irish, Indian and Russian revolutionaries, agreed whole-heartedly as he ushered Casement in to see Count von Wedel.

In those early days of high-level welcome, Casement was also charmed by Wedel's personality, his 'upright build; frank, straight brown eyes and perfect English accent', and was especially delighted by the official response to the central plank of his plan: that a corps of

Irish soldiers be raised from prison camps in Germany and sent back to fight in their own country. Meyer had enthusiastically agreed with Casement that it gave 'full "moral" value' to Germany, and would be worth 'ten army corps' in France. Casement was adamant that the soldiers needed to be persuaded that they were striking a blow for Ireland, not attempting 'merely to hit England', and that 'any Irish man might commit treason against England for the sake of Ireland' with impunity. If the Declaration he had just presented was published he had 'little or no doubt scores, perhaps hundreds, of Irish prisoners would follow him'.

The morning at Wilhelmstrasse ended with Wedel's promise to review Casement's early-morning Declaration, an instruction to Meyer to go to the Chief of the Political Police to obtain a card stating that 'Mr Hammond of New York was not to be troubled', and the suggestion that Casement and Christensen wear enamel American flags on their lapels. As the two new arrivals spent the evening wandering about the city, Casement considered himself 'fairly launched on Berlin'.

He had certainly made 'a reasonable and trustworthy impression' on Wedel, who requested the Chancellor give 'serious consideration' to the proposed Irish Brigade. If Bethmann Hollweg agreed, the first steps would be to separate out Irish prisoners and move them into one camp 'to make it possible for Irish Catholic priests and Sir Roger Casement to exert their influence upon them', and to publish Casement's Declaration that 'Germany has no intention whatsoever of bringing Ireland under German domination' and would 'stand for its liberation' in the event of victory. Casement suggested as added appeal that the document would help sway Irish-American opinion to the German side.

Casement's German diary, unlike the sketchy, indiscreet personal journals of 1903 and 1910–11, seems to have been composed with posterity in mind, as an apologia if one ever became needed; it was devoid of any sexual references, presenting more of his thoughts and feelings in response to the events he was caught up in. He was back at the heart of a campaign which, even if potentially fatal to him, had become a gloriously patriotic venture. However, in his current perilous isolation, he fell to brooding about Findlay's betrayal and decided to send the actual traitor, Christensen – the 'treasure' he clung to and the only person with whom he felt he had true connection – back to Norway with some misinformation.

He composed a fake letter to McGarrity about his 'somewhat trying journey' to Europe, the clumsiness of Findlay's plotting and 'the stupidity, laziness and cowardice of the English' in general, while praising 'our friends here' and their intention to 'go the whole road with us'. He emphasised that 'the <u>sanitary pipes</u> will be furnished on a big scale, with a plenty stock of <u>disinfectants</u>. Enough for 50,000 health officers at least . . . We shall be fully prepared here by Christmas . . . The people here are wonderful.' The second letter did not contain obvious codes for guns and ammunition: it opened 'Patrick' and was enclosed in an envelope within an envelope, the first addressed to a Philadelphia hotel manager and the second to a Philadelphia priest, Father Coghlan; 'R' wrote that everything would be in place by December, and that 'the German–Irish alliance will beat the Entente yet'. Mines would be laid in the North Sea, there were '60,000 here and ample stocks for them and a picked band of trained men to go over'. Patrick was to 'keep all ready to sail at the word' and they would 'certainly have the flag up by St Patrick's Day'. Alongside the taunts and feints for his enemies in London, there was a yearning to be home in four months' time.

On 20 November 1914, the day before Christensen left for Christiania, the Declaration was in the newspapers: 'the well-known Irish Nationalist, Sir Roger Casement' had been received in Wilhelmstrasse, and 'the Imperial Government formally declares that under no circumstance would Germany invade Ireland with a view to its conquest'. If German forces did land, it would not be 'as an army of invaders to pillage and destroy' but would be 'inspired by goodwill towards a country and a people for whom Germany desires only national prosperity and national freedom'.

Casement posed as Christensen to concoct a telegram to Findlay using the Minister's fourth-word code; when it was stripped down, it read 'Have got good letter giving names, sending through Post-office difficult. Give quickly advice, I am broke, send plenty money to Adler.' It had the desired effect on Findlay, who immediately scrawled a telegram to London stating that 'informer' was offering to 'give names' of Casement's accomplices for money, and asking how much was he authorised to offer? Nicolson authorised any reasonable sum up to £100, and Findlay replied to Christensen in the same code that he was able to offer £30, to be paid in Norway on receipt of 'reliable information'. Christensen's pretext for setting off with the two letters and some fabricated pages of Casement's diary was complete, and Nicolson's 'Irish Conspiracy with Germany' file was filling up.

Casement sent MacNeill and Alice Green copies of the Declaration, informing MacNeill that 'if Ireland will do her duty, rest assured Germany will do hers towards us, our cause and our whole future . . . Tell all to trust the Germans – and to trust me.' He signed off: 'You know who writes this', assuring 'the poor old woman'* that he was 'well, and has convincing assurance of help, recognition, friends, and comfort'; he had 'seen the big men and they are one with his views and if successful they will aid to the uttermost to redeem the four green fields', the provinces of Ireland. He exulted that even 'if we do not win today, we ensure international recognition of Irish nationality and hand on an uplifted cause for our sons'.

As there was no postal system between the combatant nations, these letters were posted by German spies in Rotterdam, and were intercepted by Scotland Yard. Casement had first been taken seriously by the British Security Service on publication of the Declaration: RIC reports of his Volunteer activities filtered back from Cork, Dublin, Belfast, Galway, Antrim and Down, and his connections were monitored. Alice Green was friendly with the Chief Secretary for Ireland, who 'put her *low down*' in the 'hierarchy of treason', but even if there had been anything treasonous in the letter, she was unlikely to have been investigated further: the woman who had played a signal part in encouraging Casement's Irish studies and developing his network through her salons, who had bankrolled him, who had been the recipient of some of his most profound and emotional letters and in whose house the gun-running had been plotted,

---

* Ireland.

was cut off from responding to him. Nevertheless, his triumphant missives to her became critical evidence less than two years later, while she re-emerged as his most proactive supporter.

Now that he was in the open, Casement could begin his last scheme. Meyer informed him that he was travelling to the French front to further the POW plan, and he entered a more ruminative, and defiantly partisan, frame of mind now that he was about to see the war at first hand. On his last evening in Berlin, he went to Hoffmann's Restaurant, where he was already a 'recognised habitué', and, strolling back, contemplated the 'several detachments of recruits' he had seen departing for battle: they had flowers in their belts, many carried brown-paper packages from home and all 'looked happy and smiling' even though they were marching 'sedately to the trenches of death'. It was the day of the overwhelming victories over the Russians at Soldau and Włocławek, yet he was struck by the 'absence of jingoism' among this 'quiet, patient and sure-hearted people', words reminiscent of his descriptions of the Putumayo Indians.

'Poor old Adler . . . nearly wept!' at being left in the hotel before his own departure the next day, while Casement, Meyer and two Prussian Junkers of the General Staff boarded the night train to Cologne at Friedrichstrasse. After coffee and bread and butter in a Cologne hotel, they set off by car for a six-hour, 170-mile drive to the front at Charleville, just over the French border from Belgium. Despite his fur-lined gloves, Casement had to sit on his hands for warmth; he was reminded again of his German motoring tour with Dick Morten in the early summer of 1912, but did not admit to any nostalgia for the life he had left behind. He revelled in the stewed beef, macaroni and boiled potatoes with 'a plain white wine' in the officers' mess at Sedan. After the meal he was taken off by a diplomat he had met in New York to discuss the 'Irish Brigade' and the movement of Irish POWs from their various camps into one place. Such was his hopeful single-mindedness and the charm of another well-born German that he got the impression that 'the matter' was 'nearest the heart of the General Staff'. Yet it was his loneliest crusade – even on his journey up the Congo he had had the sense of right-thinking

European opinion behind him. Now Devoy was unsure about the validity of his adventure, and behind the German welcome and brief enjoyment of having such a renowned defector in their midst Foreign Secretary Gottlieb von Jagow was dictating a memorandum to his deputy, Zimmermann, to say that 'The reservations about carrying out the idea are evident. The military results would be small, possibly even negative, and it would be said we had violated international law.' Although Jagow was allowing everything to proceed on the grounds that 'it would suffice to have it known that the Irish prisoners were quite ready to fight against England on our side' for the sake of British embarrassment and a weakening of the Union.

To date, no prisoner had been moved, not least because the German authorities were struggling with a central issue in the scheme – 'they don't know the difference between an Englishman and an Irishman!' Casement recognised that a persuasive chaplain would be essential and impractically proposed that a couple of the prisoners be sent back home to find one; while they were there, they could further explain to the Provisional Committee of the Volunteers what he was up to. The acknowledged solitariness of his mission was not alleviated later in the day: he checked in to Charleville's Hôtel de Commerce, which had no hot water, food or electricity, 'only a few bits of candles' which the sole remaining manservant handed out. Eventually, Meyer took him off to an officers' mess where there was some cold sausage and a piece of bread, but uncertainty as to how to explain his charge meant Casement was soon whisked back to his miserable hotel.

Another titled German civil servant, Baron Wilhelm von Stumm, head of the Wilhelmstrasse Political Department, met him for an hour the next morning. Stumm, who considered Sir Edward Grey 'an inferior man', seemed interested to hear of Findlay's trickery. They discussed the nature of the British Empire, how it would be in Germany's interest to have an independent Ireland, and how the Declaration was being received. Casement left the meeting believing that they were 'agreed in aim', even if 'the means to attain it . . . lay in the lap of the gods'. He was realising he had to trust to the 'fortunes of war', which at that point appeared to have ebbed and flowed to a stalemate. With that encounter, his brief visit to the front was over and he had official blessing to carry on plotting.

On the long car journey back to Berlin he was again witness to the great events into which he had launched himself as he passed the splintered bridges over the Meuse, the shattered civic buildings of Namur and the bloodstains on the walls in Andenne where Belgian resisters had been summarily executed. The cards on the mass graves of these men brought him close to tears, and he admitted that the Belgians were now suffering 'a national agony . . . far more than they, or their king . . . wreaked on the well-nigh defenceless people of the Congo Basin'. So necessary was his hatred of England, though, that he blamed the British rather than the Germans for the death toll, claiming that the Belgians would have allowed the Germans free passage into France had Britain not 'preferred the arbitrament of arms'. As so often at moments of self-doubt, he pumped himself up with his own rhetoric to ask 'what were the wars of Rome, the legions of Caesar compared to those of Berlin, to the army corps of the Kaiser', even as he saw the results. He reiterated that Britain was out to 'secure the trade of the world' through the sacrifice of 'Irish boys and men', and there was no benefit to Ireland in giving '300,000 men to the shambles of France and Flanders'.* As the party motored through the 'barbed-wire fields', he inveighed against Americans for their gullibility in believing English lies and the 'asinine pranks' of their press in publishing them; the overwhelming shame would have made him, had he been English, open his veins.

Nevertheless, he was bucked by the thought of the made-up letters on their way to Christiania. They should 'make Findlay's hair – such as remains of it – rise up and bless him and the day he got hold of Adler Christensen'. He began to move in society that winter, lunching with Count (later Prince) Gebhard Blücher, to his 'great joy'. Blücher was an old friend from Africa who later lived in London's Notting Hill. Jagow ducked a meeting by leaving the capital

---

* It is not possible to give an exact figure for the number of Irish soldiers who served, but the total is thought to be around 200,000 by 1918: 28,000 regular soldiers and 30,000 reservists were called up immediately and a further 148,000 signed up in the course of the war.

again, while, according to Blücher, 'adding things about Ireland and [Casement's] mission that . . . were not very favourable'. Casement consoled himself with the reflection that Blücher was always 'extraordinarily inaccurate in his versions of happenings'. The Anglo-Irish Countess Blücher, a gossip-prone, fair-weather friend, was astonished to meet her fellow countryman in Berlin: she 'knew his anti-English feelings well, and his rabid Home Rule mania, but did not expect it to have taken this intense form of becoming pro-German'. The Countess was one of many who later dissociated themselves from Casement, but he came away from their meeting with the impression that 'she really would like to see England get . . . a good birching from Germany'. In her later memoirs, she maintained that she had nothing to do with him after this meeting, citing his 'perverted tastes' and adding that Christensen's 'appearance and mannerisms' were 'very feminine'; apparently he 'habitually made up'.

The German Ambassador to the Vatican produced two priests, Fathers Canice O'Gorman and John Thomas Crotty. O'Gorman was 'a loyalist nationalist', and Crotty 'a raging Fenian!' Both swore that they would neither spy on Casement nor get involved in politics but would 'confine themselves strictly to their holy business' for diplomatically expedient reasons. Casement was angered by the news that the British wanted to establish diplomatic relations with the Holy See, which he interpreted as the Pope taking the English side on Irish matters, thus 'clear proof of the strength and reality of the national soul again uprising in Ireland' and of Britain's anxiety about that, and therefore of the 'justice of my point of view'. His idealism and its outcomes were at the mercy of the relentless wheels of politics and war, but his fragile confidence depended on keeping himself at the centre of things.

Meyer returned late in the evening of the day of the priests' arrival in a state of excitement. The military authorities had located 2,300 Irish Catholic POWs. They had sorted through nearly 20,000 French and 10,000 British soldiers to establish that around 1,500 were in the huge camp at Sennelager. Casement was triumphant: he had 'told them all along England fights with Irishmen' and that of the 17,000–18,000 prisoners captured so far – about a fifth of the British

Expeditionary Force that had crossed the Channel in August – he would have expected that 3,000–4,000 would be Irishmen and over half of those Catholics. He asked Meyer for 3,000 more copies of the English-language propaganda newspaper the *Continental Times*, which contained the Declaration, and cap badges and Irish-flag pins to be produced for the prisoners. About 300 men were already gathered at a special camp at Limburg, near Frankfurt-am-Main, and plans were being laid for his visit to remind them of their true patriotic duty.

Findlay kept his cypher clerk busy after he had debriefed Adler Christensen in a locked room with closed blinds. Christensen had gone straight to the legation in Christiania on 26 November for the first of two meetings in his three weeks away from Berlin; two 'Most Private and Secret' telegrams were on their way to London by evening. The first included the content of the fictitious letters to America with the news that Casement had seen 'friends in Berlin' who would 'co-operate in plan with all their resources' – true to an extent. London should be on high alert at the start of 1915 for an invasion of Ireland as Casement had '60,000 (rifles?)' as well as 'a picked band of trained men'; on top of which, 'two can play at laying mines' – part of the misinformation. And when Casement wrote that Redmond had suggested six months before that he 'get an Irish Republic if you can', he was simply making trouble for the party leader.

Christensen implied that Casement was deep in a conspiracy and that he planned an imminent trip to Denmark to arrange for two ships to be 'ready to sail at the word . . . Charts are excellent, localities clearly marked, clearing out can be quickly done with right men on the spot.' Casement apparently had 'absolute confidence' in trusting his 'companion' with this secret, and Findlay, who knew nothing of Casement's organisational or espionage skills, was concerned to keep as tight a lid on the information as possible for fear of 'disastrous consequences'.

Sir Arthur Nicolson got a second despatch after 'the informer' had told Findlay that Casement had charts in his possession showing 'passages through mine-fields' and had spies in the British Navy, 'among them were even Naval Officers'. Findlay was wary enough of

Christensen's integrity to 'hesitate to report these disturbing statements as they have no support', especially as under cross-questioning
Christensen was unable to remember the location of the minefields,
or even whether they were British or German, vaguely implying
'they were off the coast of Ireland as well as off British coast'. Despite
this, the Foreign Office made the first calamitous suggestion that
Findlay could 'promise informer £5,000* in the event of his supplying information leading to capture of C and his accomplices'.

If Casement had sent the minefield information as part of his subterfuge at this stage, he would have given more plausible detail; but
if Christensen's freelance double-cross was designed to get the financial reward he claimed he had been offered on his second visit to the
British legation in October, then it was a triumph: although Findlay
never told him the full extent of his authorisation, he offered £1,000
on the spot, handing over 500 Kroner† 'on account'. On hearing of
more 'liberal rewards' to come, Christensen conjured up the claim
that '600 men are working continuously at Krupp's [armaments
manufacturers] on a secret job and are not allowed to communicate
with anyone'. In their wartime panic, the Foreign Office had crossed
an ethical line in authorising such a colossal bribe to an untrustworthy, nationally neutral mole. But as the errant Casement was
clearly masterminding a devastating campaign, the pay-off seemed
warranted.

It seemed even more so when the freelance Christensen beefed up
the conspiracy even further: he had been commissioned to buy 'a
jagt . . . a large cutter-rigged Norwegian sailing vessel of about 60 or
70 tons' with a 'good skipper and crew' who would receive 'high pay'
to transport Casement to meet an American yacht; he had also heard
a rumour that the Chicago meat-packing magnate J. Ogden Armour
had ordered an ocean-going vessel from a Hamburg yacht builder to
rendezvous 'with body of conspirators . . . off Irish coast'; Casement's charts would guide it through the mines. Findlay imagined a
landing in Galway Bay was likely. Perhaps picking up on something

---

* Around £475,000 today.
† About £12.

Casement had mentioned after his meeting with Zimmermann, Christensen revealed that 'Casement has been seeing Indians at Berlin and is trying to organise rebellion in India' making use of 'much money from American Secret Society'. In fact, the Clan were adamant that their base had no interest in the British Empire outside Ireland.

The lonely Casement wrote a week after Christensen's departure to tell him that 'I miss you very much . . . Don't forget me – and be sure I don't forget you. I shall be very glad to hear from you; and to see you back again with me once more. My beard and moustache have grown a lot since you left – and I look very nearly the same as ever . . . Write soon to me, dear Adler. I think very often of you and will be glad to see you again.' He stood outside himself to admit to having qualms about his irrevocable course: 'It is not every day that even an Irishman commits high treason – especially one who has been in the service of the Sovereign he discards, and not without honour and some fame in that service.'

His mournful letter crossed with a triumphant one from Christensen, exulting that he had 'seen my friend and he was very glad to see me', and he was 'pretty keen' to do so again. He had 'got [Findlay] going all right'. He confirmed that he had 'thrown something in about the German boat and . . . suggested that that boat had been laying mines'; he asked for 'a telegram or a good letter' from Casement to back him up. That letter should also say exactly what Casement had been doing in Denmark, because that was puzzling Findlay – understandably as there was no basis for the lie. Casement should order Christensen back to Berlin as he was 'almost ready' and 'casually mention a few names' of 'High sea officers and also well-known land officers, what is going with you on your journey'. Christensen had inflated his value, but still needed 'more what you can think of that will be good' intelligence to up the price. He had let on that 'a whole lot of Americans high up is going to leave America on a big steam Yacht' owned by a millionaire, and on being asked if troops were coming from the United States had said he 'would not be surprised because it is a secret society over there' just waiting for Casement's word; he should also claim that he was willing to go 'as high as $30–40,000'* for the right vessel. Christensen wound Casement up by ending, 'I almost forgot he said he knew you are a very clever -----. And he used a bad word, and that you was very dangerous and that they must get you.'

Casement's reply was again suffused with tenderness. Christensen was staying with his parents, and his lover wished he too 'had a father and mother to go to now' as he was 'very lonely often – & get most miserable'. It ended: 'I think very often of you and will be so glad to see you again and clasp your hand,' before asking after his teeth, which had been causing him pain, and offering, without irony given the Christiania bribe, 'If you want money, tell me.' He revealed his self-disgust at the deceit he was perpetrating on Findlay and the British, which ran against his hallmark honesty: 'I *hate* what I am doing all the time and feel almost as big a cur as [Findlay] is.' Without any idea how far Christensen had exceeded his brief, Casement longed for 'dear Adler . . . to become an honest, *good* man'; he was made 'really unhappy' when he thought of the lies being told on his behalf; it would be a moral and practical mistake to touch Findlay's bribe. The long-orphaned, trusting Casement had little inkling that he had been double-crossed on top of his own duplicitous provocations and that his only long-term paramour was spinning and exaggerating in Norway. He added the requested disinformation: he had $30,000 for Christensen to charter a schooner to be kept in a Norwegian port, and that 'the shipment' was ready to go. 'Things here are moving very fast and I hope to be ready sooner than I expected' added a note of urgency; he suggested that 'the break-up of British rule' in Ireland would be emulated in Egypt and India; and mentioned that 'the yacht over the water' was nearly ready, and that senior German officers would be by his side.

Wedel endorsed this letter on the spot, and only later did Casement learn that it was never sent. The decision to withhold it might have been taken out of fear of over-egging an already unlikely conspiracy, but more likely it was prompted by official nervousness about Christensen's plausibility. On 1 December, Casement had a

---

* About £1 million today.

telephone call from Professor Theodor Schiemann, a propagandist and political agent who had lived in Britain before the war. Schiemann was translating a collection of Casement's writings, including *The Crime against Europe*, for circulation in Berlin under the title *The Achilles Heel of England*, but was ringing now to let him know that 'disquieting statements about Adler that were unwarranted and malicious' were circulating in official quarters. Casement was 'annoyed beyond words – and disgusted' by the Professor's warning. He remained loyal to his lover while not entirely blind to the impression he made: 'Poor Adler! God knows he is bad enough without these professional inquests on him.'

In fact, the unlikely conspirators had done enough. Findlay's current description of Casement as 'clean-shaven lately' and with a 'heavy jaw rather like Carson' was wired to all diplomats and consuls around the world with instructions to apprehend him. The case was now in the hands of Casement's most formidable opponents in the form of the country's highest security officers, Captain 'Blinker' Hall, Director of Naval Intelligence, and the head of the Criminal Investigation Department of the Metropolitan Police and future head of the Directorate of Intelligence, Basil Thomson. They commissioned a brief report: Casement had 'identified himself strongly with the Irish National Volunteer movement from its inception and worked energetically' for it; in a chilling foretaste of later tactics, they were waiting to hear more 'as to his habits (natural and unnatural!)'. As for Bigger, whom Christensen was to contact should anything happen to Casement, the security chiefs reckoned the 'antiquarian and enthusiast on the Irish Language' was probably acting merely as a Belfast postbox as he lacked 'the pluck to be an *active* agent for the disloyal party', owing to being 'emotional and unbalanced'.

For now, Hall and Thomson came up with their own fantastical idea to combat the conspiracy: they would charter a yacht which would then cruise off the west coast of Ireland and report on any suspicious shipping movements. Once ashore, the yachtsman would pretend to be an emissary from Casement delivering revolutionary plans to Sinn Féin – but would really gather information from that organisation about what Casement might be up to in Germany. One of those with whom the plan was discussed was Darrell Figgis, fully loyal to the Crown in wartime less than half a year after his successful role in the Howth gun-running. The yacht they found was the *Sayonara*, the property of another American multi-millionaire Anthony Drexel, whose father had founded a bank with J. Pierpont Morgan. Drexel lived in London's Carlton House Terrace and was a philanthropist, a close friend of the late King Edward VII and a keen sportsman. A soldier of fortune was put on board as 'the owner', and a young naval officer with a flair for German accents (in case they encountered the enemy) as captain. In mid-December, the *Sayonara* sailed around the west coast of Ireland, putting ashore at times in search of information, but failed to report back anything of interest to Hall in the Admiralty Signals Intelligence hub, Room 40.

Casement knew nothing of the *Sayonara*'s fruitless voyage. He felt that his month in Germany had been productive: the government had signed off his bold Declaration with its immense propaganda implications; and he believed that Christensen was confounding Findlay. As December began, he was preparing to create a fighting brigade from the Irishmen collected at Limburg. Yet he was alone, cut off from all those close to him save Christensen, out of contact with his political friends and champions, and clinging to thoughts of Ireland and Adler Christensen, the two insecure anchors left to him. He was resentful of the lack of German official enthusiasm for 'Poor Adler' and was made anxious that he had not yet been granted audiences with the Foreign Secretary or the Chancellor. He was 'broken hearted' the night before his departure that he should be encouraging other Irishmen to turn to treason; he thought of 'friends I shall never see again – and of Ireland I have looked my last on'. These highs and lows were a foretaste of the tumultuous months ahead.

10. Web of Lies

The Declaration had brought Casement back to public attention in Britain. In December 1914 the *Scotsman* ran a leader about his 'remarkable case . . . a leader of Irish sedition and, if all reports are true, a traitor to his country . . . This eccentric gentleman, who his friends tell us is a man of the highest honour and of a full-souled chivalry rare in these modern days', was now 'trafficking with the enemies of Britain and bartering away his patriotism with an inexcusable and most contemptible act of sedition'. The *Daily Mail* shied away from such full-throated condemnation of what it termed 'a mystery', out of disbelief that, 'as reported by the German wireless, he received grave assurances of Germany's warm regard for Ireland'. His 'active interest in the progress of events' had been limited, as far as the *Mail* was aware, to 'a lively interest in the fever epidemic which was then raging in Connemara'. The newspaper understood he had 'for years been in indifferent health'.

In Belfast, the *Northern Whig*, a Liberal Unionist publication, simply stated the facts, adding the mild observation: 'How a British subject succeeded in visiting Berlin without undergoing arrest is not explained.' The American papers gave the Declaration little coverage: most of the East Coast publications had 'already openly taken sides with England' and were 'engaged in the work of forcing the United States into [the war] as an ally', according to Devoy; those who promoted Irish independence were reckoned 'pro-German' anyway. One Hearst newspaper with a substantial Irish readership, the *Boston American*, commissioned several 'Irish leaders [to] repudiate Sir Roger Casement's attitude towards Germany' in no uncertain terms: a former Congressman, who had never heard of him, declared that Irishmen should be neutral; another Hearst paper, the *San Francisco Examiner*, hailed Casement as 'a leader in thought and a hero in deed'. Some claimed that Redmond was the true patriot and, since Casement had only 'lately shown any activity in Irish national matters', he carried no authority to pitch himself against the elected Irish Party in the House of Commons.

His past and future benefactor, the unstinting champion of Congo reform for over a decade, Sir Arthur Conan Doyle, responded to the *Daily Chronicle*'s report with a letter to the paper, commending it for its use of 'no stronger term than "infatuation" for Sir Roger Casement's journey to Berlin'. He 'was a man of fine character, and that he should in the full possession of his senses act as a traitor to the country which had employed and honoured him is inconceivable to anyone who knew him'. Conan Doyle emphasised to Morel that it was 'quite incredible and impossible that so noble a man could have proved a traitor' – his pre-war 'pro-German' stance had been adopted in order to challenge the Monroe Doctrine, 'the ultimate cause of all that Putumayo barbarism', and Doyle had never heard a word of disloyalty towards Great Britain. Yet his friend was 'a sick man . . . worn by tropical hardships' and his letters from Ireland had been 'so wild' that the medical man had 'expressed fears . . . as to the state of his nerves'; certainly his current 'unhappy escapade' demonstrated that he was 'not in a normal state of mind'. After all, why would 'any sane man accept an assurance about Ireland which had obviously been already broken about Belgium?' The creator of the arch-rationalist detective, whose respect for Casement's anti-slavery work never dimmed, summarised opinion at home that the Declaration, whether a manifestation of Casement's quixotic eccentricity or his ill-health, did not represent a serious threat in the war.

Attention was mostly elsewhere that week as the First Battle of Ypres had just ended, its quarter of a million casualties reinforcing the murderous failure of the new industrialised warfare. Recent naval campaigns had also resulted in a draw: the English had been defeated by Admiral Maximilian von Spee at Coronel, off Chile, at the start of November; a month later Vice-Admiral Doveton Sturdee sank all but one of Spee's South Atlantic Squadron at the Battle of the Falkland Islands. But while the prospect of a German victory that would deliver swift independence for Ireland was stalling, the prisoners and the priests were on the move.

★

The notion of an Irish Brigade may have reached back to the Boer War when Casement, at his most English and serving in the Foreign Office, had despised the Irish soldiers won over to the Boer cause. But in 1913 he had met Major John MacBride, who had raised the 500-strong Irish Transvaal Brigade that fought against their fellow countrymen in the Royal Dublin Fusiliers and the Royal Inniskilling Fusiliers in the hills around Ladysmith and on the plains of the Orange Free State, and he romanticised 'the fight that little band of Irishmen . . . made for Boer freedom', the first time that the might of the British Empire had been seriously challenged by a small, rural population.*

He left Anhalt Station at 10.20 on the night of 2 December, the day of Austria-Hungary's occupation of Belgrade. He had kept to his room for a few days as he felt unwell, not helped by Schiemann's 'disquieting statements' about Christensen. When Blücher heard these, he had taken the path of least resistance to agree with Casement that Christensen had 'an innate chivalry and sense of honour and courage'. Yet Blücher too proved himself to be untrustworthy, gossiping about 'the Christiania business' all around the capital, including to the elusive Secretary of State Jagow. Blücher even proposed taking over the deception and 'running it as a private concern' by sending an undercover agent to Christiania to publicise 'Findlay's guilt'. Casement ignored this but was still fortified by his old friend as he set off thirty-four days after his arrival with an Imperial Passport in the name of 'Irishman Sir Roger Casement'. He had finally 'become myself', soothing his chagrin about Jagow by grasping that 'the real German diplomats are not in the Foreign Office, but in the German armies and navy'.

He reached Frankfurt at 7.20 in the morning and checked into the grand Hessicher Hof, recently changed from the Englischer Hof, to his amusement. He had with him the *Gaelic American* with the headline 'Germany Pledges Friendship to Ireland' as well as copies bound

---

* MacBride, the 'drunken, vainglorious lout' of Yeats's 'Easter 1916', was subsequently court-martialled and executed for his part in the 1916 Rising (Yeats, *Collected Poems* p. 203).

by Wilhelmstrasse of seven of his essays about Ireland's place in Europe. The exquisitely mannered Commander General for Frankfurt, General de Graaff, a peacetime friend of Edward VII, received him and arranged for a car and two orderlies to attend him the next morning. He spent the rest of the day admiring the city's spaciousness and 'general air of well doing', along with 'the fine, strong well-shaped bodies' of the sailors and soldiers.

The VIP treatment continued as he travelled in a 'fine military motor' with the Prussian spreadeagle on the panels and was saluted by every soldier and every child they passed; he delighted in the journey through the 'beautiful country with sunshine lighting the hills and woods'. He was met at Limburg by two generals and eighteen other high-ranking officers, including the Harrow-educated Prince Leiningen, who had been born at his great-aunt Queen Victoria's residence on the Isle of Wight, and who would much rather have been in England than in Germany. Casement was enthused by his first sight of the camp, 'with its glorious view of the Cathedral on its rock right on the river', even though its structure was only half finished, with 400 French prisoners working to complete it.

The 300 Irishmen soon dampened his ebullience. They were a '*very* wretched lot – half clad only in a miserable thin Khaki Stuff – they were pinched with cold, dirty and miserable', particularly by comparison with the French. His idealised vision of a patriotically charged fighting band was dashed. He had not countenanced men who had mostly been raised in harsh circumstances, who had fought and been captured in battle and who were now enduring a bitter winter. In his disillusion, he transferred his disappointment into feeling 'ashamed' of them. Being confronted by the 'scum of Ireland, literally', enraged him anew about the iniquity of recruitment in the country. Twenty NCOs were taken to a separate room from the rest of the 'poor starving' men and he was shocked by one he thought 'more English than the English themselves', who was anti-German and did not mention revolution in Ireland. Most of the rest at least had the 'Irish face and eye' alongside '*horrid beards*'. He spoke to them about the 'Home Rule fake' and the 'Irish in America' and in his dismay clumsily implied that they were 'not brave enough' to follow his path. Many hoped to go to America themselves or join the Volunteers on release rather than attack Ireland with German aid.

One of the NCOs aggressively asked if this tall knight with the melodious English accent, who was accompanied by two German generals and their staff, was even Irish, but backed down when it was confirmed that he was. Casement distributed pictures of the Pope, the copies of the *Continental Times* with the Declaration and some 'English papers with the usual lies', before going to the kitchens where he admired the French soldier-cooks and in particular one 'in blue puttees showing splendid calves & with the figure of a young Hercules'. He ruminated on the pride the French could feel in having fought for their country, while the Irish were 'a mercenary army', demoralised, without the 'spark of patriotism . . . in these poor, sodden sick faces', and forced into battle. His only consolation was the healthy confidence of the German soldiers, which convinced him they would win the war and free his country.

His talks with the soldiers went better the next day without any German officers alongside him. 'Several [said] very little persuasion would be needed' to join his brigade. One sidled up to announce he had 'paraded in front of you, Sir Roger' at Six Miles Cross, Tyrone, and Casement was moved to recall standing on a church wall on a dreary Sunday evening only six months earlier to address the Volunteers. He took heart when a few believed what they read in the *Gaelic American*, that they had 'been put in the front and sacrificed' by the British generals. One man apocryphally recounted how 400 members of his Irish regiment had thrown down their weapons at Lille rather than fight on; they were 'fed up with the lies of John Bull's press bureau'. Yet 'anti-English feeling' was balanced by there being '*no* pro-German' sentiment; the men believed that 'all the destruction they saw in France – especially of churches . . . was wantonly inflicted by the Germans'. Only two, a thirty-two-year-old in financial trouble called MacMurrough and a young, intelligent corporal from Wexford called Quinlisk, signed up.

On his final visit to the camp, Casement came most starkly up against the realities of his mission, triggering fears about his future. He arrived early, accompanied by two doctors, to find that exercise books he had left behind on his first visit contained the names of 383 prisoners. Some were English Catholics, born of Irish parents and captured while serving in Middlesex and Lancashire regiments, which raised the possibility of their motivation just being a ticket home. He read aloud the conditions for joining the Brigade: its sole purpose was 'to achieve the independence of Ireland'; nobody could enrol for mercenary reasons; while they were in Germany, the members of the Brigade would be 'subject to the discipline and control of the German War Office', which would train and equip them with a distinctive uniform of their own; he would be 'in supreme command' of the men's movements on or off the field of battle; in the event of the Brigade failing to reach Ireland, or in the event of peace between Britain and Germany, then the soldiers would be sent to America. There was silence as they contemplated the terms, and perhaps the prospect of the unmilitary Casement, currently with a bad cold and hacking cough, as commanding officer. He 'pointed out the risks and dangers' and announced that he would return in a week for their answers after Fathers O'Gorman and Crotty had spoken to 'a good many of the men' in the hope of gaining their commitment. Before he set off for the two-hour drive through the snowbound Taunus woods into Frankfurt, he realised that he would have to fire their patriotic imaginations with 'further liberties' and asked Prince Leiningen for 'fuller powers' over the men's welfare, and for soap, shaving materials and tobacco.

In the mess, de Graaff pointed out that Wedel was merely a 'letter carrier' and that Casement must insist on seeing either Bethmann Hollweg or Jagow. In a four-line letter to Wedel Casement reported that he had 'little doubt that the men will do as I suggest', but that 'before committing them, however, I should like to see the Secretary of State, or the Chancellor'. He understood that he could not put 'a couple of thousand Irish soldiers into the high treason pot' without 'very precise and secure promises in their regard, and for the political future of Ireland'. By raising the stakes of his mission, he had reached the final crossroads, confiding to his diary that 'for me there is no after the war – or hereafter at all. All I am & have & shall be is here now. It is all for Ireland and I refuse to think of anything else or of any personal consequences.' Despite a sleeping tincture for his worsening cold, he lay awake, resolved that if those at the top of government did not support him, he would ask for a passport to enable him to live out his failure in Norway or Sweden.

The next morning, his anxiety had 'hardened', which he deflected into rage that the 'Findlay affair' was not being taken more seriously, and above all that Christensen was being undermined. He channelled his resentment into the areas in which he might have influence, determining to 'go on with the case against Findlay by every means in my power, & I shall do all I can to help poor Adler lead a better life'. He had shown unease when he wrote to Christensen on the night of his departure about the 'wrong we are both doing in meeting deception with deception', but he had no inkling how much his lover was enjoying his doubly deceitful role or the scale of his exaggerations in Norway. He wondered if the 'case against Findlay' was not 'more telling' than the Brigade – it would 'knock recruiting on the head in Ireland' and bring shame to 'John Bull's army'. He became aggrieved that his hosts 'are keen only on the things . . . that will help them', but also recognised that the documents Christensen had taken to Christiania gave 'Downing St. overwhelming proof' of his own guilt, so he could not 'retire from the affair' just because of German disapproval. Meanwhile, the Germans seemed to have got behind with building the camp and transporting the POWs: he had been in the country for over a month and only 'seen a few of the men in a makeshift way with *no prior* preparation of them'. His plan had been that the men would be supplied with literature and special treatment – 'their hearts would have been heated and their imaginations awake'. He scanned the British newspapers for signs of panic at his actions, combining pride and paranoia to declare that the aerial bombardment of Scarborough, Whitby and Hartlepool that first brought war to British civilians, killing over 100, would be read by the British as the product of his 'malign influence', even though the towns were on the other side of the country to Ireland.

As so often at moments of imagined catastrophe, Casement did his accounts; he would soon be 'penniless', with no sign of any more money coming from America. In his anguished realisation that he had no 'hereafter', he turned against the Germans too: they had mis-managed their '*human* problems' through not preparing the men and leaving the 'propaganda of treason' entirely up to him. His mercurial temperament lifted him from his fatalistic anxiety when he read in the *Frankfurter Zeitung* on the pre-dawn train that the British police were seizing copies of the *Irish Worker*, as well as something he was unable to translate about Sinn Féin: he remembered that Father Crotty had spoken of censorship the day before and how it would put 'all the clergy agin the Govt'. His 'defection', as he put it, was validated, and he expanded upon it as 'a serious blow to [English] pride'; he hoped he could put the country of his childhood 'in the wrong box even in America!'

He became ill, 'with a throat with a band of red-hot iron around it', and saw MacMurrough and Quinlisk in his bedroom. He had gathered 'warm things' and books and 'gave them a good dinner', and the men talked for a long time. The NCOs questioned volunteer numbers, and it came as a fresh surprise that the potential recruits could be '*very* anti-German' and suspected that his mission was 'a German trick to get them to fight for Germany'. MacMurrough and Quinlisk 'would not commit themselves to say how many would join', leading Casement to surmise that the prisoners were not true Irishmen 'but English soldiers' after all; it did not seem to occur to him that the Boer War brigade was involved in a far-off and unpopu-lar war, conscripted as the victims of overmighty imperialism; the men before him had been taken prisoner in battles in which they had lost friends to the Germans, and now they thought they were being asked to fight for that enemy in their own country.

He spent the next two days feverish and coughing in bed in a fore-taste of the illnesses that were to dog him for the rest of his troubled time in Germany. He read an account in a Cologne newspaper of a speech by John Redmond 'imploring 100,000 Irishmen to go out and die for England' which 'puts the cap on his treason to Ireland' in 'the most cowardly war even England ever waged for her selfish ends'. If his country followed Redmond's entreaties, 'she deserves the gloom of slavery'. In this mood, he decided to make another visit to the camp with the two priests so that they might hear confessions. If he could not recruit '200 or 400' of them, either he was 'not much use' or they were 'not much Irishmen'. He was at least still rational enough to question whether it was 'Ireland or tobacco' that was the appeal.

In his gloom about the future, on the train back he imagined himself as German. He mused on 'this people . . . their manliness of brow and bearing, their calm front and resolute strong chests turned to a world of Enemies', contrasted with 'the columns of trash about Prussian barbarism & English heroism'; he was 'ashamed to belong to so contemptible a race'. As his German expedition teetered and his resolve wavered, he began to use the sort of language he had once employed for Leopold's Force Publique or Arana's slave drivers to sustain his task and his identity and prop up his idealism now that it was buffeted by the realities of war and human nature.

While Casement was riding these highs and lows, Adler Christensen was giving his own account of the Irish conspiracy in a second meeting in Christiania on 7 December. He developed, peopled and confused his narrative, accelerating Findlay's alarm: he now had two jagts, the *Bródrene* and the *St Olav*, skippered by men called Alingsen and Hansen, with four crewmen apiece. In answer to the observation that keeping a rendezvous in an unmotorised sailing vessel was hard, Christensen chose to be vague: he did not know exactly what they were to be used for, maybe to put 'conspirators on board American yacht' anywhere off the coast of Schleswig-Holstein, Denmark or Norway. When Findlay suggested they might be conveying arms, Christensen agreed, before departing for Berlin thoroughly pleased with his work and the income in prospect, and had plenty of time during a hold-up at the border to hone his embellishments even further as he played each of his handlers off against the other. The semi-credulous Findlay performed his duty in sending a lengthy letter in the diplomatic pouch warning that 'the Germans have taken this business seriously in hand' and urging London to adopt 'the most prompt and drastic measures . . . to deal with the situation'.

Casement's Berlin home was now the small, noisy Hotel Eden. On his return he was cheered to hear from Wedel that 'a trusty messenger' from America had conveyed the news that the Declaration had 'produced an excellent impression' with Clan na Gael. Wedel also told him about the disastrous naval losses in the Battle of the Falklands, which enraged him as the 'British had 38 ships gathered to meet this gallant little fleet' and were accordingly 'cowards'. A later conversation with Meyer did not improve his temper when he was informed that the harp cap badges for the Brigade were too expensive to produce; 'such a niggardly conception of their obligations' cast him down to such an extent that dinner with some German grandees did not improve his perception of the intelligence of the 'governing classes', which he now regarded as inferior to that of the despised English.

When he was sorting out his trunk to be sent from the hotel a few evenings later, Adler arrived, full of his 'delightful web of lies'. He described how Findlay had been 'pale, with beads of perspiration rolling down him . . . in a state of wild excitement' when told of the steam yacht and the jagt, and had again called Casement 'clever and a very dangerous son of a b----!' Christensen claimed he had been offered an unimaginable £10,000 to turn Casement in, which he planned to donate to the Irish cause. If Casement escaped, Findlay would apparently 'go bug house', interpreted by Casement to mean 'off his chump'. Altogether the report was 'delicious' to him, dispelling his gloom.

The two men spent the next day together at the Eden. Christensen repeated that Findlay considered Casement 'a gentleman' but a 'dangerous son of a b----', putting him in such a good mood that he laughed about 'my dear Foreign Office' paying out to the near-vagrant Norwegian he had picked up on Broadway. He rejoiced in his ejection from the English establishment, regretting that he did not have a copy of Conan Doyle's letter about his 'mental malady'. He concluded that the English were 'a strange people': when he had served them, he was a 'hero . . . the most chivalrous public servant in the service of the Empire etc. etc.'; but now that he was 'doing a far braver thing and a far more chivalrous one' he was at best 'a lunatic' and certainly 'a rampant traitor'. As Dorian Gray puts it in Wilde's novel, 'to become the spectator of one's own life . . . is to escape the suffering of life' – the reunion with Christensen and his tall tales enabled Casement to climb out of his despondency and stand outside himself to accept and justify his treachery.

The lack of a meeting with the Chancellor or Foreign Secretary had led him to conclude hyperbolically that Germany did not have 'any soul for great enterprises', since it wanted 'the divine spark of imagination'. But on his return to his unsatisfactory room at midnight, he found a note from Wedel telling him to present himself to Dr von Bethmann Hollweg at noon. Adler Christensen was 'very downcast at the thought that all our plans against Findlay would come to nought' as the German government contact might well result in the Christiania sideshow being left behind. But Casement's spirits lifted even further when he arrived at Wilhelmstrasse: a document about the organisation of the Irish Brigade he had been working on was agreed, and he was told that Devoy had despatched another $1,000 for him, as well as another priest in sympathy with the cause, Father John Nicholson of Philadelphia. Wedel also showed him the latest commentary from England, exemplified by a cutting from the *Manchester Guardian* describing his 'act of treason to England and of double-dyed treason to Ireland'.

When Casement was shown into the Chancellor's office in Bismarck's Wilhelmstrasse palace, the sharply bearded Bethmann Hollweg, dressed in his field-grey uniform, advanced to shake his hand. Bethmann Hollweg had risen through the Prussian government to be appointed by the Kaiser to his current role in 1909; he had a reputation as a moderate conciliator who had fruitlessly sought accommodation with Britain over the naval arms race, but at this stage of the war he accepted that Germany needed to take any necessary steps to survive. The pair sat and smoked cigarettes, the Chancellor speaking in French and Casement in English as they discussed the Irish in America and the dream of a free Ireland. Hollweg acknowledged that an independent Ireland 'would be a good thing for Germany and for the freedoms of the seas' and at Casement's urging agreed 'to *have* an Irish policy for Germany in future'. He asked for details of the Findlay case, and was astonished by the reward and, justifiably if true, about Findlay's 'entrusting the key to the

back door of the British Legation to my rascal Adler!' Casement
expounded on 'the English character . . . Like certain chemicals –
apart harmless, brought together you get an infernal explosive or a
deadly poison.' Hollweg 'laughed' before bringing the half-hour
audience to an end with the wish for 'all success in my aims and
projects'.

In his focus on the misinformation plan, Casement had intended
for Christensen to return to Norway with another 'sham letter' full
of 'invented atrocities' to keep the Minister 'at a white heat', but now
that he had been taken seriously by the Chancellor he became '*not
sure of Adler*' after all. He had found him changed since his second
visit to Norway; his 'old, boyish eyes and smile [were] gone' and he
no longer met Casement's eye. He talked admiringly of Findlay as 'a
man who sticks at nothing' who 'would roll the God d----d Germans
up'. The trusting Casement had no idea that his lover was raising the
dramatic stakes for his own purposes, or that he had probably taken
up with a German girlfriend already. Christensen deemed himself
indispensable to Casement, was probably dazzled by what he stood
to gain financially if he could keep juggling, and resented Schiemann's 'allegations', which the ever meddling Blücher had informed
Casement had been 'conveyed to the F.O. [in Wilhelmstrasse]'. In the
end, Casement reckoned Christensen's 'rage against the Germans' for
paying so little attention to the lucrative, amplified Christiania business was 'almost swallowing up his affection' for him.

He had been made even more uneasy about the Findlay deception
by a letter from Kuno Meyer, the Celtic scholar and spy, dated 28
November, which stated in no uncertain terms that McGarrity,
Devoy and Quinn 'all disapprove the publication of the Christiania
incident'. Devoy was perceptive enough to ask 'how the enemy got
hold of the information [about his journey and backing] which they
evidently did not have when they held the ship . . . in Stornoway' in
the first place. On top of this, Casement had floated the idea that the
Irish Brigade might go to Egypt to fight the British, a notion which
led Devoy to rebuke him: 'We in America strongly object to any such
proposal, and our friends in Dublin are unalterably opposed to it.'
They had not sent their emissary to Germany to run an opportunistic

espionage plot, and did not share Casement's emotional, not very strategic response that the British Empire had to be tackled wherever it raised its flag. Now that Christensen's evasiveness seemed a potential liability to his central mission, Casement's recent affection continued to fall away; he even wondered if it might be best to get him back to the United States.

These thoughts led him to consider how cut off he was, how he had heard nothing from Ireland, particularly from Eoin MacNeill and the 'poor brave but frail' Alice Green. The press cuttings had shown how he was regarded in England, and he now considered that the 'only hope' for Ireland was that the British government 'will show their hand so openly against Irish nationality that Redmond and his gang of traitors' would have to 'repudiate England' or the cause they had 'so cruelly betrayed'. The day that he had finally achieved his goal of meeting the Imperial Chancellor was ending in a confusion of loyalty, betrayal and hope.

By Christmas Eve, Casement had swung around to decide that there was no harm in maintaining the diversion of the conspiracy. He revived his 'Mr Hammond' alias and bought a ticket to embark at Gothenburg for Christiania on 8 January on the Danish ship *Mjölnir*. He would be carrying two sketch maps of huge minefields supposedly laid by the Germans that would effectively close off the Irish Sea. The German Naval Office drew these up for him and Christensen traced them in his own hand for verisimilitude before his departure once more on Christmas Day. In his rekindled enthusiasm Casement cast aside his worries about Christensen's shiftiness.

Christensen was briefed to tell Findlay that a 'special messenger' had arrived from New York 'with good news' for his master. Dr Ewald, Vice-President of the American Truth Society, had indeed come to see Casement at the Eden the previous night to tell him that there was no chance of America getting 'roped in' to a war with Germany as 'there would be a revolution'; he also reported that the German-American press was so impressed by the Declaration that it 'said the next German Dreadnought [battleship] should be named *Sir Roger Casement*'. Another Christmas bonus was Richard Meyer bringing an Irish Brigade sample uniform: pale grey 'with a touch of green running thro' the warp', emerald green facings on the cuffs and collar, a harp on the collar flaps and another with a shamrock on the green cap band.

The renewed debriefings of Christensen in Christiania led to another flurry of telegrams to London to end Findlay's unforeseen year as an agent runner. An urgent report concerned the 'tracings of two charts which [the informer] had found in C's drawer'. The first showed four minefields: one in a circle of 'about 15 miles diameter immediately to the north of Tory Island'; the next at Tor Rocks; the third from Ballyferris Point to the Mull of Galloway, effectively sealing the Irish Sea to the north; and the last from Carnsore Point to Strumble Head in Wales, shutting off access to the south. The second chart was equally threatening, as it showed six more sites the Germans were planning to mine: one from Buckie and Spey Bay in Moray running north-east for twenty miles; another for the same distance east of Aberdeen; a third for twenty miles to the east of the Tyne's entry to the sea; two more north and south of the Humber Estuary; and one twenty-five miles north and south of Yarmouth.

While this espionage gold was being coded, Findlay composed another telegram. He was frustrated by Christensen's obfuscation: 'the informer' seemed vague about the 'sailing-boats' and what they were 'to be used for', or whether they would sail at all. Christensen also had no news of 'the American yacht', but maybe that was at sea already 'to possibly pick up Casement at or off port in South of Norway'. He was similarly vague about the 'names of Agents in Ireland'. Despite these gaps, the conspiracy was sufficiently serious for Nicolson to send copies of the material to the Prime Minister, Lord Kitchener, the First Lord of the Admiralty Winston Churchill, MO5(g) and Hall at Naval Intelligence. Hall replied, 'We have no information that would be of use to you,' but wished to know the date of Casement's rendezvous with the American yacht.

Berlin seemed untouched by war that Christmas aside from the patriotic bunting and the soldiers on the streets. The British shipping blockade had yet to make itself felt, and the traditional Christmas seasonal markets were brightly lit and crowded. Church bells had rung out in previous weeks following the collapse of Russian forces in Poland and Galicia, while failure at Ypres and the Serbian victory over Austria-Hungary at Kolubara went unacknowledged. Germany was overstretched on two long fronts in its pursuit of total victory, but Casement still hoped for a breakthrough on the Western Front and a march on the Channel ports. The British had just announced their Protectorate over Egypt as part of their war against the Ottoman Empire, news which ramped up his rhetoric as he claimed that the proclamation was 'a delightful specimen of British hypocrisy and double dealing combined with the arrogance of a successful burglar who has got his victim robbed and bound'.

Now that he had the Chancellor's blessing for his campaign, Casement asked Under-Secretary Zimmermann to go beyond the Declaration to a formal document, 'a proposal for the embodiment of an Irish Brigade, pledged to fight in that cause alone'. Five days later Zimmermann, conscious that the visitor had been received at the highest level and that his government had nothing to lose, sent the document. Its ten articles laid down that the Germans would support the Brigade, which would fight under the 'Irish Flag alone'; that Casement should have disciplinary charge of it; that German officers would be appointed until 'Irish officers can be secured'; that no member should receive 'monetary reward'; that the German Navy would transport the Brigade to Ireland when it had a 'reasonable prospect of success'; and that if the war ended before the men were deployed, they could be given passage to the United States. It also contained the near-contradictory provisions that 'The object of the Irish Brigade shall be to fight solely in the cause of Ireland', yet if the landing in Ireland could not take place 'it might be possible to employ the Irish Brigade to assist the Egyptian People to recover their freedom by driving the British out of Egypt'. Casement had inserted the clause into his new treaty despite Devoy's explicit unhappiness about it; the Germans had no problem endorsing any blow to Britain.

Casement spent the first Christmas of the war with Countess Hahn in another step in his progress through gossip-laden German society. The second half of 1914 had seen him travel from Ireland to America

to Norway and on to Germany; he had become involved in the closest relationship of his life, which in turn had led to unknown
double-cross and betrayal. His spirits had veered between hope, disappointment and resentment, and between trusting love for Adler
Christensen and suspicion, but he was ending the year positively.
Now he was brought down from his optimism again by events
beyond his control: although in France the replacements for the British Expeditionary Force were ill-trained and failing according to
German reports, the war news from the east had taken a turn for the
worse as the Russians reinforced and successfully held the Bzura line
thirty miles west of Warsaw. His physical health often mirrored his
mental well-being, and he became unwell with a heavy cold just as he
set off for Frankfurt on 30 December. He spent the advent of 1915 in
bed in Limburg, knowing that the next few weeks would be critical
in defining his reputation far beyond his achievements in Africa and
South America. Those campaigns had made a difference to the lives
of hundreds of thousands; now he had limited energy, time and
resources to change the fate of his own country.

11.   Conspiracy's End

Nineteen-fifteen was the year of digging in. Germany pursued its eastern offensive in the hope of forcing peace with Russia, which on 1 January appealed to the British to launch diversionary operations against the Ottoman Empire; Britain and France tried to expel the Germans from their western gains. As Flanders became a quagmire and the year ground on, efforts were focused on the chalklands along the River Somme and in Champagne; after a successful British, Canadian and Indian offensive at Neuve Chappelle in March, the Germans took advantage of poor communications to force yet another expensive stalemate. In April, Germany used lethal chlorine gas on the Western Front at the Second Battle of Ypres, and the British, Australians, New Zealanders and French embarked on the first disastrous amphibious landings in the Dardanelles between the Aegean and the Sea of Marmara. Success for the Irish nationalist movement in this death-dealing attritional struggle depended upon German support, ladling pressure on Casement's recruitment success at a time when his mental and physical health were perilous. His year was to reflect the frustrated stasis of the war.

The opening entry of his journal set the tone. He had been unable to write as he had 'been ill and greatly upset at the failure of my hopes', despite the acceptance of his treaty proposals by Count Zimmermann. He jotted 'friction between Irish and English troops in northern France' on the back of a coded telegram from the German Military Attaché in neutral Stockholm which noted that 'Success of statement by Casement and [German] Foreign Office excellent in Ireland' – provided an invasion was launched with no fewer than 25,000 troops and 'with 50,000 extra guns'. Even if he were to recruit every one of the men in Limburg, ten times that number would need to be supplied by his hard-pressed hosts to be successful.

He had spent the last days of 1914 encouraging the release of Irish civilian internees trapped by the war at Ruhleben, six miles from the capital. There were 4,000 British in the camp, some living in stables, others in the haylofts above with scarcely room to stand upright. A young Dubliner who had been studying German in Marburg, Bryan Kelly, was released and visited Casement in the Eden just before Christmas. They talked about County Kerry, the Irish language and the Gaelic League before Casement launched into a diatribe about how 'England was the enemy of Europe' and 'Germany the nation of the future'; he admitted he had burnt his own boats but had to stop Ireland 'falling with the ruins of the British Empire'. Kelly's impression was of an 'extreme fidget . . . a very impulsive, excitable man' as he heard of the near arrest in Stornoway, the visit to Charleville and how the British were lying in wait for him in the North Sea. Another who got home was Professor Henry Macran of Trinity College Dublin, 'a very rebel', who was glad to be 'a true and faithful witness to the truth about Germany' as he carried messages to Gertrude Bannister, Alice Green and Eoin MacNeill, and money for Nina. Casement hoped the remaining 160 Irish internees would be freed, if only to enrage the English.

Fathers O'Gorman and Crotty were 'delighted' to see Casement, professing themselves fully won over to the cause, although O'Gorman was shortly to return to Rome, to be replaced by Father Nicholson. They went to Limburg on 5 January, with Casement encouraged by Christensen's news that 'all was going very well'. Since his last visit, there had been a fresh intake, among them Michael Keogh, the son of a Royal Ulster Constabulary policeman who had gone to New York and become a Clan na Gael member; the two men had actually met in 1911 when Casement was in the United States to drum up support for his Putumayo campaign. Back in Ireland, Keogh had served a month's imprisonment for sedition in the Curragh Camp incident before joining the Royal Irish Regiment at the start of the war. Three weeks later he was captured in the 'veritable death-trap' of the Battle of Mons, where Irishmen were put 'in the breach [and] suffered most'.

The Sennelager camp held 1,500 of his countrymen and 10,000 other 'Tommies', and Keogh had been startled to be called to a parade at which an English-speaking German officer declared that 'all Irish soldiers, now prisoners of war, [would be] be assembled in one distinct camp, be treated better, have more freedom, better food and clothing and suitable games'. With the help of a corrupt guard, he got in touch with Casement to offer his support, and was among those who took the eighteen-hour train journey to Limburg at the end of the year. He was astonished at the comfort of the newly finished quarters: well-ventilated huts housing fifty men in two rooms, with real blankets on the trestle beds. Keogh was asked to recruit 'young men with a fair education' and knowledgeable about Irish subjugation; they must be bachelors to ensure that no dependants' allowance could be stopped. Casement was 'rather optimistic' on this third visit, despite Keogh coming across so many 'undesirables', Englishmen, Welshmen and Scots who had fooled the Germans and signed up for better treatment; a third of the 'Irish goods' from the camp at Döberitz had 'not a drop' of Irish Catholic blood in them but their 'gluttonous Anglo-Saxon eye' had been caught by the 'mere mention of food improvements'. One veteran of Mons, William Dooley, who had claimed to have undergone a 'very strict examination . . . of parentage, birthplace, religion and nationality', was delighted to find that the bread ration of his cohort of 245 Irishmen would be increased to '750 grammes per day with soup and coffee on our arrival'. The provisions now included 'bacon, eggs and beer', and those who adhered to their loyal oaths 'were marched by periodically during mealtimes' to rub in their mistake. Boots replaced wooden clogs, and overcoats were supplied.

Copies of *The Crime against Ireland* and the *Gaelic American*, 'which gave particulars of the dreadful treatment of Ireland by . . . the dirty English', were distributed and the men were taught what 'disgraceful things took place' in the South African War, 'another example of England's injustice'. But when Casement offered £5 a head if 'you succeed in winning the war for Germany', proposing that 'we will make Queenstown a Naval Base for the landing of troops against England', many grew uncomfortable. He claimed that Redmond was a traitor, that the Home Rule Bill 'only a pretence' and that 'England started this war and if you don't fight for Ireland you are nothing but a lot of cornerboys and spalpeens'.* This was too much for some of the prisoners: one NCO, T. R. Collins, told the 252 men in his charge 'to have nothing to do with these people', to think of their families and to ask themselves how would 'the Irish party be able to face the Government if any of you turned traitors'. Some jostled and heckled Casement, who swung his umbrella at them to keep them back. The protesters had their rations cut for the next three days, and many were dispersed to other camps with Collins's admonition to 'remain loyal to your King and Country'.

Bryan Kelly, the personable student from Ruhleben, accompanied the party to Limburg. He witnessed a crowd cheering for Redmond and barracking Casement, with one man shouting, 'How much are the Germans paying you?' Casement called the man 'a scoundrel' and walked away. Two days later, Kelly called on Casement to find him very despondent: these men were 'the last he would think of' if he was raising a brigade from scratch. They took the train to Frankfurt together, and Casement rambled on about his Foreign Office career and his warnings to Grey around the time of his Putumayo report that the government's attitude to Germany was 'bringing England to the brink of ruin'.

Casement had lost hope of raising a militia from his 'contemptible' countrymen, and concluded that his great scheme 'must be entirely abandoned'. The men 'showed clearly the utter slothful indifference of that type of debauched Irishman to any appeal but to his greed'. The ascetic was distancing himself from those he had believed to be his true countrymen, failing to comprehend how the suspicious prisoners could be complaining of hunger or lack of tobacco, or, and above all, be 'full of ill will to Germany', the foe whose soldiers they had been looking to kill only months earlier. He was despondent 'after the revelation of Irish depravity', frustrated and miserable again at the inability of others to feel the same inner grip of a cause. But four minutes after he got back to his hotel, Wilhelmstrasse relayed a

---

* Cornerboy – a disreputable street loiterer; spalpeen – a lout. Neither of these expressions sounds like Casement's style: maybe he was trying to use language that would appeal to his audience, or the soldier who reported this was exaggerating for effect.

telegram from Christensen that read: 'Meet me train 7.24 Berlin, must see you, good news.'

The telegram was swiftly followed by a call from Meyer to inform him that Christensen's return had been delayed. But also waiting at the hotel was an exultant letter from the Norwegian dated 27 December: Findlay 'still believes . . . about those little ships I told him about . . . and he is firm in the belief that you are going to land in Ireland with a whole lot of German troops'. He had again gone further than his brief to announce that there would also be three or four 'transports or battleships' making their way through the minefields to Ireland, allowing his fantasies to run wild when he suggested that there should be a man looking like Casement on the *Mjölnir* 'with a big ulster up over his ears' so that Findlay would board the vessel and become their prisoner.

Findlay and Christensen had met twice on 3 January. The first time, Christensen gave the sailing date for the *Mjölnir* as the 9th, with a recommendation that she be intercepted at Gothenburg. He reckoned he had played his part superbly, 'showing nervousness about his own safety if captured'; he would need to hide his 'master's strongbox' before the papers were transferred to a British warship. Realising that this was his moment of indispensability to his made-up scheme, Christensen then made 'impossible demands' for £1,000 on account, which were refused. He stormed out, getting as far as the gate before a footman caught up with him. He had effectively blackmailed Findlay into a guarantee in exchange for his agreement 'to meet party at Christiansand' and ensure Casement's handover. Findlay wrote on a sheet of paper with the legation's letterhead that he promised 'On behalf of the British Government . . . that if through information given by Adler Christiansen, Sir Roger Casement be captured either with or without his companions', £5,000 would be paid and Christensen would 'enjoy personal immunity and be given a passage to the United States should he desire it'. He had made the mistake that played into Casement's hands.

The deceit initiated by Christensen's deviousness and promulgated by Casement to prove that the government he had served were base resulted in a moral defeat for England. Nicolson was appalled by Findlay's actions, cabling that 'Nothing should ever be given to informer in writing. Pray be careful at this most important point.' But it was too late. The second half of the draft telegram from White-hall was in Sir Edward Grey's hand, a sign of the close interest he was taking in his former distinguished subordinate. The Foreign Secretary showed a level of compassion and solicitude: Findlay must 'make it perfectly clear that [Christensen] is on no account to have any harm or injury caused to Casement's person' during the *Mjölnir*'s interception; if the Norwegian was 'the sort of person' Grey assumed him to be, he was apprehensive that 'he may do something abominable such as assassinating or injuring Casement to secure capture of him or his papers'. While some might have seen the death of Casement as the solution to a problem, Grey abominated it for itself, and for the risk that it would create a martyr.

Christensen awaited the *Mjölnir* in the port on the night of the 8th, although she was not due to dock until the next evening. He was wearing a green necktie as a recognition signal, and spent much of the day chatting to a British agent, Everson. When the ship pulled in, Christensen boarded her, but found no sign of 'Mr Hammond'. After midnight on the 9th, Findlay passed on the no-show to London, along with Everson's unverified observation that a German U-boat had been in the port, presumably to intercept any Royal Navy ship intent on grabbing Casement. Christensen and Everson stayed for another three days, allegedly awaiting orders for the former from Berlin, which naturally failed to arrive. The two men travelled to Christiania together, and as they parted Christensen left the agent with a letter for Findlay in which he 'confessed': he had been so enraged by Findlay refusing to give him '£1000 down' when they last met that he had reported to Berlin that his letter of instructions about the *Mjölnir* had been stolen in Norway, 'he did not know by whom'. Plans had changed as a result, and he had not dared tell the British for fear of detention. But they 'cannot do any harm now'. If Christensen's confessional letter ever existed, it never made it to Nicolson's 'Irish Conspiracy' file.

Findlay was despondent after the failure of the 'coup we had hoped to bring off in the Casement Case'. He had gone over and over it in his head and did not see how he could have 'acted otherwise' to prevent rebellion and invasion in Ireland and to halt the prospective minefields. He once again rehearsed the circumstances which had led him to the fateful written guarantee, justified as 'simply an offer of reward for capture of self-confessed traitor such as might be posted in every police office in Great Britain'. It would never have been made in peacetime, and had only been done to keep hold of his informer. In what seemed a weak defence of his actions at the time but turned out to be a shrewd calculation, he claimed that 'we have nothing to fear from publicity'. He had apparently told Christensen that he was 'a fool to ask for it, as it would be his death-warrant if Germans or Fenians got hold of it', a warning which he did not report, and which Christensen, eager to give himself every dramatic opening, had not passed on.

The diplomat found it hard to comprehend that he might have been the victim of an implausible double-cross that had started on the morning Christensen first arrived in his legation. He minuted that it was 'impossible to follow the workings of a mind absolutely ~~devoid of~~ unregulated by any rules of morality or intelligence but subject to intense suspiciousness and guided by low cunning'. The British espionage operation had failed, but he clung to the conviction that all the information he had passed on had been 'correct', signing off on the business that had consumed him for months by saying 'I deeply regret failure but have done my best' in handling 'a most loathsome beast'. He pleaded that the authorities at least take seriously the threats 'to lay mines, to run arms, and to land men in Ireland from Germany and America'.

Casement's most recent visit to Limburg had cast him down to such an extent that for the first time he failed to mention the city's medieval beauty or its cathedral in his journal. He told John Quinn that he was now 'a refugee, an outcast with no place to lay my head when this present war is over. The enemy would hang me – I know.' Kelly too found the potential recruits 'quite contemptible', despised by French and German alike – many of them still signing up only for the free passage home. Casement informed Meyer that 'there was no hope of getting the soldiers to do anything' and immediately tacked to his emotional escape route in wondering if the telegram about Adler's return signified that 'these scoundrels have fallen into their despicable plot to kidnap' him; he stressed his own influence once more after reading about English mines around Norway in the newspaper – 'clearly' part of the 'British action to prevent my contemplated Wolfe Tone descent on the coast of Ireland'. Between the anxiety engendered by Christensen's reports and his failing belief in the Irish Brigade, he needed to fix his own self-worth high to maintain his equilibrium.

Quinlisk reported that some of the men were threatening to ensure Casement's execution for treason if he got home. Quinlisk was prepared to be a martyr, but Casement promised him safe passage to America if need be; the corporal's courage plainly showed that the rest were 'cowards', but the sensation of being 'very sad . . . despondent' was being channelled into a 'long-contemplated' open letter to his former boss. He had read of Grey's confirmation that his pension had been stopped, and the statement made by the Secretary of State for the Colonies in the Lords that he should undergo 'severe penalties': it was 'a melancholy reflection that a man who did some good service in the past should, assuming him to be in the possession of all his faculties, have fallen so low'.

He was embarked on another, increasingly isolated week in Limburg. He had heard nothing from 'Berlin at all and so nothing from Christiania'. He assumed Adler's 'fooling' of Findlay had been exposed, and planned to take some form of unspecified legal action against the Foreign Office for 'criminal conspiracy'. The rain continued, his teeth necessitated dental work and Father O'Gorman returned to Rome, but not before condemning the prisoners as 'miserable specimens of Irishmen'. Despondency deepened with the rumour that Kitchener was landing in France with 2 million soldiers to 'smash' Germany, at which point the prisoners would return home to receive their accumulated 'blood money'. His handwriting, always unschooled and hurried, began to deteriorate as he contemplated the 'demoralised and Anglicised' soldiers; he returned to Berlin on 21

January without much hope of further success or usefulness in Germany.

Yet, against the odds, Christensen's immorality and betrayal had nevertheless delivered into his hands the moral weapon he required to fight back against the English – Findlay's handwritten promise and threat were 'the most damning piece of evidence ever given by a Government against itself'. He was outraged that the document had been in Wilhelmstrasse for nearly three weeks without his knowledge; he did not pause to consider that the silence might have been the result of waning German interest, but chose to believe that the diplomats had their own, unstated plans for it. He insisted that the paper was his property, and he intended to use it to publicise Grey's wickedness. Wedel agreed to hand it over, as well as offering to pay Christensen's travel expenses, but Casement was adamant that 'the matter was between me and the British Government . . . Adler was my servant and I could not allow him to accept money from the German Government.' When he saw Christensen at their hotel that evening, he dismissed the idea of continuing the Findlay deception as he had the only bit of paper he needed to expose the whole 'dastardly criminal conspiracy'.

Over the next week, he drafted and redrafted his letter to Grey; it consumed all his thoughts. Now he had 'the final proof of the actual punishment [the English] sought', his capture at Christiansand, he could expose the British perfidy; it was worth the loss of 'pension and honours and was even worth the commission of an act of technical "treason" . . . to save Ireland from some of the calamities of war'; he was prepared to 'face charges in a Court of Law' but not to find himself confronted by 'waylaying, kidnapping, suborning of dependents or "knocking on the head"' in the North Sea. The rest of the letter demonstrated his fury at what he still believed to be the original British approach by one of the 'secret agents of the British Minister'. He played down his own deceptions which, alongside Christensen's embellishments, had brought the situation – and his mental state – to this tangled pass.

If it had been true that Findlay had suggested to 'my dependent that were I to "disappear it would be a very good thing for whoever brought it about"', or that Christensen had been induced to 'knock him on the head', his outrage would have been justified. But he was still tragically blind to Christensen's venal untrustworthiness; he was more concerned about the effect on his lover than about the threat to himself. He believed Christensen had continued the conversation only 'to become more fully aware of the plot', and it was Findlay who had built 'the conspiracy against my life, my liberty, the public law of Norway and the happiness of the young man he sought to tempt by monstrous bribes to the commission of a dastardly crime against his admitted benefactor'. It was 'a triumph of Norwegian integrity' that his 'faithful follower' had escaped the country unscathed.

The remaining third of the 3,000-word, self-deluding letter reprised the charge that Britain had gone to war with Germany on the false premise of 'atrocious crimes in Belgium' and had coerced the Irish into abandoning Home Rule by warning them 'that their fate would be the same, did Germany win this war'. The Declaration had been designed 'to relieve my countrymen from the apprehensions this campaign of calumny was designed to provoke', and should not have engendered a conspiracy to 'take my life with public indignity'. As for his own part in the clumsy double-cross, those stories 'should not have deceived a schoolboy' and were only part of his 'necessary self-defence to lay bare' the government's entrapment. In due course he would put Findlay's written promise to pay Christensen 'before the legitimate authorities'. Meanwhile, he wished to give up his honours, and return the insignia.

The letter was timed to coincide with the opening of Parliament; he was confident of being the subject of questions. He was determined to be 'first in the field *& expose them*' before the government could take the high ground of 'moral indignation' about his now admitted 'treason'. Meyer was enjoying the conspiracy so much that he offered Casement three detectives to travel with him to Norway: the pair conjured a scenario in which somehow Findlay would be encouraged to kidnap Casement, at which point the men would pounce to seize the British Minister and his accomplices, turning them over to the Norwegian police on an unspecified charge. The excitable Casement allowed himself to be talked out of this espionage extravaganza by the unlikely calming influence of Blücher, but he still intended to travel openly with his escort, challenge Findlay and then pass the matter to the police.

On the last day of January, he signed the typed and corrected copies of his letter, walked through the thick snow to the Stettinbahnhof and set off for Sassnitz; the ferry to Norway had been stopped so they would have to travel on the mailboat. Christensen accompanied him in first class, the detectives were in second class. Meyer had delivered an Admiralty warning, without any intelligence basis, that a British submarine might try to stop the mailboat to Norway and demand his surrender, engendering a sleepless night in his bunk contemplating that he was travelling 'to challenge the mightiest Govt. in the world and to charge them with infamous criminal conspiracy . . . a desperate act'. He himself had 'no Govt., save that of the one bent on destroying' him. At their hotel breakfast the following morning, Christensen dissuaded him from continuing, presumably partly because he did not want the story of his own meddling to emerge. The combination of this appeal, his realisation that he could not win the fight he was taking to them and his own fear persuaded Casement to turn back. He sent Christensen to Norway to 'get his things' before rejoining him, though he was anxious that the British would seize the 'poor penniless wretch' as a hostage for his own liberty.

The Grey letter, accompanied by a photograph of Findlay's pledge, was despatched to a dozen embassies and legations, to Devoy, to the State Department in America and to the German press. It was posted from the Hague to its addressee, the Foreign Secretary, and to the British newspapers. Casement spent the ensuing days in a fretful mix of fear and excitement; he decided to leave his hotel to avoid the expected international furore and went to stay with Baron and Baroness von Nordenflycht, diplomat friends from Rio days. After that, he booked into a hotel in Potsdam but returned to Berlin in despair after the concierge was rude to him for speaking English. Next, he called on Mrs White, the Viennese wife of the English proprietor of the *Continental Times* who, after a brief conversation with her overwrought visitor, advised a rest in a Grunewald sanatorium.

The next day brought the news that the Portuguese Minister had refused to forward his letter to Lisbon as it 'exceeded the legal rights' of his legation, but there was no other reaction. Meyer agreed that the Portuguese was a '*cochon*', but in his nervous state Casement now turned against his protector and handler, finding Meyer 'secretive and lacking in frankness', keeping important things from him. Now that his exposure of the illegal international conspiracy was failing to get immediate traction, alongside the disappointment of the Irish Brigade, he felt he had lost control of his mission and was being treated 'as a kind of tool or agent – to be directed & used – but never kept informed or referred to – or consulted'. At this outpouring, Meyer too recommended a rest cure, offering to 'arrange all with the police'. Although the exhausted Casement had 'lost all faith' in Wilhelmstrasse's 'good sense and action', he agreed. Adler accompanied him to one of the large Victorian villas in the forest to the west of the city, but decided, by his account, at the last minute to stay behind with the head waiter of the Continental. Despite the sanatorium staff being 'all very friendly and polite', Casement felt 'so lonely and abandoned'. In his paranoid depletion, he wanted only to 'get away from police spies & military and all the rest of it'.

Late that same evening he heard that England had prohibited cables to and from Europe as Kitchener's new army needed the security protection of a news blackout, but in his state of enraged depression, grieving for what was slipping away from him and knowing that his boats were comprehensively burnt, the broken man saw the decision by the 'Bitch & Harlot of the North Sea' as firmly directed at him, 'a part of their d----d conspiracy'. England 'fear mightily my charge' being published in America, 'and have arranged their version and publicly branded me a "traitor" before' he could tell his side of the story. Meanwhile he was 'a semi-prisoner', mistrustful of the German government and 'their hopeless ineptitude' and expecting to be arrested the following morning.

The man who had analysed the English character with the German Chancellor a matter of weeks earlier was unrecognisable in the figure who was pouring out his misery, much of it inflicted by his devotion to someone others had mistrusted from the start. His Treaty, now 'signed with the Seal of State', was 'the *only* thing I had to show for all my sacrifice (& folly)', an acknowledgement of the German pledge to help Ireland achieve 'complete independence'; but so far he had achieved little with the Brigade. 'Since a possible German victory faded further & further into the limbo of the lost', the Treaty – a significant diplomatic achievement – might be all he had to show for his months in Germany. He was 'disillusioned and miserable'. While he was writing up his diary and 'eating my heart out', the next day 'an agent of the secret police' called and ask for the pass he had been given four months earlier which had allowed him to travel freely; this deprivation exemplified his status, he decided – that he was being 'used by a most selfish and unscrupulous government for its own sole petty interests'. His last journal entry for 1915 was for 10 February: he expected the Germans 'to bungle things' to the extent that he would 'be hauled off to jail'. He did not pick his pen up again for nearly fourteen months, by which time he was counting down his German days to make a last-ditch attempt to save his country.

12.   The Great Tale

Time was running short for Clan na Gael. There was little public appetite for initiating a revolution, and few funds for it, 'when the greatest war in history was going on', as John Devoy bluntly stated. Devoy recognised that his emissary 'was so upset by Findlay's attempt to kidnap and murder him' that he had 'lost for a time his sense of proportion' and was not focusing his energies on arms procurement. In Berlin, Casement was feeling betrayed by the Germans and betrayed by the British establishment in Christiania, but was still clinging to Adler Christensen. In Ireland the secretive inner group of Irish Republican Brotherhood strategists had decided that the government's Home Rule offer was too little, too late, and that a rising must take place the following year. The restless, enthusiastic, tubercular young poet Joseph Mary Plunkett, Director of Military Operations of the Irish Volunteers, was sent to Germany to negotiate for arms and officers.

Plunkett left Dublin on St Patrick's Day 1915. For fear of spies and interception, he took a circuitous route via Liverpool, Paris, San Sebastián (where he was overcome by bronchitis, treated with quinine and creosote), Barcelona (where he celebrated Palm Sunday and went to his first bullfight), Genoa, Florence (where he saw masterpieces of the Renaissance and went to the Easter services in the Duomo), Milan, Lausanne and Berne. He finally reached Berlin under the name of Johann M. Peters, visiting from San Francisco, over a month later and made himself known to Wedel, who immediately rang Casement.

The two men met at Casement's hotel, where they were briefly joined by naval lieutenant Hans Boehm, the Abteilung IIIb* agent dealing with separatist groups in Ireland and India. Boehm had spied

---

* The military intelligence wing of the Imperial German Army.

in America and was now seconded to Casement's operations. Plunkett was not entirely open at the meeting, only hinting at the Rising as 'a great tale of planned revolution'. Casement, recovering from a bout of flu, believed he had come with 'important news . . . from my friends in Ireland', and was horrified by the diluted message. No rebellion stood a chance without 'the military (& naval) support of a great Continental power'; he 'sat on [the idea] as often and as vigorously as was possible', citing precedents from Hugh O'Neill in 1598 to Wolfe Tone in 1798 to reinforce his point. Privately, he considered 'A Rising in the streets of Dublin . . . criminal stupidity', an act of pointless sacrificial violence. Yet his emotional patriotism was rekindled even as he disdained such talk; he 'who had always stood for action . . . could not stay in safety in this land while those in Ireland who cherished a manly soul were laying down their lives for an ideal'. However, by the time he wrote these words his options were radically limited, his expectations narrowed and his life scrutinised.

British intelligence was building its dossier: its officers took a look around Casement's occasional London lodgings at 50 Ebury Street, Pimlico, and accessed his bank account. His siblings were frequent recipients of cheques, as were Bigger and Bulmer Hobson in Ireland; they worked out McGarrity, and Quinn after a period of uncertainty. Payments to his doctor were analysed, but those to an A. Doubleday were a source of confusion and anticipation, until active reconnaissance located a fishmonger of that name a few doors down. But however unrevealing this trawl might have been, Ebury Street already contained a much more damaging, arguably fatal, secret.

Bryan Kelly considered it his duty to make a statement at Dublin Castle on 8 February. He felt guilty that he owed his return to Casement's intervention, and was assured that nothing he said would be used in evidence against him. He recounted his first meeting at the Eden Hotel with the nervy man who had lectured him on the collapsing British Empire and on how Germany was the 'nation of the future', and who explained how he had got better treatment for 'the poor Irish fellows who had been sent to the shambles in Flanders'. The heart-stopping days at Stornoway and Charleville and Casement's meeting with the Imperial Chancellor were news to London, and Casement's version of the Christiania imbroglio gave the British officials pause for thought. Kelly recalled that, on their journey back from Frankfurt, Casement had expounded on his warning to Grey and Tyrrell that the British attitude towards Germany was bringing the country 'to the brink of ruin'. In his opinion, Casement's frequent statements 'which seemed strangely at variance with other utterances of his' suggested 'some nervous affection', even that he was 'unhinged'. Grey forwarded the report to Lloyd George, Kitchener and Asquith with the admonition that 'The promise must be kept and the information treated as confidential.'

Prisoner swaps were under way by the summer, and stories of Casement's actions filtered into the press. Corporal B. Thompson had been captured serving in the King's Own Yorkshire Light Infantry, but professed to be 'a Dublin man' when interviewed for the August Bank Holiday edition of the *Daily Chronicle*. He reported (with exaggeration) that 20,000 men at Limburg had been visited 'by a tall gentleman who spoke to them for the purpose of forming an Irish brigade of prisoners of war', and who took him aside to show him the prototype of a uniform and to ask 'if he were willing to become a recruiting sergeant'. Thompson's name did not come up in either Casement's or Keogh's accounts of Limburg.

Special Branch officers interviewed Casement's associates in London. The Anglo-Irish Lady Margaret Jenkins, a supporter of the Congo campaign, asserted that Casement's remarks were 'at times very revolutionary', and that his 'great friend' Mrs Green was 'a red-hot revolutionist'. Lady Margaret had been in Ireland through the summer and autumn of 1914 and concocted a story that Casement was visiting Galway at a time when he was actually in the United States, 'as it would make an ideal spot for the landing of rifles, or for use as a submarine base'.

British spies engaged in double-think. A report was prepared for Sir Mansfield Smith-Cumming, 'C', head of foreign intelligence, which opened: 'There is a curious, yet nonetheless persistent feeling among quite important persons in Germany, that [Casement] is in the pay of the British Government.' The main justifications for this theory, and its author claimed to have many more, were that he seemed to be mixing in 'the best circles', yet if he was being paid by the Germans they would not have given him this access; his 'attempted assassination' must have been 'an extremely well-laid scheme' set up by the British as a feint, or Findlay would have been sacked; finally, if Casement escaped with his life ('unlikely') he would apparently be given 'a high position in the English government . . . to carry out with success a law sanctioning Home Rule'. C was being asked if he would support an unstated counter-intelligence scheme 'by which the position of the man would be rendered untenable', but the request received no annotation in the Chief's green ink. Despite these diversions, the Casement dossiers were building into a clear, if not always straightforwardly defined, portrait of a traitor.

Devoy and Quinn remained concerned. The news of the Brigade was not encouraging; the Treaty with Germany still contained the wording about Egypt; there were no offers of arms; and their emissary, obsessed with his questionable servant and Findlay, appeared to be cracking up. In response to Father Nicholson's request that Casement come back to Limburg to continue recruitment, his excuse of his flu covered up the real reason – he would 'not return . . . to be insulted by a handful of recreant Irishmen . . . cads and cowards'. The language of Irish nationalism he had imbibed through the Gaelic League and intellectual debate with Mrs Green did not translate easily into a POW camp.

At the same time as he was distancing himself from his countrymen, Casement was writing to Gertrude Bannister that 'I am well still, and busy for the Poor Old Woman – I have made friends for *her* here and all are devoted to me . . . I am guarded and cared for like a National Treasure!' Despite this bravado, he did not hide his loneliness, how often he thought of Gertrude and Nina 'and all the old times – Like a dream now'; he attributed the sadness to the war rather than to anything within him: 'Some day peace will come again to the world and men's minds will be restored to sanity.' He enclosed a copy of his letter to Grey, complete with a photograph of Findlay's pledge, to forward to Ireland; it had caused an 'enormous sensation' in Europe.

There had actually been very little coverage of the convoluted case. Various newspapers in Norway published Casement's charges, which were a revelation to Findlay: he cabled Nicolson on 17 February insisting that the letter to Grey was 'an extraordinary mixture of fact and falsehood'. Still mortified by the business, he suggested 'prompt action be taken, as the accusation that I bribed an innocent young Norwegian servant to betray his master is calculated to do great harm'. He wished to issue a statement that Christensen had come to him of his own free will, and 'offered documents for money' to show 'that Casement was organising a hostile expedition to U.K.'

The affair got only a brief mention in *The Times*'s round-up of propaganda from the Berlin newspapers; a piece in the *Observer* was headlined 'An Absurd Story: Sir R. Casement Alleges Plot Against His Life' over a condensed version of the allegations; the *Daily News* ran with 'Absurd Plot Story'. A week later, Findlay was reporting that 'the matter has practically died a natural death' in Norway when he received the presumptive message from Casement demanding 'a guarantee of protection' – given what he had heard about being kidnapped and knocked on the head – for him to travel to the neutral country to confront the British government 'with conspiracy to procure my death or capture by treachery', as well as with bribing his 'faithful servant to violate Norwegian laws . . . an act of utmost baseness'. Findlay was concerned about salvaging his own reputation and proposed 'Refutation of charge that [he] sought out and corrupted servant and of conspiracy to murder without touching other points would be sufficient.' But the curt response from Whitehall was to say: 'Your tel of yesterday. It is best to leave matter quite alone.' Findlay's career did not suffer from the discomfort of the bribe: he became Sir Mansfeldt the following year and was awarded the Grand Cross of the Order of St Olaf by the King of Norway for his work in maintaining the essential flow of goods and munitions to Russia through the German blockade.

Casement's obsession with Christiania continued well into March. More internees arrived from Ruhleben at the start of the month, including William Coyne, Gerald Hoy and John Patrick Bradshaw. On the grounds that Bradshaw came from Ballymoney, Casement believed he would be a good man 'in spreading the Findlay tale throughout the land', and he asked Wedel to ensure a copy of the report in the *Continental Times* went back with him. Nothing came of this approach: as with Kelly, it was a presumption that the released Irishmen would promote the Irish cause any more than the Limburg soldiers.

Gerald Hoy, a teacher, certainly felt no such allegiance. He had got to know several Hussar officers in his three years of living in Germany, in particular Braumüller of the Great General Staff, who showed him a photograph of the Grey letter, which Hoy 'did not believe . . . because English diplomats were too clever to leave any incriminating documents in the hands of other people'. Even when Hoy met the 'Foreign Advisor to the Great General Staff Sir Roger Casement' and got the story at first hand, he was sceptical that Casement 'was compelled to hide himself in Berlin as he had information that British agents were preparing against his life'. In London, Hoy told all to his uncle Hugh Cleland Hoy of Naval Intelligence, as he reckoned that 'if once Germany got England down it might be a bad look-out' for Ireland after all. Room 40 chose not even to listen to Hoy's 'good plan by which the whole [Casement] organisation can be rooted out', far less 'lay it before the Admiralty'. (No record of the plan has survived.) Loyalty to country counted for far more than loyalist rebellion in what had become a global war.

Although it was essential for Casement's delicate mental equilibrium that he did not know of these frequent individual acts of treachery, newspapers on both sides of the Atlantic were now freely making allegations. The London *Graphic* ran a front-page cartoon of the immaculately dressed and hatted Casement talking to a group of shorter, scruffy Irish soldiers, their caps at all angles, with the caption 'The Voice of the Traitor!' in Gothic script. The text declared he had 'sounded the very depths of vileness since he sold himself body and soul to the enemy', and that he was offering his recruits either 'a German farm, a German wife' and a salary, or 'a free passage to America, employment there, and £20'. A copy of the weekly found its way to Limburg, where the loyal Father Crotty reassured Casement that 'everyone knows it to be a lie'.

The *New York World*, an anti-Irish newspaper, took up the charge on 10 February to assert that the German government had paid large sums to Casement to foment rebellion. He was outraged and, as the piece came out a couple of days after Grey would have received his letter, assumed that this was the latest extension of the underhand Foreign Office plot. The American Consul General in Munich, the Irish-born T. St John Gaffney, urged him 'to push the case to the bitter end' and expose the treachery; he should demand damages of $100,000.* In mid-March, Casement asked Quinn to act for him against this 'absolute lie' – he had rejected offers from publishers, lecture agents and even a tobacco company which wanted to bring out a new cigar using his name and picture, which proved he was not out for money. His accusers 'were reduced to the elemental weapons of British warfare against an Irishman – the Black Lie and the Silver Bullet'.

Quinn took some time to reply that silence was the best option: bringing a case would be expensive, would demand Casement's presence in New York and would have little chance of success anyway by that stage: 'it would be no crime for Sir Roger to have been paid by Germany. It does not reflect upon his integrity or his honour or his personal reputation.' Casement fired back that it should be 'abundantly clear that I was acting, not "for Germany", but for Ireland'. He had thought 'that every Irishman would understand, at least, that much, even if a restricted political development might not permit him to sympathise with the end in view'. Quinn, his benefactor in the previous summer of politically charged excitement, chose not to engage further while telling his associates that if Casement 'wanted to serve Ireland his place was in Ireland'. The contact between the two men was over as far as Quinn was concerned. Casement's dislocation had become an embarrassment. He was more than ever isolated.

May brought strategic peril. Against Bethmann Hollweg's advice, Germany declared the seas around Britain a war zone in which all shipping could be attacked, while Britain continued to use the same

---

* Over $2.5 million at today's values.

naval codes despite the near certainty that they had been cracked. On the 7th, the submarine *U-20* sank the fast passenger liner *Lusitania*, travelling from New York to Liverpool, off the Old Head of Kinsale, with the loss of 1,201 lives, including 128 American citizens. The Germans justified the attack on the grounds that the ship was carrying ammunition, and the British swiftly posted recruitment posters in the west of Ireland. Casement was alarmed by the possible effect on pro-German Irish-American sentiment, and was unconvinced by Devoy's reassurance that Clan na Gael was 'confident it will come out alright' and Americans would simply conclude that they should not travel on English ships. In the same week, Casement's Ulsterman ally from Putumayo days, the former Ambassador (now Lord) Bryce, undermined any lingering pro-German sympathies with his investigation into atrocities perpetrated by the Germans in Belgium; in response, Casement accused the Foreign Office of falsifying documents to suit Bryce's narrative.

The rising political tension in Britain over Asquith's handling of the war led the Liberals into a coalition with the Unionists in the last week of the month; the IRB Supreme Council founded its Military Committee in the same week. Redmond lost influence by declining a Cabinet seat, and when Carson became Attorney General, from which post he described the Home Rule Act as a mere 'scrap of paper', the Irish Party was weakened further. The losses on the Western Front and the slaughter of the Royal Munster Fusiliers and the Royal Dublin Fusiliers at Cape Helles on the Gallipoli peninsula were blows to the party's standing inside Ireland even before the events of the following year.

Against this background, Casement and Clan na Gael were falling further out of step. At times he was convinced, as he wrote to Joe McGarrity, that 'Germany *cannot* beat England . . . all my hopes for *the present* war are gone.' Devoy was clear that 'our most essential task was to furnish, to the utmost, means whereby the men in Ireland could arm and equip themselves'. Greater risks were needed 'in the teeth of the British Government' to achieve their ends, especially because in America the 'more and more venomous . . . antagonism of the [Woodrow] Wilson Administration' to Irish nationalism was sapping support.

Devoy remained irritated by the inclusion of the Egyptian clause in the Treaty, and reckoned Casement needed to maintain that 'his mission was the really important part' of throwing off the British yoke.

Plunkett was holding meetings to negotiate for arms with Hans Boehm and the sinister Count Rudolf von Nadolny, then head of Abteilung IIIb, later to run a sabotage operation involving explosives and anthrax shipments to Spain, the United States, Argentina and Romania, and currently enraging Plunkett by insisting that any arms should be provided from America. Plunkett was ill again at the start of May, but was under pressure from Boehm to finish his draft agreement to secure arms and officers for the uprising. He spent his evenings with Casement and Adler Christensen, as well as meeting Keogh and Quinlisk when they were in Berlin on Brigade business. Despite Casement's protestations, Plunkett distrusted Christensen, finding his face 'curiously immobile', and maintained his pseudonym in the Norwegian's presence. The agreement was finished on the day the *Lusitania* went down, just before Boehm, Casement and Plunkett set off on the twelve-hour night train to Frankfurt.

They were in Limburg for eight days. Boehm, who had weeded out sixty-six 'undesirables', told Plunkett that the Irish Brigade would be worth a division to the Germans, although Plunkett's speech in the camp, 'The Betrayal of Ireland by England Since the Passing of the Home Rule Act', did little to galvanise the men. The NCOs were currently reporting just thirty-six recruits. Plunkett, who had been in Ireland at the outbreak of war, understood the motivations pushing Irishmen to enlist in a way that had never penetrated Casement's often romanticised nationalism, including the threat to their way of life and nationhood, regardless of their loyalties or the process of Home Rule; some were living and working in England and joined Irish regiments without any deep nationalist convictions; many were in financial need and soldiering was a better-paid job than any they could get at home; many believed the invasion of Belgium enough reason to fight Germany. The oath of allegiance on signing up in 1914 troubled the more moral, and Casement's philosophical argument to allow them to break that oath – that kings owed a duty to their people as much as the other way around – was hard to digest.

But on this first visit to the camp since January's disappointment, Casement continued to recruit by referring to history and using emotive language about the evils of the British Empire. Although the German government had stipulated that publication of the Treaty required a minimum of 200 recruits, he 'should not be justified in doing anything more than I had already done to induce men to join'. Plunkett was clearer about the needs of the times and 'far less scrupulous' in his approach, urging 'We'll have to get them, if we kidnap them', which Casement countered in his unrealistically ethical way with 'We must continue only and *solely* to appeal to their patriotism'. He was unable to give those who had fought in the horrific early battles of the Great War much confidence in their future: 'When Patrick Sarsfield died . . . in Flanders in 1693, he said on the field of his death, "Would that this blood were shed for Ireland." He was giving his life for France . . . not for Ireland. Well, today, the case is very different, and if any Irishman in the Irish Brigade today loses his life, he can at least say that he is giving his blood for Ireland.' The qualities of passion and personal sacrifice that had served him so well in his illustrious past, and his growing realisation that martyrdom was his own best future, did not translate to his current audience.

One of those who joined for the wrong reasons but who was to be at Casement's side through the dramatic events of the following spring was Daniel Bailey. Bailey had been born in Dublin but had not seen Ireland since 1906. He had joined the Royal Irish Rifles in 1904 and been stationed in India, then lived in Canada before coming to London to work in a Paddington Station goods shed. He was called up as a reservist and captured in September 1914 at the Marne. When Bailey heard Casement speak, he signed up 'to see if I could possibly get out of the country', but entered his name as D. J. Beverley in case things went wrong. A Daniel O'Brien was one of those who despised Bailey, and once he was 'in his green uniform with a harp and shamrock on the collar . . . we all refused to speak to him'.

By the end of the high-level recruitment week, there were fifty-three names on the list, to Nadolny's scornful dismay as he had ordered a hundred uniforms, and the Treaty remained unpublished. Casement returned to Berlin on 10 June for a 'council of war' with

Plunkett and Boehm, which raised further difficulties. Plunkett had been negotiating for 12,000 German soldiers and 40,000 rifles, but these were 'contemptuously refused by Nadolny who said they had plenty of goodwill for Ireland (his very words!) but would give no arms. Arms must be provided by the Irish in America.' Plunkett, raging, left for Switzerland, writing a poem called 'The Spark' just before his departure, which ended:

> Now Death and I embark
> And sail into the dark
> With Laughter on our lips.

Casement 'felt the last link with hope was going from me for ever' as Plunkett left; the poet became the youngest signatory of the Proclamation of the Irish Republic to face the firing squad a year later.

Father Nicholson also concluded that he could do no more and returned to America, signing off after his four months' unrewarding work in Limburg with the verdict that 'our wrestling here was not so much against present conditions as against the disintegration of the last twenty years'. The downcast Casement suggested to McGarrity that 'Without the Brigade there is nothing between' the Germans and Clan na Gael that would prevent them talking direct, and he was now 'wholly useless here . . . Let me go back.' Despite his narrowed focus he grasped that Germany didn't 'care a fig for our cause by itself . . . they know nothing of us or of our country'. Kind Joe McGarrity displayed understanding of his former guest's character when he wrote to Devoy, who was pressing Casement to abandon the Brigade and concentrate on winning practical armed support, telling him that it was important to recognise that Casement 'was an idealist and it is well that he is one, even if we cannot live up to his ideals'. His personal sensitivity and cut-off situation needed to be allowed for, as well as his 'keen disappointment with the "Poor Brothers"', as Casement, to Devoy's annoyance, called the Irish. But Boehm hurried a memorandum to the Great General Staff warning that they risked 'turning even the Irish into enemies' and must treat the small number of men 'who volunteered for the Irish Legion exactly as planned originally' with uniforms and the promise of passage to America. If Casement were to leave Germany as their 'enemy', it would cause them 'enormous damage' in the Irish-American lobby at a point when that power's neutrality was essential.

The Brigade Volunteers were taken to Zossen, twenty miles south of Berlin, and given their uniforms, while a few were promoted to NCO ranks; payments of two Marks per week were made to 'each destitute Irishman' and the Commandant 'tried, as much as possible . . . to carry out plans for the promotion of their welfare'. Zossen, ringed with barbed wire and with sentries posted all around, was the largest training camp in Germany, made up of many different nationalities. The Irishmen's quarters were a newly built wooden hut with beds for a hundred, smaller rooms for the warrant officers, and washing facilities. The Brigade's men messed with the German soldiers, and were issued with rifles, side arms, five Maxim machine guns and two trench mortars for drilling and training.

By the third week of June, Casement had had enough of the Brigade, officialdom and Berlin, and retreated to Riederau, on the Ammersee near Munich, leaving Boehm to run the Zossen operation. He stayed in small hotels and often visited the city; he always felt at home out of doors and he was admired for his deep knowledge of the flowers and shrubs of the Botanic Gardens. An author who interviewed those who met him there heard of a hard-working, self-contained dreamer: 'What his mouth did not utter, his eyes said. Those eyes had unlimited things to say.' His close friends there were Dr Charles Curry, an Irish-American professor at Munich University whom he nicknamed 'the Rebel' as they circled the lake for hours, and Consul General Gaffney, the Limerick Irish lawyer with a reputation as a loudmouthed bore but sympathetic to him 'personally and politically'. The British Envoy to the Swiss Federation, Sir Evelyn Grant Duff, the type of entitled English diplomat Casement loathed, sent an appraisal of Gaffney to the Foreign Office which dripped with disdain: 'Complexion, fair, usually puffy, subcutaneous reddish type of hard drinkers; Face, fat and round, bloated; Hands, large and puffy, wears several rings with jewels.'

Being surrounded by 'true, warm friendship' soothed Casement as he wrote an emotional farewell to Adler Christensen, who was returning to the States after their convoluted and ultimately destructive relationship: 'I cannot get your face out of my head – I thought of you all the time – I know what you felt and I love you for it, you faithful, loving soul . . . in life and death I will never forget you and your devotion, affection and fidelity to me . . . God bless you, dear faithful friend of my heart – you who are true to the death . . .' They had parted in Berlin at the start of July, with Casement still believing the version of events told to him by probably the only man he ever loved, and almost certainly unaware that Christensen had at some point in the previous nine months bigamously acquired a German wife, Margaretta, whom he was taking back to America. It was not Christensen's final appearance, but it was the end of his twin roles as romantic solace and strategic distraction.

Casement's disconnection that summer was indicative of a waning interest on both sides, just as it underlined his unaccustomed sensation of being without a galvanic campaign. Gaffney realised the personal toll experienced by Casement, as well as deploring the political cost to the Irish cause, when he wrote to Under-Secretary Zimmermann in early August to ask if Casement might be allowed to return to America on the 'warship of some friendly neutral power' as 'his presence there and his personal support of the cause he had so much at heart' might convince the US to stay out of the war. Two days later, Casement himself asked Wedel to issue him a passport for Sweden and thence to America; he felt 'idle and useless'. Wedel had already thanked Casement for sending him a photograph with a valedictory 'it will always remind me . . . of a friend['s] heroic efforts in struggling against fearful odds'; he now backed Casement's passport so that he could 'at least be active in an anti-British way . . . As matters stand with the Irish Legion at this point, he cannot be of use here to either the Irish or the German side.' Richard Meyer confirmed that he would be given 'every possible support for his journey'.

But Casement could not desert the men or his mission, however restless and withdrawn he had become. He fretted over every detail to do with the Brigade, telling Keogh that he could not 'possibly send you money for clothes and boots' while the uniforms were still pending, yet still passing on three weeks' pay to help with the arrears. He pointed out that 'the [German] authorities are greatly disappointed' at the numbers, and the Volunteers were 'cut off and alone' unless help came from America. The 'shame and failure' fell on his shoulders, but it was important to remember 'that all our trials are part of *the* trial . . . to *do* something for Ireland'.

Boehm needed to reinforce the Brigade with officers. The first of these was Franz Zerhusen, a German married to an Irish woman, whose Hamburg business had been ruined by the war. Zerhusen and Boehm did their best to improve conditions, requesting football outfits and running shoes, but the men remained bored, ill-disciplined and verging on the mutinous. Devoy had maintained that the presence of an Irish officer was essential, although quashing Casement's idealistic plan of a West Point graduate 'whose rank should not be less than that of Colonel', and it was to fill this vacancy that Robert Monteith arrived. Casement initially considered him a stopgap until a more senior man could be found, but it was not long before he was describing the new arrival as 'invaluable . . . Loyal, brave, untiring and of a great fidelity'. That last quality, one he had repeatedly ascribed to Christensen, was fully justified in Monteith's case. The two men, and Bailey, were to be at each other's side in the extraordinary events of the following spring.

The burly, heavy-jowled and resourceful Monteith was the third son of a Wicklow farmer, and was, as described by one of Franz von Papen's aides, '36 years old, about 5 feet 9 inches tall, formerly sergeant major in the royal riding artillery* in the English army. Participated in the Boer War and the Indian border wars, served in Egypt and was wounded twice.' At the outbreak of the war Monteith had held a position in the armoury in Dublin simultaneously with being a captain in the Irish Volunteers after signing on at the inaugural meeting at the Rotunda Rink. He had been dismissed when he declined the rank of captain in the British Army and made his way to New York. Although Devoy considered Adler Christensen 'one of the worst crooks ever', even speculating that he was in

* The Royal Horse Artillery.

the pay of the English, he commissioned the treacherous Norwegian to spirit Monteith over to Germany.

Christensen admitted that they had only a 60 per cent chance of success, while Monteith was aware his courier was 'known to secret service men on both sides of the water and . . . was a dangerous man to travel with'. The plan was that Monteith should stow away under Christensen's bunk to Christiania, where passports were not checked; the cabin steward would be bribed to turn a blind eye. Monteith left his wife and two daughters and duly hid himself as the ship steamed out of New York. There was no bathroom in the cabin, and he endured misery as seasickness overcame him; otherwise, all went well until the eighth night, when Christensen, who had been sustaining him with sandwiches and water, told him there was a British patrol on board and one stowaway had already been arrested. Monteith was smuggled between empty cabins as each one was searched, and managed to suppress his cough as the vessel was taken into Kirkwall in Orkney and the passengers and crew examined. On reaching Christiania he was horrified to see that Norwegian officials were checking passports after all; he had not a word of the language and Christensen had already disembarked. He had decided there was nothing to be done but chance it, when a stumble over a rope gave him an idea: he came down to meet the officials staggering and muttering like a drunkard, to be steadied on his feet and waved on with a polite bow. He was grateful that the Norwegians 'know how to handle drunken men'.

He was surprised that Casement was not in Berlin to meet him on 22 October; Wedel told him he was ill, thanks to his tendency 'to take too little care of himself'. In a marker of the progress of the war since Casement's arrival a year earlier, Monteith noticed that regiments on their way to the front were not cheered or given flowers; going to battle was an 'unpleasant job', nothing for 'undue advertisement or demonstration'. He headed to Munich, where he was profoundly moved to be confronted with 'one of the outstanding figures in the titanic conflict of arms and brains; it was the proudest moment of my life' to meet 'a man who had saved millions of lives'. He had never seen 'eyes more beautiful . . . blazing when he spoke of man's humanity to man; soft and wistful when pleading the cause so dear to his heart'; he was struck by Casement's deep tan, by his wiriness and by 'his downheartedness about the war'.

Casement's retreat had brought him to a difficult but realistic point: he recognised that the United States would eventually join the British, and that following the German losses at Ypres his hosts would not reach the Channel ports. When Monteith mentioned recruitment for the Brigade, he only got a weary 'Very well, if you want to do so, go ahead' from his despondent hero. Monteith breakfasted, bought clothes and turned back north.

Monteith interviewed fifty men a day during his three-week stay in Limburg. He could only offer them 'an opportunity to fight for Ireland in Ireland' and found it hard to convince his audience, most of them exhausted and made suspicious by the repeated approaches, that he was not a German fifth columnist; he had yet to be issued an officer's uniform, despite requests. His diary entries included: 'Men seem indifferent. A lot of them are absolutely impossible'; and 'A little hostility today', with only the occasional 'Two more men for Zossen'. Reports of ill-discipline as the Irishmen scrapped among themselves and with the other nationalities, particularly the Russians, continued to travel the short distance to Berlin.

Part of the reason for Casement's lack of interest was that he had lost his friend and prop. The *New York Herald*, out to get Consul General Gaffney for his long-standing criticism of President Woodrow Wilson's foreign policy, had picked up a story from a Munich newspaper of the two men being at a pre-war dinner. The *Herald* ran the headline 'Gaffney Friend of Irish Traitor', with the subhead 'Accused of Entertaining Sir Roger Casement, Who Went Over to the Germans'. Gaffney was fired from the consular service, while Casement took the blame for 'having given a dinner in my honour at which anti-British speeches were made'. In addition, spiteful letters had arrived in Wilhelmstrasse on *Gaelic American* stationery from a busybody named Freeman, who had no contact with Clan na Gael but claimed that the movement had lost faith in Casement and regretted sending him. Although Devoy was to take Freeman to task and insist that they retained the fullest confidence in their man, yet more damage was done to Casement's fragile sense of himself.

Monteith, Zerhusen, Keogh and Bailey visited him on the morning of 23 November after his arrival back in Berlin. Monteith was appalled when he saw 'SRC on verge of collapse, disappointment of his hope time after time has almost killed him – I am seriously afraid he contemplates self-destruction'. But Casement would never give up while there was any cause: he was again planning on taking the Brigade east. Influenced by a resident Turkish friend, Halil Hadid, and without discussion with Devoy, he asked Meyer for papers and letters of recommendation to negotiate in Constantinople to 'assist the Ottoman forces to expel the British from Egypt'. But he was still overestimating the desire of the men to fight at a time when the Turks were dealing slaughter on the beaches of Gallipoli, and he had to acknowledge that the disheartening thirty or so who were desperate enough to commit to this change of plan could not make a difference. Yet he clung to the hope that the force 'might have a moral effect and be of political value . . . out of all proportion to their actual number'. Devoy witheringly suggested that the unauthorised alternative plan was intended 'to impress the world by sending sixty [*sic*] men to a place where they could do nothing'.

On 10 December, Casement finally admitted to Wedel that there was no point in supplying German aid to Ireland as 'the few men armed there are insufficient . . . and have far too little equipment to make any successful fight. It would not only be hopeless but a crime to urge them to an armed effort.' He still proposed action in the east in the hope of bringing inspiration to those fighting the British in India and Persia, despite the newly appointed Lieutenant Monteith's opinion that encouraging his men towards 'helping to free another small nationality which England strangely enough omits to free – nobody seems very enthusiastic about the prospect'. Nadolny saw his way clear of a problem when he submitted the scheme for government approval: 'The deployment of the men would be a relief for us. There is hardly a danger of desertion because the British are informed about their joining the Irish Brigade and they know it.'

Monteith was worried by this time: 'No arms have yet arrived . . .

SRC very ill. I am afraid his mind is going, disappointment after disappointment has broken him.' His next visit to Casement's over-heated, oppressively furnished rooms proved even more alarming: 'He presented a deathlike appearance. His bronzed face had turned an almost ashen colour, his features were pinched and haggard and he lay so still that his breathing was barely perceptible.' For Casement the contrast with the previous German Christmas, with its validation from the recent audience with the Chancellor and the promising Christiania double-cross schemes, could not have been greater. Now he was without Christensen, without an Irish Brigade and with his resentment against the conduct of the Foreign Office unvindicated.

Casement wrote to another Meyer sibling, Antonie, from the Hotel Golden Lion in Zossen to comment that the war 'has killed Christianity in the life of nations' and that he did 'not like to think of the future – it is all dark and hopeless and forbidding – and I think the dead are best'. He was 'sick at heart and soul, with mind and nerves threatening a complete collapse'. Above all, a torment to such a moral man, he reckoned 'no man was ever in such a false position' as him. In this melodramatic vein, he believed he was in his last days, as was 'Civilisation', which 'ends in an orgie of Hatred, Lying and organized Murder'. A further Meyer sibling, Eduard, could not be sent the greetings of the season as 'Everything looks dark and dreary', and a Berlin friend was wished only 'a hopeful Christmas' in the war that was now just 'a massacre'. He could 'see no daylight'.

He spent a miserable Christmas Day with German friends in Dres-den, but in his mercurial fashion had recovered himself sufficiently by his last New Year's Eve to sing 'Irish songs in a magnificent voice'. One that stood out was a setting of Thomas Moore's 'Come, Rest in This Bosom'. The poem's first stanza speaks loudly of his isolation:

> Come, rest in this bosom, my own stricken deer,
> Though the herd have fled from thee, thy home is still here;
> Here still is the smile, that no cloud can o'ercast,
> And a heart and a hand all thy own to the last.

In January it was back to 'dreary deadly dull Zossen' and a slump. He was 'too lonely' and took little exercise as his heart was troubling him; he yearned to do something 'in the open air – as of old in Africa where my happiest days were spent'. But, despite this dream of his former, anonymous life, he had taken the first steps on the road to martyrdom as he gave voice to his understanding that if 'in Ireland today, I would make it the last act of my life to see that the resistance was offered with every ounce of strength and courage'.

Monteith suggested he see a mental health specialist, who on 14 January ordered him to a sanatorium. He checked into Munich's Kuranstalt Neuwittelsbach, specialising in nervous diseases, a year after his last rest cure. He was under the care of the distinguished Dr Rudolf von Hoesslin, author of *The Handbook of Neurasthenia* and a believer in hydrotherapy and cold baths, a psychologically restorative experience for one who was used to swimming off the coast of Antrim. Father Crotty sent a telegram to Joe McGarrity saying 'He may *or may not* recover', and Clan na Gael acknowledged that the mission was over. Just before Casement was hospitalised, Devoy had spread himself over seven pages of a letter to Casement to complain that Christensen had returned from delivering Monteith with a fistful of false expenses claims, although he let him off because 'the outstanding feature' of his involvement had been the infiltration; he added that Nina was now safely in New York away from the abuse she had been receiving in England as the sister of a traitor.

Devoy marked his emissary's performance against his objectives: in seeking 'to secure military help for Ireland when the opportunity offered', he had been decidedly 'ineffective'; in attempting 'to educate German public opinion on the Irish situation', he had 'succeeded admirably'; and in organising 'Irish prisoners of war into a military unit', he had 'failed badly'. But Devoy recognised, at least in hindsight, that he 'did his best in all these things'.

A telegram from Ambassador von Bernstorff arrived in Wilhelmstrasse at 2.15 p.m. on 20 February 1916: 'Irish leader John Devoy informs me that revolution shall begin Easter Sunday Ireland. Requests arms between Good Friday and Easter Sunday Limerick, West Coast of Ireland. Longer waiting impossible, request wire reply whether I may promise help from Germany.' The letter from Devoy which had sparked the message calculated that there were about 40,000 Volunteers in Ireland; of these the 'Redmondites' had enlisted, leaving a defending force of 30,000 poorly trained men with 'very few competent officers'. Clan na Gael hoped for 25,000–50,000 rifles, 'with a proportionate number of machine guns and field artillery and a few superior officers'. But they knew enough 'to respectfully request that Sir Roger Casement be informed that in case an expedition should be sent to Ireland, we wish him to remain in Germany as Ireland's accredited Representative until such time' as it was decided otherwise. In the healthful security of his Munich sanatorium, Casement had no inkling of these discussions, or that he was not invited to leave the country he now hated. His recent defiance had collapsed and he would be unable to resist 'with every ounce of strength and courage' that he had recently envisioned as his 'last act'.

13.   Homecoming

It was Robert Monteith who was summoned to the headquarters of the German General Staff to discuss the Rising in six weeks' time. He was shown a letter from Devoy requesting 100,000 rifles, an estimated one per Volunteer, with additional artillery, trained artillerymen and German officers – support for a whole rising which came as a bombshell. In return, however, Nadolny had suggested to the Foreign Ministry that 'two or three fishing trawlers could land about 20,000 rifles and 10 machine guns with ammunition and explosives at Fenit Pier in Tralee Bay', in the crook of Dingle on the south-west coast. At the time, Germany was producing 250,000 high-quality rifles and 2,300 machine guns each month – and its troops would need everything they could obtain as they commenced the 1,220-gun bombardment of the twelve-mile front along the River Meuse west of Verdun that heralded the next phase of the battle for the city. Monteith was left crestfallen by the meagre support and wired Casement to come to Berlin, only to receive the reply that he was still too ill to travel. Monteith set off for Munich again to find Casement improved since his last visit, but still 'a shadow of his former self' after two months in the Kuranstalt, allowed out of bed for only four hours each day. But the news of the Rising 'came upon [him] like a thunder clap' and he 'jumped to life – or tried to – for there was not much jump in [him]'. The few weeks remaining to him in Germany were to exhilarate, enrage and exhaust him as his last mission drew near.

He discharged himself, arriving in the capital on 7 March 1916. Clan na Gael were wary of him acting alone, and had already vetoed his plan to go ahead of the arms by submarine to supervise the landing. An appeal to Nadolny was rebuffed by the impatient spymaster on the grounds that if an advance U-boat was spotted the whole operation would be blown. At that point Casement admitted to himself after eighteen months of negotiation that Germany had no 'idealistic' interest in Ireland whatsoever and was simply sending the rifles in the hope that they would be 'at once used' as an irritant and a gamble, without any underlying strategy or any hope of success. It was 'an underhand trick' that meant 'no revolution, no arms' – the Brigade numbers were tiny, and they would be steaming into disaster with unknown weaponry and unsupported by essential 'strong foreign military help'. As always, his first concern was for the 'appalling consequences for Ireland'. The only other recruit apart from Monteith to have got through from Clan na Gael was John McGoey; and Casement decided to despatch him in his place to Dublin to warn the Supreme Council of the shipment. Much to his surprise, and almost certainly because it was risk- and expense-free compared to a U-boat voyage, Nadolny agreed, and the young Irish-American left via Denmark. Casement did not necessarily inform Nadolny of the other part of McGoey's mission, 'to try and get the heads in Ireland to call off the rising'. Before he left, McGoey wrote a note on Hotel Saxonia paper to his comrades in the Irish Brigade, of which only a fragment survives: 'let us trust a brighter morning for Ireland and her children', for on that day 'we will have a fuller and truer conception of the motives that imperatively [*sic*] demanded my apparently cold and feelingless departure'. He was never heard from again.

Casement started to fantasise that the 'cowardly, dastardly' Germans expected, even wanted, the arms ship to be captured with him aboard and his 'countrymen to be shot down'; he wondered if the English would let the men of the Brigade go free to America if he would shoulder all the blame. He saw little chance of his own survival, but vowed to 'make all clear' for posterity and travelled to Munich in febrile misery to put his affairs in order. But he was too tightly wound to rest even in Riederau, and was about to return to Berlin when he was felled by a fever, possibly his recurrent malaria. In a single day at the Baseler Hof in Munich, he wrote the forty-five-page 'Last Word for my true friend Charles Curry', a frantic, often paranoid work of justification which included instructions to bury a copy of the Treaty in silk and only exhume it to give to Devoy or McGarrity: it would stand as proof of the German undertaking and

their current attitude of manoeuvring 'to get rid of the whole thing at cheapest cost to themselves – a tramp steamer, 20,000 old rifles, 5,000,000 cartridges and 10 machine guns'. He and Monteith 'go to our dooms – if the German government washes its hand of all responsibility – because it is only complying with the request of John Devoy'. McGarrity was bequeathed his trunks of papers and instructed to publish them to 'save my reputation after I am gone'; the royalties were to be divided between his sister Nina and Devoy, who had 'helped me nobly' notwithstanding his moral and strategic desertion at this turning point. The man who regarded him as a hero when last heard from, E. D. Morel, was to be his biographer, assisted by Alice Stopford Green. He was convinced that the British would not put him on trial but would find another way to '*humiliate &*
degrade' him in order to prevent him becoming either 'a Martyr or a Hero of Revolutionary Ireland'.

In this outpouring, virtually a suicide note, Casement let on that another cherished bond had evaporated: he had learnt that Christensen had 'turned out very badly' – he had kept some of the Clan na Gael money they had arrived with and, worse, £5 intended for Nina; his erstwhile lover, sent off with such affection, had 'apparently turned into a regular scoundrel. I trusted him absolutely. I was a fool.' Yet for what remained of his self-esteem Casement needed to persist in the belief that Christensen's dealings with Findlay had been 'all right', even if Findlay had also realised his visitor was 'a scoundrel'. Casement was still ignorant of the truth, and drew a line under it by pointing out that, although German publishers had offered him as much as 50,000 Marks* for a book, he 'felt it was beneath' him, although there was no wavering from the fact that the British government 'did a low-down dirty thing' with their 'cowardly act'. German diplomacy also came in for abuse in his miserable catalogue of shattered ideals: he was about to be 'sacrificed', and begged that Curry, to whom he entrusted his German papers and diaries for safekeeping, should show '*much* later . . . how innocent he is – and how his action throughout, if mistaken, was

---

* 50,000 Marks was about £2,000 at the time, about £200,000 today.

based on unselfish regard for what he thought to be the welfare of his country'. Alice Green knew 'the truth . . . Some day it will all be made clear.'

He undertook more farewells in Berlin, 'the victim of grave doubt and a prey to extreme anxiety'. He begged Princess Blücher to ensure everyone understood that his every action had been in the Irish cause. The unreliable Princess described him as 'beside himself with terror and grief', but Gilbert Hirsch, an American journalist, depicted a more poised, self-abrogating figure alert to the flickerings of martyr-dom as he fully grasped his loss of influence: his 'sensitive lips and nostrils; something shy about his manner; something abstracted . . . about his way of speaking – all indicated a man extremely susceptible to suffering. But the perpetual sparkle of humour and intrepidity in the clear grey eyes made it clear that it was the suffering of others to which he was quivering, rather than his own.'

Nadolny was now 'a complete and perfect scoundrel . . . the instru-ment of a policy of scoundrels' for his withdrawal of support. The few Brigade members had finally lost heart, and of the thirty-eight who had volunteered for service in the east, twenty-four now with-drew. Reports came from Zossen that 'almost all of them have taken to drink, hanging about or other excesses'. When Monteith had seen Nadolny in January to discuss their fate, the German 'went into a towering rage and said *he would send them all to the Western Front*' should they refuse to return to Ireland. The next meeting with Casement also soon became acrimonious as the spymaster threatened that, since the Brigade did not meet the numerical conditions of the Treaty of December 1914, unless Casement agreed to accompany the arms himself now that their dealings had come to an end, Devoy would be informed that they would not be sent. Casement could carry poison for himself in case the ship was intercepted by the Royal Navy, but pointed out that he was not 'at liberty to make arrangements . . . for shielding from a felon's fate the band of Irish soldiers'. His 'position was a hideous one'; the obsessions, breakdowns and isolation of the previous few months had combined to leave him 'so completely in the dark as to what is really being planned in Ireland, in America, that I dare not accept the responsibility' for the Brigade – yet that was being forced on him. He was 'being used as a tool for purposes' that were now 'very plain . . . practically a prisoner with no means of communicating with . . . America or Ireland', and could only reiterate his plea to travel alone.

Back in his hotel room, he began 'a record of my mind and understanding' that would 'live after' him in his morbid state. He lamented that the 'scheme' in which he had invested so much 'can only bring failure – and probably something far worse than failure – disaster'; it was 'beneath contempt', no longer a military enterprise but 'a piece of gun-running', such as he had set up himself almost two years earlier. He considered the predominantly 'law abiding and peace loving' Irish would be drawn into 'bloodshed and civil strife' by this 'filibustering expedition'. 'All that is solid and respectable in Ireland will be moved to the deepest resentment . . . wrath and contempt', eclipsing the reaction to 'the rape of Belgium'. Morality counted most, and on those grounds the German decisions were 'indefensible'. Advantage was being taken of him, yet he could do nothing to prevent Germany being branded with 'the far graver charge of treachery'. Nurse Edith Cavell had been shot for treason by the Germans six months earlier for helping British troops escape from Belgium and her execution had become a symbol of 'German barbarism'; but her murder 'will not be in it with "the betrayal of Sir Roger Casement"'. On all three counts, military, political and moral, 'the *right* thing to do even now is to stop the whole thing', otherwise his country, and even America, would be 'launched into the war' by his own failure, as he saw it. He tried to sum up his unmoored, self-aggrandising emotional state: he was carrying on 'because I am fool enough, or brave enough, or coward enough . . . while I know it is hopeless'.

The next few days were hectic. Casement made a final visit to the Brigade and Father Crotty on 5 April which was 'dreadful'. He 'could not tell them the truth', that the strategy he had expounded so passionately had been 'a ghastly folly'. He pretended that he, Monteith and Bailey, the latter chosen for his expertise in Morse signalling and machine-gunnery, were simply going on ahead 'to clear the way for deployment in the east', but he loathed the deceit and 'could scarcely refrain from crying'; he stressed that rather than bear the loss of honour he was inflicting on them, the 'sooner my life was taken from me the better'.

A letter from Plunkett's father in Berne to the German Staff came on 6 April. Its four points carried an 'urgent message from Ireland': that the Rising had been fixed for Easter Sunday, now less than three weeks' away; that the 'large consignment of arms' must arrive in Tralee Bay no later than dawn of Easter Monday; that German officers were 'imperative' for the Volunteers; and that 'a German submarine will be required in Dublin harbour'. Plunkett acknowledged that 'the time is very short [but] delays are dangerous'. Nadolny wired back that he knew about the first two points but as for '3 and 4: Execution not possible'; furthermore, should Casement attempt to reply, Nadolny 'humbly requested' the Wilhelmstrasse officials that he be shown any such document before it left Berlin. Casement never received Plunkett's follow-up demand that he press harder for the officers and the submarine; it arrived the day he left the country.

He spent a sleepless night after Plunkett's letter; he even hoped that the English might seize his ship so that he could put an end to the Rising. He was convinced '*all* is indeed lost', and sent for the voluble, beringed St John Gaffney, now running an organisation called the Friends of Irish Freedom for Europe, to share his 'ever-growing anxiety about the consequences in Ireland'. Gaffney contacted Jacob Nöggerath, a wealthy German-American 'confidential agent of the FO', who was shown the passage in Casement's diary about the disaster that would unfold if the German government plans were carried out; he hastened to talk to Count Zimmermann. Zimmermann, who later spoke of his 'private grief' that Casement had left the country on his 'fantastic' expedition, in turn tried to see the Chancellor. Bethmann Hollweg could not spare the time, but authorised Nöggerath to deal with the General Staff, 'hopeless' though Nöggerath considered them to be. But at least the 'low-minded intriguer' Nadolny and the Admiralty would have to reconsider under this degree of political pressure. Casement was summoned at 4 p.m. on 7 April: they had had 'a full-dress debate and the thing was settled' – he was to go home by submarine. His hopes of preventing the wreck of his dreams and the catastrophe of an under-supported Easter Rising quivered back to life.

The genial Reserve-Lieutenant Karl Spindler of the German Navy was ordered from his command of a half-flotilla of patrol boats at Wilhelmshaven to Hamburg. Expecting to be given the captaincy of a 'patrol boat equipped with all the newest devices', he was surprised to see instead 'a stately vessel' in the evening sun, although the *Libau* appeared larger than she was because of her 'lofty upper works'. She was a 1,228-ton ship that had sailed under the flag of the Wilson Line of Hull as the *Castro* before being captured in German waters in the early days of the war. The Admiralty had decided that, for the purposes of the weapon transportation, one sizeable ship would be more economical and less visible than the two or three trawlers they had been considering.

Only her crew of sixteen were allowed on board as the *Libau* set off the next morning through the Kiel Canal to Lübeck, where she and they were transformed. Mysterious cases marked as cargo for Genoa and Naples were lowered into the hold with extraordinary care for fear of one of them breaking open to reveal the rifles and ammunition inside. All sorts of items, including tin baths, wooden doors and window frames labelled for Italian ports, as well as a consignment of pit props labelled for Cardiff, were then placed in position to cover up the inner, illicit goods. The *Libau* was made over as a Norwegian ship: seamen's uniforms arrived, complete with buttons stamped with the name of a Scandinavian manufacturer; Norwegian books replaced anything in English or German; Christiania newspapers came on board; even the sardine tins bore the names of Norwegian producers; maps, charts, flags, log books and manifests, torches and surgical dressings were all replaced, and German arms and explosives were hidden away. Linen, china and anything else bearing the Wilson Line insignia were pitched overboard. Documents were aged with soot, oil and grease from the engine rooms, and the crew were ordered to start growing beards (those who struggled were helped to look the part by the application of oil and coal dust) and to strew old Norwegian meat tins around their cabins. Finally, the comparatively new vessel was made to look like a common tramp steamer: red lead paint was applied to her funnel and sides under cover of darkness, giving the impression that rusty tattiness was showing through, and her name was painted over to read *Aud-Norge* in five-foot letters. The last element of the disguise was ultimately the most significant: she did not carry a radio.

On 9 April, two weeks before the scheduled Rising, the *Aud*, now a dinghy vessel flying the Norwegian flag on a trading run from Scandinavia to the Mediterranean, steamed out of Lübeck heading for the busy commercial port of Warnemünde at Rostock. She left German waters the following day. Her crew adopted a rolling gait, clamped short pipes into their mouths and shoved their hands into their pockets as she set a leisurely pace across the North Sea between Norway and the Shetland Islands, ducking south of the Faroes and passing the Hebrides to head for Tralee Bay and the rendezvous with Casement's U-boat.

The same day as the *Aud* left Lübeck, Sergeant Sean Francis Kavanagh was called from Zossen to the Hotel Saxonia on Friedrichstrasse. Casement looked 'nervous and worried' as he handed him an envelope containing a note to be read to the men after his departure. He was 'setting out on a mission and may never see' any of the Brigade again, but wanted them to carry on training 'for the time may come when they will be required to fulfil their promise'. As Kavanagh left, Casement 'raised his right hand in salute, whilst the word "Courage" floated . . . across the room as if it had been pronounced in a whisper'.

Casement's fears for the fate of the Brigade had increased after Nadolny riled him during one of their bitter discussions by stating that the men would be regarded as deserters or at best as 'disgraced' prisoners of war if they did not leave with him. On 11 April, he wrote to Bethmann Hollweg to 'bring to [his] notice the small body of Irish soldiers who volunteered . . . to fight for Irish freedom, with the whole-hearted freedom and support of the Imperial German Government', asking for them to remain 'as guests of Germany in the highest sense of the word'; he appointed Gaffney as the arbiter of their interests, not least with regard to any money coming from America, and sent Wedel a list of the fifty-five Brigade members. His final farewell was co-signed by Monteith and Bailey: it explained that the three men were 'going on a very perilous journey' and that the chief reason the soldiers were not accompanying them was to 'keep them out of the very grave danger we have to face'. If they were not heard from again, the Brigade would know they had 'gone to do our part in our country's cause according to what we deemed was right'. The 'brave stout Irish hearts' of the Brigade members could not have given more; their names would be honoured in history.*

That day saw the final entry in the diary that had charted Casement's swings from patriotic elation to personal despair over the previous eighteen months; that had misapprehended the machinations of his lover and both praised and railed against the German government; and that had been silent in the periods when he was loath to plumb and record his thoughts. 'My last day in Berlin! Thank God,' he wrote; he preferred the 'English scaffold' that was likely to be his fate 'than to dwell with these people longer'. He went out for some clothes, because for travelling he had only the thin suit in which he had arrived in the capital; he had given his other one to Bailey. He wrote letters and paid bills, complaining that he had been 'swindled' over the doctor's many hotel visits. One of his last acts was to send Bailey's Brigade uniform to Gaffney as a souvenir: it was the only one to reach Ireland when Gaffney gave it to the National Museum in Dublin.

A car transported Casement, Monteith and Bailey to the General Staff building, where they were issued with Mauser pistols, poison capsules and railway tickets. They were briefed that the *Aud* would rendezvous with them at Inishtooskert, an island just outside Tralee Bay, at midnight on 20 April; they would be met by a pilot boat showing two green lights. Casement was given a set of codes in case

---

* The Irishmen were indeed better treated than most POWs and were put to work in the Baltic coastal towns. Some joined the 16th Bavarian Infantry Regiment, and Michael Keogh was awarded the Hindenburg Cross at Ligny.

he needed to communicate with the Germans 'should operations be prolonged, necessitating further supplies': 'Sectpol' was the call signal, and any German operator picking up this word between 22 April and 20 May would transmit it immediately to the General Staff. After that, there would be no lines of communication. The men were driven to the Zoo Station to board the 9.30 p.m. train to Wilhelms-haven, with each allocated a separate sleeping compartment. They were instructed to empty their pockets of any incriminating 'litter', an instruction that Casement ignored, with consequences he may even have subconsciously desired in order to satisfy his need to bear witness to his own narrowing story.

He was expecting the journey to take twelve days and to be a 'dreadful voyage – confined and airless and full of oil smells'. But the 'first fear' for the tall, nervous figure who needed constant exercise was not claustrophobia but, as the closing sentence of his last journal read, 'that we shall never land – but be kept off the shore until the "rebellion" breaks out', and his final, self-sacrificial campaign to avoid bloodshed remain unfulfilled.

The British Admiralty's Room 40 intercepted at least thirty-two signals between Berlin and the German embassy in Washington about Irish nationalism from the start of the war up to the Easter Rising. A shipment of arms was suspected, but there had been radio silence over the past few days. On 12 April, 'Oats' came to Room 40's attention, the code that meant a sailing was imminent; 'Hay' would have signified a delay. In the main German naval port of Wil-helmshaven, the Irish trio boarded *U-20* under the command of Captain Raimund Weisbach, who eleven months earlier had been the torpedo officer who sank the *Lusitania*. The party was photo-graphed standing against the conning tower, with Casement looking older than his years, the removal of his beard for reasons of disguise accentuating his haggard features. The passengers crammed into officers' sleeping quarters under the torpedo tubes; the oil fumes when *U-20* was on the surface (electric engines were only used underwater) were almost overpowering.

A faulty diving-fin crank forced a return to Heligoland and a fresh

North Sea departure on *U-19*, with the loss of two days. They hit heavy seas off the Shetland Islands and Casement was horribly sick; the thought of the daily diet of tinned smoked ham and salmon, war bread and coffee, did nothing to help. He was exhausted yet unable to sleep with his mix of adrenaline and misery. Monteith hurt his wrist practising on the outboard motor that would power the small dinghy for their approach to land and Casement had to cut up his rations for him. They sang Irish songs, and hung up the city flag of Limerick they were carrying at Gaffney's behest. Monteith clambered through the small manhole in the tower in borrowed oilskins to get air whenever possible, but Casement mostly remained in his bunk for the five-day voyage.

Just after midnight on the morning of Good Friday, 21 April, *U-19* was on the surface, awaiting the rendezvous with the *Aud*. The moon shone brightly on the glassy sea, but there was no sign of the ship and no lights on the shore. The *Aud* had in fact already arrived in the area after battling through a hurricane that nearly wrecked her on Rockall Bank, and more than once a British cruiser had steamed alongside for a look. Captain Spindler's men spent Holy Thursday jettisoning the tin baths, pit props and assorted pails to access the true cargo before lying off Tralee Bay until their assignation.

Spindler had scrutinised the town through his field glasses and was puzzled that there were no lights and no signs of a shore party. But, even if he was in the right spot at the right time, his part in the expedition was doomed owing to his lack of radio. He had been at sea for nearly a week when John Devoy in New York received a message from Dublin about the Rising's delay: 'Arms must not be landed before midnight of Sunday, 23rd. This is vital.' On the *Aud*'s arrival off Tralee under the Norwegian ensign three days earlier, the Royal Naval sloop HMS *Bluebell* flashed a signal asking her to identify herself, which she did as bound for Genoa from Bergen. The suspicious British captain ordered her to follow him the 138 miles to Queenstown; a shot across her bows forced Spindler's compliance, and he instructed his men to put on their naval uniforms under their seaman's clothes and plant explosives. Three and a half miles out from Queenstown, Spindler stopped the engines, and the watching British saw a cloud of white smoke billow from a fourteen-foot hole in her starboard side; German ensigns were hoisted and the men ripped off their outer clothing and made for the two lifeboats. *Bluebell* fired a warning shot over their heads, at which the now German officers and ratings raised their hands and were taken aboard the sloop under armed guard. Ten minutes later, there was another dull explosion, a burst of flame and the *Aud* dived towards the seabed. An Admiralty diver later recovered 'one rifle complete, several broken butts, a rifle cartridge and a bayonet scabbard' from the debris, all that was needed to establish her intent.

As *U-19*'s officers scanned the darkness for the *Aud* or the pilot boat's green lights, the three Irishmen were also straining their eyes, imagining flashes of light with each white-topped wave. They had no idea of what reception the Volunteers might have arranged, or what help had come from America; 'an ugly thought' crossed their minds that they had been double-crossed and the *Aud* had never existed: their own countrymen would not be so careless about a rendezvous. On the mainland, the only person to notice any activity was a labourer, Michael Hussey, who saw a red light shining out at sea for a few seconds as he walked home from visiting a friend.

Monteith watched 'the cold, drawn, hopeless look on Casement's face' as the minutes passed. The crew were impassive. After a while, Weisbach announced that he would be endangering his craft if he tarried and set course for Tralee Bay at his full surface speed of fourteen knots. The men were 'sick at heart' as they went below to collect their packs. Monteith retrieved the Mausers, only then asking Casement if he knew how to use one. Casement replied that he 'had never killed anything in his life'. As Monteith loaded Casement's weapon and issued him with a sheath knife, 'an expression of intense pain and loathing crossed his face'.

Fearful that Casement might collapse, Monteith was encouraging him to lie back against his locker for what remained of the journey when an officer came in to ask that they prepare to go ashore. The submarine lolled in the swell of the hazy night as the canvas dinghy, about nine feet long by three feet at its widest point, was lifted from the hatch. They made their farewells, put on their life jackets and climbed in, Casement in the stern, Bailey in the centre and Monteith in the bow. Weisbach would not let them use the motor for fear the coastguard would hear, so the younger men took to the oars. They were going around in circles, pushed by the tide towards jagged rocks, when Monteith realised the oars were different lengths; he took over the pulling single-handed, ignoring the pain from his wrist. After an hour in the hostile darkness, Casement announced that he could see the white tops of waves breaking on a beach; they heard the surf shortly afterwards.

The closer they got, the rougher the waves, until at one point a six-footer knocked them into the bitterly cold Atlantic. They struggled back into the boat, only to lodge on a sandbank. Monteith nearly lost an oar as he poled off. Eventually, they got near enough to the shore to crawl out of the boat into the waist-deep water. As Bailey helped Casement stagger up the beach, Monteith tried to scuttle the boat, but the canvas proved too hard to rip with his knife. He stumbled up the sand as the waves broke noisily behind him in the blackness, and found his companions lying down, the emaciated Casement barely conscious and Bailey little better after eighteen months of enervating prison conditions. It was not yet 4 a.m. Monteith encouraged his ingloriously 'weak army of invasion' to walk up and down to restore their circulation before they wrung out their clothing as best they could. He tried to cheer them up by saying that they had 'got through . . . their adventure alright', to which Casement gave the ambiguous response that they were indeed 'much nearer the end of the chapter'. When he remembered this conversation in later life, Monteith found himself wishing that his hero's story could have ended there, that he had let Casement 'sleep into eternity in the foaming water of Banna Strand' in the shadowy monochrome of the morning.

PART FOUR

Traitor

14.   The Tower

From the Congo horrors on, Casement tended to place a cheerful gloss on unhappiness when he contacted his sister and his niece. Yet his letter to Nina about that morning rings true. As he 'landed in Ireland . . . (about 3 a.m.) swamped and swimming ashore on an unknown strand I was happy for the first time for over a year . . . for one brief spell happy and smiling once more'. As dawn broke over the grassy sand dunes above the beach, 'all around were primroses and wild violets and the singing of skylarks in the air'. His bucolic spring-time in his own country was to last for only a few hours.

The other reality was that the cold, grey and miserable dawn rendered the normally picturesque sweep of Banna Strand, between the gorse-topped arms of the Slieve Mish mountains as far as Mount Brandon and Ireland's most westerly point to the south, and Kerry Head to the north, forlorn territory for the three men's perilous and inauspicious homecoming. There was no reception committee. Despite their exhaustion, they needed to move fast to cover the ten miles south-east to Tralee and then on to Dublin. They buried their Mausers, ammunition belts and field glasses in a tin box in case they were intercepted, keeping only their overcoats.

'The Chief', as Monteith called Casement, would not manage the trek, so needed to be hidden until a vehicle could be found. They decided on an old ruin along the coast which they had spotted on the map. Monteith was for taking the straightest line along the beach, but Casement wanted to be out of sight as soon as possible, and insisted they go directly inland before turning towards their goal. After half an hour's walk, they hit a stinking marshy patch, through which they stumbled up to their knees. Soon the sun broke through and they found a freshwater stream which gave them 'new life and vigour'. But the ruin was too small and exposed. They continued, passing a farm-house over whose low drystone wall an untidy, tousle-haired servant girl stared at them 'in a manner which showed it was unusual for strangers to pass along that road so early in the morning'. Monteith cursed once they had passed her, but was gently upbraided by Casement for doing so. Casement was next to see Mary Gorman in court.

They ducked down to hide from a farm cart transporting seaweed, and soon encountered a ring fort about sixty yards in diameter, a shallow, sunken, fern-filled ditch within sheltering wild hedges surrounded by fields. They sat to make plans: each man should try to get an inventory of the *Aud*'s contents to the Volunteers to prepare for the unloading; 'no consideration of the fate of his companions should turn him from this course'. Monteith and Bailey abandoned their sodden overcoats, first checking the pockets. Monteith found a packet of sandwiches made of war bread and German sausage, soaked with salt water; he started to grind them into the mud but Casement asked if he might try to eat the sludge, though it proved to be a challenge too disgusting even for the famished man.

The Chief refused to hold up his able-bodied companions. Monteith entrusted him with the code sheet, as well as with the photographs of his wife and children which were drying on the grass. He and Bailey arrived in Tralee just before 8 a.m. when many of its few thousand inhabitants were on their way to Good Friday Mass. In their first piece of luck, they came upon a newsagent-cum-hairdresser who could be identified as a patriot by his display of the *Volunteer* and *Honesty*, another nationalist paper. He ushered them to a back room for a breakfast of eggs, bread and butter before escorting them to the head of the Kerry Volunteers, Austin Stack. Stack sent for a friend of Monteith's, Con Collins, to identify him, which took another hour. When the notoriously inefficient Stack was told that the arms ship must be in the bay, he countered that his instructions were that she would not be arriving until the night of Easter Sunday. The cause of the failed rendezvous became clear.

The urgent business was to rescue Casement, so Stack escorted Bailey to a waiting car on the Ardfert road with a parcel of clean clothes for 'Mr Rice' while Monteith hid out. Bailey, his detractors afterwards thought suspiciously, struggled to locate the spot where they had left Casement, unaware that it was a well-known local landmark called McKenna's Fort. They went up and down the lanes, at one point changing a punctured tyre, and were twice stopped by the police before abandoning the car and taking to bicycles lent by a Volunteer. Bailey spent the night in a farmhouse before being directed 'to a Castle', where he was told to 'knock about'; a short while later, he was arrested. Monteith, who needed to be on the Dublin train in the afternoon, had to abandon his Chief.

Their arrival turned out not to have been unobserved after all. John McCarthy, a farmer from Curragh Head, who lived a quarter of a mile from the ocean, left his house at about 2 a.m. to walk along the shore to a holy well a mile distant, although as he was later unable to name the well he was possibly on a less pious mission. On his return journey a few hours later, he noticed a boat bobbing on the incoming tide. It was too heavy for him to lift, so he sent for his neighbour, Pat Driscoll, to help shift it to higher ground. McCarthy saw a knife at the bottom of the dinghy and, following some footprints up the beach, a partially buried tin box tied up with string. When his young daughter appeared, opened the box and started to play with the three pistols inside it, McCarthy despatched Driscoll to the police barracks a few miles away at Ardfert.

Sergeant Hearn of the Royal Irish Constabulary rushed down with Constable Macklin to find several excited men around the trove. The boat was hauled yet further up the beach and the pistols, which turned out to be loaded Mausers, were impounded along with a brown leather satchel containing a flashlight, a partial map and twenty rounds of ammunition; a further hunt turned up another bag with *A Simple Confession Book* by Mother Mary Loyola, more maps and forty rounds; the tin box held 900 bullets. All this and the dinghy were loaded on to McCarthy's cart to be taken to Ardfert by Macklin, while Hearn cycled back to the barracks, collected Constable Reilly and two carbines and started searching the country inland.

At 1.20 p.m., after Casement had been alone for some hours, Reilly came upon McKenna's Fort. He saw the back of a man's head and shoulders above the brambles and blackthorn and 'called upon him to come out'. Casement met this challenge by saying, 'This is a nice way to treat an English traveller.' Reilly blew his whistle to summon Hearn, to whom Casement identified himself as Richard Morten of Denham, Buckinghamshire, an author currently engaged on writing a life of St Brendan; he had left Mount Brandon two nights previously and spent Good Friday lodging at a farm. He 'could not give a reason why' he was in the fort without any identification. When Hearn noticed that the man's boots and trousers were wet and covered in sand, he arrested him for illegally bringing weapons into the country contrary to the Defence of the Realm Act.

The two policemen and their prisoner set off across the field to the public road. A sharp-eyed twelve-year-old boy, Martin Collins, who had halted his pony and trap to watch the activity was still hovering nearby when Reilly returned to the fort. Collins revealed that he had observed Casement tear a piece of paper in half and drop it behind him. He gave the two pieces to Reilly, who saw strings of numbers, all beginning with oo followed by three digits, and, against each number, phrases such as 'Further ammunition is needed' or 'Last wire is not understood' or 'Begin always "Sectpol" and the rest by cipher'. Casement's matches had been too wet to destroy the codes.

At the Ardfert police barracks, his pockets and knapsack were turned out. He was carrying four gold sovereigns and 12s 9d in silver, a six-foot-square green and yellow flag 'with a representation of a castle in the middle and some foreign language underneath',* a pair of field glasses, forty rounds of ammunition, 'some wearing apparel', a few maps and 'some kind of diary'. This last item was a series of easily decoded jottings where '11th April: Left Dublin for Wicklow' was later translated with only a modicum of code-breaking skill as 'Left Berlin for Wilhelmshaven', for example; 'Willie's yacht' could only mean Kaiser Wilhelm's U-boat. By the end of Good Friday, these exhibits had been joined by three overcoats, the longest of which contained in a pocket a first-class rail ticket from Berlin to Wilhelmshaven.

Casement asserted his right to remain silent at Ardfert, and in the late afternoon was driven the five miles to Tralee barracks. A sergeant

---

* Irish, as it turned out, on Gaffney's Limerick flag.

called for a doctor to look over a prisoner who 'had got into some sort of trouble', and Michael Shanahan found a 'man of distinguished appearance' who looked 'jittery and exhausted' in front of a smoky peat fire in a room with a billiards table. He sensed the man wanted to say something privately to him, so he asked the two policemen present to leave the room, at which point Casement identified himself in the hope that the doctor was 'in sympathy with the Irish cause'. Shanahan affirmed that he was. Casement whispered that he was tired out 'after twelve terrible nights in a U-boat' and would like to be set free. Shanahan, noting that the barrack doors were wide open and that a few armed men might fight their way in, said he would 'see what he could do'.

But the astute Head Constable Kearney waylaid the doctor to show him a newspaper cutting about Casement. He placed a piece of paper across the beard and asked if 'the top part of the face did not remind him of the man inside'. Shanahan answered no, and hurried into town to try to enlist some Volunteers to spring Casement, but they all refused, some saying that they had heard the prisoner was just 'some Norwegian sailor'. Since the barrister, writer and headmaster of St Enda's School in the seemingly far-off days of Omarino, Patrick Pearse, had recently been in town to stipulate that 'not a shot was to be fired before the agreed date for the Rising', they were sticking to their orders.

As the afternoon of the long day turned into evening, Casement was desperately working out how to contact Dublin. He called for a priest to attend to his spiritual needs, in the expectation that the man would be a patriot. Kearney, a staunch Catholic himself, obliged and shortly after 9 p.m. Father Ryan arrived. After disclosing his identity, Casement asked him to get word to the Volunteers: 'Tell them I am a prisoner and that the rebellion will be a dismal hopeless failure, as the help they expect will not arrive.' Ryan 'demurred' – he was not a 'political ambassador'. Appealing directly to his priestly calling – he would 'bring God's blessing on the country' – Casement persuaded him that the avoidance of bloodshed lay within his remit. Ryan sought out Stack, who had just read in the *Kerry News* that 'a strange tall man of unknown nationality had been arrested'. The message eventually reached Pearse and Eoin MacNeill, now Chief of Staff of the Volunteers.

The leadership had been in frantic, stormy meetings all week: Mac-Neill had instructed the men 'to prepare for defensive warfare' two days earlier, but had been informed by Hobson and others that this was a cover for the Rising to start on Easter Day. An angry confrontation with Patrick Pearse now took place: Pearse took the view that it was too late for the Rising to be called off, even without the German aid, while MacNeill had reported rumours of a German landing in Kerry on Friday. But by Saturday night he had changed tack to countermand the mobilisation orders, and put coded notices in the newspapers that there would be a twenty-four-hour delay. There ensued a brief, confused, anticlimactic respite which might have allowed the cut-off captive to believe that his ordeal was not in vain.

Assistant Commissioner Basil Thomson had been head of the Metropolitan Police's Criminal Investigation Department for three years. Born in 1861 in Oxford where his father was the Provost of Queen's College (he was later Archbishop of York), he spent the 1880s as a colonial administrator, even at one stage becoming Prime Minister of Tonga; he went on to publish some long-forgotten novels, including *The Diversions of a Prime Minister* and *The Indiscretions of Lady Asenath*, then read for the London Bar and became Governor of Dartmoor Prison before joining the Met. As spy mania swept the country with the advent of war, the flamboyant self-publicist set himself up in direct competition with the more retiring Vernon Kell of MO5(g) to earn the enduring enmity of the new organisation.

On Easter Saturday, Thomson was on late-night 'Zeppelin Duty' at New Scotland Yard when his telephone rang. It appeared that the 'stranger who arrived in the collapsible boat [sic] at Curraghane' might be the man he had been expecting for a while, Sir Roger Casement. The man would be delivered to London's Euston Station at 6.10 the next morning, Easter Sunday. The previous day, Casement had been uncuffed and moved with an escort of six constables to Arbour Hill Barracks, Dublin. He did not speak until his train came close to Killarney Station, when he asked if he could get a newspaper.

He was denied this privilege, but the Head Constable of Killarney came to the carriage door to gossip with the policemen, asking if they had heard 'what happened to the two lads at Puck'; it emerged that a car had been driven off the road into the sea containing the bodies of two men wearing Sinn Féin badges and carrying revolvers and a 'field message book'. Casement, believing the dead men to be Monteith and Bailey, began to 'sob and cry' and kept it up 'for some time' as the train pulled out, to the consternation of his escort. When he had collected himself, he asked if Puck was near Castlemaine Bay, about seven miles from Tralee; on being told it was, he said, 'I am very sorry for these two men, it was on my account that they came over, they were two very good Irishmen.' When the party reached Dublin's Kingsbridge Railway Station (now Heuston), Casement asked if he might be allowed to go to bed soon; he was 'very tired, as he had got no sleep for the past twelve nights'.

Inspector John Sandercock of the CID was the first official to whom Casement disclosed his identity. Sandercock had been sent by Thomson to meet the Irish Mail and convey his prisoner to New Scotland Yard. On the platform at Euston, Casement asked, 'Do you know who I am?' Sandercock replied that he did, but Casement anyway went on, 'I am Sir Roger Casement and the only person to whom I have disclosed my identity is a priest at Tralee', as a prelude to a request that 'the fact of his arrest be published in Ireland at once in order to "show the poor boys that the game is up and so avoid useless bloodshed"'. Thomson refused as he considered it better 'to keep the whole matter as secret as possible until further action has been decided upon'.

Casement was cautioned, taken to Brixton Prison and told he would be interviewed at 10 o'clock that same morning. A message went to Army Command in Dublin to say that all they had learnt from 'C.R.', as his identity was disguised in the message, was that the two 'men who escaped were wet through' and 'probably members of the Irish Brigade'; Casement had not 'incriminated any individuals in Ireland so far' and apparently his 'one desire [was] to stop any action on the part of his friends at the present time as he feels they have been duped by the Germans'.

Casement was brought before Thomson, Blinker Hall, the proud imperialist Major Frank Hall of MO5(g) – himself a County Down landowner and previously Military Secretary of the UVF and a gun-runner – and Superintendent Patrick Quinn. The prisoner entered the room 'rather theatrically', and his interrogators encountered 'a tall, thin, cadaverous man with thick black hair turning grey, a pointed beard and thin, nervous hands, mahogany coloured from long tropical service. His forehead was a network of wrinkles, his complexion deeply sunburnt.' They began their jousting: Casement backtracked on confirming his name, although admitting there were not 'many people who would care to impersonate' him. He asked for Sir William Tyrrell, his friend and defender in the Foreign Office but more recently one of the establishment 'scoundrels' he had been ranting against from Germany. Thomson doubted if Tyrrell was 'in town' that Easter Day and asked why Casement wanted him. The answer was that he was 'in great difficulty' although 'not about myself . . . It may involve other people.' The request was denied.

Thomson proceeded to ask about the items found in McKenna's Fort, such as the weakly coded diary. Casement agreed 'they are names meaning some other places', but did not expand. When Thomson produced a copy of the Buenos Aires newspaper *Deutsche La Plata Zeitung* which carried an interview with Casement under the headline '*England zu Spät*' ('England Too Late'), in which he criticised Britain's motives for entering the war, he at first denied giving the interview, then angrily insisted that he had never concealed his opinions 'regarding the righteousness of England's war with Germany'. He reasserted his reasonableness and prejudged his honourable martyrdom by saying that 'Some Irishmen are afraid to act, but I was not afraid to commit High Treason . . . I face all the consequences . . . I have done nothing treacherous to my country. I have committed many follies in endeavouring to help my country.' He had known that he was 'bound' to be caught if he returned but had 'come from a sense of duty'.

Thomson continued to produce evidence that Casement had been employed by the German government to 'seduce the loyalties' of the prisoners of war from their 'allegiance to the King'. Casement

Julio César Arana, the Devil of
the Putumayo and founder of the
London-listed Peruvian
Amazon Company.

Casement with Juan Tizón,
the Company's chief overseer,
at La Chorrera, 1910.

The Company steamer *Liberal*, which delivered
the Putumayo commissioners to Iquitos.

A Putumayo youth with his heavy load of rubber, in a photograph taken by Casement with his box camera.

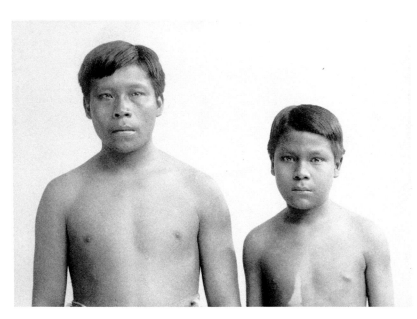

Omarino and Ricudo, the two youths Casement took to England in an unhappy experiment.

Molly Childers and Mary Spring
Rice smuggling rifles for the Irish
Volunteers on the *Asgard*, 1914.

Alice Stopford Green, the
well-connected scholar who
backed Casement to the end.

With John Devoy, head of Clan na Gael, on his way to a packed
meeting in Philadelphia just as Europe was descending into war.

Eivind Adler Christensen, Casement's lover, helper, spy and betrayer. The men met on Broadway soon after Casement's arrival in New York and travelled to Europe together.

Rudolf Nadolny, the sinister head of the military intelligence unit Abteilung IIIb.

The German authorities gathered the Irish prisoners of war at Limburg, near Frankfurt.

Casement wanted to sue the London *Graphic* for implying that he and the Irish Brigade recruits were gaining financially from the German government.

Recruits in their uniforms at Zossen, 1915.

A tea party with his champion, the American Consul General in Munich T. St John Gaffney (second from left).

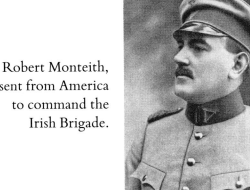

Robert Monteith,
sent from America
to command the
Irish Brigade.

On *U-19* off the
Hebrides, April 1916.
From left: Monteith,
Bailey, Lieutenant
Walter, Casement and
Captain Weisbach.

The SS *Libau*, shortly to be disguised as the *Aud*.

The dinghy in which the three men
rowed ashore at Banna Strand.

Reginald 'Blinker' Hall,
Director of Naval Intelligence
(above), and head of the CID
Basil Thomson (below),
Casement's interrogators.

The Unionist F. E. Smith,
Attorney General.

George Gavan Duffy and J. H. Morgan, representing Casement.

Serjeant Sullivan, the lead counsel who failed to make it through the trial.

In the dock.

Leaving court.

retorted that the men had signed contracts with their eyes open and had never been going to fight for Germany, but for Ireland. He 'didn't care twopence for Germany' and again asked for Tyrrell, in vain.

The preliminary, unproductive interrogation ended with Casement's return to Brixton. He was 'dazed' by events and by lack of sleep; he later remembered that he was 'incapable of thinking clearly on any subject but the one – how in the name of God to still stop the Rising without doing a mean or cowardly thing or giving any man away'.

The capture and the non-arrival of German weapons had allowed the authorities in London to breathe more easily. Casement's anxiety also subsided somewhat as he established with Thomson that 'there was not a word in the papers of any trouble in Ireland'. Thomson's first question in the interrogation had touched on an issue that had been central to Casement in a more abstract sense for the previous decade: 'Do you claim to be a British subject?' The answer was that in law he supposed he was, but he would never 'put forward the plea that I was a British subject' to seek protection, even though he was reminded that under the wartime emergency legislation 'British subjects are treated or can be treated differently from aliens of any kind'. Casement, still without legal representation, announced that his captors could deal with him as they pleased, just as Hall interrupted the skirmish to say that Bailey had been arrested and had given a full confession, including that Monteith had been with them. Casement offered as proof of Monteith's commitment that he had wanted to come alone on the 'most hopeless enterprise', sparing his companions.

He saw no point in dissembling as all seemed quiet in Dublin. He revealed the nature of the *Aud*'s cargo, although the German proposal to send the ship had come as a 'thunder clap'. As he grew more passionate, he forgot that he was being questioned in London and addressed the Germans directly, just as he had harangued Nadolny in Berlin: 'I have been here for a year and a half and begged you again and again to send rifles to Ireland and you refused always. Now you spring it at my head at the eleventh hour, when I have long given it up . . . The belated help synchronises with what I can only regard as

a hopeless rising in Ireland where my countrymen will be shot down.'
After a 'terrible fight' he had 'won the day' in not taking to Ireland
the fifty men of the Brigade. His interrogators let on that they had
statements from the soldiers who had returned in prisoner swaps, but
Casement dismissed these as 'base falsehoods' without even hearing
their content, referring to the *Graphic*'s 'Voice of the Traitor!' slur.

Thomson read aloud the triumphantly defiant letter to Alice
Green that had accompanied the December 1914 Declaration in
which Casement had claimed that thanks to his actions the Germans
would 'aid to the uttermost to redeem the four green fields'. In
response to this incriminating evidence, Casement complained that
he was being denied 'communications with any legal authority'.
That elicited a confession from Thomson that he had a 'difficulty' in
establishing whether he would be tried in a military or a civil court,
as it depended on the politically vexing nature of the charge. The
second interrogation petered out in a discussion of trial venues and
possible solicitors.

By the time the men met the following day, hostilities had opened in
Dublin after 1,200 rebels, men and women, occupied the iconic
imperial Georgian edifice of the General Post Office on Sackville
Street, as well as City Hall, Boland's Mill, Jacob's Biscuit Factory and
other buildings, although the symbolic home of British rule, Dublin
Castle, remained unbreached. Lethal snipers, machine guns and field
artillery opened up around the city centre; a gunboat on the Liffey
was brought up to shell the insurgents' largely improvised strong-
holds and the 1,269 troops already in the city were reinforced to
16,000 by the end of the week. Five days later, on Saturday 29 April,
Patrick Pearse offered unconditional surrender in order to prevent
more civilian bloodshed;* the area around Sackville Street reminded
observers of 'the shelled remains of Louvain, Amiens or Ypres'. The
Rising had been the military shambles Casement foresaw, made

---

* A total of 260 civilians, 126 members of British armed forces, 82 Irish rebels and
17 policemen died during the week. Some 2,600, including 2,200 civilians, were
wounded.

worse by the punitive English response: Yeats's 'terrible beauty' had been born in the new cityscape of violence and martyrdom.

Thomson opened the final bout in a fury against the prisoner and the unfolding disaster. He wasted no time: 'Since I saw you yesterday what we thought would happen has happened. There has been more or less a rising in Dublin, and a good many have been killed, and that is all the good that has proceeded from your expedition . . . I understand that what you did tell us yesterday or the day before . . . was not the whole facts of the case as regards the ship.' Another shipment of arms must have been on the way, otherwise how could the rebellion succeed? Casement replied there was no possibility of further cargo unless he telegraphed for it; he offered the empty hope that there would not be retaliatory German Zeppelin attacks on Dublin. Once again, he started to dramatise his testimony as he remembered that he had said to the Germans, 'If my friends can organise a rising on April 23rd, I'll go myself first and I landed in Ireland and knew the thing to be hopeless . . . They said, not at all. It will be a success and you will be able to dictate terms to the British Government.' Even his syntax collapsed as the final ruination of his hopes was brought home to him.

Without any prospect of influencing events in Ireland, Casement remained in his dissociated state, ruminating on German attitudes to him: 'They sometimes called me a dreamer but they were willing to profit by my foolishness.' He attacked the British for putting Home Rule on the statute book only 'to trap Ireland into arms' and quash his people once and for all, even though a conscription bill had only been passed in January; he had become a nationalist thanks to the Boer War and his experiences in the Congo; he wished he had refused his honours.

A police officer entered and held a whispered conference with Superintendent Quinn, who in turn muttered something to Thomson. Thomson now threw in what seemed a non sequitur. He asked, 'Have you got some trunks at 50 Ebury Street? I propose having them down and examined.' Casement replied that there was 'nothing in them', before Blinker Hall took the interrogation back to the question of future arms shipments, and whether Casement knew what the contents of the *Aud*'s hold were. In an attempt to get him to open up, Hall suggested that the crew of the German ship would be 'shot as pirates' as they were acting 'without a commission from the Emperor'. In fact, the seamen were treated as prisoners of war.

At this point, with such speed as to suggest that he had known about the trunks since the police investigated the Ebury Street fish-monger as far back as December 1914,* Thomson announced the arrival of them, although without their keys. Casement's 'Break them open' showed his nonchalance about the contents, which were inventoried as trinket boxes, patent medicines, books, a magnifying glass, scissors, photographs and mounts, newspaper cuttings, cotton wool, a canvas holdall, a ledger and '3 diaries'. This side event of his last appearance in New Scotland Yard was to have resounding consequences.

As he was still without either lawyer or charge, Casement requested that nothing he said 'be used against me', to which Thomson assented. The first day of the chaotic and bloody fighting in Dublin ended with the policeman announcing that 'instead of going back to Brixton Prison you are to be taken into military custody with a view to a military trial and you will now go to the Tower of London'. Incarceration in the fortress that had housed Anne Boleyn, Sir Walter Raleigh and Guy Fawkes before their deaths made his likely fate historically obvious.

News of the arrest had reached the newspapers. *The Times* printed a tight-lipped Admiralty statement about 'an attempt to land arms and ammunition . . . by a vessel under the guise of a neutral merchant ship, but in reality a German auxiliary, in conjunction with a German submarine. The auxiliary sank and a number of prisoners were made, amongst whom was Sir Roger Casement. Sir Roger Casement has acquired remarkable notoriety since the outbreak of war through his attempts to associate Irishmen with the cause of Germany.' Other papers went for more sensational headlines such as 'Farcical Invasion of Ireland. Notorious Traitor Captured'.

* Thomson confirmed this in a moment of forgetfulness in 1922.

The Commons was packed after the Easter Recess, with many MPs in uniform. Augustine Birrell, Secretary of State for Ireland, declared martial law on the island, and in a debate about the need for a secret sitting the maverick Noel Pemberton Billing asked the Prime Minister if it was true that Casement was in London and 'could he give the House and the nation the assurance that the traitor would be shot forthwith?' Once the cheers had subsided, Asquith replied that that was 'not a question which should be put'.

Casement's Bannister cousins, Gertrude and Elizabeth, both schoolteachers, were spending the holiday weekend in Frinton-on-Sea, Essex. Two days earlier, Gertrude's bedroom windows had been made to rattle by the German bombardment of Lowestoft. Elizabeth went for a walk on Easter Monday and returned 'white-faced and scared' on seeing the news 'on the posters'. They jumped on the next train to London, desperate to contact their cousin. Gertrude suggested that Alice Green 'who knew so many people in London' might help, and they checked into the Wilton Hotel to be near her Grosvenor Street home. Gertrude had spent the past eighteen months trying to navigate her way through the rumours and the hostile claims in the press about Cousin Roger; now he was back in the country, and presumably facing a capital charge.

The sisters found Alice Green 'in despair at all the events; the Rebellion in Dublin she characterised as "madness"', and Casement's return 'a calamity brought on by an insane desire of Roger's' to emulate the eighteenth-century founding father of Irish separatism Wolfe Tone, whom he often referenced. In her own shocked misery, the 'wise woman' could offer no hope or advice. Gertrude wrote to Herbert Samuel, the Home Secretary, asking to visit her cousin, and the sisters set off for the Home Office. Whether or not their request even reached his desk, Casement's Commons champion over the Congo atrocities refused an audience, and his messenger pointed out that the department anyway had no jurisdiction as Casement was in a military rather than a civil prison. A trip to the War Office met with a similar rebuff from Asquith's brother-in-law Jack Tennant, accompanied by the suggestion that they apply to the Home Office. When they protested, a junior recommended Scotland Yard. Their letter to

Thomson was acknowledged, but nothing more. They spent day after day 'of weary trudging from Public office to Public office, always refused with absolutely blank, stony indifference'. Gertrude wrote Casement a brief note to say they were trying to see him and were praying for him, but the Governor of the Tower did not pass it on. MI5 had stipulated that all correspondence should be forwarded to the War Office, unless the prisoner was transferred to the civil authorities, at which point it should be sent to New Scotland Yard instead.

By this time, Mrs Green had rallied to suggest a lawyer, George Gavan Duffy of 4 Raymond Buildings, Gray's Inn. Gavan Duffy was the son of Charles Gavan Duffy, one of the founders of the Young Ireland Movement and the *Nation* in the 1840s before his emigration to Australia, where he became Premier of Victoria. George was a nationalist to his core, later becoming Irish Minister for Foreign Affairs and ultimately President of the High Court in Dublin, and he agreed to take Casement's case despite his partners' threat that if he did so he would have to leave the firm. Gavan Duffy applied to see the prisoner, but was himself refused.

The sisters went around the Home and War Office loop once more before it was suggested that they should get in touch with Treasury Counsel, who were compiling the case against Casement. To their astonishment, Sir Charles Mathews, the sociable Director of Public Prosecutions, agreed to a meeting, but only to say, when Gertrude pleaded that she had heard her cousin was due to be shot any day, that no civil authority had any influence. Gertrude was beginning to learn her way around the system that was so cruelly denying her access, and countered by asking why, if that was so, had he been taken on 'two occasions to Scotland Yard? And why are you engaged in draw-ing up a case against him?' Mathews's demeanour changed, and he became 'cold and harsh' as he asked how she knew this (the police had told her); she walked out.

On their next circuit in what Gertrude described as their ten days of cruelty, someone told the sisters that Casement was in the custody of the Life Guards. The regiment's courteous, sympathetic Major Arbuthnot suggested they write to the Governor of the Tower, which they had already done. Arbuthnot then revealed that he had himself seen Casement and that he needed clothes, but he withheld the full depths of his miserable situation. The prisoner was in a windowless cell with two soldiers present at all times, a third looking in through the pane in the door. These men changed every hour and the one dim overhead light was permanently left on so he found it hard to sleep. Despite repeated requests, he was still in the clothes and underclothes in which he had waded ashore on Banna Strand. His writing materials had been taken away. He had tried to poison himself by scratching his arm with a broken spectacle lens and applying the curare he had brought from Germany, but succeeded only in raising a painful sore; he refused to eat, and was threatened with force-feeding by the regimental doctor. The only person who showed him any kindness was one of his guards, a Welsh corporal, who muttered that he was a very brave man he hoped would be released. On 3 May, the corporal was overheard informing Casement that the rebel leaders had been executed in Dublin,* after which he never reappeared. On the same day, Augustine Birrell resigned and John Redmond declared that the leaders of the rebellion had been primarily traitors to Home Rule and to Ireland more than to England, adding that the Germans had committed an act as heinous as the invasion of Belgium in supporting the Uprising.

By the time Gavan Duffy was allowed in, Casement had eaten nothing but hunks of bread for days, and looked dreadful, his eyes bloodshot and red-rimmed from exhaustion; he was collarless, his new beard ragged, his boots were flapping without their laces, and his arms, head and neck were blotchy from insect bites. He spoke hesitatingly, and often stumbled over his words. When Gavan Duffy painted this picture to Alice Green, she wasted no time in conveying her influential disgust to Asquith, with the result that a Downing

---

* Pearse, MacDonagh and Thomas Clarke were executed at once, eleven others (including Plunkett) over the next ten days. Seventy-five of the ninety death sentences were commuted. Some 2,000 suspects from around the country were shipped to British prisons and internment camps. Pearse wrote the night before he was hanged, 'The help I expected from Germany failed. The British sank the ships.' (MacColl, *Roger Casement* p. 220.)

Street official telephoned Major Arbuthnot, who suggested that the cousins prepare a clothing parcel.

Two days later, Gertrude and her sister were granted a permit to visit. After an hour's wait, they were shown into a room with a horse-hair sofa, a table and some chairs, and Casement entered, accompanied by Arbuthnot and two soldiers. The women clung to their cousin, and, after a while, asked to be alone with him. Arbuthnot ordered the soldiers to stand outside but to keep looking in, and absented himself. The meeting was 'terrible': Casement had been told, punitively, that none of his family or friends wanted to see him as they were all 'disgusted by his treachery'; now that the women were here, he was sure it was to say farewell before he was shot. He recounted his landing and capture, and the interrogation by Thomson and Hall. Gertrude was outraged that 'these two high-minded, chivalrous English gentlemen were dressed with all care and deliberately humiliated their prisoner by making him appear before them in a filthy condition'. After three-quarters of an hour, their time was up. The next time the Bannisters saw him was in Bow Street Magistrates' Court as his courtroom drama commenced its painful, complex and often powerfully moving process.

15.   Some Neglected Morals

The Attorney General, Casement's enemy in the matter of Home Rule and promoter of gun-running for the UVF, was the lead prosecutor to open the hearings at Bow Street on 15 May 1916. F. E. Smith had taken over his post from the man he had galloped alongside, Sir Edward Carson, who was now Leader of the Opposition. It was a succession that enraged Casement's supporters: H. G. Wells blamed Asquith's 'moral feebleness' for leading a government in which 'this Sir Edward Carson figured as Attorney General (with a salary of £7,000 and fees)* to be replaced presently by his associate in the Ulster sedition, Sir F. E. Smith. Grosser insult was never offered to a friendly people'; Smith prosecuting Casement was 'a shocking conjunction'. But Smith would never have stood aside because of his past actions – it was inconceivable to him that anyone might not want to be British.

He ran through Casement's career, applauding his loyalty to the Crown; he gave weighty reference to how 'deeply sensible of the honour done to me by His Majesty' Casement had been when he accepted his knighthood. Smith emphasised that 'it might be useful to remember at this stage that these were Casement's feelings in June 1911 towards the country which he had served for so long and towards the Sovereign of that country . . . a man who had had 19 years' experience of the methods of government of this country, and in which he himself had participated, a man of mature years and cultivated understanding and . . . considerable knowledge of history'. The Attorney General's line of attack could not have been plainer: Casement had been a loyal, rewarded and grateful servant of

---

* The fees fluctuated from year to year, but the combined salary and fees had been £18,397 6s 6d in 1914, approaching £1,800,000 at today's values.

the Crown and the government – and had then conspired against them.

Thomson had been summoned by Smith to be told of the Cabinet's decision to proceed with a civil trial. Although 'trial by court-martial would be much quicker', it was important that the case be heard in public before a jury 'lest in after years we should be reproached with having killed him secretly'. If Casement had been indicted for any other crime, such as conspiracy resulting in the Dublin insurrection, he would have been tried in Ireland after his arrest in Kerry; but high treason was always heard in London. There could be no hint of subterfuge with a figure of such prominence after the Union-rocking Easter Rising, Smith ordained. Thomson was ordered to gather his witnesses quickly, and by the time of the hearings had interviewed some of the civilians and RIC officers from Kerry, as well as many former Limburg prisoners. On 10 May, word came from the British embassy in Washington that Adler Christensen had agreed to testify. Casement's lover, whom he had consistently, ignorantly and often irrationally defended, prepared for his final betrayal.

With only a matter of days to go before the Bow Street appearance, a defence team was needed. Alice Green, fresh from stonewalling Thomson, and Gavan Duffy set to, but thanks to the notoriety of this unwinnable brief at a moment when patriotism counted, no leading barrister would take it, defying the 'cab-rank rule' which required barristers, if free, to accept instructions regardless of personal bias; it was a convention that had been introduced by the Bar Council in the previous century, ironically in response to difficulties that Irish defendants had in obtaining legal representation during the Fenian dynamite campaign of arbitrary terror in the early 1880s. Feelings were running so high in the inns of court that Gavan Duffy's firm followed through on their insistence that he resign. Eventually, a barrister on the Welsh circuit, Thomas Artemus Jones, stepped up; he was joined by Casement's liberal acquaintance John Hartman Morgan, former leader writer on the *Manchester Guardian*, Professor of Constitutional Law at University College London, and coiner of the maxim that 'Irish history is a thing for Irishmen to forget and for Englishmen to remember.'

Green reckoned £500* would be needed to pay for the defence at the committal hearings, much more for the inevitable trial, and put up £100; she wrote to Casement's long-time supporter William Cadbury, who contributed £200 with a note that he had 'no sympathy whatever with his alleged actions in Germany' but wished him 'to have every proper opportunity of stating his case'. Cadbury, like Conan Doyle, believed that until proven otherwise 'the unwisdom of recent months had been largely caused by [Casement's] serious state of health', and 'the past years of his noble and unselfish life' should not be ignored; the novelist Ford Madox Ford reckoned he had been 'driven mad by the horrors' of the Congo. Gertrude Bannister and her sister gave up their hard-earned savings.

Jones visited the Tower for a client conference and lost no time in pointing out that 'the charge is high treason and a verdict of guilty means death', to which Casement responded he 'should be glad to die a thousand times for the name of Ireland'. He had been writing notes about his past three years for his lawyers: he justified the Volunteers by blaming the government for failing to deliver Home Rule, and blamed Smith and Carson for starting the militarisation; his aim had been to keep Ireland 'out of conflict'. He had never 'contemplated an insurrection . . . when engaged in the Volunteer movement' although he had 'dreamed . . . of a possible state of European affairs that might bring effective foreign help . . . But that was only a "dream" . . . Had the war not come, the dream remained a dream.' It was a hopeless courtroom defence, a sign that he was disengaging from the current reality to take refuge in romantic, impractical patriotism – perhaps in martyrdom.

The charges laid against Casement and Bailey were that they 'at various times between 1 November 1914 and 21 April 1916 . . . unlawfully, maliciously and traitorously did commit high treason within and without the Realm of England in contempt of our Sovereign Lord

---

* Approximately £45,000 today.

the King and his laws, to the evil example of all others in the like case offending contrary to the duty and allegiance of them to our Sovereign Lord the King'. Casement proclaimed Bailey's innocence and asked Duffy to conduct his defence. Bailey's appearance in the dock had been settled only the week before at a meeting in F. E. Smith's room in the House of Commons – a member of the Brigade had to be on trial or 'the army would be dissatisfied'.

The Times set the tone of the English press for the three-day committal proceedings at which the magistrate would determine if there was sufficient evidence to commit Casement for a full trial. Its leader opined that there should have been 'an alternative and more expeditious course' to ensure justice, by implication the swift conviction and execution of the rebel leaders in Ireland. It characterised Bailey as 'simply a typical Irish peasant', and described Casement as 'more gaunt and thin than ever', appearing 'restless and ill at ease in body and mind', with his 'short and scrubby beard'. He wore an ill-fitting tweed suit bought by his cousins, scratched his neck, bit his nails and never let his gaze settle. Presiding was the Chief Magistrate Sir John Dickinson, Smith was prosecuting, and Mathews and Frank Hall were also in the court. The Bannister sisters had to queue for nine hours to be sure of places in the public gallery. Bailey, playing a minor role alongside Casement in the dock, had no supporters.

The first two days of the hearing were an abbreviated rehearsal by the prosecution for the inevitable trial: after setting Casement up as the grateful knight, Smith read out Bailey's statement about their journey on *U-19* and what was known about the scuttling of the *Aud*; RIC officers recounted Casement's few hours in Kerry and described what was found in McKenna's Fort; and six soldiers back home after prisoner swaps gave evidence about the Limburg visits. Jones had little to add on the third day, merely expressing the wish that the defence would at least be given proper preparation time for the trial, at which Junior Treasury Counsel Travers Humphreys informed the court that 'the authorities consider it most important that this trial should take place at the earliest possible moment'. Dickinson noted that that would be in about three weeks, and committed the accused for trial 'at a place and time to be fixed hereafter'. On being asked if he had anything to say, Casement shook his head and answered, 'No, Sir John.'

The authorities recognised that Casement was unwell and put him into the Brixton Prison hospital where he could benefit from an improved diet. The medical officer applied insecticide to deal with the lice that still plagued him, and awarded him the rare privilege of tobacco after Gavan Duffy wrote to say that his client's 'suffering is undoubtedly aggravated by the prohibition against smoking'. Casement's first letter was to Inspector Sandercock, his Euston greeter and escort to and from Bow Street, thanking him for his 'unfailing courtesy, manliness and kindness'. Sandercock had shown the 'best side of an Englishman's character – his native good heart', and the prisoner implored the young policeman to keep in mind 'that a man may hate a country and its policy and yet not hate any individual of that country'.

Gavan Duffy visited often, as did Alice Green and Gertrude Bannister. Henry Nevinson, a distinguished war correspondent as well as a campaigner against slavery, who had met Casement at Dick Morten's house eleven years earlier, was struck by how much he had aged: he was 'wrinkled and careworn; his hands at first worked nervously, sometimes being passed quickly over his face and eyes, to hide or suppress emotion and even tears . . . But his eyes were straight and frank and blue as ever, his manner charmingly polite.' When William Cadbury's wife Emmeline asked him why he did 'it', he replied that he had to try to stop the English 'doing cruel things to the Irish'. One person who did not visit was E. D. Morel: he felt that his new anti-military foreign policy pressure group, the Union for Democratic Control, would suffer if he acted on his 'personal feelings' and came; he hoped that Mrs Green would not consider him 'a moral coward'.

Gavan Duffy counselled against Casement defending himself, a desire born from his penury and his conviction that only he could get across the rightness of his actions; quite apart from the potential legal disaster of this course, he was physically and emotionally too fragile. Gertrude Bannister made the first approach to Charlotte Shaw, the heiress wife of the Irish playwright and political activist George Bernard. The Shaws had been 'much moved' at Casement's arrest 'but did not pay much attention to the matter, as we only knew him in a general way', until Gertrude called on them at their Adelphi Terrace house. They thought her 'an Irishwoman of a fine type – sensible, shrewd, capable, responsible . . . She came to us first to ask for some money help, and in the second, to ask if we would work with her to get together a little group of people to attempt to work up some real defence.'

The sixty-year-old Shaw, whose copious plays, novels and polemics about personal, political and social wrongs had already encompassed *Arms and the Man*, *Man and Superman* and *Pygmalion*, had been a consistent critic of Sinn Féin, warning before the Rising that the consequence of executing the nationalist leaders would be to hand the cause over to the movement: 'It is absolutely impossible to slaughter a man in this position without making him a martyr and a hero, even though the day before the rising he may have only been "a minor poet".' He wrote an excoriating article in the *New Statesman* headlined 'Some Neglected Morals of the Easter Rising', which argued that 'no wise man now uses the word Traitor at all' because 'All the slain men and women of the Sinn Féin Volunteers fought and died for their country as sincerely as any soldier in Flanders.'

The Fabian reformer Beatrice Webb threw 'a painful luncheon party' to bring the future Nobel laureate and Alice Green together, at which Shaw announced that the most effective course was for Casement 'to defend his own case and make a great oration of defiance which would "bring down the house"'. Alice Green almost collapsed in tears at this proposition as 'the man was desperately ill . . . quite incapable of handling a court full of lawyers'. Shaw calculated that for Casement to 'plead not guilty but admit all the facts; to assert his complete right to act as he had done . . . to be eloquent about his right to take up arms for the independence of his country . . . would at least [have] a chance of [prompting] disagreement in the jury', and he set off after lunch to write this speech: the only way to reconcile Casement's work for the British government, 'a diplomat by profession', with his Irish views was to proclaim that he had long believed

in an independent Ireland, so that at the outbreak of the war, reckoning Germany would win, he had concentrated on getting support
there 'as a considered diplomatic policy and not a mere gush of patriotic sentiment'. Shaw proposed that in 'a very humble way' Casement
might have unified Ireland as Garibaldi had Italy in 1848, a feat
applauded by the British government. Casement did not advocate a
German occupation of Ireland, and had only asked for Irish soldiers
and German arms; nobody could be loyal to more than one country.

As he warmed to his task, the dramatist took over: 'I am neither an
Englishman nor a traitor; I am an Irishman, captured in a fair attempt
to achieve the independence of my country.' Casement should ask
the jury to ignore the facts of the case, and instead ask themselves the
only thing that mattered – was Casement a traitor, 'in the wider
sense', to his country? When he saw the document a few days later,
Casement was moved to learn of Shaw's involvement. In many ways
the speech accorded with what he himself had been working on, but
'with this exception – that I should never suggest to an English court
of jury that they should let me off as a prisoner of war, but [would]
tell them "You may hang me and be damned to you" '. Since the English 'have my body, they may do with it what they please . . . but the
rest of me will remain unconvicted still'. Alice Green and Gertrude
Bannister told Shaw that Casement would certainly need counsel,
while Beatrice Webb rejected Shaw's suggestion that he produce the
piece 'as a national dramatic event' to stir up feeling from the stage.
Shaw, who anyway insisted that only Casement could speak his lines
'with the necessary wholeheartedness', lost interest and did not con-
tribute to his defence out of meanness and for fear of compromising
his own celebrity status.

Casement's own inspiration was more historical and emotional
than practical: he wanted to establish 'not that I did not commit high
treason, because that of course I committed it openly and knowingly,
but that I did not act dishonourably or "treacherously" . . . I want to
show that the very thing I did has been done again and again by *far*
greater men, by the noblest men in history, whom the English nation
are asked to honour and praise for ever.' He considered calling Garibaldi's biographer G. M. Trevelyan to argue that he was following

the example of the revolutionary, patriotic Young Italians; he requested research into William of Orange, the Dutch Protestant victor of the 1690 Battle of the Boyne who had taken the English and Scottish thrones to end the bitter conflict between Crown and Parliament. He cited Tomáš Masaryk, the Czech legislator who had pledged allegiance to Emperor Franz Joseph and became a traitor to his country by campaigning for independence on the outbreak of war in 1914, then received a declaration of support from Asquith when he raised a Czech Legion to fight the Austro-Hungarians with money from overseas. He suggested that he was being tried for his 'rebel views about Ireland', no more the business of the law than if he held 'certain religious or atheistical views', and that 'the only thing the law has a right to assail me on is when I did translate my (well-known) rebel views into action'. He knew what the outcome of his trial would be and wanted to maximise the propaganda potential of his last public forum.

As always, Alice Green was the staunchest as well as the best-connected figure in his life. The Prime Minister received a blistering letter the day the Bow Street hearings ended, stating that 'Prejudice had overturned the honourable tradition of English justice that every prisoner should have a fair trial, more especially when his life is in question.' She said she would be raising money for Casement's defence in America, as he was poor and his only relatives in England were schoolteachers; she raged against his incarceration in the Tower which had 'gravely [affected] his physical endurance'. Asquith, wary of her influence and wanting to do the right thing by his high-profile prisoner, forwarded her broadside to the War Office, which declared that Casement had been offered a change of clothes on his arrival and that he 'was apparently satisfied under the circumstances'. The officials even had a memorandum from the General Officer Commanding, London District, stating that there was 'a Medical Certificate that the Quarters where the prisoner was confined were suitable for his detention'.

Green attempted to drum up international support, writing to General Louis Botha, who had been guerrilla leader in the Boer War (and captor of the young Winston Churchill) before he worked for peace with his enemies and became the first Prime Minister of South

Africa and a loyal British ally. She said that Botha must intervene when the inevitable sentence was pronounced as 'no voice would be as powerful as yours in its effect on turning the public mind to clemency and generosity . . . All the dice are loaded in a very singular degree against the prisoner. I have therefore ventured to appeal to you if you could give your work at the critical moment on behalf of mercy.' She stressed how ill Casement had become after his Amazon journey, and how impoverished and time-pressured his defence was.

She secured the services of an Irish-American lawyer, Michael Francis Doyle, a friend of Gaffney's. Gertrude had written to Doyle on 17 May at Green's suggestion, after which he met the now widowed Nina Casement Newman in Philadelphia and agreed to represent her brother, gratis if need be. Clan na Gael had sent its last $25,000 to Dublin just before the Rising, but Devoy had on deposit the $5,000 proceeds of the sale of his brother's estate in New Mexico, so he gave that for the defence fund. Casement had felt utterly abandoned by his American friends, forming 'hasty and wholly unjustifiable conclusions about [them] and the Germans', so he 'looked surprised . . . and tears came into his eyes' when Doyle appeared in the prison with the money.*

The *Daily Mail* ran a story about the 'young man well on the right side of forty' who had 'come over at the express desire of Sir Roger' and who had been in conference with Gavan Duffy within a half-hour of his arrival; the *Evening News* described how Doyle was present 'by special permission of the British Government'. From the American perspective, it helped raise interest in what was becoming a politically charged event even before the inevitable sentence was passed: McGarrity put out a statement that 'England will hesitate to execute Sir Roger knowing that . . . three Englishmen [are] only

---

* Total contributions to the defence fund came to £1,750 (about £160,000 today). Contributors included: Doyle £700; Alice Green £200; William Cadbury £200; Sidney Parry £100; Gertrude Bannister £100; Elizabeth Bannister £50; Roger Casement, cousin, £25; Jane Cobden Unwin £5; Henry Nevinson £5. A total of £1,086 6s 0d went to counsel; £537 7s 2d to Duffy 'on account of costs'; and £15 7s 9d to 'Sir Roger Casement and for his refreshments at Court (including payments at his request for Defendant Bailey)'. (Reid, *The Lives of Roger Casement* p. 368.)

equal to one Irishman'; it would be 'proof that with England there is no love for an Irishman, no matter what his creed unless he become and remain her tool and turn his back on his own country and her people'. Meanwhile the British Ambassador in Washington, Sir Cecil Spring Rice, telegraphed on 1 May that 'execution of Casement would cause many protests'.

The Home Office was alarmed by Spring Rice's reference to Doyle's 'reputation of being a self-advertiser and of no particular standing', and planned to tread softly. Herbert Samuel feared provoking antagonism if he stuck rigidly to the rules regarding foreign representation in British courts, and made various further concessions: Doyle's 'papers would not be subjected to examination' on arrival in the country or in the prison, but a warder needed always to be present when he was in conference. Although it remained 'very undesirable that this gentleman should be given any recognition as one of the prisoner's legal advisers', he was granted dispensation to sit silently alongside counsel.

Gavan Duffy continued to cast around for barristers to make the case in court, and leading English practitioners continued to turn him down. He eventually turned to his agile-minded brother-in-law, Serjeant A. M. Sullivan KC, son of a Nationalist MP and historian, and the last Serjeant-at-Law* to be appointed at the Irish Bar. Sullivan was leading counsel in the Irish courts and had been admitted to the English Bar, but could appear in London only as a junior. Beyond this disadvantage, he was at best lukewarm towards Casement, writing after the trial that 'he was a man of supreme energy, great physical courage, and of intellectual audacity', but 'he had undermined his mental balance', and his 'vanity, inconsistent with reason', was a 'weakness that wrecked what might have been the most daring project of the Great War'. Sullivan categorically rejected Shaw's speech, and was not helped by Casement's own views about his best defence: Sullivan was forbidden to depart from his admission of his 'full responsibility', by which he meant 'not only responsibility for the

---

* A small, originally elite group of lawyers in England and Ireland, eventually replaced by King's or Queen's Counsel.

rising in Ireland which was, without question, based on my prior teaching', but also his 'responsibility *vis-à-vis* the German Government and my duty to defend them'. Although the lines played into the prosecution's hands, they satisfied Casement's now heightened sense of grandiose self-sacrifice. Sullivan dismissed all this as 'sentiment', further antagonising Casement who called the lawyer's proposed defence 'dishonourable . . . to my past attitude and all my actions'. After their conference, Casement was clear that there could 'only be one verdict', without any 'hope of acquittal or annulment or pleas of error or on technical grounds', and he asserted once again that it would be better for him 'to go my road alone' to get the 'same finding . . . and save much good money'.

The government examined precedents. Because the law under which Casement was being tried was so ancient, the methods of punishment were similarly archaic. The chief legal adviser to the Cabinet, the pale, thin-lipped Sir Ernley Blackwell, pointed out that 'in certain cases of high treason . . . "by law" the sentence against persons convicted . . . was "that they should be drawn on a hurdle to the place of execution and there be hanged by the neck, but not until they are dead, but they should be taken down again, and that when they are yet alive their bowels should be taken out and burnt before their faces, and that afterwards their heads should be severed from their bodies . . ." Blackwell's understanding of 'drawn on a hurdle' was that the sentence had to be carried out in public; the drawing and quartering had been rendered superfluous by a law of 1870, which required hanging only. The Director of Public Prosecutions weighed in to ask whether shooting might be allowed: 'since the king could substitute beheading for hanging, there seems no reason why he should not be empowered to substitute shooting for hanging' to give a more militaristic air and fit in with the executions in Dublin. Nobody – government, defence, the prisoner himself – appeared in any doubt about the trial's outcome. Casement wanted to take upon himself the full burden of guilt for the conspiracy, yet he did not believe he would be executed: his forthcoming ordeal was a 'sham trial for my shame and humiliation'; the English 'dare not hang me' and thereby ensure martyrdom. Yet in his same pencilled jottings in his cell he seemed to welcome death, as the alternative was worse: 'I have no hope, or expectation, or wish to live. The life of a British convict to me is far more dreadful than death.'

For both government and prisoner, reconnections were made during the preparation period. One person whom Casement's team might have preferred remain silent was Adler Christensen. A Chief Inspector Ward made the journey to Philadelphia during the Bow Street hearings and Christensen began his statement with the revelation that he had first met his lover in 1905 or 1906 in Montevideo. Casement's only recorded visit to the city was in 1910, which would make Christensen eighteen at the time, rather than the fifteen or sixteen of his own account. He claimed he had been on leave from his ship, and was followed by the Consul into a lavatory; afterwards 'they met in a hotel bar', and he deserted, remaining in the city for a month, often seeing Casement, who was there visiting his friend, the German diplomat Baron von Nordenflycht. When Christensen left for the United States, Casement gave him 'jewellery and money to the value of about $900'.*

Casement could never have afforded such largesse. He was in Uruguay for only a few days, with the rest of the month full of recorded consular work that acted as a cast-iron alibi; Nordenflycht, a friend known to Christensen in Berlin, had been Minister in Montevideo, but at the time of his visit Casement made no reference to either Nordenflycht or Christensen in his diary, or to any sexual encounters, while his next destination, Bahia, has the one-word sentence 'Stevedore'. Christensen's account is at best exaggerated, but there is enough incidental detail, such as that Casement was briefly in Montevideo (and likely to be looking for sex), not to categorically rule out the possibility that they had met before their 1914 encounter on Broadway. On an unrelated scrap of undated paper, Christensen claimed that he had met Casement in a 'South American port' when he was a starving deserter; he had visited the British consulate 'where there are always sailors engaged and wanted', but was not taken on

* About $30, 000 today.

without discharge papers. Apparently Casement 'helped' him on this occasion, which might refer to paid sex, but the testimony remains far-fetched.

Christensen's account of the rest of his time with Casement was reasonably factual, although he failed to acknowledge his damaging embellishments in the Findlay affair. He let slip that he had kept one of the copies of the Irish Brigade Treaty with Jagow's signature as a form of insurance, and did not shrink from boasting about the successful shipboard concealment of Monteith. He offered to testify against Casement if he was given $200 and his wife a stipend of $15 per week during his time in England 'and [provided] his liberty would not be interfered with'. Ward refused to discuss any reward until the Treaty was produced, which Christensen was unable to do a week later. At that second encounter, the Norwegian claimed that his 'sole object in giving information was to get even with Devoy': further digging elicited the claim that Devoy had tried to prevent Christensen associating with his current wife and had 'remonstrated with him as to his gambling habits'. They 'came to blows' when Devoy 'threatened to expose him' as a bigamist. Devoy wrote cryptically to a correspondent that 'Christensen was going over to testify against him – and incidently [*sic*] give away all our secrets that he had got from Roger, *but we kept him here.*'

Casement never heard about the Philadelphia interviews, and they were not deemed worthy of use in the courts, but Devoy had written to him in December 1915 outlining his lover's crookedness in America, revealing that he 'has been swindling us and recklessly and foolishly lying', all down to 'a woman', the daughter of a Berlin banker, whom he had 'brought back with him the first time' but who was now 'across the River' in Europe with 'a new-born baby'. Christensen had stolen money from Clan na Gael through claims of robbery and fabricated expenses, and had attempted blackmail in the pursuit of his bigamous (and short-lived) marriage to Margaretta; Joe McGarrity had spent money and time paying off Margaretta's debts and sorting out the divorce papers. Despite all that he had learnt about his lover and companion through the most psychologically and practically complex months of his life, Casement never openly disowned him. He confessed to Alice Stopford Green in Brixton that 'he never suspected Christensen of treachery to himself until this year', but 'made no other comment'.*

Some people from Casement's past were more sympathetic than others. His American journalist contact from his days in Lourenço Marques, Poultney Bigelow, was savage in the *New York Times*, crediting the start of his 'career of madness' to 'a too strenuous study of Irish mythology masquerading under the name of history'. Bigelow posited that Casement's letters to the papers and about Grey were 'proofs of insanity' and accused him of helping 'the Hun to enter at our gates: for every sane American knows that Prussian rule in Ireland would be followed by a Prussian raid across the Atlantic'. Julio Arana sent an expensive telegram in which the murderous businessman, soon to become a senator, was:

> asking you to be fully just confessing before the human tribunal your guilt only known by Divine Justice regarding your details in the Putumayo business . . . You tried by all means to appear a humanizer in order to obtain titles [and] fortune. Not caring for the consequences of your calumnies and defamation against Peru and myself doing me enormous damage. I pardon you, but it is necessary that you should be just and declare now fully and truly all the true facts.

Basil Thomson continued to build his case. No doubt influenced by the diaries, he concluded that Casement 'had a strong strain of the feminine in [his] character . . . the quick intuition of a woman as to the effect he was making on the people around him. He had a strong histrionic instinct.' He was not alone in thinking that Casement was driven more by instinctive sympathy than by reason, but only he suggested that these traits had led the reformer to exaggerate 'his revelations about the Congo and Putumayo'. Arana's document fed his theory, and inspired a chilling one: that the reforming 'obsessions

---

* Christensen married for a third time in 1928, to a nineteen-year-old in Winnipeg. He was, as Ivan Christensen, convicted of several charges of robbery and avoiding deportation from France, and died in Fresnes Prison, Paris, in 1935, vomiting blood. His personal effects consisted of a cheap watch and forty francs.

disclosed in the pages of his diary . . . would seem to show that some mental disintegration had begun to set in' around 1910. The police-man, not wanting a retrospective plea or pardon on the grounds of diminished responsibility, was quick to add that any such disintegra-tion 'was not sufficient to impair his judgement or his knowledge of right and wrong'.

Other letters were more welcome. South London's most notorious prisoner thanked his cousin Roger of Magherintemple for his contri-bution of £25 to the defence fund; and in his brother Tom's absence in the war in East Africa, he told his wife – without any mention of his own perilous situation – that he often thought about Tom 'and par-ticularly of the last look I had of him at the railway station . . . more than three years ago now – and the world has gone to wreck and ruin since then'. He contacted Richard Morten to say that he would 'be so glad to see your dear honest old *English* face again!' and recalled their idyllic Rhine holiday, just as he had on his first trip to Limburg. He had been in the area 'this very day last year in the garden of an old Catholic priest who had been many years in Ireland'.

But by the time Morten came to visit, the English establishment had set a dark chain of events in motion. Blinker Hall, Director of Naval Intelligence, summoned six journalists to his office, including the editors of the *Daily Chronicle* and the *Sphere*, and Mary Boyle O'Reilly. She was the daughter of a Fenian poet, very influential in Irish-American philanthropist circles and a journalistic hero since she entered Belgium in 1914 disguised as a peasant to witness the German pillaging and brutality and the burning of Louvain. Hall gathered the group to look at photographs of Casement's 1903 diary, almost cer-tainly seized from his Ebury Street lodging house in advance of the charade over the key in New Scotland Yard. The photographs were of entries up until 13 February, complete with annotations of his homosexual encounters on the streets of London. They were crudely torn out, and are still missing from the archives, but entries from the remainder of Casement's time in London before his final return to the Congo and from his 1910–11 diary give a flavour of what the jour-nalists saw to ensure that his posthumous reputation was forever bound up in his private passions: on 17 February, he went to a 'club

dinner . . . Then walk. Papers. Saw (Enormous – youthful). Home.'
Three days later, he visited his aunt, Grace Bannister, before returning to his hotel 'by Frederick St. at Sailor's Home. Henry Abrahams
from Demerara 6".' The last three words of an entry for 13 May 1911,
when he was in Ireland with Millar Gordon, were not on display but
were underlined three times by the police: 'Arr[ive] Newcastle.
Huge! In Bath Splendid. Millar into me'.

In early June, O'Reilly wrote to Alice Green to warn that the
material 'of Sir Roger Casement's . . . proved him to be a moral
offender unworthy of public sympathy. One of these journalists, a
man without knowledge or sympathy about Irish affairs, but with a
spirit of fair play, informed me that this incriminating evidence will
be brought forward early in the trial by way of divorcing public sympathy from the accused.' Mrs Green immediately asked for a meeting
with Sir John Simon, Asquith's Home Secretary until January when
he had resigned over the introduction of conscription for single men.
Although he had been among those who had declined to represent
Casement, he was appalled by the move, telling Mrs Green that 'such
an outrage on justice would be a dreadful slur, and that, if known to
judge and jury, would have the opposite effect from what was
intended'. A few days later another Liberal legal grandee, the past and
future Lord Chancellor Viscount Haldane, got in touch to say he too
was shocked, and regarded the leak 'as contempt of Court, and with
deep indignation'; it was so 'clumsily' done that it would discredit
the prosecution if presented as evidence. Green remarked to Gavan
Duffy that 'I rather think the action as regards the journalists has
become the talk in the high places of justice.'

Smith offered to enter the diaries into evidence. At the end of his
long life, Sullivan claimed that Smith was hoping to short-circuit the
trial and its potential to create conflict at home and in the United
States, by encouraging the plea of 'guilty but insane' as evidenced by
the 'perversion'. But homosexuality would not have been regarded in
court as a manifestation of insanity – as the successful prosecution of
the few hundred cases a year of sodomy and gross indecency showed –
so more plausible explanations for Smith's strategy include basically
blackmailing the defence into a guilty plea that would spare the

embarrassment of a full public trial, or producing the diary in court as evidence of illegality and moral turpitude to defame Casement's character even further in the eyes of the jury, the press and his fellow Irishmen. Sullivan refused even to look at the material and never mentioned it to Casement; he understood his client well enough to appreciate that even if the admission of the diaries 'might save his life . . . death was better than dishonour'. Though they were not used just then, the few pages were to play a contentious role in what remained of the prisoner's life and had a lasting effect on his reputation.

For now, though, the rumours were circulating and nearly ruptured Casement's longest friendship. Professor Morgan accompanied Dick Morten on a visit to Brixton, leaving the room so the two men could talk more intimately. Morten, who had 'said not a word about it being common talk', finally asked, 'What about the other thing, Roddy?' – presumably the revelation about his sexuality – to which Casement simply replied, 'Dick, you've upset me.' This elliptical exchange and the whole imbroglio of treachery, secrets and the near certainty that they would not meet again must have been too much for Morten. Casement afterwards wrote to his best friend for over half his life, the man whose name came first into his head on his arrest at McKenna's Fort and whose idyllic Buckinghamshire manor house was the nearest thing he had to a true home in England, to say, 'I am very sorry you came. It upset us both . . . Please dismiss from your mind all that was said . . . It had been one of the true joys of my life to have had you as a friend for so many years – and one of the bitter griefs to lose you. Goodbye, and may it all rest in peace between us for ever and ever.'

16. The Forfeit

The weather on 26 June 1916 was dull, even chilly for the time of year, as it had been all month. But Sir Roger Casement was transformed since his last public appearance: he was wearing a dark suit sent from his trunk at F. J. Bigger's house in Belfast, and a white shirt with a newly starched collar and a dark tie. His health had improved and, now that the moment was upon him and events were beyond his control, he was serene. He had his last platform. Gertrude thought him 'wonderfully tall and dignified and noble . . . looking away over the heads of the judges and advocates and sightseers, away to Ireland'; while the lower-flown Artemus Jones recalled 'a tall, slender, handsome man, his dark beard helping to emphasise the intellectual cast of his features'; he retained his 'dignified courtesy' and 'imperturbable demeanour'.

Court Four of the Royal Courts of Justice in the Strand, with its Gothic windows set in lofty stone walls above the panelling of the well of the court and illuminated by two chandeliers of a dozen globe lights, was packed. The Lord Chief Justice, Viscount Reading (formerly Sir Rufus Isaacs), sat in what was his personal courtroom under the royal coat of arms flanked on the bench by Mr Justice Avory and Mr Justice Horridge. For cases of treason, the law stated that the hearing should be before the Court of the King's Bench rather than before a single judge. Appearing for the Crown in the trial of the only Briton to be prosecuted for treason in the Great War was the formidable line-up of the Attorney General, the Solicitor General Sir George Cave and three barristers – in all, five counsel against Casement's team of Sullivan, Jones and Morgan, with Gavan Duffy on the solicitors' bench, assisted by Doyle. The Bannister sisters, the 'best and truest' Alice Green, Henry Nevinson and the ever loyal Ada McNeill were in the gallery, as was Eva Gore-Booth, the suffragist, theologian, dramatist, poet and, along with her sister Constance

Markievicz, friend and muse to Yeats. Eva and Casement had never met, but when he looked up and saw her he smiled and waved.

The jury had been selected and sworn in by the time the accused was led in. The right of the defence to challenge potential jurors enabled Casement's lawyers to reject thirty-seven of them; they were trying to ensure a humble panel in the hope that twelve such men would be more conscious of oppression and accordingly be in greater sympathy with their client. But as the jurors were drawn from the electoral register it was necessarily a standard panel of householders from the London suburbs of Willesden, Hackney, Palmers Green and Ealing with the most English of names; among them were four clerks, a warehouseman, a leather merchant, a mechanical engineer, a baker, a tailor and a coachman.

The proceedings began with a unique feature of a high treason trial, the appearance of the King's Coroner to read out the indictment: Leonard Kershaw listed the six allegations that were contrary to the Treason Act of 1351: 'soliciting and inciting' soldiers to join the armed forces of . . . [the King's] enemies, and to fight against our Lord the King' on 31 December 1914, 6 January 1915 and 19 February 1915; circulating leaflets in Limburg in January and February 1915; persuading around fifty soldiers including Keogh, Bailey and Quinlisk to forsake their allegiance to the King in order to fight against him 'and his subjects'; and in April 'setting forth from the Empire of Germany as a member of a warlike and hostile expedition' equipped by the King's enemies to land arms and ammunition 'intended for use in the prosecution of said war'. Sullivan leapt to his feet in an attempt quash the indictment on the grounds that there was nowhere in it 'an allegation of any act done anywhere within the King's domains', but the judges advised him that his time would come. His client pleaded not guilty in a clear and steady voice.

F. E. Smith was silkily urbane, surgically brief and viciously ironic in his opening statement, his every word underscoring the Unionist's triumph. The political undertones were emphasised by the fact that he had telegraphed his entire speech to the American press the previous evening, to establish the strength of the prosecution case before any pro-Irish media could spin the proceedings. He returned to his

line that Casement's alleged crimes 'are aggravated by the relationship in which he formerly stood to the Sovereign whom he has
betrayed and the country at which he has struck', before embarking
on a summary of the defendant's 'considerable career of public usefulness' resulting in his handsome pension. Most of his remarks
would have not been out of place in a hagiographical obituary. The
bold, central structure of his speech became a legal masterclass as he
read, in full, Casement's letter to Sir Edward Grey accepting his
knighthood, establishing that he had expressed his gratitude in terms
'a little unusual, perhaps', in their warmth. He affected puzzlement
over how things could have changed between 1911, when he was
grateful to the 'ruler of a great and mighty nation', and 1914, when
'the same nation was struggling . . . for its very existence'. From
someone who had been involved in the struggle as Carson's 'Galloper' in the Union camp, this was a well-crafted and disingenuous
courtroom tactic, as well as a sizeable rhetorical edifice to build on a
slender, gracious letter in response to a deserved honour.

By the time Britain was 'involved in the most prodigious
war which has ever tested human fortitude', Casement was 'an honoured guest of the German nation' intending to 'seduce from their
allegiance . . . the Irish prisoners of war who, after fighting valiantly
for the Empire, had been captured' – men who, 'like the prisoner,
had embraced the service and eaten the bread of this country'. He
wondered whether it had entered Casement's head that 'he was
exposing poor men, his inferiors in education, age and knowledge of
the world, to the penalties of high treason'. Having played the patriotic card, Smith now presented Ireland as an 'unhappy country which
has been the victim in its history of so many cruel and cynical con-
spiracies, but surely never of a conspiracy more cynical and cruel
than this'. He outlined the way some prisoners had been bribed with
food, money, the green uniform and the possibility of free passage to
America, while those remaining loyal to the Crown were put on
short rations. He named the men the court would be hearing from,
all of whom were probably unknown to Casement as they had never
come close to joining his Brigade.

Nearly half of Smith's speech was about the landing in Ireland, the

Aud and HMS *Bluebell*, the discovery of the codes and Casement's self-identification to Inspector Sandercock. The recital was given full dramatic value, yet was spoken, as he himself said, 'without heat and without feeling . . . fortunately neither is required'. The Attorney General closed with a sonorous death knell: 'The prisoner, blinded by a hatred to this country, as malignant in quality as it was sudden in origin, has played a desperate hazard. He has played it and he has lost it. Today the forfeit is claimed.'

The rest of that day was spent establishing the prosecution case. The Chief Clerk of the Foreign Office confirmed the cessation of Casement's pension before Cave questioned some of the soldiers who had spurned the chance of signing up for the Irish Brigade. Private Cronin of the Royal Munster Fusiliers described Casement distributing copies of the *Gaelic American* and the *Continental Times* and apparently asking questions along the lines of 'Why live any longer in hunger and misery in this camp when you can better yourselves by joining the Irish Brigade?' When Cronin declined, his rations were cut from 750 to 300 grams of bread, and mangolds were substituted for potatoes. Sullivan's cross-examination later established that rations had been reduced for all prisoners then and that Cronin had become a Volunteer after hearing Casement speak at the Cork Meeting in 1913. These were small gains in his bid to discredit the witness, but they were far from undermining the substance of his testimony.

Seven more soldiers followed, all telling of Casement's failure to recruit them and the resulting privations. They named Keogh and others, and credited the camp rumours that they were going to be sent to help the Germans against the British, or even fight the Russians alongside the Turks. Sullivan tried to get across that none of this contained evidence of Casement conspiring with the Germans, he was simply 'doing an act which is the act of the man himself' and 'the statements and acts of persons . . . he has never seen in his life cannot be introduced'. The Lord Chief Justice ruled that the 'evidence is said to be given as a step in proving he adhered to the King's enemies', before the prosecution continued its portrayal of a man 'seducing and corrupting' those who had sworn allegiance to Britain. When the last soldier alleged that Casement had addressed the prisoners forty-six times during his seven months in Limburg, it went unchallenged by the defence. The usually emotional defendant appeared completely indifferent to the potent evidence he was hearing.

In the last few minutes of that first day, Michael Hussey testified about the light at sea on Holy Thursday and the dinghy on the sand at Banna. In the morning, the prosecution continued the focus on the landing, with John McCarthy, Mary Gorman and young Martin Collins taking the stand in their Sunday best. Next up was Sergeant Hearn to describe the events in McKenna's Fort and the journey to Tralee. He was asked by Sullivan whether newspapers containing exhortations by the Ulster leaders, including Carson and the Attorney General, whom he did not refer to by name, encouraging the local Volunteers to resist Home Rule by force if necessary were available in Ardfert Barracks; he also questioned him about the pre-war arrival of arms in the area and an August 1916 proclamation which forbade trafficking. Sullivan was attempting to get the tension around Home Rule across to the jury, but his inability to bring his client into the story of those machinations meant Smith's opening speech and the loaded Mauser pistols left on the beach for young girls to discover hung heavy in the air.

Constable Reilly was shown the tatty code sheet given to him by Martin Collins: the pencilled message on the back in Casement's hand that 'the friends' station' for receiving messages 'will be closed for good' after 20 May was incriminating evidence of a wider espionage conspiracy. RIC men who had dealt with Casement on Good Friday and Easter Saturday successfully got it on the record that they had followed the law at all times. A seaman from the *Bluebell* recounted the interception of the *Aud* and the arrest of her crew in German uniform; a diver described the damage to the formerly British ship as she was scuttled and the weaponry strewn on the seabed. A colonel from the Imperial Russian Guard identified the 1905 Russian rifle that had been recovered, and another from the War Office's Directorate of Military Intelligence declared the torn maps found in Kerry to be of foreign origin.

Sandercock and others carried the narrative up to the Tower of

London, at which point the prosecution's final witness appeared. Inspector Parker of Scotland Yard recounted how he had rearrested Casement in the Tower on the current charge. After he had stepped down, the Solicitor General asked for 'the document which was circulated throughout [Limburg] camp by German soldiers' to persuade the Irish prisoners to join the Brigade. Sullivan objected, because the recruitment poster in question was 'not brought into contact with the prisoner or under his observation', but Reading admitted it into evidence. Cave left the London jury with the poster's exhortations ringing in their ears: 'Irishmen! . . . You have fought for Belgium in England's interest, although it was no more to you than the Fiji Islands! Are you willing to fight for your own country? . . . The Irish Brigade shall be clothed, fed and efficiently equipped with arms and ammunition by the German Government . . . Join the Irish Brigade and win Ireland's independence! Remember Bachelor's Walk! God Save Ireland!'

Serjeant Sullivan's defence took up the rest of the second day and most of the third. He had little to come back with against the weighty evidence the jury had heard, and his only tactic was to attempt to quash the indictment altogether – on the basis of punctuation. The charge was that Casement had committed treason, in the wording of the 1351 Act, 'by adhering to the King's enemies elsewhere than in the King's realm', in this case meaning the German Empire. The fourteenth-century statute on which the indictment was based was unpunctuated and in Norman French; it defined treason as 'levying war against the King or being adherent to the King's enemies in his realm giving to them aid and comfort in his realm or elsewhere'. Sullivan argued that the wording limited treason to acts 'in his realm'; a comma would be required between the second 'realm' and 'or elsewhere' for the statute to be read otherwise. So in his submission Casement could not be charged under the Act since he was not in the realm when he tried to persuade the Irish Brigade to 'adhere to the King's enemies'.

Sullivan spent over two hours putting his case, replete with precedents, and Morgan, the constitutional expert, continued on the morning of the third day; he contended that until the reign of Henry

VIII, nearly 200 years after Edward III's statute was drafted, there was no such offence as treason outside the realm, as there was no means of trying it. 'The authorities on the point are overwhelming, and no medieval lawyer would come to any other conclusion.' The Lord Chief Justice and the two other judges conferred before Reading gave a lengthy judgment to overrule the keenly argued but doomed attempt to halt the trial on the thin, semantically legalistic point. Their interpretation of the Act was that treason encompassed acts 'in his realm or elsewhere'. The defence had no witnesses to call and there was no point in putting Casement on the stand to be mauled by F. E. Smith. However, Sullivan requested that, before his closing speech in what appeared more than ever a lost cause, the prisoner be allowed to make a statement.

Reading warned the jurors that what they were about to hear was not spoken under oath, so there would be no cross-examination. Casement drew some folded papers from his waistcoat pocket and began to speak in his low, well-modulated voice still 'untinged by any hint of an Irish accent'. His hands trembled as he turned his pages, and at times he was barely audible through nerves, but his reading, which took about five minutes, 'always showed a mixture of diffidence and courtesy'. He had earned his pension 'by services rendered, and it was assigned by law'; his knighthood was 'not in my power to refuse'. Beyond that, he simply wanted to correct 'four misstatements': he had never asked any Irishmen to fight with the Turks against the Russians, nor on the Western Front; he had never asked 'an Irishman to fight for Germany'; it was 'an abominable falsehood' that he got anyone's rations 'reduced to starvation' for not joining the Brigade: they had been reduced for all prisoners, and indeed for the entire German population owing to the British naval blockade. Finally, and what had hurt him most, was the 'malicious invention' of 'German gold'. He had never taken money in Germany, aside from that offered by his fellow Irishmen; the imputation was a slander. He had none of his own and was grateful to those who had helped him on the continent, just as he had 'been touched by the generosity and loyalty of those English friends of mine who have given me proof of their abiding friendship during these last dark weeks of strain and trial'. He hoped that the jury might 'comprehend that a man who in the newspapers is said to be just another Irish traitor, may be a gentleman'. Finally, he wished to preserve his 'honour' by saying that the Rising 'was not made in Germany, and not one penny of German gold went to finance it'. It was a thoughtful speech which could not sway the jury's deliberations, but showed an honourable, measured man who wanted to correct the record. It was the Casement who had suffered from depression after the failure of his endeavours in the past two years who spoke, not the feted emotional campaigner of the past.

His private, amused comment on the lengthy discussions of the Treason Act was 'God save me from such antiquaries as these to hang a man's life upon a comma, and throttle him with a semi-colon'. The disconnection between client and counsel became more apparent as the lawyer began his closing speech by calling it 'a matter of congratulation that such a trial as this at such a time is taking place in the capital city of your nation in open Court'. It was 'a great tribute to the confidence and courage of your race', and the verdict should not be 'coloured by passion, prejudice, or preconception arising from matters outside this Court'. Sullivan emphasised that the knight before them was different, 'a stranger within your gates' who 'comes from another country where people, though they use the same words, perhaps speak differently; they think differently; they act differently'. The jury might justifiably have found it startling enough to be deciding the fate of such a well-known figure; they had just heard the seemingly English Casement speak without stressing his Irishness, yet his counsel was pointing out that he was far removed from them, albeit reliant on their English 'spirit of fair play'.

The court was at its fullest as the end of the trial approached, and *The Times* reported that 'many more ladies were present'. With his rich brogue and serjeant's wig distinguishing him from any of the others present, the bearded Sullivan appeared the most foreign figure in the room. A contemporary reporter noted that his oratory was 'spellbinding . . . of a kind not often heard in English Courts of Law' as he developed his theme that 'no Irishman has a right to take up views or risk his life for any cause that is not in the service of Ireland'. Yet the Ireland to which he was referring had yet to come into

existence. Sullivan contorted political reality in stating that Casement had worked for the empire, not for England, in achieving his
consular successes. He attempted to knock down the Crown's case
that the prisoner had adhered to the King's enemies in Germany by
proposing that it was his motives, his 'view of his own acts which
must justify him or condemn him. Unless he intends treachery to the
King, the fact that others may use with advantage that which he does,
against his intention, perhaps to the public detriment of the realm,
does not make him guilty of treason.' He had never asked an Irishman to take the German side; rather he had made it plain that they
would be fighting only for Ireland. Of course, the German government wanted the Irish Brigade to succeed, but 'What cared he? He
was not a German.'

Sullivan ran into trouble with the bench by raising matters that
had not been brought into the trial as evidence, and he irritated Smith
by mingling politics with the law in a way that the prosecution had
been at pains to avoid: his client was planning to use the Irish Brigade
'in connection with the National Volunteer movement' and was justified in doing so in the light of the resistance of the Ulster Volunteers
to the Home Rule Bill, an obviously illegal opposition to an Act of
Parliament; as they 'armed . . . drilled . . . marched and counter-
marched the authorities stood by and looked at them'. He came close
to naming Smith and Carson when he referred to the 'great names
and men of high position' backing the UVF. Casement had recruited
the Brigade on the basis that they would fight for no other country
but their own. They would be supporting the Irish Volunteers as
they responded to the Ulster Volunteers' resistance to the Home
Rule Bill – the UVF having armed themselves 'to resist the King and
Commons and to blow the statute off the books with powder',
thereby turning the island into 'two hells'; the only response to such
provocation 'for any man in the protection of his constitutional freedom is to stand with arms in his hands'.

It was when Sullivan stated that on the outbreak of war 'one man
would observe that his neighbour had not given up his rifle' so 'would
arm himself, and one by one and in small quantities you have the
danger of the arms coming in', that the Lord Chief Justice finally

intervened to ask for evidence of such claims, swiftly followed by a peeved Attorney General complaining that he had heard a great many uncorroborated statements about rifles coming into Ulster. Sullivan referred them to Sergeant Hearn's testimony about the pre-war arrival of weapons, but Reading shot back that they were dealing with the present. Sullivan apologised, explaining that all he was trying to do was to show how when the war was over 'the Irish Brigade was to be used in Ireland . . . to secure Home Rule . . . and for no German purpose'.

Sullivan's tenuous thread had been broken by the judicial rebuke. After two hours on his feet, his eloquence deserted him. The press noted that he was 'beginning to suffer from the strain which his heavy work on behalf of his client had imposed'. He stumbled through his words, frequently halting. The lead advocate's last statements in the trial were to say, 'The matters I have spoken of had occurred since Sir Roger Casement left the Consular Service. They would explain the position. As I say, those matters had occurred since Sir Roger Casement left the Consular Service.' After a long pause, he ended, 'I regret, my lord, to say that I have completely broken down,' and sank into his seat, his head in his hands. 'The intensity of his useless pleading', the disgruntled George Bernard Shaw suggested, had overcome him.

Afterwards, Casement wished he had 'stuck to my two Welshmen', Jones and Morgan, 'and not brought the other in at all'. The Serjeant-at-Law's doctors diagnosed his collapse as caused by stress and lack of sleep and advised him to stay away from the Royal Courts on the fourth and final day. Artemus Jones was granted permission to take up the slack of his leader's address to reinforce more aggressively the argument that Casement had been in Germany 'not for the purpose of helping Germany to fight England, but for the purpose of forming an Irish Brigade to strive for something they had a right to strive for, the protection of their countrymen if they were coerced or tyrannised by armed forces in Ireland which were not controlled by the Executive Government' – the same as the Volunteers in 1913. Jones tried to shift the explosive piece of evidence that the code sheet represented, connecting Casement to the *Aud*'s mission to land arms:

being involved in that was 'wrong and possibly wicked', but it was chargeable under the Defence of the Realm Act rather than the capital crime of high treason.

At times, Jones was making the moral and emotional case Casement wanted rather than a legal one. He exhorted the jury to accept that the prosecution had failed to prove the prisoner had any desire 'to strengthen the position of Germany in her war against England' as the Irish Brigade was plainly formed to fight for Ireland alone. He reminded them that 'life is a comedy to those that look on, and it is a tragedy to those that feel' – and Casement felt in abundance. Jones did not intend to make 'an emotional plea' for his client; there was no point as 'The ancient and valiant race from which this man springs does not produce the type of man who shrinks from death for the sake of his country' – so many of that race had already 'gone to the scaffold . . . for the sake of their native land'. In the end they had to make their decision based on the evidence, and Jones left them with the proposition that, as the Crown had been unable to provide proof of treachery 'up to the hilt', it was open to them to reach 'a verdict which would be none the less just because it is humane'.

In his closing speech F. E. Smith devastated the defence anew. He praised Serjeant Sullivan's 'ability and propriety and eloquence' and regretted his 'indisposition', before taking his case apart. He scornfully summarised it as claiming that 'the prisoner did not attempt to seduce Irish prisoners from their admitted allegiance to the King in order that they might assist Germany . . . [or] in order that they might fight against England; but he was so struck, his mind was so affected by the growing lawlessness in Ireland, by the constantly increasing accession of military equipment to the Volunteers in the North', that he was planning to assemble the Brigade to balance out the post-war power of the UVF, which in his view 'had attained excessive proportions'. Smith reminded the court not only that Home Rule was on the statute book, but that 'From the moment that Germany made her tiger spring at the throat of Europe . . . the past was the past in the eyes of every man who wished well to England.' With this argument, Smith made his pre-war support for Ulster irrelevant. He rammed home the point that his earlier question as to how the prisoner could reconcile his journey to Germany with 'the duty which he owed, and which he so recently professed to his Sovereign and to his country', had not been answered – because there was no admissible answer. He dismissed as 'belated after-thoughts and sophistries' the arguments that Germany had no military interest in these men they were showing 'hospitality' towards, and that they would be content to wait until after the war to make Ireland a different place.

The jury was taken through the evidence of the soldiers, and the fact that the red lights of either the *Aud* or some other vessel had been spotted by Michael Hussey in the very early hours of Good Friday: it was important that the rifles were closely linked to Casement. That brought Smith to the crucial evidence of the code sheet: 'Why is the prisoner arranging that Germany shall send ammunition to Ireland, not at the end of the war, but during the war and at the very moment of the bitterest struggles in the war?' The phrases on the sheet such as 'Send another ship' and 'Cannons and plenty of ammunition are needed' spoke for themselves. Before telling the jury that they had to do their duty to return a verdict according to the evidence, however painful it was, Smith laid it out before them: 'If those facts taken together, his journey to Germany, his speeches when in Germany, the inducements he held out to these soldiers, the freedom which he there enjoyed, the course which he pursued in Ireland, the messages which he contemplated as likely to take place between himself and the Germans, satisfy you of his guilt you must give expression to that view in your verdict.'

The court broke for lunch. After the adjournment, the Lord Chief Justice summed up the case in a speech of just under an hour, longer than the Attorney General's rapier thrusts. He reminded the jurors that nothing they had heard or read outside the court could be brought into their deliberations and that 'where the defence have thought it right and necessary to introduce political considerations' they should nevertheless look solely to the evidence. They were considering treason, 'a most odious charge' wherever it arose, but in wartime 'almost too grave for expression', and had to do so dispassionately, as justice and emotion never mixed well. He explained that Casement needed to be found guilty on only one of the six charges to be judged a traitor, pointed out that the defence had not challenged any of the salient facts, and dismantled Sullivan's plea that the jury had 'to arrive in the mind' of the prisoner. He suggested that it was 'difficult, almost impossible, for an Englishman to divine what was passing through the mind of an Irishman, or to understand it'. His definition of assisting the enemy left little room for doubt: if Casement 'knew or believed that the Irish Brigade was to be sent to Ireland during the war with a view to securing the national freedom of Ireland, that is, to engage in a civil war which would necessarily weaken and embarrass this country, then he was contriving and intending to assist the enemy'.

Casement was removed to a private room, where he sat in conversation with Jones for the fifty-three minutes of the jurors' deliberations. The jurors asked the Clerk of the Court for the exhibits of the code sheet and the torn map, and later for a copy of the indictment. When Casement was brought back, the press reported, he 'looked around the Court with a smile and comported himself with the same urbanity of manner' he had shown throughout. He held out his hand to Gavan Duffy and 'nodded a greeting to some friends in the well of the Court'. The jurors filed in, and the King's Coroner ran through the roll call of their names before asking the foreman for the verdict 'on the high treason'. The answer, arrived at unanimously, was 'Guilty.' The King's Coroner turned to Casement to ask, 'What have you to say for yourself why the Court should not pass sentence and judgment upon you to die according to law?' At that the prisoner took several closely written sheets of blue prison foolscap, the product of twenty days of drafting and redrafting, leant across the dock and said that 'as I wish to reach a much wider audience than I see before me here' he would 'read all that I propose to say'.

He had nothing to lose and little to gain as he stood to perform the greatest piece of oratory of his life. It was heard in silence, though he was in breach of the convention that such speeches from one about to be sentenced to death should restrict themselves to matters which might affect the judge's sentence, such as in the case of a murderer claiming she was pregnant. He opened by saying that 'the argument that I am now going to read is addressed not to this Court, but to my own countrymen', with its implied protest against the jurisdiction in which he was about to be sentenced to death. The first part of his speech lasted for half an hour, and poked at the statute and its immorality when applied to him, because in 1351 Edward III was not King of Ireland. 'I am being tried, in truth, not by my peers of the live present, but by the peers of the dead past; not by the civilisation of the twentieth century, but by the brutality of the fourteenth; not even by a statute framed in the language of an enemy land – so antiquated is the law that must be sought today to slay an Irishman, whose offence is he puts Ireland first . . .' The jury, and England, 'cannot but be prejudiced in varying degree against me, most of all in time of war . . . Place me before a jury of my own countrymen, be it Protestant or Catholic, Unionist or Nationalist, Sinn Feineach [Feiners] or Orangemen, and I shall accept the verdict and bow to the statute and all its penalties.' In what sounded like a commentary on his own romantic character rather than on the relationship between England and Ireland, he stated his belief that 'Loyalty is a sentiment, not a law. It rests on love, not on restraint.'

He overcame his 'nervous and overwrought' start and, in marked contrast to his brief speech from the dock on the second day, gained in 'confidence and self-possession', which *The Times* reporter thought indicated a lack of contrition. He was in full command of his passionate beliefs and looming martyrdom as he spoke of Ireland's sons and daughters 'meeting always the same fate, and always at the hands of the same power . . . through centuries of misery', while preserving 'the remembrance of lost liberty . . . the noblest cause men ever strove for, ever lived for, ever died for'. He stood before them 'in a goodly company and a right noble succession'.

He became more current and specific as he spoke about the Ulster Volunteer Movement, making it clear that he had no quarrel with its members, had rather 'aimed at winning [them] to the cause of a

United Ireland' and away from the 'English party' by exhibiting 'affection and goodwill' so that Protestant and Unionist, Catholic and Nationalist, could all live together free from the oppression of the past. In his view, 'unscrupulous English Conservative politicians' had inflamed northern passions for their own political ends. So it became the Irish Volunteers' 'bounden duty to get arms before all else', hence his trip to America; surely the diaspora there had more of a 'right to appeal to Irishmen . . . than those envoys of "Empire" could assert for their weekend descents upon Ireland'.

He squared up to Smith as he answered the question the Attorney General had put to the court about why he had gone to Germany. He had realised in America that 'my first duty was to keep Irishmen at home in the only army that could safeguard our national existence. If small nationalities were to be the pawns in this game of embattled giants, I saw no reason why Ireland should shed her blood in any cause but her own, and if that be treason beyond the seas I am not ashamed to avow it or to answer it here with my life.' He declared tauntingly that the difference between him and Smith was 'that the Unionist champions chose a path they felt would lead to the wool-sack [i.e. the Lord Chancellorship]; while I went a road I knew must lead to the dock'. His 'treason was based on a ruthless sincerity' whereas the Unionists' 'lay in verbal incitements that they knew need never be made good in their bodies', for reasons of personal and political ambition rather than for any belief deeply held. He was proud to be on trial rather than 'fill the place of my right honourable accusers'. At this, the Attorney General dropped his courteous courtroom demeanour to show his true contempt for the prisoner: he audibly muttered, 'Change places with him? Nothing doing,' before sauntering out of the Court with his hands in his pockets and, as Gertrude Bannister observed, 'a most unpleasant sneer upon his face'.

Casement was not put off. He became yet more fervent and eloquent as he declared that if Irishmen were sent 'by the thousand to die, not for Ireland, but for Flanders, for Belgium, for a patch of sand in the deserts of Mesopotamia, or a rocky trench on the heights of Gallipoli, they are winning self-government for Ireland', or so they were told by England. 'But if they lay down their lives on their native soil, if they dare to dream even that freedom can only be won at home by men resolved to fight for it there, then they are traitors to their country, and their dreams and their deaths alike are phases of a dishonourable phantasy.' Ireland took on the personality that he had perceived in it back in the days of his romantic poetry, and that personality became his as he said that the country had 'wronged no man, injured no land, sought no dominion over others', yet was 'treated among the nations of the world as if she was a convicted criminal'. If it was treason to fight against 'such an unnatural fate' as this, he would cling to his ' "rebellion" with the last drop of my blood'.

He brought himself back from his oratory into the court proceedings to thank the jury for their verdict, hoping they would not 'take amiss what I said, or think I made any imputation upon your truthfulness or your integrity' by suggesting he had the right to be tried in Ireland by his true peers. His last words were to ask them 'How would you feel yourselves as Englishmen' if one of their own 'was to be submitted to trial by jury in a land inflamed against him and believing him to be a criminal, when his only crime was that he had cared for England more than for Ireland?'

There was no need for the Usher to call for silence when Casement finished. The black caps were placed upon the wigs of the three judges and the Lord Chief Justice sentenced him to 'be taken hence to a lawful prison, and thence to a place of execution, and that you be there hanged by the neck until you be dead'. Casement bowed towards the bench and smiled before being led away.

The next day, the start of the First Battle of the Somme, it was announced in the *London Gazette* that the King 'had been pleased to degrade Roger David Casement from the Order of Knights Bachelor'. He was the first felon for three centuries to be stripped of his honours.

The trial ended with the case of his submarine mate Bailey, against whom no evidence was offered and who was allowed to walk free. It emerged that when he was first questioned he had bargained his knowledge in exchange for protection in the courts, leading to lasting accusations of treachery to the nationalist cause. Within a few weeks, he was on his way to East Africa to rejoin the war. The third member of the party, Monteith, remained on the run, hidden on a farm in Limerick and subsequently by Capuchin nuns in Cork. He eventually found his way back to his family in New York a few days before Christmas. His memoirs were dedicated 'To the Memory of My Chief and Friend Sir Roger Casement, The Man Who Eliminated Self'.

17. The Quality of Mercy

Prisoner 1270 was cheerful after his moment of rhetorical glory. He was taken to the condemned cell at Pentonville Prison in the north London suburb of Barnsbury and given a blue serge convict's uniform. He quipped to Gertrude Bannister that 'A felon's cap's the brightest crown an Irish head can wear.' He was allowed only one visitor per day but corresponded freely. He renewed his friendship with 'Dear Old' Dick Morten after their upset, describing his routine as 'eat and sleep and read books and say prayers'. He longed for his ordeal to be over: 'Today chains are not laid upon our bodies, and the physical lot of a prisoner is easier, but the mental death must be the same. Indeed, in some ways it was perhaps better, as the body didn't last so long to bear the troubled spirit in its pain.' He was 'not mad', simply did not 'believe any more in lies and hatred than I did'. His final farewell to his oldest friend was to wish him and his wife long lives 'to grow old together and grow nearer as you grow older. We shall never meet again – but I shall often meet you in my heart – often think of you as of old in the sunny days when we bathed together' in the River Colne.

His supporters rallied once more. Gertrude pointed out to Sir Edward Grey that throughout the whole 'long and ghastly tragedy, when his deed has been painted in the blackest hues that journalistic power could mount . . . no voice has been raised to point to his past great record of selfless devotion to the cause of suffering humanity'; her cousin had 'injured no man, has taken no man's life . . . brought no weakening to England, no strength to Germany. He still stands as the man who helped to right those who suffered wrong & who fed the hungry.'

Eva Gore-Booth maintained that 'Casement came to Ireland in a frantic attempt to dissuade the Sinn Fein leaders from what he considered the fatal mistake of the Rising.' It was 'an intolerably ghastly idea that he should be hung as a result of this self-sacrificing and devoted effort, facing, as he did, almost certain death for the sake of preventing bloodshed and misery in Ireland . . . An act of grace now would do more to conciliate the ordinary Irish people than any concessions to political leaders.' Grey shared her letter with his Cabinet colleagues, remaining as open-minded as possible to Casement's service and friendship. He regarded the letter addressed to him from Berlin ranting about Findlay as a sign of madness rather than malice, and was revolted by the 'stealthy slander' around his former employee.

Other establishment figures were not so generous. Five days after his death sentence, Casement sent Alice Green a sonnet he had written in 1914 that proclaimed his religious serenity. It opened:

> Weep not that you no longer feel the tide
> High breasting sun and storm that bore along
> Your youth on currents of perpetual song;

And ended:

> And on this lonely waste we find it true
> Lost youth and love, not lost, are hid with Christ.

Major Frank Hall of Room 40 attached to the intercepted poem a note addressed to Basil Thomson asking, 'Is this working up a plea for insanity, think you?!!'

Serjeant Sullivan had asked that the appeal should not be heard for a fortnight as his brain would 'not respond to work' following his collapse. Casement saw little prospect of success: he knew 'the reasons for everything in my actions' and had 'not attempted to tell my side . . . I must just let it be, and bear the fate.' This time, he would have no voice in the legal roundabouts, writing resignedly to Alice Green, 'I am advised I *should* go', as at least 'I shall see you and the others . . . again – and I shall be a spectator this time – sitting in a reserved box and looking upon the actors with a quite detached and cynical smile – especially the wigs.' His great speech had been delivered; the rest should unfold without him.

The two-day hearing began on 17 July 1916, with counsel on both sides lined up in Court Four again. Sullivan reargued his position throughout the first day and into the morning of the second: Casement had committed no treasonable act within the language of the statute because to do so required his presence 'in the realm', yet he had been in Germany. Sullivan plundered the historical precedents, including the origins of the statute, designed to prevent Edward III's barons raising armies from their French estates, and that of the last Welsh Prince of Wales, Owain Glyndŵr; he acknowledged that Sir Edward Coke, Attorney General during the trial of Sir Walter Raleigh, had disagreed with his position, but his ruling had been non-binding. Sullivan cited the more recent case of the Irish-Australian Colonel Arthur Lynch, who had commanded an Irish Brigade to fight against England in the Boer War. Lynch had been elected MP for Galway during his absence in South Africa, but was arrested for treason and sentenced to death on his return in 1903. His sentence was commuted to life imprisonment, before he was released and pardoned; he was currently Nationalist MP for West Clare. Sullivan argued that between 1351 and 1903 there had been no decision concerning 'adhering' outside the realm, and that the Lynch judgment was incorrect. The Serjeant admitted in his memoirs that his speech was 'a very dull legal argument intelligible only to myself'.

When the judges returned, Mr Justice Darling indicated that the Attorney General did not need to reply to Sullivan's case, meaning the appeal had failed. Darling was quick to praise Sullivan's argument as 'in every way worthy of the greatest traditions of the King's Courts', before he cited authorities that disagreed with some of Sullivan's interpretations. As regards the all-important question of punctuation, it transpired that Darling and Mr Justice Atkin had been to the Public Record Office to inspect the statute and Parliamentary rolls. Sullivan proposed that the scribe who enrolled the statute had inserted breaks in the form of two transverse lines where commas would be inserted in later documents. The judges had scrutinised the vellum on both rolls with a magnifying glass to conclude that the break on the primary, statute roll had been caused by folding and refolding over six centuries and was not a part of the text.

Gavan Duffy knew the appeal would be a lost cause, but retained 'every hope that it will succeed if the Attorney-General gives leave for an appeal to the House of Lords . . . the only Court where there is even a trace of intellectual honesty left'. By a quirk in the order of things, such leave could only be given by F. E. Smith, and then only if he believed the case involved a point of law of exceptional public importance and interest. As soon as Casement was returned to Pentonville on 18 July, Gavan Duffy, Artemus Jones and J. H. Morgan put in their applications. Doyle wrote a fifteen-point letter to the Home Secretary from the Savoy Hotel which was cuttingly annotated by the Cabinet legal adviser Sir Ernley Blackwell to the effect that neither Casement nor his counsel had said 'that his purpose was to induce Germany in case it should land troops in Ireland not to destroy Ireland'. Two days later, Smith called in the other four counsel with whom had prosecuted the case, and in turn each of them told him that they did not see grounds for referral to the Lords. Smith himself had already had his opinion typed up and could now say 'the decision was mine alone, but I shall add that having consulted you afterwards you were all of the same mind'.

The execution date was set for 3 August, under two weeks away. Sir Arthur Conan Doyle, who had never wavered in his admiration for 'Congo Casement's' efforts, had written to Clement Shorter, the editor of the *Sphere* and one of those at the press viewing of selections from Casement's diaries, the day after the trial ended. He maintained his previous position that Casement's 'mind was unhinged, and that his honourable nature would in a normal condition have revolted from such an action' as treason. Now he gathered thirty-six influential signatories, including the Regius Professor of Physics at Cambridge, the President of the Royal College of Physicians, Arnold Bennett, Hall Caine, G. K. Chesterton, Sir James Frazer, John Galsworthy, Jerome K. Jerome, John Masefield, the President of the Baptist Union, C. P. Scott of the *Manchester Guardian*, the Webbs and the Bishop of Winchester, to petition Asquith.

The influential group advocated leniency on three grounds: the first was that an 'allowance needed to be made for [Casement's] abnormal physical and mental state' because he had 'for many years been exposed to severe strain ... and several tropical fevers ... during his honourable career of public service'; the second was political expediency, that execution would 'be helpful to German policy by accentuating the differences between us and some of our fellow subjects in Ireland'; and finally, there was an 'object lesson' in the way the American Civil War had ended, when 'the leaders of the South were entirely in the power of the North', yet none of them were executed, 'a policy of mercy' that ensured 'a breach which seemed to be irreparable has now been happily healed over'. There were two notable signatures missing: Casement's Congo friend Herbert Ward could not forgive him and had just changed his son's name to excise his former friend's; E. D. Morel was again warned off by his fellow committee members on the Union for Democratic Control, which had been arguing that the war was the fault of the Foreign Office as much as it was the Kaiser's; he did not want to make their situation with the government worse by siding with a traitor.*

Blackwell was characteristically brutal in his next report to the Cabinet. He doubted 'a violent change has taken place in the prisoner's previous sentiments towards Great Britain', citing the entry in Casement's diary for the day of the award of the knighthood: 'Letter from Sir E. Grey telling me of knighthood. Alack.' Blackwell underlined 'Alack' twice and proposed that Casement should not have held public office since his diaries testified that he was 'addicted to gross unnatural practices ... It is certain that throughout his work in connection with the Putumayo atrocities his private life was of the filthiest description ... His diaries and ledgers of 1910–11 show that ... his leisure was entirely taken up in finding accomplices or victims and there are several instances where he succeeded in corrupting youths and one of his attempting to corrupt a child of 11 years of age.' The youngest person with whom Casement had sex in South America was sixteen, another two were seventeen, the rest

---

* Morel was to serve six months in Pentonville the following year for an offence against the Defence of the Realm Act after sending a UDC pamphlet to the 1915 Nobel Prize Laureate in Literature Romain Rolland.

older, often soldiers and policemen. British sensibilities would also have found it hard to comprehend the unabashed nakedness in the Amazon and Casement did not hide his admiration for the physique of boys bathing in the river or on the streets of the towns, or for the erection of a boy sleeping in a lifeboat of his ship. Blackwell was right to maintain that, if any of this had been known, Casement's 'honourable career in public service would have come to a sudden termination'. He ended his rant with the assertion that although the prisoner's 'physical and mental state' might be abnormal, his 'crime and the faculties he has displayed in carrying it out and justifying it' gave no room for leniency. He had written an earlier memorandum to the Cabinet about Casement being 'addicted to the grossest sod-omitical practices. Of late years he seems to have completed the full cycle of sexual degeneracy and from a pervert had become an invert – a woman or pathic who derives his satisfaction from attracting men and inducing them to use him.' Yet none of this would seem to have any bearing on the legal discussion of whether Casement might be reprieved.

The legal adviser also arguably exceeded his brief on the other two points of Conan Doyle's letter: he opined that 'Casement's reprieve would be more helpful to German policy than his execu-tion' on the grounds that it would have a 'prejudicial effect . . . upon British public opinion and upon the opinion of our Allies', while not affecting 'Irish opinion in the United States' which was 'not hostile to us already'; a reprieve would look like 'an act of weakness' abroad, and would not be 'favourably received through-out the Empire'. Blackwell rejected out of hand the parallel with post-Civil War America, dismissing the petitioners who 'find it convenient to regard him merely as a misguided Sinn Feiner. They forget . . . his primary object was to "help Germany".' Blackwell addressed the possibility that the petitioners might publish their letter by concluding that the distinguished men 'overestimate . . . the weight their names would have with British public opinion'. Blackwell's Secretary of State, Herbert Samuel, whose early Com-mons triumph had been to move the motion depriving King

Leopold of his colony in 1903, now regarded Casement as 'a man of atrocious moral character'. Asquith's secretary replied to Conan Doyle 'that the Government prefer that [the petition] should not be published'. There was a week to go.

In a display of the lasting respect in which Casement was held for his humanitarian work, heavyweight names at home and abroad also sent appeals. Gertrude Bannister got up a fresh petition signed by Bloomsbury aesthetes, Irish nationalists, socialites and Quaker luminaries including Mary Childers, Duncan Grant, William Cadbury, Arnold Rowntree, Lytton Strachey, Francis Meynell and Ottoline Morrell. Morrell had met Casement at Alice Green's and 'wrote to all the influential people that I knew, Asquith, Violet Bonham Carter, Bernard Shaw' and others. She 'could not believe it possible that they would hang a man who had done such noble and self-sacrificing work for humanity'. Bernard Shaw created his own petition, but did not sign it for fear of 'prejudicing its chances of attracting other names'; he wrote a letter to both *The Times* and the *Daily News*, but neither would publish it, 'the D.N. because it wishes to prevent the sentence being carried out', he thought, 'and the T. probably for the opposite reason'. He pointed out to Asquith, with some truth, that up until his trial Casement had had no 'serious hold on the Irish people'; his political writings had had a mainly American circulation and his projects were 'too technical' to be understood in Ireland. Asquith had not found Casement a 'national hero' on a recent visit to Ireland and the petitioners 'venture to assume that you did not wish him to become' one; if he hanged, that would be 'the one infallible way'. If the government followed the Arthur Lynch route and commuted the death sentence, Casement would 'be harmless, disabled by his own failure. On a British scaffold, he will do endless mischief.'

Petitions came from Ireland, including from Ulster. In the United States, the Negro Fellowship League pleaded that 'There are so few heroic souls in the world who dare to lift their voices in defence of those who are born with black skins, that the entire Negro race would be guilty of the blackest ingratitude did we not raise our voices on behalf of the unfortunate man who permitted himself in an evil

hour to raise his hands against his own Government.' The President
of the League addressed King George V personally, quoting *The
Merchant of Venice*: 'The quality of mercy is not strained.'

John Quinn had been 'disgusted and depressed by the horrible
fiasco in Ireland . . . The whole thing was sheer lunacy. Of all the
idiotic asses that ever were these Sinn Feiners are the worst.' He had
advocated a steady increase in the stock of arms, and drilling, so that
after the war 'they would have been in a position to take up their
claim to a fuller measure of Home Rule with some show of force'.
He now occupied himself with 'exhausting telephoning' for three
days to get 'twenty-five prominent Americans . . . to join in a cable to
Grey' which stated that the signatories were 'profoundly convinced
that clemency would be wise policy on the part of the British Government at this juncture and in this great crisis in the history of our
race'. The worldly Quinn believed that Casement, whom he knew
'intimately', was 'a man of the utmost austerity and purity in his personal life'. He had got to hear the rumours before the end of the trial
but regarded 'the damn insinuations that came out of England that
they had something on him in the way of degeneration of some kind
were too filthy and nauseating to even think of'. Quinn was a herald
of those who to this day believe the diaries are forgeries, despite con-
clusive scientific analysis demonstrating their authenticity.

W. B. Yeats had 'never before written to an English minister over
Irish questions' but was convinced that 'the execution of Sir Roger
Casement will have so evil an effect that I break this habit of years'.
He warned of the 'young people' of Ireland who 'under the belief
that the late rebellion was repressed with great harshness [were]
becoming more and more disaffected'. These, 'on whom the intellectual life of Ireland depends, are less likely to be restrained by fear than
excited by sympathy'. The evil had been done, and, in a resonant
Yeatsian phrase, the author pointed out that there was 'such a thing
as the vertigo of self-sacrifice' – anti-British feeling would be inflamed
by the hanging, whereas 'The pardon of Sir Roger Casement . . .
may give an opportunity for moderate opinion to recover something
of its weight.' Yeats added that he had recently heard from 'a keen
unpolitical observer' protesting that the execution of the Irish rebel

leaders was 'a greater shock to American opinion than the sinking of the *Lusitania*'.

Eva Gore-Booth continued her campaign, writing to the former Home Secretary Herbert Gladstone and copying in the current incumbent, Herbert Samuel, plus Lord Bryce, Lord Emmott and the Prime Minister. Blackwell delivered an opinion to the 21 July Cabinet meeting that 'it is impossible to believe Casement came to Ireland for the purpose of stopping the rising . . . if all had gone well, there can be little doubt [he] would have taken an active part'. According to Blackwell, he came up with the idea of cancelling the Rising only after his capture; apparently Basil Thomson had denied that anyone had said in Casement's interrogations that Ireland 'is a festering sore, it is much better that it came to a head', a tawdry and literal evasion of Blinker Hall's remark in the first interrogation after Casement's arrival in London that 'It is better that a cankering sore like this should be cut out.'

Although Asquith had informed the King the day after the Court of Appeal hearing that the Cabinet had decided that Casement should be hanged, the case came up in each of the four Cabinet meetings in July and the first in August as the pressure mounted to find some other way of dealing with the verdict. Mercy was the Home Secretary's prerogative, but not a decision he could take alone. At the 5 July meeting, it was decided to submit Casement's diaries to an 'alienist', as psychiatrists and psychologists were called, to assess their legal potential in an insanity plea. Asquith recorded that 'Several members of the Cabinet (including Sir E. Grey and Lord Lansdowne) were strongly of opinion it would be better (if possible) that [Casement] should be kept in confinement as a criminal lunatic than that he should be executed without any smirch on his character and then canonized as a martyr both in Ireland and America.' Grey had been pushing back on the notion of using the diaries in any way, and his Cabinet colleague, Smith, found the whole idea 'rather a ghoulish proposal'. The following week the 'alienist's report', which concluded that the prisoner was 'abnormal but not certifiably insane', was brought to the Cabinet table.

Blackwell resisted the groundswell of petitioners by manipulating the media. Casement's attorney, Doyle, had been promoting the line that, as the *Manchester Guardian* headline put it, Casement was 'A Victim of Circumstances': he had come to the country he loved with 'a burning passion' to stop the Rising, in which he had had no hand. If Doyle had been able, 'being an American and a neutral', to get documents and witnesses to prove that Casement was not helping Germany, the outcome of the trial would have been different, but that was impossible in wartime. Blackwell scrawled in the margin of the press cutting, 'This is somewhat different to saying that application was made to the H[ome] O[ffice] & was refused!!' As the execution date came closer, Blackwell wrote to F. E. Smith to say that he had been instructed by Samuel 'that some attempt was to be made by unofficial communication to the Press to meet the story put about . . . that Casement came to Ireland with the intention of stopping the Sinn Fein rising'. Blackwell had accordingly arranged that the *Morning Post* and the *Daily Chronicle* would be given information about the *Aud* and its cargo, as well as details of the code sheet with 'extracts'. He felt, on the evidence, that it was 'impossible to contend that he came with the intention of stopping the rising'. F. E. Smith approved the scheme but pointed out that it needed to be 'carefully considered' whether disclosure should take place '*before his execution*'; he did not have 'a strong view'.

Ever since the first pages of the 1903 diary had been copied by the police and shown to selected members of the press, initially by Blinker Hall, rumours and false denials had been in circulation. The day after the trial, the *Daily Express* ran the headline 'Paltry Traitor Meets His Just Deserts. Death for Sir Roger Casement. The Diaries of a Degenerate'. Two days later, Mrs Dryhurst, one of Gertrude Bannister's signatories, asked the Fabian civil servant Sir Sydney Olivier to make representations about 'an abominable slander' which until the *Express* splash had 'only been whispered or hinted at in secret . . . We Irish naturally concluded that they were the usual forged documents that have hitherto been used in every political trial, but they were not produced.' When challenged, Basil Thomson countered with a lie that, to his knowledge, no journalist had seen the diaries. A few days later, the *News of the World* contended that nobody who read them 'would ever mention Casement's name again without loathing and contempt'.

Conan Doyle was not deflected; he regarded the diaries as 'very sad, and an additional sign of mental disorder'. It was similar to the line taken by the most powerful moral voice in the land. Many people had approached the Archbishop of Canterbury, Randall Davidson, to canvass his support, and on 14 July the prelate wrote to Herbert Samuel with reference to Casement's Congo and Putumayo work that 'At each of these times I saw something of Casement and was always impressed by his capacity, his enthusiasm, and his apparent straightforwardness. I find it difficult not to think that he has been mentally affected, for the man now revealed to us in the evidence which has been made public seems a different creature from the man whose actions I knew and watched.' He had no means himself of judging 'the accusations which are current against him respecting unnatural vice', but deferred to the Reverend John Harris, later Sir John, Secretary of the Aborigines Protection and Anti-Slavery Society, who had 'assured' him 'that from intimate knowledge of Casement's life . . . during the Congo days he is able to say without hesitation that . . . he was one of the purest of men at a time when opportunity of vice was not only easy but was commonly yielded to'.

Harris was 'absolutely convinced *and with solid reason* that Casement is innocent of moral depravity' and 'could give [the Home Secretary] good ground for saying so' if Samuel could spare him 'a few minutes'. Blackwell arranged a meeting for 19 July, the day after the failed appeal, at which he showed the campaigner the photographs of the extracts. Harris thanked Blackwell for his 'kind consideration under the extremely painful circumstances', and advised the Archbishop 'with the most painful reluctance that the Roger Casement revealed in this evidence is a very different man from the one up to whom I have looked as an ideal character for over fifteen years'. Harris's only comfort was that 'there appears to be no evidence that these abominable things were practised in the Congo'.

With the diaries out in the world of influence, Blackwell could safely advise the Cabinet that 'So far as I can judge, it would be far wiser from every point of view to allow the law to take its course, and by judicious means to use these diaries to prevent Casement attaining martyrdom.' Certainly among Casement's liberal supporters the news was the talk of the town: Charlotte Shaw could 'go nowhere in London without hearing this scandal whispered. It was put about in influential people's houses; discussed in low tones in drawing-rooms; shouted in clubs.' To modern eyes the use of the diaries to turn the petitioners against Casement, or at least to give them pause, was brutal. Blackwell's campaign to cement the punishment for Casement's greater crime appears merciless, despite being rooted in the prevailing morality and legality around homosexuality, with the possible added stigma of a premium being placed on perceived masculinity at a time of war. It is unclear to what extent Herbert Samuel agreed with his adviser's view that execution had to take place, or even on what grounds a reprieve might have been granted, but the propagation of the diaries from before the trial up to the final decision remains a stain on the official treatment of Casement, a disclosure that got out of hand and which had a lasting effect on his posthumous reputation.

The government were sensitive to American opinion given their hope that the US would join the war and were aware of the clout of the Irish-American lobby. As 3 August loomed ever closer, representations were arriving in the White House and Downing Street on top of the petition from the Negro Fellowship. John Quinn sent Ambassador Spring Rice a letter signed by a persuasive list of newspaper editors, businessmen, academics, the Leader of the American Bar and a former Attorney General. There was an angry debate in the Senate on 29 July in which the proposer of clemency, Senator Martine, shouted, 'God help our country. Alas, Sir Roger Casement, patriot, statesman, author, and poet, thy name must not even be lisped in the Senate of the United States lest the British lion may growl disapproval!' Another speaker declared, 'the English ministry would be madmen if they executed Sir Roger Casement; they would be fit subjects for incarceration as lunatics; they would not be statesmen; they would show themselves so shortcoming as not to be possessed even of the ordinary shrewdness of a "peanut politician"'. Senators highlighted the similarities of Casement's and Pearse's selflessness in struggling for liberation to that of Washington, Jefferson, Hamilton and other Founding Fathers. A resolution that the President and the State Department should lodge a protest against the possibility of execution was passed and found its way to the Committee on Foreign Affairs, where Spring Rice believed 'it will probably remain'. He echoed Casement's diplomat friend Alfred Mitchell-Innes, now Minister to Uruguay, who telegraphed immediately after the trial: 'exercise of mercy would be received with rejoicing in S. America where Casement was greatly respected'. Yet, when Spring Rice got wind of the telegram, he asked 'for copy of Casement's journal to be confidentially shown here'. Blackwell proposed that the Foreign Office send 'two photos of specimen pages . . . to convince anyone [Spring Rice] may show the copies [to] that the diary is not a fake or forgery', and a copy crossed the Atlantic in the Admiralty bag a few days later.

In London, Basil Thomson and Blackwell kept up their own campaigns with some success. The policeman told the civil servant that he had shown the diary to the US Ambassador, Walter Page, and 'pointed out the innocuous passages that identified the writer as well as the filthy part . . . [Page] said that he considered the matter of international importance in view of the pressure that was being brought to bear on the President . . . he felt sure he would be in time.' Thomson then forwarded Adler Christensen's mendacious statement to Blackwell.*

From her home in Philadelphia, Nina wrote a personal plea to President Woodrow Wilson asking him to intervene on the grounds of her brother's service to humanity, but Wilson confided to his secretary, Joseph Tumulty, that 'We have no choice in a matter of this

---

* Sir Basil Thomson was to fall from grace in his own scandal in 1925: he was charged with 'committing an act in violation of public decency' with a young woman, Thelma de Lava, whom he had been kissing on a bench in Hyde Park. Thomson insisted that he was researching a book on London vice but was found guilty and fined £5.

sort. It is absolutely necessary to say that I could take no action of any kind regarding it.' Doyle made representation to Tumulty that 'a word from the President would be enough to save Casement', but Wilson was determined not to get involved in Britain's predicament and was adamant that it would be 'inexcusable to touch this. It would involve serious international embarrassment.' Some months later, the often paranoid Spring Rice, the author of the hymn 'I Vow to Thee, My Country', concluded that 'the President is by descent an Orange-man and by education a Presbyterian', his tribal loyalties fixed to Ulster and the Allies. When the Vatican diplomat Cardinal Früwirth sent a telegram warning about the outrage to Irish-American opinion that would result from the execution and advising reprieve as 'an act of high policy', the Foreign Office minuted, 'Execution will not make the slightest difference to the Irish in America; they are much too far gone already.' Ambassador Page had lunch at Downing Street two days before Casement's date with the hangman, and was told by Asquith that he 'could not in good conscience interfere . . . in spite of the shoal of telegrams that he was receiving from the United States'. The Prime Minister was keen to stress that anything that 'affects our relations with the United States is always a fundamental consideration'. It had been a matter of days since the Senate resolution gave faint hope for clemency, but the normal business of international politics was prevailing as Casement's life expectancy began to be measured in hours rather than days or weeks.

Casement began his final farewells. The most painful was to his sister Nina, who had played the critical maternal role in his upbringing, and whom he had not seen for years: 'it wrings my heart to leave you beyond all else on earth, and to leave you thus, without being able to show you all I feel for you, and all the keen and bitter sorrow I feel at having left you, neglected you, and gone from you without a word'. He apologised for a bitter, long-ago argument and reverted to child-hood to write, 'I bow my head in your lap, as I did when a little boy, and say Kiss me and say Goodnight.' He had 'prayed for death often in Germany . . . for I had lost all hope, something had broken in me . . . I was so lonely and I could do nothing and go nowhere.'

When Father Crotty saw him just before his departure from Wilhelmshaven, Casement had not indicated his desire to convert to
Catholicism, but early in his London incarceration he asked for a
priest. He told Father Carey of Clerkenwell that he wished to die a
Catholic, and had the memory of his mother taking her children on
holiday in North Wales when he was four; she had brought them to
a Catholic chapel, and he recalled that the priest 'had splashed water
over them'. He was channelling his passion into religion and signed
off to Nina with 'Goodbye, Goodbye and may the friendship of
Christ be yours, may His blessing be yours and His pardon and peace
be mine and bring us together in the land where He dwells and where
pardon comes to the sorrowful. Your loving brother – loving you, I
hope, far more deeply hereafter, when the grace of God has cleansed
his heart, than he ever did on earth, but loving you now with his best
heart . . . Roddie – or as you always called me – Scodgie.' He told a
visitor that he 'felt the loss of my mother more than I have felt anything in my life'; Nina had taken on the role.

He thanked William and Emmeline Cadbury for their kindness,
but they received only a heavily censored version of his letter. When
they requested the whole thing a few weeks later, Blackwell refused
as 'it contains a great deal that is false and which Casement might
have said on oath but did not'. A letter to the Irish novelist Agnes
O'Farrelly, who had contributed £50 to his defence fund, was
destroyed on the grounds that it might make a martyr of him and 'it
is treasonable as well'; the same fate met his farewell to his brother
Tom, as well as most of his prison writings. In the absence of any
drafts of these letters, we might assume that they accused British officials of wrongdoing, as in the missive to Sir Edward Grey sent at
Casement's lowest point in Germany, as well as inflammatory statements about Ireland, the Rising, the treatment of the rebels and the
country. Blackwell's conduct in leaking the diaries and suppressing
these writings may all have sprung from a determination to ensure
that Casement did not become an Irish martyr.

Writing to Richard Morten, Casement mocked the indictment:
'You'll hear me clanking up the Avenue – because I'll be in armour of
course – look at the date: 1351! – and I'll ask (in Norman-French) if

one Dick de Morten lives there . . . The whole world is a sorry place, Dick, but it is our fault, our fault. We reap what we sow – not altogether, but we get our deserts – all except the Indians and such like.' Possibly the letter contained a veiled hint of the homosexuality that had been the cause of their falling-out on the last occasion they spoke; possibly it was a rare flash of self-pity alongside a Putumayo reference.

On 27 July Gertrude Bannister came to see the beloved cousin who had written her jokey descriptions of the Congo fauna. Her devotion had incurred her dismissal from her job of seventeen years at Queen Anne's School, Caversham. She wrote to Bernard Shaw thanking him 'for everything'; it had been 'always a consolation to Roger to find you understood so absolutely'. She told Shaw the school 'had no further use for me. When he was "sick and in prison" & I dared to visit him & to go on doing it, it became too much for their respectability & they firmly removed me!' On this last visit, her cousin was doubly upset as the prison's Governor had told him 'how abhorrent his action had been', and he had been rebuffed in his final attempt to contact Herbert Ward. He instructed Gertrude to 'Go back to Ireland . . . when it is all over' with his body and 'let it lie in the old churchyard in Murlough Bay'. They wept as they parted, Casement saying, 'I don't want to die and leave you and the rest of you dear ones, but I must.' Gertrude 'staggered outside . . . crying out loud'. She wanted 'to scream out, but what's the good . . . he was inside waiting for death, such a death. I was outside and wanted to die.' His last letter to her ended with a plea to 'think of me just as we were all away back in the old days'.

On the day of Gertrude's devastating farewell, news arrived that Captain Charles Fryatt, commander of the merchant ship *Brussels*, had been executed by the Germans. The *Brussels* had attempted to ram a U-boat in the Channel, and Fryatt had been seized and court-martialled. Bernard Shaw wrote a letter to the *Daily News*: 'The extraordinary luck which never seems to desert England has ordained that the Lusitanicide Germans should again select just the wrong moment (for themselves) to produce a new revulsion in our favour by shooting, on technical grounds, a man whom all the rest of the world regards as a prisoner of war', as well as a non-combatant. The Americans were furious about the killing of Fryatt, and Shaw wondered if the hope that they might join the war would 'be extinguished again . . . by the execution of Casement?'

The Cabinet paid no attention to Shaw's homily, but the Foreign Office had just received a plea for mercy from the senior Senator Henry Cabot Lodge on the same grounds; Cabot Lodge, Spring Rice cabled, 'thinks contrast between last German atrocity and British clemency would be a striking object lesson to the general public'. In the Ambassador's view, there was a risk of 'a great explosion of anti-British sentiment' in the US if the execution went ahead. Nina fired off a last, blunter telegram to Downing Street, 'If you execute my brother it is murder', alongside an excoriating letter in which she insisted that 'my brother's blood is upon the heads of all you cowards'.

The final Cabinet meeting was on the day before the scheduled execution. It was exactly a month since the Battle of the Somme had begun to inflict its devastating toll on the British Army. The Ministers spent 'the greater part of the sitting' discussing Casement, and at 4.00 p.m. a telegram was sent from the Foreign Office to Washington. Grey asked his Ambassador to 'tell Lodge . . . his friendly message about Casement and the consideration he urges have been carefully weighed by His Majesty's Government. The Government feel that there is no ground except that of political expediency on which Casement can be reprieved and it will not be consistent with justice or tolerable to public opinion here to reprieve him on this ground . . . Casement is clearly proved to have done all in his power to instigate the rising with German aid.' Because of the German angle, Casement's 'whole action in the matter was more peculiarly hostile and malevolent than that of any of the leaders, extreme though some of these were in Ireland'. The diaries that had been used to manipulate public and international opinion were disingenuously referenced as Grey continued: 'Such material as might have been alleged to point to insanity, including extracts from his diary, was at the disposal of his Counsel, who never raised this plea on his behalf.'

Grey concluded that 'Casement's demeanour and proceedings throughout the trial gave no ground for suggesting insanity and indeed were sufficient to disprove it'. That same day the Prime Minister wrote to Jane Cobden Unwin, the Liberal politician and campaigner for the rights of indigenous populations under colonial rule, and wife of the publisher of *The Dream of the Celt*, that it was 'with sincere pain' that he now informed her that Casement was not to be reprieved.

18.   Strange Fate

The Governor of Pentonville Prison informed the prisoner on 2 August 1916 that he would be hanged at nine o'clock the following morning. Casement wrote his brief will, witnessed by his warder, leaving everything to Gertrude Bannister, and so superseding a testament written in Brixton which had his sister Nina as the main legatee. His final dispositions were all of a modest piece with his lifetime disregard for material comfort when there was so much to be accomplished for others;* his bequests included his copy of *The Confessions of St Augustine* to his uncle Edward Bannister, the former Vice-Consul in the Congo who had secured him the job at Elder Dempster's Liverpool offices and then on the *Bonny* in 1883; *Meditations for Lay Folk* was for Gertrude's husband-to-be, Sidney Parry, a wealthy investor in sustainable rubber and a distinguished soldier as well as a long-term supporter of Casement; oddly, his spectacles were for Ada McNeill: they were accompanied by a note expressing the hope that she 'would never have any need to use them'. Ada also inherited his remaining books, which she instructed should be burnt after her own death. Casement's original copy of the Treaty, in Dr Curry's care in Germany, should be sent to Joe McGarrity in Philadelphia. There was an envelope of photographs of Africa at his solicitor's office with instructions that it was to be given to Herbert Ward at his death, but in the earlier will written in Brixton Prison Casement had instructed: 'Don't give them to him now. He has turned against me and would only insult me now.' In his final letter to his Bannister cousins, he asked for 'a roll of Congo tobacco' in his trunk to be given to Inspector Sandercock. There was no mention of Adler Christensen.

He wrote a postcard to Gertrude: 'Tomorrow, St Stephen's Day, I shall die the death I sought, and may God forgive the mistakes and

---

* The value of his estate was £135, approximately £12,250 at today's values.

receive the intent.' He also composed a farewell to his 'friends and well-wishers' that read: 'My last message to everyone is "*Sursum corda*",* and for the rest, my good will to those who have taken my life, equally to all those who tried to save it. All are my brothers now.' He was unaware of the full extent of the bitter wranglings outside the condemned cell and the use to which his diaries had been put over the past weeks to discredit his name.

For some months he had been considering converting to Catholicism, aided by the ministry of Father Murnane in Brixton and Father Carey in Pentonville. He did not 'want to rush, or jump, or do anything hastily just because time is short. It must be my deliberate act, unwavering and confirmed by all my intelligence.' He was beset by doubts when he wrote these words, 'not on a rock – but on a bed of thorns'. According to Gavan Duffy, he hesitated because he finally understood his own impulsiveness, a by-product of the early divisions which had driven him for so much of his life: 'his mind was imprisoned as well as his body, and his love for his country and his mother, who was a Catholic, made him so eager to be reconciled that he feared to be carried away by emotion at a time when his reason was clouded'. His sin of homosexuality might have weighed upon him as well. But by 20 July he was ready to resolve his double, barely remembered baptism.

Father Carey applied to the Archbishop of Westminster, Cardinal Bourne, for permission to accept Casement's conversion, but the Cardinal, fully aware of the climate surrounding Casement, demanded that before he issued the paperwork Casement must sign an apology 'expressing sorrow for any scandal he might have caused by his acts, public or private'. Casement declined, 'in all humility', telling Gertrude at their agonising last meeting that 'they are trying to make me betray my soul'. But now, as he was *in articulo mortis*, at the point of death, the priests had authority to act independently. Father Carey heard his first and last confession in the prison chapel on that final evening, and recorded that the penitent sobbed like a child afterwards; 'his contrition for any sins he may have committed was intense'.

---

* 'Lift up your hearts', from the Catholic liturgy.

On his return to the condemned cell Casement asked for pen and paper to compose his last wishes and thoughts for his friends and family. The prison authorities impounded this document on Sir Ernley Blackwell's instructions as being propagandist in character, but another priest, Father McCarroll, hastily made at least a partial copy. Its uncharacteristically clipped tone was due either to the hurried note-taking of the father or to Casement's own urgency and rhetorical exhaustion. His 'dominating thought was to keep Ireland out of the war. England has no claim on us. Law, Morality or Right. Ireland should not sell her soul for any mess of Empire.' He wanted to be buried in Ireland, away from 'Protestant coldness'. He realised that what he loved about the Irish was 'the chivalry of Christ speaking through human eyes', and was relieved that he would die 'with my sins forgiven and God's pardon on my soul'.

He acknowledged the essential gentleness of his nature in a paragraph which also displays the worldly innocence that had helped bring him to the gallows: 'It is a strange, strange fate, and now as I stand face to face with death, I feel just as if they were going to kill a boy. For I feel like a boy – and my hands so free from blood and my heart always so compassionate and pitiful that I cannot comprehend how anyone wants to hang me . . .' It was 'they' who were the traitors, not him, 'filled with a lust of blood – of hatred of their fellows'. He gave thanks for his friendships in the last few weeks, and believed that 'truth and right lives on in the hearts of the brave and lowly'. His death was 'glorious . . . for Ireland's sake . . . the most glorious one in history'. The Congo, the Amazon and the anguish of Germany had never seemed further away as he embraced his martyrdom.

Archibald Fenner Brockway,* gazing from his cell window that evening, saw Casement walk out of his own cell looking perfectly calm although his 'complexion was sallow. He came out seeing nothing but the sky and the sun.' The warders allowed him to stay out in the small garden with its hollyhocks and other flowers for an hour.

---

* The future Labour MP, peer and peace campaigner was in gaol for handing out anti-conscription leaflets.

Just before he came back in, he 'turned again to the sun, which was setting'. In the last sunset, 'one could see that his spirit and his personality became united with the infinite beauty of that scene'.

Alice Stopford Green, the stalwart figure who underpinned Casement's intellectual path as well as his finances, held a vigil at the Grosvenor Road house where he had attended salons and plotted to run guns. Among the watchers was Henry Nevinson, who recorded: 'We sat with Mrs Green through the night, and while he in his cell was watching for the dawn of his death, she continued to speak to us of life and of death with a courage and wisdom beyond all that I have known. It was as though we were listening to the discourse of Socrates in the hours before his own execution. So profoundly wise she was, so cheerful and humorous through it all.'

Casement was not watching for the dawn; he did not awake until after sunrise. He commented to his gaoler that it was a beautiful day, and was handed his ordinary clothes in place of his prison uniform. He took Holy Communion in the chapel at 7.30, and was given the Last Rites in the same service. Afterwards, he refused breakfast 'so that his God might be the last food he took on earth'. He spent the last hour between Mass and nine o'clock 'in earnest and fervent prayer' with Father Carey in his cell, and, as far as the priest could judge, he had 'all the dispositions, faith, hope, charity, resignation to God's will, etc., etc., to meet his Creator . . . It was an edifying Catholic death and it is wonderful how he grasped the Catholic faith at the end.'

Just before nine o'clock, the prison doctor came into the cell to ask if he could do anything for the prisoner, by which he meant a dose of sedatives. Casement cheerfully answered that he needed nothing. On the stroke of the hour, the Governor, the Sheriff, the executioner, John Ellis, and his assistant appeared. Casement's hands were bound behind his back by a leather strap and Father Carey began to recite the litany for the dying as the party walked the few yards to the scaffold. Ellis, a hairdresser and newsagent in Rochdale and Chief Executioner since 1907, believed Casement to 'be the bravest man it fell to my unhappy lot to execute'. He recalled 'the composure of his noble countenance, the smile of contentment and happiness as he willingly helped my assistant, the steady martial tread of his six feet four inches and soldierly appearance adding to the solemn echo of his prompt and coherent answers to the Roman Catholic chaplain'.

The tolling of the prison bell alerted a crowd of around 200 who waited on the Caledonian Road, mostly children on their school holidays enjoying the ghoulishness of the event and munitions workers on their way to the local armaments factory. Some cheered as a warder afterwards pinned the notice of execution on the prison gate. Casement's body was left hanging for an hour before an autopsy which found death to have been instantaneous. Gavan Duffy formally identified Casement's body in the afternoon for the Coroner's inquest. The day before he had asked the Home Office that it be released to Gertrude Bannister for burial in accordance with the prisoner's wishes, on the basis that he had not been a murderer; there was no precedent for executions for treason. Blackwell insisted that the relevant act from 1868 stipulated that 'the body of every offender executed shall be buried within the walls of the prison within which judgement of death is executed on him'. Roger Casement's body was wrapped in a shroud and buried in quicklime in the yard of Pentonville, a resting place he shared with Dr Crippen, among other murderers, whose notoriety he had so resented on his emergence from the Amazon jungle six years earlier.

In 1937 Yeats wrote that:

> The ghost of Roger Casement
> Is beating on the door

as another war with Germany was on the horizon. The Irish Free State, still within the British Empire,* had been in existence for fifteen years following the Irish War of Independence; a self-governing Irish state would be achieved only after the Irish Civil War of 1922–3, with Ulster remaining part of the United Kingdom. Through all this turmoil, Casement's body had:

---

* In 1937, the year of Yeats's poem, it became Éire/Ireland.

> never crossed the sea because
> John Bull and the sea are friends,

just as they had been in 1914. Yeats wrote another poem, 'Roger Casement', after reading *The Forged Casement Diaries* by Daniel Maloney in the same year. He implored Irishmen to:

> Come speak your bit in public
> That some amends be made
> To this most gallant gentleman
> That is in quicklime laid.

Yeats's wife knew nothing of the publication of this poem in a newspaper and was surprised to find herself being treated with great deference by the Dublin shopkeepers as she went her rounds the next day. Even if Casement was not part of the official discourse of the time, there was an obvious unofficial longing to acknowledge the poem's subject's life and impact.

Yet Casement's remains were not exhumed from Pentonville's yard until 1965, in time for the fiftieth anniversary of the Rising; that the honour was only accorded Casement nearly half a century after his death was in no small part down to the revelations of his homosexuality. As many as 165,000 people filed past the coffin as it lay in state in Dublin, although Charles Casement's two elderly daughters were the only family present, flown in from Australia. Gertrude Bannister had died in 1950. President Éamon de Valera, who had known Casement decades before, arose from his sick bed to praise him as 'a noble champion of the oppressed and helpless', emphasising his Ulster origins and looking forward to 'this great man's' dream of a united Ireland. The coffin was buried not in Murlough Bay where his plot, bought by Nina, remains empty still, but in Glasnevin Cemetery alongside other heroes including Daniel O'Connell and Charles Stewart Parnell.

In the years since his interment, as attitudes and legislation around homosexuality have changed, and as debates about the nature of empire and its effects on indigenous peoples have developed, Casement's standing in the Irish pantheon continues to rise: Tralee Station,

Baldonnel Airport, Dublin, and the Gaelic Athletic Association playing fields in Belfast have all been renamed after him; he is more widely written about than any of the others who died in 1916. In the Republic of Ireland today, he is celebrated primarily as a humanitarian: a century on from Good Friday 1916, President Higgins gave an address to thousands on Banna Strand to:

> celebrate, in the name of the Irish people, the great contribution of Roger Casement, not only to Irish Freedom, but to the universal struggle for justice and human dignity. [He] was not just a great Irish patriot, he was also one of the great humanitarians of the early 20th century – a man who is remembered fondly by so many people across the world for his courageous work in exposing the darkness that lay at the heart of European imperialism.

The President recalled 'Casement's idealism, his courage, his passionate defence of the human dignity of those who were the victims of a brutal world order'. A statue erected in neighbouring Ballyheigue bears the inscription that he was an 'early pioneer of human rights in the Congo and Amazon and knighted in 1911', and that he was 'a founder of the Irish Volunteers in 1913' and was 'captured at Banna Strand on Good Friday, 1916'. The first Irish contribution to United Nations peacekeeping was in the Congo when the new republic was plunged into civil war in the aftermath of independence from Belgium in 1960.

Casement had been in Joseph Conrad's mind since their first Congo contact in 1890, although the novelist refused to lend his support publicly to the Congo Reform Association, and was a notable absentee from the list of literary petitioners.* After their three weeks in Matadi, Conrad went to assume command of the *Roi des Belges* while Casement remained on the coast; they did not meet again until 1896, at a dinner in London, following which they talked until three in the morning. They had only two other encounters after that:

---

* Another was Rudyard Kipling, the scribe of empire in many ways, whose adored only son had been killed the previous September. Kipling found himself 'unable to sign' the document (BL MSS63596).

Casement took a day trip to the Conrads in Kent shortly after his first report was published, a time when 'Certain liberal circles were making rather a pet of him: well-connected Irishman, Protestant Home-ruler, of romantic aspect – and so on'. On the second occasion they ran into one another in Surrey Street, off the Strand, in 1911: the novelist noted that Casement was 'more gaunt than ever and his eyes more sunk into his head. There was a strange austerity in his aspect.' Conrad had written to congratulate him on his short-lived Lisbon appointment and hoped to visit him there; he inscribed a copy of *Typhoon* to him. Apart from hearing of the Putumayo report and the knighthood, Conrad knew nothing more until he 'read the news of [Casement] being in Germany'.

They had 'never talked politics', but the events of 1916 brought a rush of 'old reminiscences'. Conrad's fictional themes encompassed imperialism and colonialism and their effects on individuals; maybe he had an inherent antipathy to nationalism after his father's disastrous attempts at revolution in Poland in 1863. He now wondered 'in one's grief, what it was all for? With Britain smashed and the German fleet riding the seas, the very shadow of Irish independence would have passed away. The Island Republic (if that is what they wanted) would have been merely a strongly held German outpost . . .' He believed the whole Irish Brigade adventure was 'a mere intrigue' on the part of the Germans: 'they would have seen Ireland drained to the last drop of blood with perfect equanimity as long as it helped their military action on the continent forward an inch or two'. Nevertheless, Conrad never thought that Casement would 'swing in any case'.

The novelist considered Casement 'a creature of sheer temperament – a truly tragic personality', who had made his way through life 'by emotional force'. When the two men had spent time together before the world had heard of either of them, Conrad saw no signs of 'the greatness' Casement achieved, as his emotional force had not yet found its outlet. The Congo and Putumayo reports were products of this passionate engagement, but so was the over-extension of his questing that led him to Germany. It was the 'sheer emotionalism that has undone him'. John Quinn, to whom these views were expressed, agreed that his emissary was 'not a profound thinker, either on politics or anything else. He was all emotion and sentiment and temperament, but honest and honorable.' Quinn defended Casement's memory by asserting that 'Neither by word or act, by tone of the voice, by a gesture or the slightest syllable or letter was there a shadow of a shade of anything of a degenerate about him'; and until he was shown photographs of the diaries by the British Naval Attaché Quinn was convinced they must be forgeries.

Another author who took a close interest in Casement was T. E. Lawrence. Lawrence was twenty-four years younger than Casement, and his background carried similar secrets and divisions that contributed to his later ambitions and obsessions: he was born illegitimate, the son of an Anglo-Irish father and a governess mother; his sexuality remained hidden from the world and his humanitarian instincts carried echoes of Roger Casement's; he was a man of courage who experienced strong emotions; he worked in military intelligence and the Foreign Office, but came to dislike colonial administrations which benefited only the administrators. In the last year of his life, the hero of the Arab Revolt in the Great War was considering penning a biography of Casement. He wrote to Charlotte Shaw in mid-December 1934, 'I still hanker after the thought of writing a short book on him. As I see it, his was a heroic nature. I should like to write upon him subtly, so that his enemies would think I was with them till they had finished reading it and rose from my book to call him a hero. He had the appeal of a broken archangel.'

Lawrence's well-turned phrase captures so much of the importance and legacy of Roger Casement: the idealist, the missionary humanitarian, brought crashing to earth by flaws that were also his assets. Romanticism coloured everything he did – until it became no longer sustainable owing to external political forces; the trait, a relation to the less attractive naivety, was Casement's guiding force, as well as a leading factor in his tragedy. His was a character fragmented by upbringing, religion, sexuality, geography and identity, often forces in opposition to one another which he fought to unify. His move from knighted Protestant scion of the Foreign Office at the height of the British Empire to Catholic Irish rebel, gun-runner and champion of a language that he could barely speak himself was the outward manifestation of his inner divisions. His nobility, idealism, courage and energy led him to greatness and the saving of countless lives in Africa and South America, as well as to the foundation of the Irish Volunteers; but those abstract qualities, essential to the compassionate reformer, counted for little in the avalanche of events which overtook his last two crowded years. He was entirely without the intellectual underpinning, cynicism and instinct to compromise to be able to strategise through the rough seas of wartime.

Casement's dichotomies have made him a figure of fascination to novelists. Authors as varied as James Joyce, Neil Jordan, Stevie Smith, Agatha Christie and W. G. Sebald have written him into their work. The Peruvian Mario Vargas Llosa crafted an entire novel around Casement with the same title as his volume of poems, *The Dream of the Celt*, published in 2010 – the year in which Vargas Llosa was awarded the Nobel Prize in Literature. These fictional resurrections and reworkings over decades are testament to the modernity of Casement and the currency of his concerns. Perhaps only now can we gain perspective on a man whose reputation as the first modern human rights campaigner, an anti-colonialist fifty years before the winds of change finally collapsed European colonisation, an early harbinger of the Irish state and a martyred target of homophobia has been so buffeted by twentieth-century politics that he has been reduced to a series of symbolic, frequently misguided deeds instead of being viewed and accepted in all his complexity.

At the end, Casement understood how those divisions of his early life and attributes had made him who he was and taken him to the gallows. He wrote in his final letter to his longest-serving friend, Richard Morten: 'I made awful mistakes, and did heaps of things wrong, confused much and failed at much – but I *very near* came to doing some big things . . . It was only a shadow they tried on June 26; the real man was gone.' In an undated poem, 'The Love of Heaven', are two lines that he might have liked to stand for his own life of emotion:

> The epitaph of brave men all
> Is in our hearts and tear-dimmed eyes.

Acknowledgements

Jeffrey Dudgeon's editing and annotation of Roger Casement's 'Black Diaries', his research into other documents around Casement in Ireland, England and the United States and the generosity with which he has shared material on his website have been invaluable to me. I am also grateful to Angus Mitchell, particularly for his editions of the Amazon journals and Casement's writings during his time in Germany. Among other kindnesses and along with discussion of points of family history and lore, Patrick Casement of Magherintemple transcribed his relative's letters from Africa which gave me new insights into his time there and his family relationships.

In the course of writing this book I have enjoyed many fruitful conversations and much useful correspondence with: Rupert Christiansen, Roy Foster, Flora Hood, Jonathan Keates, Simon Littlewood, Ben Macintyre, Fintan O'Toole, Anthony Sattin and Matthew Sturgis. Angus Grahame loaned me rare Victorian books of African exploration. Christopher Terrington discussed medical matters and Thomas Grant KC kindly answered my legal queries and took me on a tour of the Royal Courts of Justice. A chance encounter on Banna Strand with Tommy Commane helped to bring the events of Good Friday 1916 to life.

Natasha Fairweather of Rogers, Coleridge and White has been a staunch champion and guide for this book since its earliest inception. Stuart Williams of the Bodley Head has once again been an outstandingly wise, deft, persuasive and insightful editor and publisher, supported by his excellent team; Laura Reeves's work on the text has been astute and wide-ranging, and her and Leah Boulton's calm steering of the many elements of the book through production is greatly appreciated. Peter James's copy-editing is deservedly celebrated and it has been a privilege to have his knowledgeable and clear attention and skill applied to the book, as it has been to be the beneficiary of Kit Shepherd's eagle-eyed proofreading. It is always a reassuring pleasure to have Juliet Brightmore as a picture researcher. Needless to say, any errors are entirely my own.

Finally, and very much not least, I would like to thank my wife Felicity for her great patience over the three years she has put up with me talking about Roger Casement, and for her love for much longer than that.

List of Illustrations

Section One

The infant Roger: Photographer unknown; Roger's sister: Courtesy of the National Library of Ireland (Call No MS 49,154/20); Magherintemple, Co. Antrim: Courtesy of the National Library of Ireland (Call No L_ROY_10131); Henry Morton Stanley: Alamy Stock Photo / CPA Media Pte Ltd; King Leopold II of the Belgians: Public domain; First sight of the Congo at Boma: Royal Geographical Society via Getty Images; Matadi: Alamy Stock Photo / Chronicle; Resigned from his work on the railway: (above) Alamy Stock Photo / Reading Room 2020 (below) Alamy Stock Photo / Svintage Archive; Colleagues who left their mark on the Congo: Bridgeman Images / © British Library Board / All Rights Reserved; Wathen Station: William Holman Bentley, *Pioneering in the Congo*, Vol II, 1900; Roger Casement in 1890: Courtesy of the National Library of Ireland (Call No MS 36,208/1); Joseph Conrad: Alamy Stock Photo / Archivio GBB; In his consular uniform: René MacColl, *Roger Casement, A New Judgment*, 1956; E. D. Morel: Alamy Stock Photo / History Collection 2016; Rubber workers left for dead and mutilated: (left) Alamy Stock Photo / World History Archive (right) Presbyterian Historical Society, Philadelphia, PA / William H. Sheppard Papers; The steamboat *Henry Reed*: Public domain; May French Sheldon: Wellcome Collection / Photograph by W. L. Royburgh, 1904.

Section Two

Julio César Arana: Photographer unknown; Juan Tizón: Mirrorpix via Getty Images; The Company steamer *Liberal*: Wikimedia Commons / Creative Commons Attribution-ShareAlike 4.0 International License / Public domain; A Putumayo youth: Courtesy of the National Library of Ireland (Call No NPA CAS 198); Omarino and Ricudo: Museum of Archaeology and Anthropology, Cambridge;

Molly Childers and Mary Spring Rice: The Board of Trinity College Dublin; Alice Stopford Green: Courtesy of the National Library of Ireland (Call No NPA PERS20); John Devoy: Villanova University Digital Library; Eivind Adler Christensen: Courtesy of the National Library of Ireland (Call No NPA CAS7A); Rudolf Nadolny: Alamy Stock Photo / Sueddeutsche Zeitung Photo; Limburg: Reproduced by kind permission of UCD Archives, James Joyce Library, University College Dublin (Ref:P127/17); Sue the London *Graphic*: *The Graphic*, 20 May 1916 / Illustration by W. Hatherell; Recruits in their uniforms at Zossen: Courtesy of the National Library of Ireland (MS.18,081); T. St John Gaffney: Alamy Stock Photo / Sueddeutsche Zeitung Photo; Robert Monteith: Bridgeman Images / © British Library Board / All Rights Reserved; On *U-19* off the Hebrides: Photographer unknown; The SS *Libau*: Public domain; Dinghy: *Trial of Roger Casement*, Notable English trials, 1917; Reginald 'Blinker' Hall: Alamy Stock Photo / The History Collection; F. E. Smith: Alamy Stock Photo / Granger Historical Picture Archive; Basil Thomson: Getty Images / Keystone / Hulton Archive; George Gavan Duffy and J. H. Morgan: Getty Images / Bettmann Archive; Serjeant Sullivan: Serjeant A. M. Sullivan, *The Last Serjeant, The Memoirs of Serjeant A. M. Sullivan, Q.C.*, 1952; In the dock: Alamy Stock Photo / Pictorial Press Ltd; Leaving court: Bridgeman Images / Hulton Archive.

Bibliography

Archives

British Library Newspaper Archive, London
The National Archives, Kew
National Library of Ireland, Dublin
New York Public Library

Books

Andrew, Christopher *The Defence of the Realm: The Authorised History of MI5* (London, 2009)
Bentley, W. Holman *Pioneering on the Congo* 2 vols (London, 1900)
Butcher, Tim *Blood River: A Journey to Africa's Broken Heart* (London, 2008)
Campbell, John *F. E. Smith: First Earl of Birkenhead* (London, 2013)
Carroll, Rory *Killing Thatcher: The IRA, the Manhunt and the Long War on the Crown* (London, 2023)
Casement, Roger *The Amazon Journal* ed. Angus Mitchell (Dublin, 1997)
——*The Black Diaries* ed. Jeffrey Dudgeon (Belfast, 2019)
——*The Crime against Europe: A Possible Outcome of the War of 1914* (Laverne, Tennessee, 2019)
——*The Crime against Ireland: Writings and Poems* ed. Herbert O. Mackey (Dublin, 1958)
——*Diaries 1910: The Black and the White* ed. Roger Sawyer (London, 1997)
——*The Eyes of Another Race: Congo Report and 1903 Diary* ed. Séamas Ó Síocháin and Michael O'Sullivan (Dublin, 2003)
——*One Bold Deed of Open Treason: The Berlin Diary 1914–16* ed. Angus Mitchell (Sallins, Co. Kildare, 2016)
——*Sir Roger Casement's Diaries* ed. Charles Curry (Munich, 1922)
——*Sir Roger Casement's Heart of Darkness: The 1911 Documents* ed. Angus Mitchell (Dublin, 2003)

Childers, Erskine *The Riddle of the Sands* (London, 1995)

Chronicle of the Twentieth Century (London, 1988)

Conan Doyle, Arthur *The Crime of the Congo* (Milton Keynes, 2020)

Conrad, Joseph *Heart of Darkness* ed. Paul Armstrong (New York, 2017)

Coote, Stephen *Yeats: A Life* (London, 1997)

De Courcy Ireland, John *The Sea and the Easter Rising, 1916* (Dublin, 1966)

Devoy, John *Recollections of a Rebel* (Dublin, 1929)

Dickey, H. S. *The Misadventures of a Tropical Medico* (London, 1929)

Doerries, Reinhard R. *Prelude to the Easter Rising: Sir Roger Casement in Imperial Germany* (London, 2000)

Doherty, Gabriel and Keogh, Dermot (eds) *1916: The Long Revolution* (Dublin, 2007)

Figgis, Darrell *Recollections of the Irish War* (New York, 1929)

Ford, Ford Madox *A History of Our Own Times* (Manchester, 1989)

Foster, R. F. *Vivid Faces: The Revolutionary Generation in Ireland, 1890–1923* (London, 2015)

Golway, Terry *Irish Rebel: John Devoy and America's Fight for Ireland's Freedom* (New York, 1998)

Greene, Graham *A Burnt-Out Case* (London, 1961)

Gwynn, Denis *The Life and Death of Roger Casement* (London, 1930)

Hambloch, Ernest *British Consul* (London, 1938)

Hardenburg, Walter *The Putumayo: The Devil's Paradise* (Milton Keynes, 2021)

Harms, Robert *Land of Tears: The Exploration and Exploitation of Equatorial Africa* (New York, 2019)

Hay, Marnie *Bulmer Hobson and the Nationalist Movement in Twentieth-Century Ireland* (Manchester, 2009)

Hochschild, Adam *King Leopold's Ghost: A Story of Greed, Terror and Heroism in Colonial Africa* (London, 2019)

Humphreys, Travers *Criminal Days: Recollections and Reflections* (London, 1946)

Hyde, H. Montgomery *Famous Trials 9: Roger Casement* (London, 1964)

——*The Other Love: An Historical and Contemporary Survey of Homosexuality in Britain* (London, 1970)

Inglis, Brian *Roger Casement* (London, 1974)

Jackson, Alvin *Home Rule* (London, 2004)

Jasanoff, Maya *The Dawn Watch: Joseph Conrad in a Global World* (London, 2017)

Jeal, Tim *Stanley: The Impossible Life of Africa's Greatest Explorer* (London, 2007)

Jenkins, Roy *Asquith* (London, 1964)

Jones, Thomas Artemus *Without My Wig* (Liverpool, 1944)

Keogh, Michael *With Casement's Irish Brigade* (Drogheda, 2010)

Knott, George H. (ed.) *Trial of Roger Casement* (Edinburgh, 1926)

Korda, Michael *Hero: The Life and Legend of Lawrence of Arabia* (London, 2010)

Lawrence, T. E. *The Selected Letters*, ed. Malcolm Brown (New York, 1988)

Leslie, Shane *The Irish Issue in Its American Aspect* (London, 1919)

Lindqvist, Sven *Exterminate All the Brutes* (London, 2018)

Louis, W. R. and Stengers, J. *E. D. Morel's History of the Congo Reform Movement* (Oxford, 1968)

Lynch, Florence Monteith *The Mystery Man of Banna Strand: The Life and Death of Captain Robert Monteith* (New Delhi, 2022)

MacColl, René *Roger Casement* (London, 1956)

McDiarmid, Lucy *The Irish Art of Controversy* (Dublin, 2005)

MacDonagh, Michael *The Irish at the Front* (Milton Keynes, 2017)

Meyers, Jeffrey *Joseph Conrad: A Biography* (London, 1991)

Mitchell, Angus *Casement* (London, 2003)

——*Roger Casement* (Dublin, 2013)

——*Sir Roger Casement's Heart of Darkness: The 1911 Documents* (Dublin, 2003)

Monteith, Robert *Casement's Last Adventure* (Dublin, 1953)

Morris, James *Farewell the Trumpets: An Imperial Retreat* (London, 1979)

Noyes, Alfred *The Accusing Ghost or Justice for Casement* (London, 1957)

Ó Broin, Leon *Revolutionary Underground: The Story of the Irish Republican Brotherhood, 1858–1924* (Totowa, New Jersey, 1976)

O Brolchain, Honor *Joseph Plunkett* (Dublin, 2012)

Ó Síocháin, Séamas *Roger Casement: Imperialist, Rebel, Revolutionary* (Dublin, 2008)

Pakenham, Thomas *The Scramble for Africa, 1876–1912* (London, 1992)

Parmiter, Geoffrey *Roger Casement* (London, 1936)

Piper, Leonard *Dangerous Waters: The Tragedy of Erskine Childers* (London, 2003)

Porter, Bernard *Critics of Empire: British Radicals and the Imperial Challenge* (London, 2008)

Redmond-Howard, L. G. *Sir Roger Casement: A Character Sketch without Prejudice* (Dublin, 1916)

Reid, B. L. *The Lives of Roger Casement* (London, 1976)

——*The Man from New York: John Quinn and His Friends* (New York, 1968)

Ridley, Jane *George V: Never a Dull Moment* (London, 2021)

Robb, Graham *Strangers: Homosexual Love in the Nineteenth Century* (London, 2003)

Sawyer, Roger *Casement: The Flawed Hero* (London, 1984)

Sebald, W. G. *The Rings of Saturn* (London, 2002)

Spindler, Captain Karl *The Mystery of the Casement Ship* (Tralee, 1965)

Stewart, A. T. Q. *The Ulster Crisis: Resistance to Home Rule, 1912–14* (London, 1969)

Strachan, Hew *The First World War* (London, 2014)

Sturgis, Matthew *Oscar: A Life* (London, 2018)

Sullivan, Serjeant A. M. *The Last Serjeant: Memoirs* (London, 1952)

Thomson, Basil *Odd People: Hunting Spies in the First World War* (London, 2015)

Twain, Mark *King Leopold's Soliloquy* (New York, 1970)

Van Reybrouck, David *Congo: An Epic History of a People* trans. Sam Garrett (London, 2015)

Vargas Llosa, Mario *The Dream of the Celt* (London, 2012)

Ward, Herbert *A Voice from the Congo* (London, 1910)

Wilde, Oscar *The Picture of Dorian Gray* (Ware, 2003)

Wrong, Michela *In the Footsteps of Mr Kurtz* (London, 2001)

Yeats, W. B. *Collected Poems* (London, 1950)

British Government Papers

Correspondence and Report from His Majesty's Consul at Boma Respecting the Administration of the Independent State of the Congo (London, 1904)

Documents Relative to the Sinn Féin Movement (London, 1921)

Articles

Aitken, Robert 'Rex v. Casement', *Litigation* Vol. 23 No. 4, 1997

Bew, Paul 'The Real Importance of Roger Casement', *History Ireland* Vol. 2 No. 2, Summer 1994

Broeker, Galen 'Roger Casement: Background to Treason', *Journal of Modern History* Vol. 29 No. 3, September 1957

C.B. 'Roger Casement: A Problem in Psychology', *British Medical Journal* Vol. 1 No. 3670, 9 May 1931

Costigan, Giovanni 'The Treason of Sir Roger Casement', *American Historical Review* Vol. 60 No. 2, January 1955

Dudgeon, Jeffrey 'A Gay View of Roger Casement', *Fortnight* No. 209, 1984

Dudley Edwards, Owen 'Divided Treason and Divided Loyalties: Roger Casement and Others', *Transactions of the Royal Historical Society* Vol. 32, 1982

Gwynn, Denis 'Roger Casement's Last Weeks', *Studies: An Irish Quarterly Review* Vol. 54 No. 213, Spring 1965

Hawkins, Hunt 'Joseph Conrad, Roger Casement and the Congo Reform Movement', *Journal of Modern Literature* Vol. 9 No. 1, 1981–2

Leary, William M., Jr 'Woodrow Wilson, Irish Americans and the Election of 1916', *Journal of American History* Vol. 54 No. 1, June 1967

Lewis, Brian 'The Queer Life and Afterlife of Roger Casement', *Journal of the History of Sexuality* Vol. 14 No. 4, 2005

Louis, William Roger 'Roger Casement and the Congo', *Journal of African History* Vol. 5 No. 1, 1964

Meyers, Jeffrey 'Conrad and Roger Casement', *Conradiana* Vol. 5 No. 3, 1973

Mitchell, Angus 'Black Diaries: Roger Casement and the History Question', *History Ireland* Vol. 24 No. 4, 2016

——'A Strange Chapter of Irish History: Sir Roger Casement, Germany and the 1916 Rising', *Field Day Review* Vol. 8, 2012

Nevinson, Henry W. 'Sir Roger Casement and Sinn Féin: Some Personal Notes', *Atlantic*, August 1916

Ranger, Terence 'Roger Casement and Africa', *Transactions* No. 6, 1966

Shaw, G. B. 'The Roger Casement Trial', *Massachusetts Review* Vol. 5 No. 2, 1964

——'Some Neglected Morals of the Easter Rising', *New Statesman*, 2 May 1916

Tóibín, Colm 'A Whale of a Time', *London Review of Books* Vol. 19 No. 19, 1997

Notes and Sources

Abbreviations

Prologue

p. xv   a beautiful morning – Hyde, *Roger Casement* p. 158

p. xv   Ireland's freedom – Parmiter, *Roger Casement* p. 321

p. xvi   grief of others – Casement, *The Black Diaries* p. xxii

p. xvi   for my country – Parmiter, *op. cit.* p. 321

p. xvi   broken archangel – Lawrence, *The Selected Letters* p. 508

1. Conquistador

p. 3   seem commonplace – Inglis, *Roger Casement* p. 24

p. 3   my own bat – Reid, *The Lives of Roger Casement* p. 7

p. 4   intense, speaking little – Inglis, *op. cit.* p. 24

p. 4   vast and gaunt – Reid, *op. cit.* p. 12

p. 4   Exploration of Africa – Pakenham, *The Scramble for Africa* p. 36

p. 4   four score villages – Hochschild, *King Leopold's Ghost* p. 49

p. 5   Christianity and Civilization – Pakenham, *op. cit.* p. xxiv

p. 5   a proper gentleman – Hochschild, *op. cit.* p. 31

p. 6   *Kolonialtummel* – Pakenham, *op. cit.* p. xxv

p. 6   and civilising others – *Ibid.* p. 13

p. 8   and pacification bases – Hochschild, *op. cit.* p. 45

p. 9   of superior quality – Harms, *Land of Tears* p. 140

p. 10   believe in kings forever – Hochschild, *op. cit.* pp. 66–7

p. 10   tribes put together – *Ibid.* p. 71

p. 11   take in a herring – Wrong, *In the Footsteps of Mr Kurtz* p. 43

p. 12   its illustrious creator – Hochschild, *op. cit.* p. 86

p. 12   Freedom and Peace – Pakenham, *op. cit.* p. 255

p. 12   That would be absurd – Hochschild, *op. cit.* p. 67

p. 13   lessen its deficit – *Ibid.* p. 118

p. 14   wild forest productions – Harms, *op. cit.* p. 365

p. 14   what was to be got – Conrad, *Heart of Darkness* pp. 6–7

p. 14   desk and pen – Reid, *op. cit.* p. 10

p. 15   is the head – ML 20 June 1884

p. 15   any man living – Reid, *op. cit.* p. 8

p. 16   his oatmeal biscuits – Sawyer, *Casement* pp. 21–2

p. 16   some principle about him – Inglis, *op. cit.* p. 28

p. 16   from S.E. Africa – Ó Síocháin, *Roger Casement* p. 32

p. 16   to overcome barbarism – Hochschild, *op. cit.* p. 97

p. 17   the capable Englishman – *Ibid.* p. 98

p. 17   beads of rain – Greene, *A Burnt-Out Case* pp. 3–5

p. 18   face of the enemy – Hochschild, *op. cit.* p. 196

p. 18   poor old Ted Glave – Inglis, *op. cit.* p. 75

p. 19   slumber, duty-crowned – *Ibid.* p. 49

p. 19   turn him down forever – Ward, *A Voice from the Congo* p. 223

p. 20   repressing their bad – Inglis, *op. cit.* p. 20

p. 20   some of the tribes – Bentley, *Pioneering on the Congo* Vol. 2 p. 10

p. 21   anywhere to help – Inglis, *op. cit.* p. 31

p. 22   measly – Bentley, *op. cit.* Vol. 2 p. 323

p. 22   good-hearted he was – Inglis, *op. cit.* pp. 30–1

p. 22   and sympathetic nature – Reid, *op. cit.* p. 11

p. 22   honourable and loyal – Inglis, *op. cit.* p. 27

p. 22   poor souls – *Ibid.* pp. 27–31

p. 23   2nd with blacks – ML letter to Susan Casement 2 March 1901

p. 23   only friends – Inglis, *op. cit.* p. 31

p. 23   up to the job – Hochschild, *op. cit.* p. 119

p. 24   still upon me – Reid, *op. cit.* p. 12

p. 25   somewhere or other – *Ibid.* pp. 12–15

p. 25 a perfect animal – Hawkins, 'Conrad, Casement and the Congo Reform Movement' p. 66

p. 26 idiotic employment – Jasanoff, *The Dawn Watch* p. 188

p. 26 and very sympathetic – Meyers, *Joseph Conrad* p. 97

p. 26 unspeakable wilderness – *Ibid.* p. 99

p. 26 never did know – *Ibid.*

p. 27 undone him – *Ibid.* p. 313

p. 27 limpid personality – Hawkins, *op. cit.* p. 66

2. Breakfast with Leopold

p. 28 fair play – Mitchell, *Casement* p. 23

p. 28 an occupying power – Ó Síocháin, *op. cit.* p. 46

p. 29 a botanical man – ML 2 January 1893

p. 29 Director-General of Customs – Reid, *op. cit.* p. 17

p. 29 in our faces – Inglis, *op. cit.* p. 33

p. 29 of broken trust – Casement, *The Crime against Europe* p. 178

p. 30 suited to the work – Inglis, *op. cit.* p. 35

p. 30 fashion of their fathers – Reid, *op. cit.* p. 20

p. 31 conduct of the Germans – Mitchell, *Roger Casement* p. 53

p. 31 the German government – Mitchell, *Casement* p. 23

p. 31 nothing to do – Reid, *op. cit.* p. 21

p. 32 reckless and brave – Sawyer, *op. cit.* pp. 4–6

p. 32 Her Majesty's pleasure – Inglis, *op. cit.* p. 35

p. 33 hunger and exposure – ML 2 March 1896

p. 33 unimportant details – Inglis, *op. cit.* p. 41

p. 33 series of thunderbolts – Pakenham, *op. cit.* p. 490

p. 34 South East Africa – Inglis, *op. cit.* p. 39

p. 34 that is pleasant – ML 2 March 1896

p. 34 any other white man – Mitchell, *Roger Casement* p. 63

p. 35 and weak circulation – Inglis, *op. cit.* p. 40

p. 35 behind the world – ML 26 September 1899

p. 35 recently been despatched – Inglis, *op. cit.* p. 44

p. 36 law of labour – Louis and Stengers, *Morel's History of the Congo Reform Movement* p. 16

p. 37   the last man – Hochschild, *op. cit.* p. 229

p. 37   Exterminate all the brutes! – Conrad, *op. cit.* p. 50

p. 38   and undefined powers – Inglis, *op. cit.* p. 51

p. 38   not wasted cartridges – *Ibid.* pp. 46–7

p. 38   forests without shelter – Hochschild, *op. cit.* p. 229

p. 39   most harshly treated – Conan Doyle, *The Crime of the Congo* p. xxviii

p. 39   its worst form – Inglis, *op. cit.* p. 49

p. 39   Freed Them from Porterage – Hochschild, *op. cit.* p. 171

p. 39   and ignorant policy – *Inglis, op. cit.* pp. 49–50

p. 40   tutor to his hand – Reid, *op. cit.* p. 25

p. 40   & S. Africa generally – *Ibid.*

p. 40   the Boers' terms – ML 2 March 1901

p. 40   false to themselves – Inglis, *op. cit.* pp. 54–5

p. 40   early May 1900 – Reid, *op. cit.* p. 29

p. 41   are too much – ML 2 March 1901

p. 41   and worse food – Reid, *op. cit.* p. 29

p. 41   a Horrid Hole – *Ibid.* p. 31

p. 41   such transcendent importance – Inglis, *op. cit.* p. 54

p. 41   a very big fight – Parmiter, *op. cit.* p. 5

p. 41   not have been stopped – Reid, *op. cit.* p. 27

p. 42   Early Paradise – *Ibid.* p. 29

p. 42   King Leopold II – Hochschild, *op. cit.* p. 178

p. 43   love of Leopold – Louis and Stengers, *op. cit.* p. 36

p. 43   no turning back – Hochschild, *op. cit.* p. 186

p. 43   terror which exists – Mitchell, *Roger Casement* pp. 75–6

p. 44   a cultivated people – Hochschild, *op. cit.* p. 204

p. 44   in lieu of tax – TNA FO 2/336

p. 45   mistrustful of me – *Ibid.*

p. 45   advise him of – Hochschild, *op. cit.* p. 198

p. 45   and Your Majesty – Reid, *op. cit.* p. 30

3. A Man among Thorns

p. 46   eyes of another race – Casement, *The Black Diaries* p. 98

p. 46   ever left before – ML letter to Susan Casement 2 March 1901

p. 46   loafs for four – Ó Síocháin, *op. cit.* p. 100

p. 47   a beastly hole – Parmiter, *op. cit.* p. 5

p. 47   all the furniture – Reid, *op. cit.* p. 31

p. 47   should be profitable – *Ibid.* p. 32

p. 47   forced to foreign flight – Casement, *The Crime against Europe* p. 172

p. 47   the tale divine – NLI MS 13,082/2iii/7

p. 47   a remunerative sale – NLI MS 13,073/23i/1

p. 48   attention and care – Reid, *op. cit.* pp. 32–3

p. 48   a splendid story – Inglis, *op. cit.* p. 72

p. 48   mended or ended – Mitchell, *Roger Casement* pp. 80–1

p. 48   his serious attention – Inglis, *op. cit.* p. 62

p. 48   and well-treated – Louis, 'Roger Casement and the Congo' p. 99

p. 48   be some progress! – Inglis, *op. cit.* p. 65

p. 49   conscience of Europe – Hawkins, *op. cit.* p. 70

p. 49   large jaws – Hochschild, *op. cit.* p. 199

p. 49   Sovereign of the country – Inglis, *op. cit.* p. 61

p. 49   surrounding the Congo – Louis and Stengers, *op. cit.* p. 52

p. 50   misgovernment and oppression – Inglis, *op. cit.* p. 65

p. 50   source of information – Louis, *op. cit.* p. 101

p. 50   black or white – Inglis, *op. cit.* p. 63

p. 50   other sources too! – Hansard 20 May 1903

p. 51   the evils prevalent – *Ibid.*

p. 51   taking action! – Casement, *The Black Diaries* p. 131

p. 51   authentic information – *Ibid.* p. 135

p. 52   turning in early – *Ibid.* pp. 112–13

p. 54   more than me – Robb, *Strangers* p. 103

p. 54   art and the artist – *Ibid.* p. 38

p. 54   some call 'Boo-line' – *Ibid.* pp. 101–2

p. 54   unnatural union – *Ibid.* p. 38

p. 55   by criminal legislation – Casement, *The Black Diaries* p. 124

p. 55   place for its consideration – Robb, *op. cit.* p. 261

p. 55   MacDonald's terrible end – Casement, *The Black Diaries* p. 127

p. 55   5 francs per room – *Ibid.* p. 129

p. 55   sailing for . . . Barcelona – *Ibid.* p. 655

p. 56   To heavenly eyes – *Ibid.* pp. 645–6

p. 56   vilify the individual – Reid, *op. cit.* p. 53

p. 56   on their track – Louis, *op. cit.* p. 104

p. 57   Transports!! – Casement, *The Black Diaries* p. 134

p. 57   energetic European intervention – Casement, *The Eyes of Another Race* p. 49

p. 57   their own seeking – *Ibid.* p. 52

p. 57   you are *nyama* – *Ibid.* p. 119

p. 58   not well-cooked – *Ibid.* p. 57

p. 58   cold in eveg – *Ibid.* p. 243

p. 58   warm and running – Casement, *The Black Diaries* p. 143

p. 59   shadow of death – Casement, *The Eyes of Another Race* pp. 129–33

p. 59   Fortunato – *Ibid.* p. 252

p. 60   a white stranger – *Ibid.* pp. 71–2

p. 60   there looking on – TNA FO 10/807

p. 60   divided her – Casement, *The Eyes of Another Race* pp. 51–4

p. 61   would be killed – *Ibid.* p. 72

p. 61   fingers were destroyed – *Ibid.* p. 161

p. 61   not at all well – *Ibid.* p. 255

p. 61   the European table – *Ibid.* p. 86

p. 62   production of india-rubber – *Ibid.* p. 87

p. 63   came before me – *Ibid.* pp. 90–2

p. 64   shadowed – Louis, *op. cit.* p. 106

p. 64   the thieves' kitchen – TNA FO 10/801

p. 64   my own future – Mitchell, *Roger Casement* p. 98

4. Those in High Places

p. 65   go overboard – Mitchell, *Roger Casement* pp. 98–9

p. 65   me for help – *Ibid.* p. 98

p. 65   a terrible indictment – Ó Síocháin, *op. cit.* pp. 177–8

p. 66   Upper Congo life – *Ibid.* p. 237

p. 66   seen in the Congo – Hochschild, *op. cit.* pp. 238–9

p. 66   against native populations – HMG, *Correspondence and Report from His Majesty's Consul* p. 16

p. 67   type man – Casement, *The Black Diaries* p. 160

p. 67   at least eight millions – Louis and Stengers, *op. cit.* p. 252

p. 67   I saw him – Casement, *The Black Diaries* p. 161

p. 68   no one else could do – Louis and Stengers, *op. cit.* pp. 160–1

p. 68   as honest as day – Hochschild, *op. cit.* p. 205

p. 68   and noble-minded – Louis and Stengers, *op. cit.* p. 159

p. 68   anti-Casement campaign – Inglis, *op. cit.* pp. 162–3

p. 69   commencement of operations – TNA FO 10/807

p. 69   a simple surgical operation – Hochschild, *op. cit.* p. 204

p. 69   our local life – Inglis, *op. cit.* p. 79

p. 69   must be laid – Casement, *The Black Diaries* p. 110

p. 69   the human effects – *Ibid.* p. 109

p. 70   humanitarian declarations – Reid, *op. cit.* pp. 53–5

p. 70   cold and black – *Ibid.* p. 55

p. 70   in this campaign – *Ibid.*

p. 70   will only do harm – Louis, *op. cit.* p. 111

p. 71   incompetent noodles – Hochschild, *op. cit.* p. 204

p. 71   Irish blackthorn – Casement, *The Black Diaries* p. 179

p. 71   tyrants and victims – Louis, *op. cit.* p. 111

p. 71   TTT and not KK – HMG, *Correspondence and Report from His Majesty's Consul* pp. 78–9

p. 71   resignation is called for – Louis, *op. cit.* pp. 111–12

p. 71   benefit of its shareholders – Inglis, *op. cit.* p. 91

p. 72   revolting beyond belief – Ford, *A History of Our Own Times* p. 126

p. 72   systematic oppression – TNA FO 10/773

p. 72   rather it doesn't – Inglis, *op. cit.* p. 91

p. 72   redresser of wrongs – *Ibid.* p. 92

p. 73   compassion for the weak – *The Times* 10 June 1904

p. 73   a deliberate lie! – Inglis, *op. cit.* pp. 93–4

p. 73   an alternative power structure – Casement, *The Black Diaries* p. 179

p. 73   intended – Reid, *op. cit.* p. 59

p. 73   resign from the Service – Casement, *The Black Diaries* p. 95

p. 74   white & clear – Louis and Stengers, *op. cit.* p. 215

p. 74   fervid support – *Ibid.* p. 163

p. 74   heart of hers – *Ibid.* pp. 163–5

p. 75   King of Beasts – Costigan, 'The Treason of Sir Roger Casement' p. 286

p. 75   amongst the natives – Jasanoff, *op. cit.* p. 213

p. 75   sorry I was born – Louis, *op. cit.* pp. 116–17

p. 76   *La Vérité sur le Congo* – Inglis, *op. cit.* p. 104

p. 76 just and correct – *Ibid.* p. 105

p. 77 might otherwise attach – *Ibid.* p. 106

p. 77 to be leaving it – Reid, *op. cit.* p. 62

p. 77 like a rascal – Inglis, *op. cit.* p. 107

5. Foundations

p. 80 message from Widdin – Sawyer, *op. cit.* p. 14

p. 81 a shocking position – Casement, *The Black Diaries* pp. 42–4

p. 81 lived on his debts – interview Patrick Casement 3 May 2022

p. 81 their future conduct – *Morning Post* 26 January 1876

p. 81 got married yourself? – Reid, *op. cit.* p. 67

p. 82 the Catholic Church – Ó Síocháin, *op. cit.* p. 8

p. 82 and religious feeling – NLI MS 13,079

p. 82 that suppressed – Casement, *The Black Diaries* p. 53

p. 83 even slightly remunerative – *Ibid.* pp. 45–6

p. 83 nevertheless inspired them – *Ibid.* p. 47

p. 83 and tender-heartedness – Mitchell, *Roger Casement* p. 32

p. 83 poor sort of life – Reid, *op. cit.* p. 5

p. 83 continuing pulmonary disease – *Ibid.* pp. 59–60

p. 84 British army in India – NLI MS 13,077/3/6

p. 84 a mercantile house – Reid, *op. cit.* p. 61

p. 84 youth of any country – *Ibid.* p. 68

p. 85 dark old library – *Ibid.* p. 31

p. 85 extent . . . desirable – ML 27 January 1893

p. 85 expensive surgical operation – ML 10 October 1893

p. 85 Your affectionate nephew – ML 2 January 1893

p. 85 shall never depart – Casement, *The Crime against Europe* p. 187

p. 85 walked and scribbled – Reid, *op. cit.* p. 21

p. 86 at English hands – Casement, *The Black Diaries* p. 71

p. 86 almost by myself – Reid, *op. cit.* p. 83

p. 87 not a stranger – Ó Síocháin, *op. cit.* p. 16

p. 87 a high chivalry – Mitchell, *Casement* p. 43

p. 87 the War Office – Inglis, *op. cit.* p. 120

p. 88 inspiration and resolve – *Ibid.* p. 134

p. 88 evils of Irish misrule – Sawyer, *op. cit.* p. 15

p. 88	our nameless desires – Casement, *The Crime against Europe* p. 170
p. 88	& the Gaelic League – Reid, *op. cit.* p. 60
p. 88	in generous emotions – *Ibid.* p. 61
p. 89	correspondence in Irish – *Ibid.* p. 74
p. 89	extraordinary success – Inglis, *op. cit.* pp. 109–10
p. 89	devote themselves to their work – Hochschild, *op. cit.* p. 237
p. 89	Mr Casement – Inglis, *op. cit.* p. 121
p. 89	a betterment of things – *Ibid.* p. 110
p. 89	Congo cannibals – Costigan, *op. cit.* p. 287
p. 89	Congo Reform Society – Inglis, *op. cit.* p. 141
p. 90	horror of the truth – Nevinson, 'Sir Roger Casement and Sinn Féin' p. 236
p. 90	pair of paupers – Costigan, *op. cit.* p. 293
p. 90	begging pauper – *Ibid.* p. 187
p. 90	blow him into suds – Reid, *op. cit.* p. 69
p. 91	quarter of Ireland – *Ibid.* pp. 71–2
p. 92	religion and art – Twain, *King Leopold's Soliloquy* p. 2
p. 92	every foolish trifle – *Ibid.* p. 14
p. 92	Irish question is nearer – Porter, *Critics of Empire* p. 268
p. 92	the CONGO EVIL – Louis and Stengers, *op. cit.* p. 176
p. 93	vinegar-sharp – MacColl, *Roger Casement* pp. 50–1
p. 93	an introduction to you – Sawyer, *op. cit.* p. 47
p. 93	attitude on the subject – MacColl, *op. cit.* p. 65
p. 93	required from Belgium – Louis and Stengers, *op. cit.* p. 190
p. 94	international wrong-doing – *Ibid.* pp. 186–8
p. 94	Infamous Cruelties – Hochschild, *op. cit.* p. 249
p. 94	honest but weak – Inglis, *op. cit.* p. 145
p. 95	a friend of Leopold – Louis and Stengers, *op. cit.* p. 188
p. 95	barely civil reply – Inglis, *op. cit.* p. 145
p. 95	ask for its accounts – Hochschild, *op. cit.* p. 258
p. 95	den of devils – Louis, *op. cit.* p. 119
p. 95	always very discouraging – Reid, *op. cit.* p. 75
p. 96	grievously injured too – Hay, *Bulmer Hobson* p. 57
p. 96	this outraged land – Inglis, *op. cit.* p. 155
p. 97	subsequent actions – *Ibid.* p. 154
p. 97	Britain and *Ireland* – Reid, *op. cit.* p. 78

p. 97   made for the Congo – Hochschild, *op. cit.* p. 259

p. 97   made him unreliable – Casement, *The Black Diaries* p. 163

p. 98   damaged Irish tongue? – Noyes, *The Accusing Ghost* p. 41

p. 98   nearly accomplished – Louis, *op. cit.* p. 199

p. 98   as wide as the world – Mitchell, *Roger Casement* pp. 124–5

p. 98   need look abroad – Nevinson, *op. cit.* p. 237

6. *The Devil's Paradise*

p. 99   covered with sandflies – Inglis, *op. cit.* pp. 157–8

p. 99   in this environment – Reid, *op. cit.* p. 80

p. 100   *Hole* – *Ibid.* p. 81

p. 100   lead me personally – Mitchell, *Casement* p. 41

p. 101   national self-respect – *Ibid.* p. 55

p. 101   Suit of Clothes – Reid, *op. cit.* p. 84

p. 101   before Millar came! – Casement, *The Black Diaries* p. 452

p. 102   menials and bottlewashers – Reid, *op. cit.* p. 87

p. 102   immoral in Brazil – Ó Síocháin, *op. cit.* p. 250

p. 102   Peruvians and Colombians – Casement, *The Black Diaries* p. 222

p. 102   future of their country – Mitchell, *Casement* p. 54

p. 103   a cauliflower occasionally – MacColl, *op. cit.* p. 77

p. 103   sores and eruptions – Reid, *op. cit.* p. 87

p. 103   Irish Home Rule – MacColl, *op. cit.* p. 73

p. 103   I hate Brazil – Reid, *op. cit.* p. 88

p. 103   and good judgement – *Ibid.* p. 81

p. 104   fourteen years a Consul – ML 15 August 1909

p. 104   powers of persuasion – Hambloch, *British Consul* p. 71

p. 104   sense of proportion – *Ibid.* p. 76

p. 105   John Bull's basement – Reid, *op. cit.* p. 90

p. 105   people against misrule – Broeker, 'Roger Casement: Background to Treason' p. 245

p. 105   laws and institutions – Reid, *op. cit.* p. 92

p. 105   as if for cooking – Inglis, *op. cit.* p. 237

p. 106   Japan – Casement, *The Black Diaries* pp. 242–3

p. 106   Lisbon July 1904 – *Ibid.* p. 227

p. 106   and wrote also – Ó Síocháin, *op. cit.* p. 267

p. 106   splendid talk – Reid, *op. cit.* p. 96

p. 107   a pigsty – Casement, *The Amazon Journal* p. 487

p. 108   a most cowardly manner – Hardenburg, *The Devil's Paradise* p. 49

p. 108   back to their tribes – *Ibid.* pp. 51–2

p. 108   await their punishment – *Ibid.* p. 54

p. 109   a fear of the 'whites' – *Ibid.* p. 59

p. 109   shifty-eyed half-breed – *Ibid.* p. 50

p. 109   preparation of codfish – *Ibid.* p. 55

p. 109   British-Owned Congo – Inglis, *op. cit.* p. 178

p. 109   Company's kindly agents – *Ibid.* p. 179

p. 110   prosperity to Peru – Casement, *The Black Diaries* p. 257

p. 110   old and smelling – Inglis, *op. cit.* p. 101

p. 110   no regions of the unknown – Casement, *The Amazon Journal* p. 67

p. 111   places and affairs – *Ibid.* p. 83

p. 111   one decent man up there – *Ibid.* p. 108

p. 111   chucked up the sponge – Inglis, *op. cit.* p. 184

p. 112   crime-stained forests – Casement, *The Amazon Journal* p. 291

p. 112   infamous ruffians – *Ibid.* p. 131

p. 112   dreadful nightmare – Casement, *The Black Diaries* pp. 266–7

p. 112   shuddered – Reid, *op. cit.* p. 119

p. 113   *alone* can aid? – Casement, *The Amazon Journal* p. 373

p. 113   Bought Omarino – Reid, *op. cit.* p. 117

p. 113   beautiful coffee limbs – *Ibid.* pp. 117–18

p. 114   sniffed – *Ibid.* p. 123

p. 114   ghastly and horrible tale – MacColl, *op. cit.* p. 95

p. 114   one place for long – NLI MS13073/38/3

p. 114   gone since then – Reid, *op. cit.* p. 151

p. 114   affected millions – Casement, *The Amazon Journal* p. 183

p. 115   flogging, beheading, burning – Reid, *op. cit.* p. 123

p. 115   their cruel burden – Casement, *The Amazon Journal* pp. 183–4

p. 115   international obloquy – *Ibid.* p. 459

p. 115   Noisy Nick – Casement, *The Black Diaries* p. 380

p. 116   The swine! – Reid, *op. cit.* p. 130

p. 116   ought to be hanged – Gwynn, *The Life and Death of Roger Casement*
         p. 177

p. 116   keeps me going – Inglis, *op. cit.* p. 189

p. 116 goodness still survived – Hardenburg, *op. cit.* p. 91

p. 117 flogging to death – Gwynn, *op. cit.* p. 177

p. 117 unofficially and privately – Inglis, *op. cit.* p. 192

p. 117 make it here – Mitchell, *Sir Roger Casement's Heart of Darkness* p. i

p. 118 esteem and support – Reid, *op. cit.* p. 136

p. 118 he left us – *Ibid.* p. 137

p. 119 splendid – *Ibid.* p. 141

p. 119 humblest rubber gatherer – Dickey, *The Misadventures of a Tropical Medico* p. 149

p. 120 youth and joy – Reid, *op. cit.* p. 145

p. 120 two inches in diameter – Dickey, *op. cit.* p. 161

p. 121 disputed regions – Inglis, *op. cit.* pp. 203–4

p. 121 an appalling iniquity – *The Times* 15 July 1912

p. 121 a book yet – NLI MS 13,073/23i/9

p. 122 are very scared – Inglis, *op. cit.* p. 209

p. 122 rest of the earth – *Ibid.* p. 235

p. 122 return home – Casement, *One Bold Deed* p. 236

p. 123 last person in the world – Inglis, *op. cit.* p. 221

p. 123 if not criminal – NLI MS 13,073/28ii/9

p. 123 might have happened – Inglis, *op. cit.* p. 225

p. 124 to the Crown – *Ibid.* p. 235

p. 124 quite the same – Costigan, *op. cit.* p. 292

p. 124 Private & Confidential – Sawyer, *op. cit.* p. 109

7. *The Soul of a Felon*

p. 128 an end of talking – Figgis, *Recollections of the Irish War* pp. 11–18

p. 129 meekly ambitious – Stewart, *The Ulster Crisis* p. 38

p. 129 dark and foreboding – Casement, *The Black Diaries* p. 482

p. 130 bade him farewell – *Chronicle of the Twentieth Century* p. 170

p. 130 Redmond and Company – Gwynn, *op. cit.* p. 185

p. 130 under a trick – *Ibid.* p. 186

p. 130 be closed again – Hay, *op. cit.* p. 109

p. 131 fought against of old – Stewart, *op. cit.* pp. 48–55

p. 131 present conspiracy – Morris, *Farewell the Trumpets* p. 225

p. 132 wound to my soul – MacColl, *op. cit.* pp. 120–1

p. 132 her people – Reid, *op. cit.* p. 179

p. 133 and falling apart – Mitchell, *Roger Casement* pp. 178–9

p. 133 citizen of Ulster – *The Times* 29 October 1913

p. 133 an Ulsterman – *The Times* 31 October 1913

p. 134 out of the reckoning – Inglis, *op. cit.* p. 244

p. 134 a friendly state – MacColl, *op. cit.* pp. 78–9

p. 135 an island beyond an island – Casement, *The Crime against Europe* pp. 72–80

p. 136 maledictions of history – Reid, *op. cit.* p. 183

p. 136 battle here ourselves – Foster, *Vivid Faces* p. 198

p. 136 America and Ireland – Casement, *The Crime against Europe* pp. 81–7

p. 136 citizen force – *Ibid.* p. 87

p. 137 people of Ireland – Mitchell, *Roger Casement* pp. 183–6

p. 137 character of the people – Carroll, *Killing Thatcher* p. 16

p. 138 whatever . . . be taken – Reid, *op. cit.* p. 187

p. 138 Sean Buide has won! – Inglis, *op. cit.* p. 256

p. 138 a foreign state – Casement, *One Bold Deed* p. 236

p. 138 had just left – Inglis, *op. cit.* pp. 256–7

p. 139 fuel to the flame – Childers, *The Riddle of the Sands* p. 96

p. 139 danger of civil war – Piper, *Dangerous Waters* p. 112

p. 139 unpractical – *Ibid.* p. 116

p. 139 Anglo-Saxon alliance anyhow – Reid, *op. cit.* p. 188

p. 140 wanted her taxes – Hansard 11 February 1914

p. 140 a bitter speech – Ridley, *George V* p. 210

p. 140 exclusion of Ulster – Stewart, *op. cit.* p. 107

p. 140 Sean Fear – HMG, *Documents Relative to the Sinn Féin Movement* p. 3

p. 141 fight in us still – Inglis, *op. cit.* pp. 258–9

p. 141 strong and good – *Ibid.* p. 261

p. 142 laughing-stock of Europe – Hansard 31 March 1914

p. 142 British military domination – Parmiter, *op. cit.* pp. 125–6

p. 142 and their patriotism – Redmond-Howard, *Sir Roger Casement* p. 26

p. 142 bluff and blackmail – *Ibid.*

p. 143 prison for it – Stewart, *op. cit.* p. 177

p. 143 minds of the people – Mitchell, *Roger Casement* pp. 199–200

p. 143 apparent dejection – Figgis, *op. cit.* pp. 16–17

p. 144 a pattern downright antique – *Ibid.* p. 21

p. 144   thrown lightly aside – *Ibid*. p. 23

p. 144   bumptious ass – Doerries, *Prelude to the Easter Rising* p. 56

p. 145   and burdened man – NLI MS 10,763/19/9

p. 145   a cracked voice – Mitchell, *Roger Casement* p. 201

p. 146   possibly Erskine Childers – MacColl, *op. cit.* p. 129

p. 146   and overwhelming sorrow – NYPL Maloney IHP 9

p. 146   *our* Imperial history? – MacColl, *op. cit.* p. 129

8. Circle of Treachery

p. 147   only possess *things* – Inglis, *op. cit.* p. 275

p. 147   have fatal results – NYPL 14 September 1914

p. 147   may ruin it – NYPL 16 August 1914

p. 147   estuary of smiles – Casement, *Sir Roger Casement's Diaries* p. 25

p. 147   fleshy, dissipated appearance – Inglis, *op. cit.* pp. 289–90

p. 148   starving almost and homeless – Reid, *op. cit.* p. 197

p. 148   out of their mouths – Doerries, *op. cit.* p. 47

p. 148   sincerity of the man – Inglis, *op. cit.* p. 276

p. 149   trustful as a child – Devoy, *Recollections of a Rebel* p. 406

p. 149   School of Paris – Reid, *op. cit.* p. 197

p. 149   all over the place – Casement, *The Black Diaries* p. 492

p. 149   a Protestant leader – Reid, *op. cit.* p. 198

p. 149   on the sea – *Ibid*. p. 199

p. 150   old, old manhood – *Ibid*. p. 200

p. 150   Mr Asquith – *Ibid*.

p. 150   but no corpses – Mitchell, *Casement* p. 92

p. 150   unknown to them – Devoy, *op. cit.* p. 417

p. 151   up to the neck – Casement, *One Bold Deed* p. 29

p. 151   the man we want – Reid, *op. cit.* p. 200

p. 151   War of Devils – MacColl, *op. cit.* p. 134

p. 151   shores of Ireland – Inglis, *op. cit.* p. 277

p. 151   things in Ireland – Mitchell, *Casement* p. 95

p. 151   'national freedom' to Ireland – Casement, *The Crime against Europe* p. 147

p. 152   buried out in Belgium – Morris, *op. cit.* p. 236

p. 152   tears in his voice – Inglis, *op. cit.* pp. 279–80

p. 152   his own friends – Foster, *op. cit.* p. 224

p. 153   mostly Irish! – Casement, *Sir Roger Casement's Diaries* p. 15

p. 153   ruined national life – Inglis, *op. cit.* p. 281

p. 153   under the Crown – Casement, *Sir Roger Casement's Diaries* p. 16

p. 153   unscrupulous anti-Germans – MacColl, *op. cit.* p. 137

p. 154   a great World power – Reid, *op. cit.* pp. 203–4

p. 154   rotten papers – *Ibid.* p. 204

p. 154   get arms there – *Ibid.* p. 208

p. 154   of the Rising – Mitchell, *Roger Casement* p. 215

p. 155   English mammon – *Ibid.* p. 206

p. 155   associations in America – Mitchell, *Roger Casement* p. 221

p. 156   cause on earth – Devoy, *op. cit.* p. 209

p. 156   shackled to a corpse – Strachan, *The First World War* p. 27

p. 158   reading about so much – NLI MS 13,084/2/1

p. 158   London week-enders – *Ibid.*

p. 158   split his sides – Casement, *Sir Roger Casement's Diaries* pp. 32–4

p. 158   papers of a sort – *Ibid.*

p. 159   facilities to enter Germany – *Ibid.* p. 45

p. 159   with great deference – *Ibid.* p. 46

p. 159   name and address – *Ibid.*

p. 160   take every precaution – *Ibid.* p. 47

p. 160   kidnapping or waylaying – *Ibid.*

p. 160   reassure – *Ibid.* p. 48

p. 161   taking a stroll – *Ibid.* p. 47

p. 161   an improper character – TNA FO 133/107

p. 161   ask for money – TNA KV 2/6

p. 161   story was true – TNA FO 133/107

p. 162   brushed against – Casement, *Sir Roger Casement's Diaries* pp. 49–50

p. 162   trouble for England – *Ibid.* p. 50

p. 163   for taxi fares – *Ibid.* p. 51

p. 163   much pressure – TNA FO 337/107

p. 164   a high one – Casement, *Sir Roger Casement's Diaries* p. 52

p. 164   real message intended – *Ibid.* pp. 52–4

p. 164   blackguards of that class – TNA KV 2/6

p. 165   dangerous rascals – TNA FO 337/107

p. 165   paid by results – TNA KV 2/6

9. *On Manoeuvres*

p. 169 some blood spilling – NLI MS 17,582/1/8

p. 169 flight to the hills – Reid, *op. cit.* pp. 204–5

p. 169 usefulness in Ireland – Reid, *The Man from New York* p. 189

p. 169 felt in Germany – Casement, *One Bold Deed* p. 39

p. 170 than to Ireland – *Ibid.* p. 41

p. 170 fine steam yacht – Casement, *Sir Roger Casement's Diaries* p. 70

p. 171 all for Ireland – *Ibid.* pp. 70–4

p. 171 British commercial mind – *Ibid.* pp. 70–1

p. 171 towards my country – *Ibid.* p. 72

p. 172 would follow him – *Ibid.* pp. 72–3

p. 172 launched on Berlin – *Ibid.* p. 74

p. 172 stand for its liberation – MacColl, *op. cit.* p. 147

p. 173 treasure – NLI MS 13,084/1/5

p. 173 cowardice of the English – TNA KV 2/6

p. 173 people here are wonderful – NLI MS 13,084/1/11

p. 173 St Patrick's Day – TNA FO 337/107

p. 173 national freedom – Inglis, *op. cit.* p. 293

p. 174 money to Adler – Casement, *Sir Roger Casement's Diaries* pp. 76–7

p. 174 give names – TNA FO 337/107

p. 174 reliable information – *Ibid.* p. 79

p. 174 four green fields – TNA HO 144/1636/311643/3A

p. 174 for our sons – Inglis, *op. cit.* pp. 293–4

p. 174 hierarchy of treason – *Ibid.*

p. 175 sure-hearted people – Mitchell, 'A Strange Chapter of Irish History' p. 25

p. 175 the General Staff – *Ibid.* pp. 27–8

p. 176 on our side – Doerries, *op. cit.* p. 58

p. 176 bits of candles – Mitchell, 'A Strange Chapter of Irish History' p. 29

p. 176 fortunes of war – Casement, *One Bold Deed* p. 58

p. 177 arbitrament of arms – *Ibid.* p. 37

p. 177 asinine pranks – *Ibid.* pp. 37–44

p. 177 Adler Christensen – Casement, *Sir Roger Casement's Diaries* p. 88

p. 178 birching from Germany – *Ibid.* pp. 91–2

p. 178   habitually made up – MacColl, *op. cit.* p. 152

p. 178   their holy business – Casement, *Sir Roger Casement's Diaries* p. 91

p. 178   my point of view – Casement, *One Bold Deed* p. 75

p. 178   fights with Irishmen – *Ibid.*

p. 179   if you can – TNA FO 337/107

p. 179   disastrous consequences – *Ibid.*

p. 180   C and his accomplices – *Ibid.*

p. 180   on account – *Ibid.*

p. 180   communicate with anyone – TNA KV 2/6

p. 180   high pay – *Ibid.*

p. 181   American Secret Society – Casement, *Sir Roger Casement's Diaries* pp. 98–100

p. 181   see you again – Ó Síocháin, *op. cit.* p. 402

p. 181   in that service – Inglis, *op. cit.* p. 293

p. 182   must get you – Casement, *Sir Roger Casement's Diaries* pp. 98–100

p. 182   really unhappy – NLI MS 13,084/4/9

p. 182   over the water – Casement, *Sir Roger Casement's Diaries* pp. 111–12

p. 183   inquests on him – Reid, *The Lives of Roger Casement* p. 241

p. 183   rather like Carson – TNA FO 337/107

p. 183   emotional and unbalanced – TNA KV 2/6

p. 184   looked my last on – Reid, *The Lives of Roger Casement* p. 241

10. Web of Lies

p. 185   act of sedition – *Scotsman* 2 December 1914

p. 185   in indifferent health – *Daily Mail* 1 December 1914

p. 185   is not explained – *Northern Whig* 1 December 1914

p. 185   pro-German – Devoy, *op. cit.* p. 431

p. 185   a hero in deed – *San Francisco Examiner* 2 July 1916

p. 186   Irish national matters – *Freeman's Journal* 16 December 1914

p. 186   anyone who knew him – *Daily Chronicle* 30 November 1914

p. 186   proved a traitor – MacColl, *op. cit.* p. 160

p. 186   broken about Belgium? – *Daily Chronicle* 30 November 1914

p. 187   Boer freedom – Inglis, *op. cit.* p. 299

p. 187   armies and navy – Casement, *Sir Roger Casement's Diaries* p. 113

p. 188   well-shaped bodies – Reid, *The Lives of Roger Casement* p. 244

p. 188   right on the river – Casement, *One Bold Deed* p. 91

p. 188   not brave enough – *Ibid*. pp. 91–2

p. 189   sodden sick faces – *Ibid*. p. 92

p. 189   inflicted by the Germans – *Ibid*. p. 96

p. 190   fuller powers – *Ibid*. pp. 98–9

p. 190   letter carrier – *Ibid*. p. 100

p. 190   or the Chancellor – Doerries, *op. cit.* pp. 67–8

p. 190   future of Ireland – Inglis, *op. cit.* p. 301

p. 191   any personal consequences – Casement, *One Bold Deed* p. 101

p. 191   a better life – *Ibid*. p. 102

p. 191   deception with deception – Reid, *The Lives of Roger Casement* p. 243

p. 191   malign influence – Casement, *One Bold Deed* pp. 101–5

p. 192   propaganda of treason – *Ibid*. p. 105

p. 192   even in America! – *Ibid*. p. 106

p. 192   but English soldiers – *Ibid*. pp. 106–7

p. 192   die for England – Casement, *Sir Roger Casement's Diaries* p. 113

p. 193   Ireland or tobacco – Casement, *One Bold Deed* pp. 107–8

p. 193   so contemptible a race – *Ibid*. pp. 108–9

p. 193   on board American yacht – TNA KV 2/6

p. 193   deal with the situation – *Ibid*.

p. 194   governing classes – Casement, *One Bold Deed* pp. 110–11

p. 194   delicious – Casement, *Sir Roger Casement's Diaries* p. 125

p. 194   a rampant traitor – *Ibid*. p. 126

p. 195   the suffering of life – Wilde, *The Picture of Dorian Gray* p. 89

p. 195   spark of imagination – Casement, *One Bold Deed* p. 112

p. 195   come to nought – Casement, *Sir Roger Casement's Diaries* p. 131

p. 195   treason to Ireland – Casement, *One Bold Deed* p. 119

p. 196   aims and projects – *Ibid*. p. 120

p. 196   swallowing up his affection – *Ibid*. pp. 122–3

p. 196   the Christiania incident – Casement, *One Bold Deed* p. 126

p. 196   opposed to it – NLI MS 13,073/44/1

p. 197   so cruelly betrayed – Casement, *One Bold Deed* p. 123

p. 197   named *Sir Roger Casement* – *Ibid*. p. 130

p. 198   thro' the warp – *Ibid*. p. 117

p. 198   north of Tory Island – TNA FO 337/107

p. 198   use to you – *Ibid.*

p. 199   robbed and bound – Casement, *One Bold Deed* p. 131

p. 199   out of Egypt – Parmiter, *op. cit.* pp. 201–3

11. Conspiracy's End

p. 201   the failure of my hopes – Casement, *One Bold Deed* p. 133

p. 201   50,000 extra guns – Doerries, *op. cit.* p. 70

p. 202   impulsive, excitable man – TNA FO 337/107

p. 202   truth about Germany – Reid, *The Lives of Roger Casement* p. 259

p. 202   suffered most – Keogh, *With Casement's Irish Brigade* p. 41

p. 203   and suitable games – *Ibid.* p. 45

p. 203   food improvements – *Ibid.* pp. 78–9

p. 203   periodically during mealtimes – TNA KV 2/8

p. 204   cornerboys and spalpeens – TNA KV 2/6

p. 204   King and Country – TNA KV 2/7

p. 204   the brink of ruin – *Ibid.*

p. 205   good news – Casement, *One Bold Deed* p. 135

p. 205   over his ears – Casement, *Sir Roger Casement's Diaries* pp. 146–7

p. 205   should he desire it – TNA KV 2/6

p. 206   or his papers – *Ibid.*

p. 206   any harm now – TNA FO 337/107

p. 207   fear from publicity – TNA KV 2/6

p. 207   got hold of it – *Ibid.*

p. 207   a most loathsome beast – *Ibid.*

p. 207   Germany and America – Reid, *The Lives of Roger Casement* p. 269

p. 207   I know – Doerries, *op. cit.* p. 75

p. 208   the coast of Ireland – Casement, *Sir Roger Casement's Diaries* p. 148

p. 208   long contemplated – Casement, *One Bold Deed* p. 138

p. 208   fallen so low – Hansard 8 January 1915

p. 208   demoralised and Anglicised – Casement, *One Bold Deed* pp. 139–46

p. 209   a Government against itself – *Ibid.* pp. 143–5

p. 209   the German Government – Reid, *The Lives of Roger Casement* p. 273

p. 209   dastardly criminal conspiracy – Casement, *One Bold Deed* pp. 149–50

p. 209   the British Minister – NLI MS 17,002/3

p. 210   brought it about – *Ibid.*

p. 210 on the head – Casement, *Sir Roger Casement's Diaries* pp. 184–5

p. 210 faithful follower – *Ibid.* pp. 186–9

p. 210 the legitimate authorities – *Ibid.* pp. 188–91

p. 210 treason – Casement, *One Bold Deed* p. 156

p. 211 poor penniless wretch – *Ibid.* pp. 158–9

p. 212 all the rest of it – *Ibid.* p. 163

p. 212 their hopeless ineptitude – *Ibid.* pp. 163–4

p. 213 disillusioned and miserable – *Ibid.* p. 167

p. 213 hauled off to jail – *Ibid.* p. 164

12. The Great Tale

p. 214 sense of proportion – Devoy, *op. cit.* p. 431

p. 215 planned revolution – Casement, *One Bold Deed* p. 167

p. 215 friends in Ireland – Doerries, *op. cit.* p. 119

p. 215 a great Continental power – Casement, *One Bold Deed* p. 167

p. 215 criminal stupidity – Ó Síocháin, *op. cit.* p. 417

p. 215 their lives for an ideal – Casement, *One Bold Deed* p. 168

p. 216 treated as confidential – TNA FO 337/107

p. 216 a recruiting sergeant – TNA HO 144/1636/311643/3A

p. 216 a submarine base – *Ibid.*

p. 217 rendered untenable – TNA KV 2/6

p. 217 cads and cowards – Reid, *The Lives of Roger Casement* pp. 292–3

p. 217 restored to sanity – *Ibid.*

p. 217 enormous sensation – *Ibid.*

p. 218 expedition to U.K. – TNA FO 337/107

p. 218 Absurd Plot Story – TNA KV 2/8

p. 218 quite alone – TNA FO 337/107

p. 219 throughout the land – Doerries, *op. cit.* p. 85

p. 219 against his life – TNA HO 144/1636/311643/3A

p. 219 before the Admiralty – *Ibid.*

p. 219 employment there, and £20 – Casement, *One Bold Deed* p. 170

p. 219 to be a lie – *Ibid.* p. 226

p. 220 the Silver Bullet – Reid, *The Lives of Roger Casement* p. 287

p. 220 his personal reputation – Doerries, *op. cit.* pp. 102–3

p. 220 the end in view – Reid, *The Lives of Roger Casement* p. 289

p. 220   place was in Ireland – Reid, *The Man from New York* p. 228

p. 221   come out alright – Doerries, *op. cit.* p. 127

p. 221   scrap of paper – Inglis, *op. cit.* p. 311

p. 221   war are gone – Doerries, *op. cit.* p. 101

p. 222   the really important part – Devoy, *op. cit.* p. 437

p. 222   curiously immobile – O Brolchain, *Joseph Plunkett* p. 304

p. 223   appeal to their patriotism – Casement, *One Bold Deed* p. 171

p. 223   his blood for Ireland – Parmiter, *op. cit.* p. 220

p. 223   out of the country – TNA KV 2/8

p. 223   refused to speak to him – TNA KV 2/7

p. 224   the Irish in America – Casement, *One Bold Deed* pp. 173–5

p. 224   Laughter on our lips – O Brolchain, *op. cit.* p. 319

p. 224   from me for ever – Casement, *One Bold Deed* p. 175

p. 224   or of our country – Ó Síocháin, *op. cit.* p. 418

p. 224   the 'Poor Brothers' – Inglis, *op. cit.* p. 317

p. 225   enormous damage – Doerries, *op. cit.* p. 131

p. 225   their welfare – TNA KV 2/9

p. 225   things to say – Ó Síocháin, *op. cit.* p. 420

p. 225   rings with jewels – Reid, *The Lives of Roger Casement* p. 302

p. 226   true to the death – *Ibid.* pp. 302–3

p. 226   idle and useless – Doerries, *op. cit.* pp. 138–40

p. 226   against fearful odds – Ó Síocháin, *op. cit.* p. 420

p. 226   support for his journey – Doerries, *op. cit.* pp. 138–41

p. 227   something for Ireland – *Ibid.* pp. 136–7

p. 227   that of Colonel – Devoy, *op. cit.* p. 438

p. 227   a great fidelity – Casement, *One Bold Deed* p. 177

p. 227   was wounded twice – Doerries, *op. cit.* p. 145

p. 227   worst crooks ever – HMG, *Documents Relative to the Sinn Féin Movement* p. 20

p. 228   to travel with – Monteith, *Casement's Last Adventure* p. 63

p. 228   handle drunken men – *Ibid.* p. 70

p. 229   downheartedness about the war – *Ibid.* pp. 77–90

p. 229   go ahead – *Ibid.* p. 85

p. 229   for Ireland in Ireland – *Ibid.*

p. 229   men for Zossen – Ó Síocháin, *op. cit.* pp. 426–7

p. 229   speeches were made – Reid, *The Lives of Roger Casement* p. 311

p. 230   their actual number – Ó Síocháin, *op. cit.* p. 427

p. 230   could do nothing – HMG, *Documents Relative to the Sinn Féin Movement* p. 20

p. 230   about the prospect – Ó Síocháin, *op. cit.* p. 428

p. 230   they know it – Doerries, *op. cit.* p. 176

p. 231   has broken him – Ó Síocháin, *op. cit.* p. 428

p. 231   was barely perceptible – Monteith, *op. cit.* pp. 103–4

p. 231   such a false position – Inglis, *op. cit.* p. 321

p. 231   see no daylight – Ó Síocháin, *op. cit.* pp. 428–9

p. 232   strength and courage – *Ibid.* pp. 429–30

p. 232   *may not* recover – Doerries, *op. cit.* p. 177

p. 232   the outstanding feature – Ó Síocháin, *op. cit.* p. 439

p. 232   all these things – *Ibid.* pp. 431–2

p. 233   until such time – Doerries, *op. cit.* pp. 182–5

13. Homecoming

p. 234   in Tralee Bay – Doerries, *op. cit.* p. 186

p. 234   his former self – Monteith, *op. cit.* p. 135

p. 234   a thunder clap – TNA KV 2/7

p. 234   not much jump – Reid, *The Lives of Roger Casement* p. 329

p. 235   no revolution, no arms – *Ibid.* p. 333

p. 235   call off the rising – Ó Síocháin, *op. cit.* p. 433

p. 235   feelingless departure – Doerries, *op. cit.* p. 188

p. 235   to be shot down – TNA KV 2/7

p. 235   make all clear – Reid, *The Lives of Roger Casement* p. 333

p. 236   Hero of Revolutionary Ireland – NLI MS 17,026/1

p. 236   a scoundrel – *Ibid.*

p. 236   cowardly act – Casement, *Sir Roger Casement's Diaries* p. 200

p. 237   be made clear – Inglis, *op. cit.* p. 324

p. 237   prey to extreme anxiety – Ó Síocháin, *op. cit.* p. 433

p. 237   rather than his own – Inglis, *op. cit.* p. 325

p. 237   a policy of scoundrels – Doerries, *op. cit.* p. 203

p. 237   *the Western Front* – Ó Síocháin, *op. cit.* pp. 431–2

p. 237   a hideous one – Doerries, *op. cit.* p. 199

p. 238   America or Ireland – TNA HO 144/1637/311643/194A

p. 238   it is hopeless – Casement, *One Bold Deed* pp. 215–17

p. 239   taken from me the better – *Ibid.* p. 217

p. 239   delays are dangerous – Monteith, *op. cit.* p. 139

p. 239   humbly requested – Doerries, *op. cit.* p. 207

p. 239   the consequences in Ireland – Casement, *One Bold Deed* p. 218

p. 239   agent of the FO – *Ibid.*

p. 239   fantastic – Inglis, *op. cit.* p. 326

p. 239   low-minded intriguer – Casement, *One Bold Deed* pp. 218–19

p. 239   the thing was settled – Ó Síocháin, *op. cit.* p. 437

p. 240   lofty upper works – Spindler, *The Mystery of the Casement Ship* p. 35

p. 241   in a whisper – Ó Síocháin, *op. cit.* p. 437

p. 241   disgraced – Casement, *One Bold Deed* p. 218

p. 242   stout Irish hearts – Keogh, *op. cit.* pp. 126–7

p. 242   swindled – Casement, *One Bold Deed* p. 233

p. 243   litter – *Ibid.* pp. 232–3

p. 243   'rebellion' breaks out – *Ibid.* p. 233

p. 244   This is vital – Reid, *The Lives of Roger Casement* p. 349

p. 245   a bayonet scabbard – TNA KV 2/7

p. 245   an ugly thought – Monteith, *op. cit.* p. 147

p. 245   crossed his face – *Ibid.* pp. 147–8

p. 246   Banna Strand – *Ibid.* p. 154

14. The Tower

p. 249   skylarks in the air – Mitchell, *Roger Casement* p. 267

p. 250   early in the morning – Monteith, *op. cit.* p. 157

p. 250   from this course – *Ibid.*

p. 251   knock about – TNA KV 2/8

p. 252   a reason why – TNA KV 2/7

p. 252   the rest by cipher – Hyde, *op. cit.* p. 58

p. 252   Willie's yacht – *Ibid.* p. 48

p. 253   see what he could do – *Ibid.* p. 16

p. 253   date for the Rising – *Ibid.* pp. 16–17

p. 253   blessing on the country – *Ibid.* p. 18

p. 253   had been arrested – NLI MS 17,075/6

p. 254   defensive warfare – Foster, *op. cit.* p. 226

p. 254 boat at Curraghane – Thomson, *Odd People* p. 85

p. 255 the past twelve nights – TNA KV 2/7

p. 255 been decided upon – *Ibid.*

p. 255 duped by the Germans – *Ibid.*

p. 256 complexion deeply sunburnt – Thomson, *op. cit.* p. 85

p. 256 involve other people – TNA HO 144/1636/311643/3A

p. 256 war with Germany – Hyde, *op. cit.* pp. 24–5

p. 256 a sense of duty – TNA KV 2/7

p. 257 twopence for Germany – *Ibid.*

p. 257 giving any man away – Mitchell, *Roger Casement* p. 272

p. 257 trouble in Ireland – *Ibid.* p. 273

p. 257 most hopeless enterprise – TNA KV 2/7

p. 258 base falsehoods – *Ibid.*

p. 258 difficulty – *Ibid.*

p. 258 Amiens or Ypres – Foster, *op. cit.* p. 228

p. 259 terrible beauty – Yeats, *op. cit.* p. 202

p. 259 the British Government – TNA KV 2/7

p. 259 trap Ireland into arms – *Ibid.*

p. 259 down and examined – *Ibid.*

p. 260 commission from the Emperor – NLI MS 10,764/3A/4

p. 260 Break them open – *Ibid.*

p. 260 3 diaries – TNA MEPO 3/2145

p. 260 the Tower of London – TNA KV 2/7

p. 260 the cause of Germany – *The Times* 25 April 1916

p. 260 Notorious Traitor Captured – MacColl, *op. cit.* p. 219

p. 261 should be put – Hyde, *op. cit.* p. 40

p. 261 people in London – MacColl, *op. cit.* p. 215

p. 261 desire of Roger's – *Ibid.* p. 216

p. 262 blank, stony indifference – *Ibid.*

p. 262 cold and harsh – *Ibid.* p. 217

p. 264 in a filthy condition – *Ibid.* pp. 223–4

15. *Some Neglected Morals*

p. 265 a shocking conjunction – Jones, *Without My Wig* p. 154

p. 265 knowledge of history – *The Times* 16 May 1916

p. 266   killed him secretly – Hyde, *op. cit.* p. 40

p. 267   Englishmen to remember – https://en.wikipedia.org/wiki/J._H._Morgan

p. 267   and unselfish life – Reid, *The Lives of Roger Casement* p. 367

p. 267   by the horrors – Ford, *op. cit.* p. 122

p. 267   the name of Ireland – Jones, *op. cit.* pp. 163–4

p. 267   remained a dream – Mitchell, *Roger Casement* p. 282

p. 268   would be dissatisfied – Hyde, *op. cit.* p. 57

p. 268   more expeditious course – *The Times* 15 May 1916

p. 268   and scrubby beard – *Ibid.* 16 May 1916

p. 269   No, Sir John – Hyde, *op. cit.* pp. 63–4

p. 269   of that country – *Ibid.* pp. 65–6

p. 269   a moral coward – Ó Síocháin, *op. cit.* pp. 446–7

p. 270   some real defence – Inglis, *op. cit.* p. 340

p. 270   'a minor poet' – letter to *Daily News* 10 May 1916

p. 270   any soldier in Flanders – *New Statesman* 27 March 2016

p. 270   painful luncheon party – Costigan, *op. cit.* p. 300

p. 270   court full of lawyers – Ó Síocháin, *op. cit.* p. 447

p. 271   gush of patriotic sentiment – Shaw, 'The Roger Casement Trial' p. 311

p. 271   a very humble way – Inglis, *op. cit.* p. 342

p. 271   the wider sense – *Ibid.* pp. 342–3

p. 271   remain unconvicted still – *Ibid.* p. 344

p. 271   the necessary wholeheartedness – *Ibid.* pp. 344–5

p. 272   rebel views into action – Mitchell, *Roger Casement* pp. 289–91

p. 272   suitable for his detention – TNA WO 141/3/3

p. 273   on behalf of mercy – Ó Síocháin, *op. cit.* p. 451

p. 273   came into his eyes – Devoy, *op. cit.* p. 477

p. 273   desire of Sir Roger – *Daily Mail* 13 June 1916

p. 273   the British Government – *Evening News* 13 June 1916

p. 274   and her people – NLI MS 17,598/2

p. 274   cause many protests – Reid, *The Lives of Roger Casement* p. 368

p. 274   prisoner's legal advisers – TNA HO 144/1636/311643/16

p. 275   duty to defend them – Ó Síocháin, *op. cit.* p. 448

p. 275   much good money – Hyde, *op. cit.* pp. 77–8

p. 275   shooting for hanging – TNA HO 144/1636/311643/52

p. 276   dreadful than death – NLI MS 10, 764/3B/2

p. 276 about $900 – TNA KV 2/9

p. 276 Stevedore – Casement, *The Black Diaries* p. 231

p. 277 helped – NLI MS 17, 023/2

p. 277 *kept him here* – HMG, *Documents Relative to the Sinn Féin Movement* p. 20

p. 277 a new-born baby – NLI MS 13,073/44viii/1

p. 278 no other comment – Casement, *The Black Diaries* p. 581

p. 278 proofs of insanity – Ó Síocháin, *op. cit.* p. 450

p. 278 across the Atlantic – Inglis, *op. cit.* p. 350

p. 278 the true facts – *Ibid.* pp. 350–1

p. 279 right and wrong – Thomson, *op. cit.* pp. 88–9

p. 279 years in Ireland – Ó Síocháin, *op. cit.* pp. 449–50

p. 280 Demerara 6" – Casement, *The Black Diaries* p. 112

p. 280 Millar into me – *Ibid.* p. 335

p. 280 from the accused – Hyde, *op. cit.* p. 75

p. 280 high places of justice – *Ibid.*

p. 280 guilty but insane – Campbell, *F. E. Smith* p. 402

p. 281 better than dishonour – Hyde, *op. cit.* p. 77

p. 281 you've upset me – Mitchell, *Roger Casement* p. 299

p. 281 for ever and ever – Ó Síocháin, *op. cit.* pp. 449–50

16. The Forfeit

p. 282 away to Ireland – Ó Síocháin, *op. cit.* p. 453

p. 282 imperturbable demeanour – Reid, *The Lives of Roger Casement* p. 394

p. 282 best and truest – Ó Síocháin, *op. cit.* p. 453

p. 283 the King's domains – Knott, *Trial of Roger Casement* pp. 3–4

p. 284 its very existence – *Ibid.* pp. 7–9

p. 284 cruel than this – *Ibid.* pp. 11–13

p. 285 the forfeit is claimed – *Ibid.* p. 15

p. 285 the Irish Brigade? – *Ibid.* p. 35

p. 285 seducing and corrupting – *Ibid.*

p. 286 closed for good – Hyde, *op. cit.* p. 98

p. 287 God Save Ireland! – Knott, *op. cit.* pp. 65–6

p. 287 adhere to the King's enemies – Hyde, *op. cit.* p. 100

p. 288   in his realm or elsewhere – *Ibid.*

p. 288   an Irish accent – *The Times* 29 June 1916

p. 288   diffidence and courtesy – Hyde, *op. cit.* p. 101

p. 289   to finance it – Knott, *op. cit.* p. 134

p. 289   with a semi-colon – Hyde, *op. cit.* p. 147

p. 289   spirit of fair play – Knott, *op. cit.* p. 135

p. 289   Courts of Law – *The Times* 29 June 1916

p. 290   not a German – Hyde, *op. cit.* pp. 103–4

p. 290   arms in his hands – Knott, *op. cit.* pp. 151–2

p. 291   no German purpose – *Ibid.* pp. 154–5

p. 291   client had imposed – *The Times* 29 June 1916

p. 291   completely broken down – Knott, *op. cit.* pp. 154–5

p. 291   his useless pleading – Shaw, 'The Roger Casement Trial' p. 313

p. 292   and possibly wicked – Hyde, *op. cit.* p. 107

p. 292   it is humane – Knott, *op. cit.* pp. 161–3

p. 292   indisposition – *Ibid.* p. 163

p. 292   wished well to England – *Ibid.* pp. 163–4

p. 293   hospitality – *Ibid.* pp. 166–9

p. 293   in your verdict – *Ibid.* pp. 177–8

p. 293   introduce political considerations – *Ibid.* p. 179

p. 294   assist the enemy – *Ibid.* pp. 181–5

p. 294   well of the Court – *The Times* 30 April 1916

p. 294   propose to say – *Ibid.* p. 197

p. 295   not on restraint – *Ibid.* pp. 198–9

p. 295   and self-possession – *The Times* 30 June 1916

p. 295   right noble succession – Knott, *op. cit.* p. 199

p. 296   descents upon Ireland – Hyde, *op. cit.* pp. 118–19

p. 296   right honourable accusers – Knott, *op. cit.* pp. 203–4

p. 296   Nothing doing – Hyde, *op. cit.* pp. 120–1

p. 296   sneer upon his face – MacColl, *op. cit.* p. 269

p. 297   last drop of my blood – Hyde, *op. cit.* p. 121

p. 297   more than for Ireland? – Knott, *op. cit.* p. 205

p. 297   until you be dead – *Ibid.*

p. 297   Order of Knights Bachelor – Hyde, *op. cit.* p. 123

p. 298   Who Eliminated Self – Monteith, *op. cit.* p. v

17. The Quality of Mercy

p. 299 head can wear – Inglis, *op. cit.* p. 362

p. 299 than I did – Parmiter, *op. cit.* p. 317

p. 299 we bathed together – Ó Síocháin, *op. cit.* p. 457

p. 299 fed the hungry – Reid, *The Lives of Roger Casement* pp. 414–15

p. 300 stealthy slander – TNA CAB 37/152

p. 300 think you?!! – TNA KV 2/9

p. 300 not respond to work – Hyde, *op. cit.* p. 125

p. 300 bear the fate – Parmiter, *op. cit.* p. 317

p. 300 especially the wigs – Inglis, *op. cit.* p. 362

p. 301 intelligible only to myself – Sullivan, *The Last Serjeant* p. 273

p. 301 the King's Courts – Knott, *op. cit.* p. 280

p. 302 intellectual honesty left – Hyde, *op. cit.* p. 124

p. 302 not to destroy Ireland – TNA HO 144/1636/311643/65

p. 302 all of the same mind – Hyde, *op. cit.* p. 133

p. 302 such an action – Ó Síocháin, *op. cit.* p. 457

p. 303 happily healed over – TNA HO 144/1637/311643/79

p. 304 and justifying it – *Ibid.*

p. 304 to use him – Tóibín, 'A Whale of a Time'

p. 304 with British public opinion – TNA HO 144/1637/311643/79

p. 305 atrocious moral character – Casement, *The Black Diaries* p. 452

p. 305 should not be published – TNA HO 144/1637/311643/79

p. 305 work for humanity – Ó Síocháin, *op. cit.* p. 462

p. 305 attracting other names – Hyde, *op. cit.* p. 135

p. 305 the opposite reason – NLI MS 13,075/1/4

p. 305 do endless mischief – Hyde, *op. cit.* pp. 135–6

p. 306 his own Government – Ó Síocháin, *op. cit.* p. 465

p. 306 even think of – NYPL Quinn Papers

p. 307 sinking of the *Lusitania* – TNA HO 144/1636/311643/45

p. 307 came to a head – TNA CAB 37/152/13

p. 307 should be cut out – Andrew, *The Defence of the Realm* p. 88

p. 307 a ghoulish proposal – TNA FO 395/43

p. 307 not certifiably insane – Jenkins, *Asquith* p. 403

p. 308 & was refused!! – TNA HO 144/1637/311643/65

p. 308 a strong view – TNA HO 144/1637/311643/42

p. 309   loathing and contempt – Ó Síocháin, *op. cit.* p. 466

p. 309   commonly yielded to – *Ibid.* p. 467

p. 309   practised in the Congo – *Ibid.* pp. 467–8

p. 310   attaining martyrdom – Hyde, *op. cit.* pp. 139–40

p. 310   shouted in clubs – McDiarmid, *The Irish Art of Controversy* p. 183

p. 311   a 'peanut politician' – *Congressional Record (Senate)* 29 July 1916

p. 311   was greatly respected – Reid, *The Lives of Roger Casement* p. 419

p. 311   fake or forgery – *Ibid.* p. 421

p. 311   be in time – Ó Síocháin, *op. cit.* p. 470

p. 312   by education a Presbyterian – Inglis, *op. cit.* p. 373

p. 312   too far gone already – Reid, *The Lives of Roger Casement* p. 431

p. 312   a fundamental consideration – State Department papers

p. 312   and go nowhere – Gwynn, 'Roger Casement's Last Weeks' pp. 67–8

p. 313   splashed water over them – *Ibid.*

p. 313   Scodgie – Ó Síocháin, *op. cit.* pp. 471–2

p. 313   in my life – NLI MS 13,079

p. 313   treasonable as well – Ó Síocháin, *op. cit.* p. 472

p. 314   Indians and such like – *Ibid.* p. 473

p. 314   firmly removed me! – Shaw, 'The Roger Casement Trial' p. 314

p. 314   wanted to die – Ó Síocháin, *op. cit.* p. 473

p. 314   the old days – NLI MS 49,154/12/3

p. 315   the execution of Casement? – Inglis, *op. cit.* p. 378

p. 315   the general public – Mitchell, *Roger Casement* p. 333

p. 315   anti-British sentiment – *Ibid.*

p. 315   it is murder – Ó Síocháin, *op. cit.* p. 474

p. 315   all you cowards – NLI MS 18,008/20/9

p. 316   sufficient to disprove it – TNA CAB 37/152/13

p. 316   with sincere pain – NLI MS 13,078/7/5

18. Strange Fate

p. 317   any need to use them – NLI MS 10,763/26/39

p. 317   only insult me now – NLI MS 10, 764/3A/5

p. 317   Congo tobacco – NLI MS 49,154/12/4

p. 318   my brothers now – Hyde, *op. cit.* p. 153

p. 318   a bed of thorns – Mitchell, *Roger Casement* p. 343

p. 318   reason was clouded – Hyde, *op. cit.* p. 154

p. 318   committed was intense – *Ibid.* p. 155

p. 319   God's pardon on my soul – *Ibid.* pp. 155–6

p. 319   most glorious one in history – *Ibid.* pp. 156–7

p. 320   which was setting – NLI MS 13,088/11/1

p. 320   beauty of that scene – Mitchell, *Roger Casement* p. 346

p. 320   through it all – *Ibid.* pp. 346–7

p. 320   faith at the end – Hyde, *op. cit.* p. 157

p. 321   Roman Catholic chaplain – *Ibid.* p. 158

p. 321   executed on him – *Ibid.* p. 160

p. 322   in quicklime laid – Yeats, *op. cit.* p. 352

p. 322   this great man's – Reid, *The Lives of Roger Casement* p. 450

p. 323   a brutal world order – *Irish Times* 21 April 2016

p. 324   being in Germany – NYPL Quinn Papers

p. 324   swing in any case – *Ibid.*

p. 325   honest and honorable – *Ibid.*

p. 325   degenerate about him – Reid, *The Man from New York* p. 237

p. 325   a broken archangel – Lawrence, *op. cit.* p. 508

p. 326   the real man was gone – Reid, *The Lives of Roger Casement* p. v

p. 326   tear-dimmed eyes – NLI MS 13,082/2i/1

Index

Roland Philipps was a leading publisher for many years. *A Spy Named Orphan*, his first book, arose from lifelong connections to Donald Maclean and his story. It was shortlisted for the Slightly Foxed Best First Biography Prize 2018, was a *Daily Mail* Book of the Year and received widespread critical acclaim. His second book, *Victoire*, was published by The Bodley Head in 2021.